WILDFLOWERS
OF THE HIGH SIERRA AND
JOHN MUIR TRAIL

Elizabeth Wenk

WILDERNESS PRESS . . . *on the trail since 1967*

Cover photos copyright © by Elizabeth Wenk
Interior photos and map by Elizabeth Wenk, except as noted on page
Sketches by Evelyn Wenk
Cover design: Scott McGrew
Text design: Annie Long

Library of Congress Cataloging-in-Publication Data

Wenk, Elizabeth.
  Wildflowers of the High Sierra and John Muir Trail / by Elizabeth Wenk.
    pages cm
  Includes bibliographical references and index.
  ISBN 978-0-89997-738-6 — ISBN 0-89997-738-3
  1. Wild flowers—Ecology—Sierra Nevada Region (Calif. and Nev.) 2. Wild
flowers—Sierra Nevada Region (Calif. and Nev.)—Identification. I. Title.
  QK142.7.W46 2015
  582.13—dc23
                            2014048407

ISBN 978-0-89997-738-6; eISBN 978-0-89997-739-3

Manufactured in the United States of America

Published by: ℛ Wilderness Press
                  Keen Communications
                  PO Box 43673
                  Birmingham, AL 35243
                  800-443-7227; fax 205-326-1012
                  info@wildernesspress.com
                  wildernesspress.com

Visit our website for a complete listing of our books and for ordering information.

Distributed by Publishers Group West

Contents

Dedication

In memory of Rebecca Ciresa Wenk, my sister and favorite person to accompany me for a day of botanizing

Aquilegia hybrid

Acknowledgments

Each year I speak with many hikers on trails, telling them stories about plants or helping them identify species. They often ask what book they should carry, and I have been unable to point them to a single perfect title because there is no plant book focused on the Sierra's high-elevation flora. I thank these people for helping plant the seed in my mind and Wilderness Press for deciding to publish this title. Wilderness Press let me dictate the scope of the book, placing faith in my ability to complete a unique and useful book; I hope I have succeeded. Amber Kaye Henderson, the editor for this book, has done a superb job of clarifying my language and flagging places where I explained myself poorly. My sister Evelyn Wenk drew the sketches of flowers for the book. I have also been so pleased by the support and help received from Sierra botanists. Alison Colwell, Alisa Ellsworth, Dena Grossenbacher, Sarah Kimball, and Connie Millar pointed me toward topics and studies I overlooked and read through sections of the manuscript. Finally, a big thanks to my family for their patience and support—especially traipsing around after me in search of so many species to photograph.

Introduction

❖ Scope of This Book

I wrote this book as a complement to the several hiking guides I have written for Wilderness Press that are focused on the high-elevation Sierra Nevada between Yosemite and Mt. Whitney. These titles all contain a liberal sprinkling of natural history, including descriptions of plant communities and the flowers themselves. Readers of the books have repeatedly requested photographs of the plants, as well as more in-depth information to distinguish between species they happen across. This book is the outcome: a combination of species descriptions and ecological stories covering the plants you will encounter while hiking in the High Sierra. I hope that this book will teach you more about the Sierra's diverse plant selections and how some are unique, as well as increase your ability to identify them.

The Sierra Nevada of California is a large geographic region, spanning west to east from just above the San Joaquin Valley to 14,000-foot summits and then eastward down to the 4,000-foot Owens Valley, and north to south from Mt. Lassen (40.5°N) to Walker Pass (35.5°N). It has very rich flora, hosting nearly 3,500 species, subspecies, and varieties. This book covers only a small portion of that geographic range, the region known colloquially as the High Sierra. It is delineated as extending from northern Yosemite south to the Mt. Whitney region, just north of the Kern Plateau. The term *High Sierra* is sometimes used more broadly to include the mountains north to the Tahoe region, but this book excludes the region from the northern boundary of Yosemite to Tahoe, both because there is already an excellent title covering the Tahoe region (*Plants of the Tahoe Basin* by Michael Graf) and because a quite different collection of species grows at these more northerly latitudes. Further constraining the list of candidate species, this book covers only those whose ranges extend above 8,000 feet in elevation, because, as described below, this elevation marks a change in forest type.

Even with the restricted definition of the High Sierra adopted here, nearly 1,500 species are known to occur within the region. This title includes just 340 of them, with brief mention of another 105. The selection includes all the large, showy, common species, but I have made a special effort to include many of the high-elevation specialists that are often passed over in a book with a greater elevation range or geographic extent.

Many of these high-elevation species are common within their preferred altitude range and habitat, and a wide-ranging hiker will step across many of them. Excluded are the approximately 225 species of grasses, sedges, rushes, and related species, for most are difficult to identify. Note, however, that these species are very important from an ecological perspective, for they are the dominant species in most meadows and wetlands and are also essential forage for animals. Selecting which other species to omit was difficult; species with more restricted ranges and species that are much more common at lower elevations were omitted.

A plant ecologist by training, I have always enjoyed the wonderful stories that scientific research tells us about how plants make a living and why they look the way they do. These stories make the plants come so much more alive, so I included vignettes in sidebars throughout the book. I hope that, as you are looking up a species, you will find yourself with a few extra minutes to read an adjoining story, ensuring that you never forget the flower you just found. The sidebars are included in the table of contents. (References for these essays can be found beginning on page 248.)

❖ Vegetation Zones and Conifer Species

Flowers and shrubs with their bright, colorful blossoms are the focus of this book, but it is the quite small number of coniferous tree species that dominate the Sierra's landscapes—at least up to alpine elevations. Each conifer species has a distinct elevation range and habitat conditions where it will be found, and each hosts a different collection of understory species. The Sierra can be divided into six vegetation zones, defined by the tree or shrub community that is most common.

- **The foothill woodland and scrubland zone** occurs mostly below 4,000 feet.

- **The lower-montane or mixed conifer forest zone** occurs between 2,000 and 7,400 feet, occasionally extending higher in the far southern High Sierra, with the prevalence of white firs, a key indicator species, peaking around 6,500 feet.

- **The upper-montane forest zone** is dominated by red firs and is most widespread between 7,500 and 8,500 feet but continues to about 9,300 feet in moist locations, with occasional red fir stands existing above 10,000 feet.

- **The subalpine forest zone** with some patches occurring as low as 8,200 feet and extending up to the treeline; several different species can be dominant at these elevations.

- ❧ **The alpine meadow and shrubland zone** occurs above treeline, which can be as low as 9,000 feet in the north to as high as 12,000 feet in the south, and is defined as a region where full-size trees cannot establish; see also "Treeline," page 110.
- ❧ **The eastside forest and woodland zone** is found in the eastern Sierra, mostly between 5,200 feet and 7,200 feet.

This book mostly encompasses just two of these zones—the subalpine forest and the alpine meadow and shrubland zones—but includes a few plants restricted to the higher elevation fir forests of the upper-montane forest zone. Shifts in temperature and moisture determine the boundaries of these zones.

In a mountainous region, elevation is generally a good indicator of temperature, with temperature dropping by 3.5°F for each 1,000 feet increase in elevation, resulting in a 50°F drop in temperature from the San Joaquin Valley to the summit of Mt. Whitney. The relationship between elevation and temperature leads to the transition between vegetation zones along the Sierra's western escarpment. Temperature also decreases with increasing latitude, with estimates of a 1°F drop for each 50 miles traveled northward. Though this latter equation is by no means global, it works locally to explain the increase in treeline between the Lake Tahoe and Mt. Whitney regions. The two locations are about 180 miles apart, which results in the same cooling effect as a 1,000-foot increase in elevation. Indeed, the treeline in the Lake Tahoe Basin is between 9,000 to 10,000 feet, while it ranges from 10,000 to 12,000 feet around Mt. Whitney.

Precipitation in the Sierra follows a simple pattern: In fall, winter, and spring, nearly all weather systems begin in the Pacific Ocean and move eastward to the Sierra. As the air masses rise, they cool and can hold less moisture. This causes the moisture within them to condense and drop out as rain or snow. In the Sierra, the greatest amount of precipitation falls around 6,500 feet, declining slightly thereafter; though the air mass continues to cool, it has less and less moisture to release as it rises higher. The storm systems have had most of the moisture wrung from them by the time they cross the crest to the eastern Sierra, so this is a much drier landscape, with montane tree species becoming rare below 8,000 feet. There is little summer moisture in the mountain range, but that which does eventually occur originates in the Gulf of California, the southeast

Pacific, or even the Gulf of Mexico, and is pulled northward when there is a zone of low pressure in the southwestern United States. This so-called monsoon moisture usually brings only brief afternoon thundershowers, but occasionally the remnants of a former tropical cyclone are entrained and carried north, bringing more persistent rain to the Sierra.

While these simple patterns explain much of the variation in temperatures and moisture across the Sierra, the boundaries between vegetation zones can be more intricate, reflecting the amount of sun exposure on different aspects, varying soil depths, and more. Vegetation zones and plant communities may be interfingered near their boundaries, with dominant tree species shifting based on plant-available moisture; each species has subtly different water requirements. Though overall moisture input is quite similar at a single elevation in the western Sierra, plant-available moisture fluctuates greatly with topography and soil depth; water availability is much lower on steeper slopes, in shallow soils, or in sandy soils, for the water drains more quickly. Also influencing what vegetation community persists in a locale is evaporative demand, effectively the dryness of the surrounding environment and therefore how much water a plant will lose. Plants on sunny south-facing slopes or ridgetops have a much higher evaporative demand than those on shaded north-facing slopes or in steep drainages. This leads, for example, to red fir forests extending to considerably higher elevations when there is higher water availability and lower evaporative demand, such as in deeper soils and in sheltered draws.

By considering these secondary effects, one can fine-tune the vegetation zone maps and subdivide them into more precise vegetation types. For instance, the upper-montane forest zone can be further divided with meadows occurring at the wettest sites, red fir forest where there is slightly less water, and then Jeffrey pine forest and finally juniper woodland at the driest sites. These vegetation types will be familiar to anyone who has hiked in the mid-elevation Sierra, where lakeshores and depressions hold meadows, much of the landscape is fir forest, and the dry south-facing slopes or rocky ridges are inhabited by either Jeffrey pines or junipers.

The subalpine forest zone can be similarly divided. Across all elevations, the wettest sites contain meadows. As one moves to drier slopes, lodgepole pine forests almost always dominate in the Kings, Kern, and Kaweah River drainages, regardless of aspect. However, from Yosemite south to the San Joaquin drainage (and very sparingly farther south), wetter, cooler slopes are home to mountain hemlocks, while lodgepole pines are on the drier and warmer aspects, as well as in locations with poor soil development. At the highest subalpine elevations, whitebark pines replace lodgepole pines, especially in rocky terrain and locations with expanses of granite slabs close to the soil surface, such as lake basins. Once south of the Middle Fork of the Kings River, foxtail pines are common on dry slopes and flats between 8,500 and 12,000 feet in elevation. They occupy sites that would be home to either lodgepole pines or whitebark pines farther north. There are two additional high-elevation conifers to add to the mix: Western white pines occur scattered through both lodgepole pine and red fir forests but can grow as open monospecific stands, especially on fairly open slopes in locations with deeper soils. Limber pines are restricted to the eastern Sierra, where they grow as small stands on rocky slopes.

One final thought is to remember that species distributions are never static. Following a fire, subalpine species, including lodgepole pines, mountain hemlocks, and western white pines, will establish in habitats where red fir will eventually be the dominant species. Over time, red firs will establish and shade them out, restricting them to the less hospitable higher elevation forests. See also "The Importance of Fire," page 20, for more on fire in high-elevation forests.

See pages 6–7 for a table to help identify both these higher-elevation conifer species and a few others that are mostly restricted to the mixed conifer forests. Learning to identify these 12 common species will help give you a sense of how the growing conditions change as you saunter across the landscape, giving hints to what shrubs and herbs you may find in the area.

❖ Habitats

A *species' habitat is*, quite simply, the area where it lives. Vegetation zones, together with the added information on local soil water availability and evaporation, accurately predict which conifer species occur across the landscape. However, to define the preferred habitats of hundreds of herbs and shrubs—which may live in meadows, in talus fields, along streams, in forests, or in the middle of sandy flats—many additional variables must be considered. Ideally, a habitat is defined as the unique combination of all possible physical and chemical conditions and biological interactions at a location. Moreover, a habitat is the combination of these features across the lifetime of the plant, for the seedling must germinate, establish, and

CONIFER SPECIES

COMMON NAME	SCIENTIFIC NAMES	NEEDLES		CONES	
		# per cluster	Length (cm)	Length (cm)	Shape
White Fir	Abies concolor	1	3–5	7–12	Cylindrical, bulky
Red Fir	Abies magnificata	1	1.5–3	12–20	Cylindrical, bulky
Ponderosa Pine	Pinus ponderosa var. pacifica	3	12–20	8–15	Nearly round
Sugar Pine	Pinus lambertiana	5	5–11	20–40	Cylindrical, very long
Jeffrey Pine	Pinus jeffreyi	3	20–25	15–25	Oval; broader at base
Western Juniper	Juniperus occidentalis	Tight scales		Small blue "berry"	
Western White Pine	Pinus monticola	5	5–10	10–20	Cylindrical
Mountain Hemlock	Tsuga mertensiana	1	1.5–2	4–7	Oblong
Lodgepole Pine	Pinus contorta	2	2.5–7	3–5	Nearly round
Foxtail Pine	Pinus balfouriana	5	1.5–4	6–18	Cylindrical
Limber Pine	Pinus flexilis	5	2–9	7–12	Cylindrical, chunky
Whitebark Pine	Pinus albicaulis	5	3–7	3.5–9	Cylindrical

then continue to survive through all seasons and, for perennial plants, across drought years, excessively wet years, hot days, cold snaps, and whatever other conditions it experiences.

Species' habitats in the Sierra Nevada and elsewhere have indeed been precisely defined by vegetation studies that compare a species' distribution with knowledge of the physical, chemical, and biological conditions across the landscape. While detailed studies are essential to document the

BARK CHARACTERISTICS	ELEVATION RANGE (feet)	OTHER CHARACTERISTICS
Bright white on young trees; light gray on mature trees; thick and furrowed	3,000–8,000 (Occasionally higher)	Mature cones never fall to ground intact; needles in a fairly flat plane
Dull white on young trees; rich red on mature trees; very thick and furrowed	5,000–9,000	Mature cones never fall to ground intact; needles mostly encircle branches
Furrows not deep, but quite wide and notably darker than rest of the orange-red bark; thick bark	3,000–7,000	Prickles on each cone scale point straight out
Red-brown color; fairly shallow grooves break bark into smaller polygons than firs and Jeffrey pine	4,000–7,500	Notably long branches with cones at tips
Aromatic; thick and deeply grooved; outermost flakes like puzzle pieces	6,000–9,000	Prickles on each cone scale point straight downward
Red-brown to red-orange; fibrous, like a fraying rope	7,000–10,000	In dry, rocky locations
Patterned, similar to puzzle pieces, but not very dimensional	7,500–10,500	Airy appearance
Red-brown color, with very fine, close-together grooves	8,000–11,000	More common in north; new branch tips droop downward
Thin and scaly, not at all three-dimensional	6,500–11,000	Abundant cones at tree bases
Rich red color; broken by irregular longitudinal groves	9,000–12,000	Only south of Pinchot Pass; long branches of needles look like foxtails or bottlebrushes
Fairly smooth and gray when young, with shallow furrows when older	8,000–12,000	Restricted to the eastern Sierra; cone scales are notably thick
Quite white and rather smooth	9,500–12,000	Most common tree in higher elevation lake basins

exact prevalence of species, what growing conditions particular species require, and what communities of plant species routinely co-occur, their results are of limited use to a hiker because you cannot measure soil temperature, soil gravel content, or precise solar radiation as you walk. However, with practice and persistence, you, a casual observer, can visually distinguish between locations suited to different species. Once you know the Sierra and its large- and fine-scale landforms well, you will be able to walk across the landscape and predict which furry-leaved friends you will stumble across. You may find yourself looking at the surrounding terrain, roughly guesstimating environmental conditions that can be approximated with a quick glance, including soil depth, water availability, slope, shading, type of bedrock, and the size of the rocks on the soil surface. Once you begin to look at the landscape as a continuum of unique habitats, you will notice that some species always grow alongside boulders, while others prefer the middle of a bare sandy flat, a wet meadow, a crack in a boulder, or some other habitat. For me, finding uncommon habitats, such as a seep in the middle of an alpine fell-field or in a talus field, is always cause for celebration because I am more likely to stumble across some rarely seen species.

❖ How to Use This Book

This book is written to be accessible to a wildflower enthusiast with no technical training but contains sufficiently detailed content to be of interest to serious amateur botanists as well as a broad range of natural-resources professionals.

The greatest divide between plant books written for different audiences seems to be the organization of plants; books for the expert are organized by scientific family and often contain dichotomous keys to identify plants, while those for amateurs are sorted by flower color. If you have a general sense of the plant features in each family, you can quickly skim the photos in one family (or a few) to identify a plant, but otherwise it is much faster to peruse by color; hence this book organizes plants by flower color. Flowers are grouped into the following color categories: white, yellow and orange, red and brown, pink, purple and blue, and green, with the latter category also including species lacking petals. Within each color category, plants are divided into two groupings: dicotyledons (dicots) and monocotyledons (monocots). The monocots have flowers with 3 or 6 petals and have leaves with parallel veins. This group includes grasses, sedges, and—pertinent to this book—irises, lilies, and orchids. The dicots include all other plant families. Within each of these two classes, the plants are organized alphabetically by family name. Divisions based on flower color can be frustrating, for a number of species could be called either pink or purple, and a handful of species can be either white or purple. In most cases, these species are filed with purple flowers, as this is their more common variant.

For each of the species, the following information is included: its scientific name (the combination of genus and species names, per the online *Jepson Manual*, the authoritative source for California plant names), its common name (as indicated in *The Jepson Manual* or at **calflora.org**), its family (a taxonomic designation that groups related genera), previous scientific species and family names (with which many people are more familiar than their current names), a detailed description of its distribution, locations where it may be seen, its habitat, its elevation range in the Sierra between Yosemite and the Mt. Whitney region, its flowering season, a description of the plant (including leaves, stems, flowers, and fruits), and sometimes extra facts about the plant. Because there are no official common names for plants, many plants are referred to by multiple common names; in such cases, two names may be given. Species, subspecies, or varieties closely related to the described plant are occasionally listed at the end of the species' description, with a brief explanation of how they differ from the focal species and where they may be found. Following are more detailed descriptions of what the profile for each species includes.

SPECIES' DISTRIBUTION provides information on both commonness and geographic range. Some species occur throughout the High Sierra, but many others are restricted to a subset of the region or are distinctly more common in parts of the region. The range of species is usually restricted by geographic barriers, either major ridges (most obviously the Sierra Crest but also many of the smaller, usually east–west trending ridges in the Sierra that divide the river drainages) or the deep river drainages themselves, especially the San Joaquin River or Kern River. The most common pattern is for species to be constrained to either the eastern or western Sierra or to be more common farther north or south within the range. These range limits exist because the eastern Sierra is far drier than regions west of the Sierra Crest, and the more southerly reaches of the High Sierra are both warmer and drier than locations farther north; see page 2 for more on how the Sierra's climate influences vegetation communities.

If applicable, I list distributions separately for the lands west versus east of the Sierra Crest. In addition, for narrowly distributed species, I mostly describe their distributions based on the river drainages where they are found. Farthest north is the so-called Yosemite region, defined to include both the Tuolumne and Merced River drainages because the drainage divide between them is quite low and not a barrier to most species' dispersal. The region just to the east of Yosemite National Park in the Mono Basin is referred to as the Yosemite region east of the Sierra Crest. The next region south is called the Mammoth Lakes region and includes both the eastern Sierra around Mammoth Lakes as well as the North Fork San Joaquin and Middle Fork San Joaquin drainages, which run, respectively, to the west and east of the Ritter Range, on the north side of the main San Joaquin drainage. Once farther south, the floras of the eastern and western Sierra become increasingly distinct, and geographic ranges are described more explicitly by river drainages. In the western Sierra, from north to south, are the San Joaquin River, the Kings River, the Kern River, and the Kaweah River. In the eastern Sierra, between the towns of Mammoth Lakes and Big Pine, mention is made of the drainages containing Convict Creek, Rock Creek, Bishop Creek, and Big Pine Creek. Several smaller river basins also drain this stretch of the eastern Sierra, but none stands out as an important divide for describing species' distributions. Farther south, there are many creeks, all with quite small, steep drainages, and only two additional divisions are used: the Kearsarge Pass area, referring to the popular trail that climbs above Independence Creek; and the Mt. Whitney region, indicating the region of high peaks from Mt. Whitney south to New Army Pass, including, among others, the Lone Pine Creek and Cottonwood Creek drainages. Other geographic terms used include the Palisades, the rugged range along the Sierra Crest to the southwest of Big Pine Creek; Mineral King, a region in the far southwestern corner of the High Sierra; and the Kern Plateau, the elevated, quite flat plateau on the eastern side of the Kern River drainage once south of the Mt. Whitney region, which is just to the south of the High Sierra. Most terms used are shown on the map on page 12.

It is also mentioned if a species is generally rare or common, with special note made if it is considerably more common in part of its range than elsewhere. A species designated as common or very common is one that you are very likely to see in a day's hike within its range; a species designated as occasional is one you may find with either persistent searching or after a few hikes in the region; and you may come across a rare species only after many hikes or if you purposefully head to a location where there is a known population.

I HAVE INCLUDED AT LEAST THREE LOCATIONS WHERE YOU CAN FIND EACH SPECIES. Many of these are places where I have found the species, and others are locations where herbarium specimens have been collected. In general, I have picked sites above 8,000 feet, but for a few species that are also common at lower elevations, I have included other well-visited spots.

To the extent possible, I have, for each species, included both locations that are accessible on day hikes and ones that you would pass on a backpacking trip, with particular emphasis on spots along the well-traveled John Muir Trail corridor. I have included many entries from a few of my favorite day hike accessible locations, including, from north to south, the Virginia Lakes Basin, the Twenty Lakes Basin, the Dana Plateau and Mt. Dana, the Rock Creek Basin, and Coyote Ridge. Many of these locations are on metamorphic rock, which tends to have greater vegetation cover and often higher diversity and less common species. If you wish to search for species most common at montane elevations, Yosemite Creek and White Wolf in Yosemite and the Devils Postpile/Agnew Meadows region west of Mammoth Lakes are beautiful and easily accessible. The Convict Creek drainage, a little south of Mammoth Lakes, has predominately marble bedrock, resulting in a very unique flora, but most of those species are rare and are not included in this book. (See "Plants of Calcareous Soils," page 99, for more information.) A number of species are unique to the Kern River drainage (and sometimes the southern parts of the Kings River drainage and the adjacent eastern Sierra). Many of those species are quite common at high elevations and easily encountered by backpackers but difficult to reach on day hikes. Long day hikes in the direction of Kearsarge Pass, Mt. Whitney, or New Army Pass will bring you close to many of them, but an overnight trip in this region will give you more opportunities to search for rarer specimens. No matter where you explore, you will come across more species if you occasionally wander off-trail.

To search for additional locations to find a species, try the Consortium of California Herbaria, an online database that tabulates information on specimens in herbaria across many California institutions. You can type the name of the species and generate a list of places where it is known to occur. Alternatively, you can search for a geographic area you will be

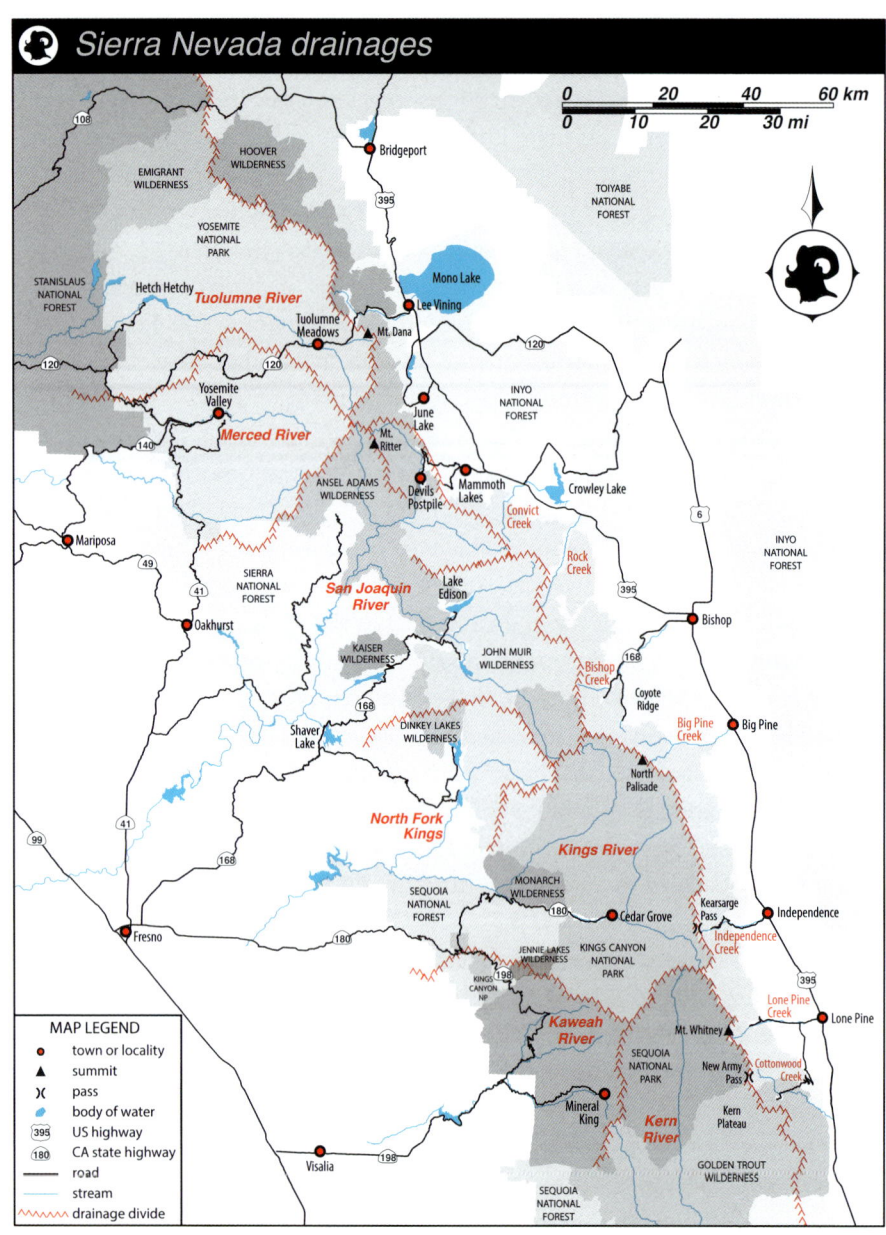

visiting and compile a list of all species that have been collected and tagged with that location; this method will not generate a complete species list but is a wonderful starting point.

HABITAT. A species' habitat is its home—the locations where it can live. The habitat descriptions given for each species are usually brief, indicating whether it is found, for example, on dry slopes, in meadows, or alongside streams. More specific information is provided only for species that live in a quite restricted collection of habitats or are very distinct in their habitat preference. Additional details on characteristics that differ between habitats are presented on page 5 and in "Generalists and Specialists" on page 184.

FLOWERING SEASON. The range of flowering times for most species spans about a month to a month and a half. Deciding how best to present this information is difficult, for there is so much variation across elevations, locations, and years that most species could be given a flowering season spanning the entire summer; in some years, at some elevations, you will find a species blooming long before or after it is "supposed" to. The flowering season ranges given for each species are the times when an individual growing in the upper montane, subalpine, or alpine zones will be in bloom during an average, or nearly average, year. Consider that a given individual will usually bloom for a period of two to three weeks, occasionally slightly more. Species of dry habitats have a short period in bloom, while those in habitats that remain moist throughout the summer, such as permanent seeps or stream banks, often continue blooming for a month or longer. Individuals of a species growing at lower elevations, where the snow melts earlier and temperatures are warmer, will usually begin blooming earlier than those at higher elevations; for a species that occurs across a wide elevation range, low-elevation individuals could begin blooming more than a month before the ones at high elevation do.

Most difficult to incorporate in the flowering times is the year-to-year variation; some people accurately joke that the Sierra has "average" precipitation but no "normal" year, with snowpack depth and time of snowmelt displaying enormous year-to-year variation. At a given subalpine location, the snow may disappear six weeks earlier in a drought year than in a high precipitation year, which will differentially affect species in separate habitats, as well as different species within a single habitat. Early flowering species in dry, exposed sites tend to launch into flower as soon as the snow vanishes and are therefore extremely variable across years. Later flowering species in these same locations will also advance their flowering times in dry years but often appear to wait for nighttime temperatures to warm a

little before the buds open and are therefore less affected by yearly variation. This means that, in the driest years, their flowers are often straggly
and few because the soils are already quite dry by the time the plants begin
flowering. Meanwhile, streamside species often thrive in years with early
snowmelt. These species are generally taller and frequently grow for several
weeks before flowering; in years with a smaller snowpack, they begin growing and flowering earlier, and because they have a continuous water source,
early snowmelt simply gives them additional weeks to continue growing
and flowering. In contrast, in the wettest years, the alpine fell-field species
and species in seasonally wet meadows typically have superb displays, while
the taller species inhabiting wet sites have a delayed start to their growth
and may actually be less showy. An added wild card is summer rainfall. In
most years, the Sierra has little summer rainfall, and species can certainly
not depend on this moisture input. However, in the odd years with considerable "monsoon" moisture from thunderstorms, species in locations that
usually dry quickly may continue flowering for longer.

Overall, above 8,000 feet, in an "average" year, few species bloom
before the beginning of June or after the beginning of September. This is
a narrow window, with 10 days making an enormous difference in what
species you will encounter. The earliest blooming species begin producing
flowers in the upper-montane forests in early June and in the subalpine
and alpine zones in mid- to late June, while the mid-season species are
showy by early July. Already by mid- to late July, the species I think of as
marking the final flush of summer color are beginning to open, with only
a few truly late-season species waiting until August to unfurl their petals.

THE SPECIES DESCRIPTIONS presented in this book are less detailed than those
in a technical book about plants. For each species, I have included sufficient
information to distinguish the species from others described in the book
but have omitted some details to minimize the use of unfamiliar terminol-
ogy and to keep the descriptions succinct. Words that may be unfamiliar
to many readers are defined and illustrated in sketches on the following
pages. Infrequently used terms are defined at each mention. Most species
described are perennials. If a species is an annual, it is noted in the description. Some perennials are herbaceous, meaning they lack woody parts, and
others are shrubs, indicating that at least part of their stems are woody.

If you are struggling to see details of plants, such as hairs or glands,
carry along a small hand lens or a camera with a good macro lens. I

increasingly find myself taking photos of plant parts with my not-too-expensive point-and-shoot camera and then looking at the screen to see the details. All dimensions are given in metric units: meters (m), centimeters (cm), and millimeters (mm). See page 265 for a ruler and conversion table (from metric to English) to help you estimate lengths.

❖ Parts of a Flower

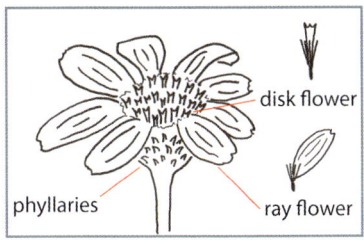

Asteraceae (sunflower family)

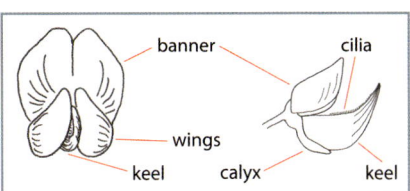

Fabaceae (pea family)

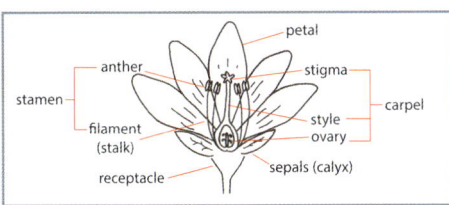

generic flower

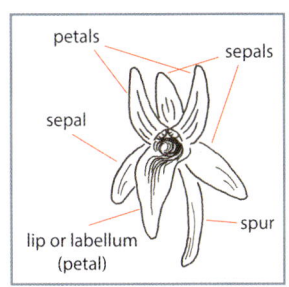

Orchidaceae (orchid family)

Glossary

annual A species that lives for only a single growing season

anther Located at the tip of a stamen, it produces and contains pollen. The term *pollen sac* is usually used in this book.

axil On a stem, the location just above the node, where a leaf is attached. Branches and flower buds grow from axils.

basal Referring to the base or lower section of a stem, leaf, or other plant part. For example, basal leaves are those toward the bottom of the stem.

calyx A flower's sepals are collectively referred to as the calyx. If the sepals are fused together, the term *calyx* is always used.

carpel Also called the pistil, carpel refers to the female floral parts—the ovary, style, and stigma—as a single unit.

caudex The basal part of a perennial plant stem, often at least partially underground, from which new growth emerges

compound leaf A leaf that is subdivided all the way to the central stalk or midrib, such that multiple leaflets are formed. See also leaflet, pinnate leaf, and palmate leaf.

corolla The flower's petals are collectively referred to as the corolla. This term is not used in species' descriptions.

disk flower In the family Asteraceae, this term refers to the flowers in the center of the inflorescence, which have a radially symmetrical flower tube and usually lack petal lobes extending far beyond its mouth. See the sketch on page 15.

filament The stalklike part of a stamen. The more generic term *stalk* is generally used in this book.

fruit Botanically, the fruit is the mature ovary, inside which are the seeds, the mature ovules. Fruits can have many forms, such as fleshy like a blueberry, a dry pod, or a capsule.

glandular When the leaf or stem surface is covered with little glands. Sometimes the glands are directly on the surface, but more often they are at the ends of hairs.

inflorescence A collection of flowers along a stem. In some flowers, this refers to a specific floral structure, such as an umbel or the characteristic inflorescences in the Asteraceae (see page 91), while in other species, it is simply a length of stem along which there are flowers.

leaflet One of the subdivisions of a compound leaf. Unlike a true leaf, leaflets do not attach to a main stem or branch but instead to a single leaf's stalk. Two common arrangements of leaflets are palmate and pinnate.

midrib The vein that runs down the middle of a leaf

node On a stem, a junction where a leaf or branch connects

ovary The female reproductive organ, located at the base of the carpel. The ovules, or eggs, are located within the ovary. The ovary develops into the fruit.

ovule The structure(s) inside the ovary that, when fertilized, becomes a seed.

palmate leaf A compound leaf in which the leaflets radiate from a central point. Imagine how fingers all connect to the palm of a hand.

perennial A species that lives for multiple years. Such species usually wait one or more years before they begin flowering.

petal A part of a flower that is often showy, with the purpose of attracting pollinators. Not all flowers have petals, and not all showy plant parts are officially petals. See also "What Is a Petal?" on page 143.

petiole The stalk that connects a leaf blade to the stem. The more generic term *stalk* is generally used in this book.

phyllary In the family Asteraceae, a ring of small leaves that surrounds the circle of ray and disk flowers. They are usually green but can be reddish.

pinnate leaf A compound leaf in which the leaflets are arranged in pairs along the central stalk. There is often one leaflet at the very end, so the total number of leaflets is usually odd.

pistil See the definition of carpel on page 15.

ray flower In the family Asteraceae, this term refers to the flowers around the outside of the inflorescence, in which one side of the flower tube is very elongate and bent outward, resembling a single long petal. See the sketch on page 15.

rhizome An underground stem from which shoots can emerge. Many plants whose leaves seemingly spread across the ground have rhizomes.

rosette An arrangement of leaves in a circle at the base of the plant. They can either lie flat against the ground or trend more upward.

sepal The leaflike (or petallike) structures that surround the petals and usually have a protective function when the flower is a bud. Together, the sepals are referred to as the calyx.

stamen The male reproductive part, composed of a stalk, also known as a filament, and the pollen sac, also known as the anther.

stigma The tip of the carpel and the location on which pollen is deposited for fertilization. It can be narrow, like the style, or much more bulbous.

style The tube (stalk) that leads from the ovary to the stigma. The pollen grains grow down this tube to reach the eggs.

umbel An umbel is an inflorescence that is a spherically (or hemispherically) arranged collection of flowers whose stalks all radiate from a single point. A compound umbel indicates that there are umbels within umbels, as is true of most Apiaceae.

whorl When leaves or flowers are connected to the stem in a series of circles, with or without a gap between the individual circles

❖ Green Flowers

Pectiantia breweri (see page 24)

❖ The Importance of Fire

Fire is an important disturbance up to an elevation of about 10,000 feet. While our impression of wildfire is often one of destruction, fires are vital to maintain the natural landscape. Many tree species, including the giant sequoias of the lower elevation Sierra, have seeds that require fire to germinate. Fires also create gaps of light in otherwise dense forests; these gaps are essential for seedlings of many species to germinate and grow. Historically, many Sierra blazes, across all elevations, have been low intensity, with lightning-caused fires creeping along the ground, burning dead branches and dry leaves, and less frequently disturbing the crowns of trees. In most patches, only the young trees with thin bark were killed. These small fires created forests that were composed of patches of various ages, leading to increased species diversity. The 1900s saw ever-increasing fire-suppression policies, with the goal of immediately extinguishing all fires to prevent "destruction" of wild areas (and, of course, human property). The results: More and more fuel built up in the forests, and fires became more and more difficult to control and also more destructive to the forest ecosystem. From the mid-1980s onward, this policy has slowly been reversed, as our understanding of the importance of fire has increased. Unfortunately, many of the lower-montane forests have so much built-up deadwood and branches that fires can be very destructive.

Many factors—including how dry the flammable material is, how much fuel is in the forest, and how many lightning strikes there are—influence the frequency and severity of fires across different elevations. The greatest number of lightning strikes is in the subalpine zone at about 10,000 feet, but at this high an elevation, the vegetation is rarely dense enough and the understory duff is too sparse and compacted to carry a fire very far. Even the red fir forests that dominate the upper-montane zone have a compact, dense duff that does not readily ignite; the largest, most severe fires are ignited in the white fir forests in the lower-montane zone. These factors lead to very different fire recurrence intervals—that is, time between fires—across elevations. At the highest subalpine elevations, in the whitebark pine–dominated areas, the fire interval is a staggering 23,000 years. Lodgepole forests at lower-subalpine zone elevations have fire every few hundred to 500 years. Prior to fire-suppression policies, the fire recurrence interval for the red fir forests of the upper-montane zone varied from 12 to 60 to more than 100 years, by locality, while for the white fir–mixed conifer forests of the lower-montane zone, it was 20–30 years.

Because the time between fires is so long in the subalpine zone, the trees in this area are not particularly adapted to fire. They do not require fire to establish and thrive. In fact, hemlocks are often killed by fire, while lodgepole pines are sometimes killed by fire. The highest elevation trees, whitebark and foxtail pines, are rarely killed by fire, due to the fact that, at these high elevations, the fires are generally very low intensity, and foxtail pines have very thick bark. Most herbaceous and shrubby species in the subalpine and alpine zones will die following a large fire. In lower elevation communities, the aboveground parts of many species die back, while their roots and large underground storage stems survive, allowing them to rapidly resprout after the fire. Resprouting is also observed in a number of high-elevation shrubs and trees, including *Chrysolepis sempervirens* (bush chinquapin), *Ceanothus cordulatus* (mountain whitethorn), *Quercus vacciniifolia* (huckleberry oak), and *Populus tremuloides* (quaking aspen). The two high-elevation manzanita species, *Arctostaphylos nevadensis* subsp. *nevadensis* (pine-mat manzanita) and *Arctostaphylos patula* (greenleaf manzanita), are both killed by fire but have seeds that readily sprout after the fire. Some herbaceous species will readily resprout from bulbs or underground stems, while others are killed and take longer to reestablish. In areas where there was once forest cover, the shrubs and herbs will all grow rapidly following a fire, and then slowly be overtopped and shaded as taller trees again establish, but this process, known as succession, takes many decades or even centuries following a severe fire.

❖ *Chrysolepis sempervirens* (bush chinquapin)
   FAMILY: Fagaceae

DISTRIBUTION Common throughout, on both sides of the Sierra Crest
HABITAT Dry, sandy to rocky slopes
ELEVATION 4,500'–11,000'
SEASON Early July–late August
LOCATIONS Lundy Canyon, Clouds Rest summit, Bear Creek, Lamarck Lakes Trail, North Fork Big Pine Creek

LEAVES AND STEMS: Usually less than 2 m in height, this shrub forms imposing thickets on dry, rocky slopes. If, however, you don't need to fight your way through them, enjoy their showy features. A golden powder covers the young stems and the underside of the leathery leaves. Because the leaves tend to be oriented in all directions, the shrubs are quite beautiful when the sun catches the underside of the leaves early or late in the day.

FLOWERS: The flowers themselves are not showy because, like most other members of the Fagaceae family, they are wind pollinated. They occur in long inflorescences, and notably, male and female flowers have separate inflorescences. The fruits are immediately noticeable because the prickly light-brown balls are up to 3.5 cm in diameter.

❖ *Quercus vacciniifolia* (huckleberry oak)
FAMILY: Fagaceae

DISTRIBUTION Common in the western Sierra in the Yosemite region and the San Joaquin drainage, becoming rarer farther south; only crossing to the eastern Sierra at Mammoth Lakes
HABITAT Dry, scrubby slopes
ELEVATION 5,000'–9,000'
SEASON Late May–early July
LOCATIONS Shadow Lake, Kaiser Meadow, White Wolf Campground, Tenaya Lake

LEAVES AND STEMS: The huckleberry oak is very common on dry, open slopes through montane elevations, often growing together with manzanita species or bush chinquapin. The densely branched shrub usually stands 1–1.5 m in height. The oval-shaped leathery leaves are 1–3 cm long and can have toothed or untoothed margins.

FLOWERS: A wind-pollinated species, the flowers are barely visible, growing along a long, narrow inflorescence. In fall, small acorns adorn the plants.

❖ *Frasera puberulenta (Swertia puberulenta)* (Inyo frasera)
FAMILY: Gentianaceae

DISTRIBUTION Fairly common in the eastern Sierra from Mammoth Lakes south through Cottonwood Creek
HABITAT Dry, often sandy, slopes
ELEVATION 7,400'–11,000'
SEASON Early July–early August
LOCATIONS Convict Creek drainage, near Brown Lake (from South Lake), North Fork Big Pine Creek, Baxter Pass Trail

LEAVES AND STEMS: The stout, often purplish stalk reaches at most 40 cm in height and is often only half that, making it easy to distinguish from the tall monument plant. Narrow leaves cover the stem and occur in pairs offset from one another at right angles. The gray-green leaves are typically somewhat folded in along their midrib and have white margins.

FLOWERS: Inflorescences grow from most leaf axils, each branched and bearing several of the decorative 4-petal flowers at the ends of the stems. The petals are green but with an ornate pattern of purplish splotches and frilly, so-called appendages toward the center of each petal. Behind, and offset from the petals by 45 degrees, are 4 narrow, greenish sepals. When in full bloom, the plant is quite striking.

❖ *Frasera speciosa (Swertia radiata)* (monument plant, deer ears) **FAMILY:** Gentianaceae

DISTRIBUTION Fairly common in the Yosemite and Mammoth Lakes regions; becoming rarer to the south; absent in the Kern River drainage
HABITAT Meadows, dry slopes, and dry flats
ELEVATION 7,000'–10,000'
SEASON Mid-July–early September
LOCATIONS Virginia Lakes Basin, Dog Lake Trail, Agnew Meadows, Blue Lake (Lake Sabrina Basin), east side of Kearsarge Pass Trail

LEAVES AND STEMS: Early in the summer there is a basal rosette of large (usually 10–30 cm), oval-shaped, soft, hairy leaves with no other identifying features. Many individuals do not develop beyond this stage in a given year; it takes several years of growth to store enough energy to flower. In July some individuals send up a 1- to 2-m-tall, very stout, shiny stalk encircled by many whorls (circles) of oval-shaped, pointy-tipped leaves.

FLOWERS: An inflorescence stalk bearing up to 10 flowers grows from each leaf axil, creating a large plant absolutely covered in flowers. The flowers have 4 thick, pale green to white petals adorned with purple dots or patterns. The fuzzy pink-purple structures on the petals are nectaries, producing a sugary solution for pollinators to harvest.

❖ *Thalictrum fendleri* var. *fendleri* (Fendler's meadow rue)
     FAMILY: Ranunculaceae

DISTRIBUTION Common throughout, on both sides of the Sierra Crest
HABITAT Stream banks, moist forest, marshy areas
ELEVATION 3,300'–11,000'
SEASON Mid-June–late July
LOCATIONS Virginia Canyon, Dana Gardens (western base of Mt. Dana), Duck Pass Trail, Rae Lakes Basin

LEAVES AND STEMS: Meadow rues produce a lot of leaves, both near the ground and along the 60- to 150-cm-tall stems. The leaves are divided into 7–9 leaflets, many of these further divided into 3 small leaflets, about 1–2 cm in width. The outer margin of each leaflet is round lobed and may be either hairless or sparsely covered in gland-dotted hairs. Each "leaf," a tall stalk of leaflets, can range 10–40 cm in length.

FLOWERS: This species is dioecious, meaning plants have only male or female flowers, not both. Moreover, both male and female flowers lack petals, with 5 green sepals cupping the stamens or pistils. Female plants look like half a pom-pom because the styles form a dome far less than 1 cm in diameter. The male flowers are more eye-catching; beneath the sepals dangle many stamens with burgundy-colored stalks and yellowish pollen at the tips. The flowers on either gender of plant occur on tall, very branched stalks; each stem can hold more than 50 flowers. The pistils soon develop into bowling pin–shaped fruits.

RELATED SPECIES: Mainly found in the Rock Creek and Convict Creek drainages, *Thalictrum alpinum* (arctic meadow rue) is a much shorter plant, reaching just 5–15 cm in height. The flower stalk bends downward once in fruit, so the fruits dangle downward.

❖ *Salix petrophila (Salix arctica)* (Rocky Mountain willow, alpine willow)
FAMILY: Salicaceae

DISTRIBUTION Common in the eastern Sierra from the Yosemite region south to the Mt. Whitney region; less common in the western Sierra
HABITAT Moist alpine tundra
ELEVATION 9,800'–12,000'
SEASON Early June–early July
LOCATIONS Gaylor Lakes, Mt. Dana Trail, Convict Creek drainage, Taboose Pass, Rae Lakes Basin

LEAVES AND STEMS: Common in wet alpine areas, this shrubby willow grows as a spreading mat, rooting at branch nodes. The stems are brownish to greenish and are sparsely hairy. Though only 2–4 cm in length, the leaves look quite similar to those of a larger willow. They are shaped like elongate ovals, are quite thick, and have a hairier underside than the top of the leaf.

FLOWERS: This is certainly not a species that you seek out for showy flowers; its inflorescence is generally 2–5 cm long with barely noticeable flowers sticking out from behind triangular leaves, known as bracts. Not only do the flowers lack petals, but like all willows, the plant is also dioecious, meaning that male and female flowers occur on separate plants. The male plants simply have stamens, while the female plants have only carpels. The female plants become showy, however, as they go to seed, for each seed has a cluster of long (long!) white hairs, so the entire plant appears to be covered in cotton stuffing.

RELATED SPECIES: *Salix planifolia,* the diamondleaf willow, is less common but easily identifiable when seen. It too crawls along the ground but has vibrant red-brown shiny stems and leaves whose upper surface is fuzzy with long white hairs. Its range also spans the length of the High Sierra.

Salix planifolia

❖ *Pectiantia breweri (Mitella breweri)*
(Brewer's miterwort)   **FAMILY:** Saxifragaceae

DISTRIBUTION Common throughout west of the Sierra Crest, and occasional east of the Sierra Crest, becoming rarer farther south
HABITAT Moist, sheltered locations, including stream banks, seeps, wet forest, and willow thickets at meadow edges
ELEVATION 6,500'–11,000'
SEASON Early June–mid-July
LOCATIONS Virginia Canyon, Dana Plateau trail, Duck Pass Trail, French Canyon, Vidette Meadow

LEAVES AND STEMS: This species consists of a basal rosette of leaves and a flowering stem. The glossy basal leaves are 3–8 cm wide, fairly circular in outline, with shallow, rounded lobes. Stiff hairs cover the stem, while the leaves are usually hairless.

FLOWERS: Up to 40 flowers grow from a 15- to 25-cm-long inflorescence stalk. The light-green 0.3- to 0.5-cm-long petals are shaped like old radio antennae: a central stalk, with 3 narrow cross-stalks on each side. These connect to a central tissue disk, the hypanthium. Quite short stamens attach between each of the petals.

RELATED SPECIES: *Pectiantia pentandra* (formerly *Mitella pentandra*; alpine miterwort) differs mainly in having stamens attached directly in front of the petals. It mostly occurs at lower elevations but has been found in the subalpine in several locations around Tioga Pass and northern Yosemite.

❖ *Urtica dioica* subsp. *holosericea* (hoary nettle, stinging nettle)
   FAMILY: Urticaceae

DISTRIBUTION Rare to occasional at montane elevations on both sides of the Sierra Crest, occasionally extending to subalpine elevations
HABITAT Wet meadows, seeps, moist disturbed areas, stream banks
ELEVATION 4,750'–10,750'
SEASON Late June–late August
LOCATIONS Shamrock Lake (Twenty Lakes Basin), Glass Creek Meadow, Sotcher Lake, Tully Hole, Long Lake (Rock Creek Basin), Baxter Pass Trail

LEAVES AND STEMS: Hoary nettle is a native stinging nettle that occurs near moisture sources, sometimes in dense thickets. The plants are tall, reaching 1–3 m in height, and the leaves and stems are both densely covered in stinging hairs, making this a plant best avoided. The plants release a chemical when the hairs are touched, which causes the sting. The elongate, serrate leaves occur in pairs along the length of the stem and are 6–10 cm in length, sometimes longer.

FLOWERS: At each leaf node is 1 or more 1- to 7-cm-long dangling inflorescences of many tiny, whitish flowers. The flowers are minuscule with 4 white to green sepals but lacking petals. Note that on a given plant, some inflorescences have stamens and others have carpels. Such a plant is labeled *monoecious,* meaning "single house." While there are separate male and female flowers, they both occur on a single plant. The longer dangling inflorescences bear the male flowers.

❖ *Platanthera sparsiflora* (sparse flowered bog orchid)
   FAMILY: Orchidaceae

DISTRIBUTION Occasional throughout, on both sides of the Sierra Crest; mostly at montane elevat▮ but occasionally occurring in the subalpine
HABITAT Seeps, stream banks, wet meadows
ELEVATION 4,000'–9,800'
SEASON Late June–early August
LOCATIONS Tenaya Lake, Minaret Lake, Rock Creek Trail, North Lake trailhead

(Continued)

(Continued)   **LEAVES AND STEMS:** Though quite common, this species is easily overlooked because its narrow leaves and green flowers blend in with the abundant vegetation of its moist locations. The fairly stout stalks rise 25–55 cm, with a few long, narrow leaves at the base and much shorter leaves along the length of the stem. The stem leaves are often shorter than 5 mm in length and quite narrow, especially at the tip.

FLOWERS: The upper section of stem bears the small green flowers, each only 1 cm long. Of the flower's 3 sepals, 2 are long and narrow and point outward, while the third forms a hood over the top of the flower. In addition, the 2 upper petals point forward, while the lower one, called the lip, is very long. At the back of the lip is the long, narrow spur, a protrusion that hangs down behind this petal and forms a very long, deep, and downward-pointed pocket at the base of the flower. All species in the genus *Platanthera* have nectar-filled spurs.

RELATED SPECIES:
A related species, *Platanthera tescamnis* (previously named *Platanthera hyperborea*; green flowered bog orchid), occurs sporadically in the eastern Sierra, though you are most likely to find it in the Convict Creek drainage. It is the only bog orchid to occur in dry locations, and its flowers are distinguished by being yellowish, having a slightly curved spur, and featuring a lip that is much longer than the hood.

Platanthera tescamnis

❖ Meanings of Latin Names

The Latin names of species are long and can be cumbersome to memorize, but they are not arbitrary, often indicating some distinguishing feature of the species—or, as described in "Some Famous Botanists" on page 135, may memorialize the person who discovered the plant or another person.

Many of the Latin (and sometimes Greek) derivations have no meaning to English speakers and are more of a curiosity than helpful in decoding or remembering a flower's scientific name. However, other Latin roots may trigger an association with a related word in the English language or are so frequently used that it is worth learning the prefix's or suffix's meaning. Sometimes knowing the meaning of a name provides extra confirmation that I have correctly identified a species, and other times it simply makes the scientific name easier to remember.

🐾 The suffix *-folia* means "having to do with leaves." There are many ways species' names incorporate this root. *Foliosa, foliosum,* and other variants mean "leafy," suggesting a plant with a profusion of leaves. Other times, an adjective combined with *folia* describes a characteristic of the leaves, such as millefolium (meaning "a thousand leaves," used for the very dissected leaves of *Achillea millefolium* and *Chamaebatiaria millefolium*), longifolia (meaning "long leaves," used for the long, narrow leaves in species such as *Arnica longifolia*), ovalifolium (meaning "oval-shaped leaves," as seen in *Eriogonum ovalifolium* var. *nivale*), densifolia (which means "having a dense clustering of leaves," as in *Draba densifolia*), paucifolius (which describes "having few leaves," as in *Rumex paucifolius*), and integrifolia (meaning "smooth leaf margins, neither toothed nor dissected," as in *Rhodiola integrifolia* subsp. *integrifolia*).

🐾 The suffixes (or occasionally prefixes) *-flora, -florus,* and similar derivations refer to traits of the flowers. Examples include *Dicentra uniflora,* where flowers occur singly, and *Thalictrum sparsiflorum* and *Platanthera sparsiflora,* where the inflorescences are sparsely flowered.

🐾 *Nevadensis* indicates that a species is from the Sierra Nevada (or possibly the state of Nevada), with many examples, including *Podistera nevadensis, Ribes nevadense, Arnica nevadensis,* and *Lewisia nevadensis.*

🐾 *Speciosus* or *speciosa* means that the flowers on a plant are particularly showy, with *Frasera speciosa* and *Penstemon speciosus* being perfect examples.

Ribes nevadense (see page 53)

🐾 *Nana* and *pygmaeus* both refer to plants that are small, and both terms are, not surprisingly, more common among the alpine species, such as *Crepis nana, Castilleja nana,* and *Erigeron pygmaeus.*

🐾 The prefix *mont-,* which is used in many forms, indicates an association with the mountains, with examples including *Ribes montigenum* and *Agoseris monticola.*

See **calflora.net/botanicalnames** for an exhaustive list of the meanings of California plant names.

❖ White Flowers

Aquilegia pubescens (see page 66)

❖ *Sambucus nigra* subsp. *caerulea (Sambucus mexicana)*
(blue elderberry)   **FAMILY:** Adoxaceae (Caprifoliaceae)

DISTRIBUTION Fairly common throughout most areas but especially common in drainages in the eastern Sierra
HABITAT Dry slopes and flats, stream banks
ELEVATION 1,000'–10,000'
SEASON Late June–late July
LOCATIONS Convict Creek drainage, Mono Creek, South Fork Big Pine Creek, Baxter Pass Trail, Mt. Whitney Trail

LEAVES AND STEMS: Though this shrub can grow quite tall—references list 8 m as the maximum—2–3 m is a more normal height at higher elevations. Multiple branches grow from the base. The branches are quite leafy; the leaves are divided into 3–9 leaflets, each 5–20 cm long, serrated around the edges, and narrowly oval shaped, but tapered to the tip. All elderberries have a characteristic pattern of leaf veins: There are no obvious veins in the last few millimeters before the leaf margin.

FLOWERS: The miniature 5-petal white flowers grow in dense heads of many hundreds of flowers, each only a few millimeters in diameter. For this species, unlike the red and black elderberries, the flowering head is flat on top, not dome-shaped. Most obvious are the berries in late fall—black but covered with white powder, so they appear blue. Meanwhile, the flowering stems have turned red. Though edible and tasty when cooked, only a few of the berries should be eaten raw.

❖ *Sambucus racemosa* var. *racemosa (Sambucus racemosa* var. *microbotrys)*
(red elderberry)   **FAMILY:** Adoxaceae (Caprifoliaceae)

DISTRIBUTION Fairly common in the eastern Sierra south to Mammoth Lakes, but absent farther south; fairly common throughout the western Sierra
HABITAT Rocky areas, including talus slopes, with some underlying moisture; meadow edges
ELEVATION 6,000'–11,800'
SEASON Early July–early August
LOCATIONS Middle Gaylor Lake, Isberg Pass, Beck Lakes, Mono Creek, Bench Lake, north of Olancha Peak

LEAVES AND STEMS: This shrub usually grows 1–2 m in height, forming a large thicket of stems and leaves. The strong-odored leaves are divided into 5–7 serrated, oval-shaped leaflets that are up to 16 cm long. As with all elderberry leaves, the main veins do not extend all the way to the edge of the leaf, instead curving parallel to the midvein.

Sambucus racemosa
var. *melanocarpa*

FLOWERS: The white 5-petal flowers are about 3 mm in diameter. They grow in large numbers on each flowering head—you will notice the tall domed column of white flowers, not the individual flowers. In fall the plant will be covered with black (var. *melanocarpa*) or red (var. *racemosa*) berries. The black elderberry is rarer, especially in the western Sierra, but the only way to distinguish between them with certainty is to wait until they are in fruit. With both varieties, it is best to eat only a small number of berries unless they are cooked.

❖ *Angelica lineariloba* (poison angelica)   **FAMILY:** Apiaceae

DISTRIBUTION Common throughout the eastern Sierra; rare in the western Sierra in the Yosemite region but becoming increasingly common farther south
HABITAT Dry slopes and flats
ELEVATION 5,600'–10,700'
SEASON Early July–mid-August
LOCATIONS Virginia Lakes Basin, Thousand Island Lake, Horton Lakes, Mt. Whitney Trail, Farewell Gap

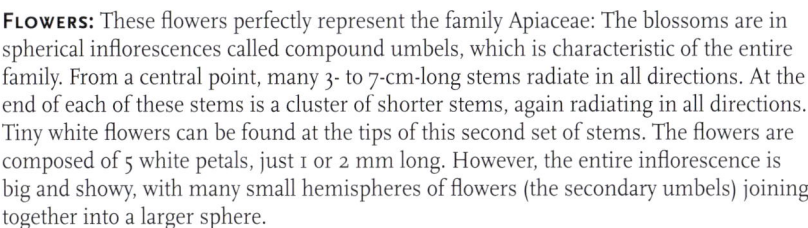

LEAVES AND STEMS: The tall, hollow stems reach 50–150 cm in height. The leaves are concentrated near the base of the plant and, as their name implies, are dissected into long linear lobes. The overall leaves are long—up to 35 cm—but are dissected multiple times, such that the final lobes are just 2–10 cm long.

FLOWERS: These flowers perfectly represent the family Apiaceae: The blossoms are in spherical inflorescences called compound umbels, which is characteristic of the entire family. From a central point, many 3- to 7-cm-long stems radiate in all directions. At the end of each of these stems is a cluster of shorter stems, again radiating in all directions. Tiny white flowers can be found at the tips of this second set of stems. The flowers are composed of 5 white petals, just 1 or 2 mm long. However, the entire inflorescence is big and showy, with many small hemispheres of flowers (the secondary umbels) joining together into a larger sphere.

❖ *Ligusticum grayi* (Gray's lovage)   **FAMILY:** Apiaceae

DISTRIBUTION Common in the western Sierra from the Yosemite region south to Mineral King; common in the eastern Sierra in the Yosemite and Mammoth Lakes regions but absent farther south
HABITAT Moist forest and forest openings
ELEVATION 6,500'–11,000'
SEASON Late June–early August
LOCATIONS Trail to Dana Plateau, Cathedral Lakes Trail, Garnet Lake, Goddard Canyon, Farewell Gap

LEAVES AND STEMS: Reaching up to 80 cm in height, this species is found in small forest openings in both the montane and subalpine zones. It is a quite slender plant, with a small cluster of basal leaves growing beside the long, narrow stalk. The leaves are twice (or three times) divided into leaflets, and the leaflets are 1–4 cm long, oval shaped, and distinctly toothed. They lack hairs and often have a shiny surface.

FLOWERS: The flowers, like the Sierra angelica, are compound umbels and are white in color. In this species, the lower stalks are long, and the secondary umbels have very short stalks, so the flowers cluster together in dense spheres, obscuring the upper stalks. The shape of the overall inflorescence is spherical to hemispherical.

❖ *Osmorhiza occidentalis* (western sweet-cicely)
      FAMILY: Apiaceae

DISTRIBUTION Occasional in the Yosemite area and
common in the Mammoth Lakes region (on both
sides of the Sierra Crest); also present at Rock Creek
but absent elsewhere
HABITAT Dry to moist conifer forests
ELEVATION 5,500'–10,200'
SEASON Early June–early July
LOCATIONS Summit Lake (above Virginia Canyon),
Lundy Canyon, San Joaquin Mountain, Sotcher Lake,
Duck Pass Trailhead, Rock Creek Lake

LEAVES AND STEMS: This plant is usually 40–80 cm in
height, occasionally taller. The leaves, including their
stalks, are 10–20 cm in length. The term *leaf blade,* as with
all members of Apiaceae, is a bit of a misnomer, for the
leaf is dissected into pinnate leaflets, which are further
divided into smaller leaflets, so most of the blade is missing. Compared to many species, the broad, flat leaflets are large, reaching 2–10 cm in length.

FLOWERS: Like other Apiaceae, this species' inflorescences are compound umbels, but
this plant has far fewer flowers than other species do, and the lower stalks are quite
long, so the inflorescences look quite open. The individual flowers are tiny, white, and
5-petaled. Because this species blooms early, you are most likely to notice the narrow,
slightly angular fruits that elongate below the flowers and are 1–2 cm long.

❖ *Perideridia parishii* subsp. *latifolia* (wide-leaved Parish's yampah)
      FAMILY: Apiaceae

DISTRIBUTION Common throughout, on both sides of
the Sierra Crest
HABITAT Forest openings, meadows
ELEVATION 4,700'–11,150'
SEASON Late June–early August
LOCATIONS Tuolumne Meadows, Rock Creek Basin,
Bear Creek, French Canyon, Lake Sabrina Basin

LEAVES AND STEMS: Large masses of this species grow
in seasonally wet meadows and in forest openings. The
stems frequently reach 15–40 cm in height, though they
are occasionally much taller. The leaves are usually split
into three long, narrow divisions, though they can be
pinnately divided.

FLOWERS: The white flowers grow as compound umbels, forming a broad and flat-
topped inflorescence, not a spherical one or a collection of tiny pom-poms like so many
other Apiaceae. The stalks disperse the flowers horizontally, with all the tiny 5-petal
flowers facing upward.

❖ *Sphenosciadium capitellatum* (ranger's buttons)   **FAMILY:** Apiaceae

DISTRIBUTION Very common throughout, on both sides of the Sierra Crest
HABITAT Diverse habitats, including moist to sandy flats, slopes, meadow edges, and lakeshores
ELEVATION 1,800'–11,200'
SEASON Early July–mid-August
LOCATIONS Twenty Lakes Basin, Rock Creek Basin, Long Lake (Bishop Pass Trail), Evolution Lake, Rae Lakes Basin

LEAVES AND STEMS: Ranger's buttons are wonderfully engaging plants—and tall as well, often exceeding 1 m in height. The long leaves are pinnately dissected multiple times into long, fairly narrow, pointed lobes. Most of the leaves are near the base of the plant, with some occurring higher along the stem.

FLOWERS: The inflorescences are true to their name and look like a wonderful collection of white spherical buttons, 1–2 cm in diameter. These inflorescences, like those of most Apiaceae, are compound umbels. The lowest sections of stalk are long, up to 10 cm length, ensuring that the inflorescence is large. The secondary umbels have small branches, however, just a few millimeters long, so the tiny white flowers are so tightly clustered together that they look like a very dense white pom-pom or a round button.

❖ *Achillea millefolium* (yarrow)   **FAMILY:** Asteraceae

DISTRIBUTION Common throughout, on both sides of the Sierra Crest
HABITAT Meadows, vegetated slopes, forest
ELEVATION 3,600'–10,500'
SEASON Late June–mid-August
LOCATIONS Tuolumne Meadows, Rock Creek Basin, Evolution Valley, Vidette Meadow, Cottonwood Lakes Basin

LEAVES AND STEMS: Because yarrow occurs across a broad elevation range, its height also varies considerably, from 10 cm up to more than 1 m in height, with 30–40 cm a very common height at higher elevations. Most leaves are densely clustered near the base, though some much smaller ones extend up the stem. The basal leaves are 5–10 cm long and divided along the midrib into small pinnate lobes. Each of these lobes is further divided into three prongs—and even these prongs are sometimes further divided, resulting in a very feathery dissected leaf, especially because it is covered in long hairs. The stems and leaves have a strong aroma.

FLOWERS: Though yarrow is a member of the sunflower family, its dense head of small white flowers is easily mistaken for a member of the carrot family. However, if you look at an individual "flower," you will see that it is actually a head made up of two flower types: outer asymmetrical ones that look like short petals (ray flowers) and central circular ones with barely visible petals (disk flowers). Yellow-colored stamens emerge from each of the central flowers. Upon close inspection, you will also notice that the head of flowers is not an umbel, but rather, the flower stalks branch off the main stem at different points.

EXTRA TIDBITS: This species has a widespread distribution, occurring across the northern reaches of Eurasia as well.

❖ *Anaphalis margaritacea* (pearly everlasting)
FAMILY: Asteraceae

DISTRIBUTION Fairly common throughout west of the Sierra Crest but rare east of the Sierra Crest
HABITAT Somewhat damp, open areas
ELEVATION 2,000'–10,500'
SEASON Mid-July–early September
LOCATIONS Yosemite Creek, Tenaya Lake, Reds Meadow, Golden Staircase, near Lake Reflection

LEAVES AND STEMS: A big patch of pearly everlasting is hard to miss, for the unbranched stems are typically about 50 cm tall, reaching twice that under good conditions. The leaves are 2–10 cm long and shaped like a very narrow triangle, rolled slightly under at the margins. White hairs cover both the leaves and stem, at times giving the stems a green-gray appearance.

FLOWERS: At the top of the branched stems are many tiny, white, papery inflorescences. Less than 1 cm in diameter, the heads have a central yellow disk surrounded by many layers of white triangular phyllaries. The latter are crisp and stiff, adding depth to the flowers. The phyllaries retain their shape and color even as they dry, lending them the name *everlasting*, while the central disk flowers turn brown.

❖ *Antennaria media* (alpine pussytoes)   **FAMILY:** Asteraceae

DISTRIBUTION Very common throughout, on both sides of the Sierra Crest
HABITAT Alpine fell-fields, dry meadows
ELEVATION 8,000'–13,500'
SEASON Early July–mid-August
LOCATIONS Donohue Pass, Evolution Basin, Bishop Pass, Kearsarge Lakes

LEAVES AND STEMS: This species grows as a mat, with its extent determined by the size of the underground stem. The mat is composed of many small tufts of gray-green leaves up to 2.5 cm in length. The leaves, which lack glands, are broadest near the tip, and they are densely covered in hairs, giving them a grayer color.

FLOWERS: At the top of each 5- to 10-cm-long stem is a collection of inflorescences. Looking at a single flower head, your eyes are drawn to the phyllaries, the papery, membranous "leaves" that surround the disk of flowers. Alpine pussytoes are distinguished from other pussytoes by phyllaries that are a black-green color. At the center are white disk flowers, all but hidden below a sea of white fluff—bristles and the yellow stigma that extend from the base of the flowers.

RELATED SPECIES: *Antennaria corymbosa* (meadow pussytoes) is common in wet meadows, especially from Yosemite south to the Rock Creek area. Its phyllaries are light-colored at the tips with a dark brown to black spot at the base. *Antennaria pulchella*, beautiful pussytoes, is widespread throughout the High Sierra up to 13,000 feet. It has completely dark phyllaries, like *Antennaria media*, but it occurs in wetter locations, has smaller flowers, and has leaves with glands. Many species of pussytoes hybridize with each other; see "Hybrids," page 233, for more information.

Antennaria corymbosa

❖ *Chaenactis alpigena* (Sharsmith pincushion,
　　southern Sierra pincushion) **FAMILY:** Asteraceae

DISTRIBUTION Fairly common throughout, mostly at
high elevations
HABITAT Alpine fell-fields; dry, gravelly slopes and flats
ELEVATION 7,500'–12,500'
SEASON Mid-July–late August
LOCATIONS Twenty Lakes Basin, Tenaya Peak,
Minaret Summit, Mono Pass Trail (Rock Creek Basin),
Coyote Ridge, Mt. Whitney Trail

LEAVES AND STEMS: This diminutive plant rarely reaches more than
7 cm in height, growing as a low rosette. The leaves are densely covered with long, cobwebby white hairs, giving them a pale mint-green
color. Each leaf is intricate, with a thick midrib surrounded by lobes
that may be lobed or toothed. Most of the plants in this region have 7 pinnate lobes, but
individuals can have fewer lobes as well.

FLOWERS: Inflorescences occur singly on stems that extend either upward or sideways
along the ground. The tall inflorescences have only disk flowers; these are white with
long, pinkish styles adding extra color. The phyllaries are long, hairy, and a purplish-
green color.

RELATED SPECIES: The lower elevation *Chaenactis douglasii* var. *douglasii*,
known as Douglas' dustymaiden, is more common in the montane fir
forests but occurs up to 11,000 feet. It is a much taller plant, with brighter
green stems. Its branched stems have many inflorescences per stalk,
but the inflorescences look quite similar to the Sharsmith pincushion.
You can find this species along Yosemite Creek, at Devils Postpile,
at the Woods Creek Crossing, on the east side of Kearsarge Pass Trail,
and at Cottonwood Lakes.

Chaenactis douglasii
var. *douglasii*

❖ *Cirsium scariosum* var. *americana* (dinnerplate thistle, elk thistle)
　　FAMILY: Asteraceae

DISTRIBUTION Fairly common throughout, on both sides
of the Sierra Crest
HABITAT Meadows, grassy sites in forest
ELEVATION 6,500'–11,500'
SEASON Mid-June–late July
LOCATIONS Gaylor Lakes Trail, Long Lake (Bishop Pass
Trail), Upper Palisade Lake, Mt. Whitney Trail

LEAVES AND STEMS: The stature of this thistle could not be
more different from that of the rose thistle—it lies flat to
the ground, with its rosette of leaves forming an enormous spiny disk reminiscent of
a dinner plate. The disk can exceed 40 cm in diameter, with the long-spined leaves
usually 10–20 cm in length but occasionally longer. The leaves are commonly covered
in long hairs and sharply toothed, with a broad, whitish midrib.　*(Continued)*

(Continued)   **FLOWERS:** At the center of the rosette, still at ground level, emerges a dense collection of white-flowered inflorescences. Each can be up to 3 cm in diameter, though they appear even wider as the disk flowers with long white stamens open and spread outward; there are no ray flowers.

❖ *Erigeron coulteri* (large mountain fleabane, Coulter's fleabane)
     FAMILY: Asteraceae

DISTRIBUTION Fairly common throughout, on both sides of the Sierra Crest
HABITAT Wet meadows, along streams
ELEVATION 6,000'–11,200'
SEASON Early July–mid-August
LOCATIONS Lundy Canyon, Tully Hole, Mono Creek, Rock Creek Basin, Rambaud Creek

LEAVES AND STEMS: Though you can find the stalks singly, the species is more often found growing en masse in moist locations; it is a common member of the streamside community. The individual stems are 20–70 cm long. The leaves are at least 5 cm long, oval shaped, quite thin, either hairy or nearly lacking hairs, and shiny.

FLOWERS: The long flowering stems may be slightly branched, but there is often just a single 10- to 16-mm-wide inflorescence on each stem. The numerous narrow, long, bright white ray flowers identify this daisy; each flowering head can have up to 140 narrow ray flowers.

❖ *Erigeron lonchophyllus (Trimorpha lonchophylla)*
     (short-rayed fleabane)   **FAMILY:** Asteraceae

DISTRIBUTION Common in the Yosemite region on both sides of the Sierra Crest and then more occasional to the south until the Kern River drainage, where it is again very common
HABITAT Meadows
ELEVATION 4,000'–11,000'
SEASON Early July–early August
LOCATIONS Tuolumne Meadows along Lyell Fork Tuolumne River, Rock Creek Trail, East Lake, John Muir Trail near Wright Creek crossing, Cottonwood Lakes, Hockett Meadow

LEAVES AND STEMS: The short-rayed fleabane is easily overlooked because it tends to be hidden beneath grass in meadows. Growing to at most 20 cm in height, the many firm green stems are covered in stiff white hairs that point outward and give the plant a bristly appearance. The elongate leaves with a rounded tip are mostly at the base. The few leaves on the stems are much smaller but the same shape.

FLOWERS: The miniature white daisies are one of my favorites—they always seem very dainty, for each of the many inflorescences has well more than 50 ray flowers, each only 2–3 mm long, surrounding the equally small yellow disk.

❖ *Sphaeromeria cana* (gray chickensage, tansy)
   FAMILY: Asteraceae

DISTRIBUTION Fairly common throughout, almost always at quite high elevations
HABITAT Rocky slopes, especially alongside talus
ELEVATION 8,800'–13,000'
SEASON Early July–late August
LOCATIONS Virginia Lakes Basin, Mt. Dana, Long Lake (Bishop Pass Trail), Kearsarge Pass Trail, Mt. Whitney Trail

LEAVES AND STEMS: A dense cluster of branches emerges from the taproot. The branches usually reach 15–40 cm in height, rarely taller. Both the stems and the small leaves are gray-green, due to the dense layer of hairs on their surface. The leaves cover the entire stem length, and some are three-pronged while others are simply oval shaped.

FLOWERS: The tops of the stems branch, each ending in an inflorescence, resulting in a cluster of inflorescences near the top of the plant. The inflorescences lack ray flowers and have a central disk about 1 cm in diameter; they resemble a collection of small, slightly fuzzy buttons. The flowers are a cream color, rapidly turning brown as they age.

❖ UV Radiation

As discussed in "A Bee's-Eye View of a Flower" on page 133, ultraviolet, or UV, radiation is, relative to visible light, shorter-wavelength, higher-energy radiation emitted by the sun. It is invisible to our eyes but, in part, visible to many insects. Many flowers, therefore, have specific patterns of UV absorption to attract insects. Insects see the lower energy UVA radiation, which is not absorbed by our atmosphere, including the ozone layer, but causes less tissue damage. The shorter wavelength UV radiation, UVB, is that which we worry most about with regard to skin cancer, and plants are, of course, also susceptible to tissue damage from excess UVB absorption. UV light causes mutations to a plant's DNA and reduces fertility. In particular, photosynthesis becomes less efficient when plants are exposed to high levels of UV light because it degrades several of the key bio-molecules involved in the reactions. (See also "Too Much Light," page 69.)

   Plants have developed a number of mechanisms to protect themselves, especially at high elevations where UV radiation is strongest. The first strategy is to reflect much of the ultraviolet light. Many plants have hairs that reflect incoming UVB light and are sometimes even able to *(Continued)*

(*Continued*)   preferentially reflect the damaging wavelengths over the useful ones. Others have waxes on the outside of their leaves, and again, some waxes reflect UV light but not longer wavelengths. An alternative solution is to create molecules that absorb the UV light and dissipate the energy before it can injure tissues and molecules in the leaf. For instance, conifers, such as pine trees, have waxy substances in the outermost (epidermal) cells of their needles that absorb the UV light. Most widespread, however, are chemical responses that are actually triggered by UV light exposure: In response to UVB light, many species begin producing molecules in their epidermal cells that harmlessly absorb and dissipate the UV light. Of particular importance are flavonoids, especially anthocyanins, the red to blue pigment molecules ubiquitous in petals. Have you ever noticed that young leaves tend to be redder? Young leaves often have high concentrations of anthocyanins because cells and the enzymes in young tissue are particularly susceptible to damage from UV radiation.

And to finish, a neat story about a non-Sierran alpine plant: Edelweiss, the famous European alpine flower, has leaves thickly covered with long hollow hairs. The exact diameter of these hairs allows them to funnel UV radiation into the hollow hairs, capturing its energy—possibly in a water reservoir. As a result, edelweiss plants absorb nearly all UVB radiation that hits their leaves but then dispose of it harmlessly. When you think of all the very hairy plants at high elevations in the Sierra, you wonder if some of them might not be playing a similar trick.

❖ *Cryptantha affinis* (side-grooved cryptantha)   **FAMILY:** Boraginaceae

DISTRIBUTION Common at montane elevations throughout the western Sierra, occasionally reaching into the subalpine or crossing to the eastern Sierra
HABITAT Open areas, forest openings, dry flats
ELEVATION 4,000'–9,000'
SEASON Mid-June–late July
LOCATIONS Tioga Crest, Tuolumne Meadows, Mammoth Lakes Basin, Hockett Meadow

LEAVES AND STEMS: This annual species usually reaches 10–30 cm in height, occasionally a little taller. The stem has few branches, each with a sparse number of narrow leaves. Bristly white hairs cover both the stem and leaves.

FLOWERS: The tiny white 5-petal flowers look like those of many *Cryptantha* species. The sepals are long and narrow, especially bristly, and point upward, holding the petals within them; only the tips of the petals stick out. The key to distinguishing *Cryptanthas* are their tiny seeds. The seeds of this species are smooth, while the co-occurring and very similar-looking *Cryptantha echinella,* the hedgehog cryptantha, has rough seeds.

❖ *Cryptantha nubigena* (Sierra cryptantha)   **FAMILY:** Boraginaceae

DISTRIBUTION Common throughout, on both sides of the
Sierra Crest, usually at quite high elevations
HABITAT Sand and talus slopes
ELEVATION 8,500'–12,800'
SEASON Late June–early August
LOCATIONS Dana Plateau, Parker Pass, Mono Pass (Rock Creek
Basin), Diamond Mesa, Mt. Whitney

LEAVES AND STEMS: This species is quite similar in appearance to
Cryptantha humilis, with 5- to 30-cm-tall stems and a large number of narrowly spoon-
shaped leaves near the base of the plant. Both the stems and leaves have long white hairs.

FLOWERS: The flowers of this species, like other cryptanthas, have 5 white fused petals,
and small yellow "appendages" form a ring in the center. The flowers are tiny, no more
than 4 mm in diameter, making them slightly smaller than those of the low cryptantha.
The flowers are concentrated near the top of the stem, though flowers sometimes occur
lower on the stem. On average, the mass of flowers is not quite as dense as it is on *Cryptantha humilis.* And if you wish to confirm your identification by looking at the seed, the top
surface of the seed is smooth, while the base varies from smooth to wrinkled.

RELATED SPECIES: A second very similar-looking species, *Cryptantha humilis,* the low
cryptantha, can be found on dry, sandy slopes through the eastern Sierra to an elevation of
12,000 feet. This species, just like *Cryptantha nubigena,* has many 5- to 30-cm-long stems
covered with long white hairs and features spoon-shaped leaves that are quite long: 1.5–6
cm in length. The flowers are nearly twice the size of the Sierra cryptantha's, and the mass
of flowers is a bit denser. The only sure way to confirm your identification is to look at the
seed: The seed of the low cryptantha is wrinkled throughout. The low cryptantha can be
found at Virginia Lakes Basin, Convict Creek drainage, Coyote Ridge, and Kearsarge Pass.

❖ *Hesperochiron pumilus* (dwarf hesperochiron)
    FAMILY: Boraginaceae (Hydrophyllaceae)

DISTRIBUTION Occasional at lower elevations in the
western Sierra, rarely reaching to montane or subalpine
elevations; rare occurrences in the eastern Sierra
HABITAT Wet meadows, damp gravelly spots
ELEVATION 4,400'–9,800'
SEASON Mid-June–mid-July
LOCATIONS Bench Canyon (near Minarets), King Creek
(near Devils Postpile), below Johnson Lake (southern
Yosemite), Hilgard Branch of Bear Creek

LEAVES AND STEMS: This species features a cluster of narrowly oval-shaped, elongate,
rounded, 1- to 7-cm-long leaves growing as a rosette. The leaves are a quite vibrant
green, and stiff, green hairs cover the leaf margins and stems.

FLOWERS: The flowers grow on short unbranched stalks, rising up just a few centimeters. The flowers are about 1–1.2 cm across and are composed of 5 broad, whitish
petals fused at the base. Pale pink to purple veins are visible in the petals, and the
stamen stalks are white with dark pollen sacks at the tip.

❖ *Nemophila spatulata* (Sierra baby blue eyes, Sierra nemophila)
    FAMILY: Boraginaceae (Hydrophyllaceae)

DISTRIBUTION Common throughout montane elevations in the western Sierra, occasionally reaching higher elevations in the Yosemite area; in the eastern Sierra only around Mammoth Lakes
HABITAT Meadows, flats, often in slightly moist locations with bare disturbed soil
ELEVATION 4,000'–10,500'
SEASON Mid-June–late July
LOCATIONS Virginia Canyon, Dana Meadows, Lembert Dome, Porcupine Flat, Hockett Meadow, Cottonwood Lakes

LEAVES AND STEMS: The thin stems of this annual tend to trend more sideways than upward, reaching a total length of 10–30 cm. The oval- to wedge-shaped leaves are 1–3 cm in length and about 1 cm in width, and they are usually coarsely toothed near their tips, forming 3–5 points. The stems are commonly covered in long hairs but can be hairless.

FLOWERS: The bowl-shaped flowers are a little under 1 cm in diameter and grow on long stalks from the leaf nodes. The 5 white petals have pale-purple veins and purple spots at their tips. Like all members of the genus, the style is deeply forked at the tip.

❖ *Plagiobothrys hispidulus* (harsh popcornflower)
    FAMILY: Boraginaceae

DISTRIBUTION Fairly common throughout, on both sides of the Sierra Crest, becoming quite common on the Kern Plateau
HABITAT Meadows, forest edges
ELEVATION 1,000'–11,100'
SEASON Mid-June–late July
LOCATIONS Dana Meadows, Agnew Meadows, Mono Creek, Rock Creek Basin, Cottonwood Lakes

photographed by Jean Pawek

LEAVES AND STEMS: This species is easily overlooked for many reasons: It is often only 5 cm tall (though plants can occasionally exceed 20 cm), its stems rarely stand upright, and because it is an annual, it may not come up at all in drier years. The 1- to 5-cm-long narrow leaves occur along the entire stem, but there are no basal leaves. Both the stem and leaves have long white hairs.

FLOWERS: The upper reaches of the stem can be sparsely to densely covered in tiny white flowers with yellow at the center. As with all *Plagiobothrys,* the 5 petals are fused into a tube, but as the flowers are only a few millimeters in length, they are virtually invisible.

RELATED SPECIES: Two additional popcornflowers occur at high elevations in the Sierra: *Plagiobothrys torreyi* var. *diffusus* (High Sierra popcornflower) and *Plagiobothrys hispidus* (cascade popcornflower), though the three species are challenging to differentiate among without closely examining the fruits, called nutlets.

❖ *Anelsonia eurycarpa* (daggerpod)
  FAMILY: Brassicaceae

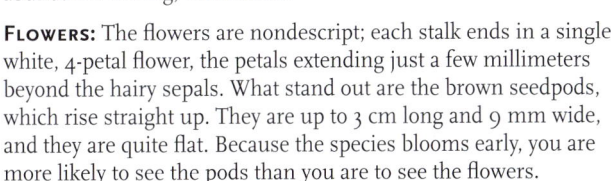

DISTRIBUTION Occasional throughout, always near the Sierra Crest
HABITAT Talus slopes, alpine fell-fields
ELEVATION 10,600'–14,000'
SEASON Early June–early July
LOCATIONS Excelsior Mountain (head of Virginia Lakes Basin), Coyote Ridge, west side of Baxter Pass, Kearsarge Pass, Mt. Whitney Trail

LEAVES AND STEMS: Small rosettes of densely hairy leaves emerge on windswept slopes and ridges. The narrow leaves are up to 2 cm long, slightly thickened, and gray due to the abundance of long, white hairs.

FLOWERS: The flowers are nondescript; each stalk ends in a single white, 4-petal flower, the petals extending just a few millimeters beyond the hairy sepals. What stand out are the brown seedpods, which rise straight up. They are up to 3 cm long and 9 mm wide, and they are quite flat. Because the species blooms early, you are more likely to see the pods than you are to see the flowers.

❖ *Draba breweri* (cushion draba)
  FAMILY: Brassicaceae

DISTRIBUTION Very common throughout, on both sides of the Sierra Crest
HABITAT Talus, alpine fell-fields, often alongside rocks
ELEVATION 9,500'–14,200'
SEASON Mid-June–early August
LOCATIONS Mt. Dana, Muir Pass, Kearsarge Pass, Shepherd Pass, Mt. Whitney

LEAVES AND STEMS: Reaching no more than 10 cm in height, this species has a dense rosette of dark to bluish-green, elongate, oval-shaped, hairy leaves. The hairs are generally branched, or stellate. The few stem leaves are similarly hairy and closely hug the green-to-purplish flowering stalk.

FLOWERS: This is one of just two species of white (to cream-colored) draba in the high-elevation Sierra; like all drabas, it has 4-petal flowers. Its twisted pods distinguish it from the tall draba (*Draba praealta*). In particularly robust individuals with long seedpods, the pods form delightful corkscrews, but a single twist is more commonly observed.

RELATED SPECIES: *Draba praealta,* the tall draba, is also white flowered. However, these plants are much taller, rising 8–30 mm; the fruit pods are not twisted; and its distribution is mostly restricted to the Virginia Lakes Basin, the region around Mt. Dana, and the Convict Creek drainage.

Draba praealta

❖ *Eremogone congesta* var. *suffrutescens* *(Arenaria congesta* var. *suffrutescens)*
(suffrutescent sandwort)   **FAMILY:** Caryophyllaceae

DISTRIBUTION Occasional in the western Sierra south from the San Joaquin River drainage, becoming common along the Great Western Divide south of Colby Pass and on the Kern Plateau; only present in the eastern Sierra once south of Mt. Whitney
HABITAT Alongside rocks on dry slopes
ELEVATION 6,900'–11,300'
SEASON Late June–early August
LOCATIONS Courtright Reservoir, base of Diamond Mesa, John Muir Trail near Mt. Young, near Mt. Guyot, Farewell Gap, Little Cottonwood Creek

LEAVES AND STEMS: The tufts of needlelike leaves form an open carpet; this is not a dense cushion plant. The leaves, usually 1–2 cm in length but occasionally longer, point upward. The flowering stems, stretching upward from the cushion of leaves, are usually about 10–20 cm in length.

FLOWERS: The crowded inflorescence of white flowers is an umbel—each flower is connected to a short stalk that radiates from a central point. The flowers have 5 narrow white petals that form a star, less than 1 cm in diameter, with long white stamens extending far above the flower.

❖ *Eremogone kingii* var. *glabrescens* *(Arenaria kingii* var. *glabrescens)* (King's sandwort)
FAMILY: Caryophyllaceae

DISTRIBUTION Common throughout, on both sides of the Sierra Crest
HABITAT Slopes, including dry forested locations; alpine fell-fields; gravelly flats
ELEVATION 6,000'–12,500'
SEASON Early July–mid-August
LOCATIONS Dana Plateau, Minaret Lake, Humphreys Basin, Lamarck Col, top of New Army Pass

LEAVES AND STEMS: A common member of all dry high-elevation communities, King's sandwort grows as a classic cushion, often radiating from the central taproot in a perfect circle. The cushion is mostly covered in tuft after tuft of miniature leaves (0.3–2 cm long), shaped like very acute triangles and usually without hairs, making them a glossy green.

FLOWERS: In a good flowering year, a long stalk, covered in gland-tipped hairs, grows from the center of each leaf tuft and then branches. The 5 small, slightly elongate petals form a cup-shaped flower, sitting within 5 narrow sepals. Only the rounded tips of the petals bend outward, making the flowers much less open than those of Nuttall sandwort. However, the 10 stamens—with red to pink pollen and the green ovary—are still visible in the center.

RELATED SPECIES: Related species *Eremogone macradenia* var. *macradenia,* known as Mojave or desert sandwort, occurs in the eastern Sierra from the Big Pine Creek drainage south, often below the subalpine zone. The flowers are similar to King's sandwort, but the plant is quite large—up to 50 cm in height and diameter— and is a tangle of thin, bright-green branches. It occurs on the Taboose Pass and Baxter Pass Trails.

Eremogone macradenia var. *macradenia*

❖ Leaf Size and Plant Size at High Elevations

The higher you climb into the mountains, the smaller the plants—and their leaves—become. The plants inhabiting an alpine fell-field have the smallest leaves. Look at *Phlox condensata, Eremogone kingii* var. *glabrescens,* or many members of the genus *Draba*; note that their leaves are nearly needles, and the plants grow as compact cushions. Overall, the leaves of alpine plants are, on average, only 10% as big as their lowland counterparts. In the bright alpine environment, these plants don't need to worry about intercepting sufficient sunlight, but they are subjected to leaf-battering winds, cool growing-season temperatures, and frigid winter temperatures, which all favor their growth form. A small, compact cushion shape increases both the soil and leaf temperatures to many degrees above the air temperature, allowing for faster growth and faster conversion of dead material to soil. Amazingly, on a sunny summer day, the leaf temperature may even be *above* its ideal temperature. A cushion form also retains more soil moisture around the roots by protecting the soil from desiccating winds, and the form captures dry leaves, creating a more nutrient-rich soil locally. Interestingly, alpine plants actually grow at the same rate (relative to their leaf area) as lowland plants grow, implying that, to some extent, small leaves, small plants, and limited yearly growth exist at high elevations because they are beneficial to the plant's growth and survival, not because the plants are constrained to grow slowly. They do, of course, have a much shorter growing season.

❖ *Minuartia nuttallii* var. *gracilis* (Nuttall sandwort)
  FAMILY: Caryophyllaceae

DISTRIBUTION Common throughout, mostly at high elevations (on both eastern and western sides), with its range extending farther west once south of the Bishop Creek drainage
HABITAT Alpine fell-fields, dry open areas, often alongside rocks
ELEVATION 7,500'–12,500'
SEASON Early July–mid-August
LOCATIONS Dana Plateau, Mono Pass (Rock Creek Basin), Rae Lakes Basin, near summit of Kearsarge Pass

(Continued)

(Continued) **LEAVES AND STEMS:** The spreading, somewhat woody stems of this sandwort don't quite form a cushion but instead create more of a carpet. The individual stems, which range from a few centimeters up to 20 cm in length, often have some dead leaves at the base, followed by a tight cluster of green leaves, always densely covered in gland-tipped hairs. The leaves are narrow but not quite needlelike, rather thick, and slightly folded upward along the midrib.

FLOWERS: One to a few flowers grow at the top of each stem, their stalks reddish with gland-tipped hairs. The flowers are tiny—generally 1–1.5 cm in diameter—but exquisite. The 5 sepals are wide open and form a sharp-pointed star, while the 5 white petals are slightly less pointed—and offset from the sepals to reveal both. At the center is the bulbous, glossy green ovary surrounded by 10 white stamens with pinkish pollen.

❖ *Minuartia rubella* (beautiful sandwort, red seeded sandwort)
    FAMILY: Caryophyllaceae

DISTRIBUTION Occasional along the Sierra Crest from the Yosemite region south to the Mt. Whitney area; absent elsewhere
HABITAT Alpine slopes and fell-fields, mostly in locations that have not been glaciated; occasionally found on open slopes at lower elevations
ELEVATION 8,500'–13,100'
SEASON Late June–early August
LOCATIONS Dana Plateau, Koip Peak Pass, Coyote Ridge, Baxter Pass, Sawmill Pass, Mt. Whitney Trail

LEAVES AND STEMS: With a compact growth form, this species would be easy to confuse with other cushion plants in the family Caryophyllaceae. This species grows as small tufts, reaching just a few centimeters in height. The narrow, sharply pointed, reddish leaves are at most 1 cm in length and are covered with gland-tipped hairs.

FLOWERS: A cluster of white 5-petal flowers occurs at the end of a short stalk. The 2- to 3-mm-long petals are narrowly oval and pointed at the tip, with the green ovary readily visible at the center of the flower. The narrow, pointed sepals are usually slightly longer than the petals and curve inward. The stems and leaves turn reddish as it goes to seed.

RELATED SPECIES: *Minuartia obtusiloba,* the alpine sandwort, is another rare species restricted to high-elevation fell-fields. This species has petals notably longer than the sepals, and the sepals curve inward along the midrib, forming a hood. Its leaves are quite thick and a distinctly bright green. It is found on the west slope of Mt. Dana, Mono Pass (Rock Creek Basin), Humphreys Basin, and Taboose Pass.

Minuartia obtusiloba

❖ *Sagina saginoides* (arctic pearlwort)
    FAMILY: Caryophyllaceae

DISTRIBUTION Fairly common throughout, on both sides of the Sierra Crest
HABITAT Vegetated banks of narrow streams, seeps, beneath moist boulders

ELEVATION 4,000'–12,100'
SEASON Mid-June–early August
LOCATIONS Twenty Lakes Basin, Devils
Postpile, Bishop Pass Trail, Bullfrog Lake,
Mt. Whitney Trail

LEAVES AND STEMS: This easily overlooked
species grows to at most 10 cm in height,
but most individuals I have found have been
half that height. A small cluster of very short
stems emerges from the ground, each with
a basal tuft of narrow leaves, as well as several
pairs of needlelike stem leaves, usually about
1 cm long. All leaves are bright green and
somewhat shiny.

FLOWERS: At the top of each stem is a single flower with 5 white petals, just 1–2 mm in
length and narrow. Behind, and slightly longer than, the petals are the 5 sepals, slightly
bowl shaped, tapered at the tip, and with a translucent edge. At the center are 10 white
stamens and a rather round, green ovary.

❖ *Silene bernardina* (Palmer's catchfly)
      FAMILY: Caryophyllaceae

DISTRIBUTION Common throughout the eastern Sierra,
occasionally crossing to the west side of the Sierra Crest;
also in the far southern Great Western Divide
HABITAT Dry slopes, forest
ELEVATION 5,000'–11,500'
SEASON Early July–early August
LOCATIONS Virginia Lakes Basin, Rock Creek Basin,
Palisade Creek, Kearsarge Pass Trail

LEAVES AND STEMS: This plant reaches 15–55 cm in height and
is only slightly branched. Gland-tipped hairs cover part or all of
the stem. The leaves are mostly near the base of the plant and
are shaped like elongate ovals.

FLOWERS: The calyx and petals are equally prominent in this
species. The calyx tube is 1.2–1.5 cm long, quite narrow, covered in
gland-tipped hairs, and decorated with 10 prominent purple lines,
or veins. The floral tube extends slightly beyond the calyx, and the
5 white petal lobes then open outward, with the stamens extending
well beyond the floral tube. Each petal is deeply notched into
4 narrow segments. The tips and backs of the petals are often
tinged a pale pink.

❖ *Silene sargentii* (Sargent's catchfly)   **FAMILY:** Caryophyllaceae

DISTRIBUTION Common throughout, on both sides of the Sierra Crest,
especially at high elevations   *(Continued)*

(Continued)   **HABITAT** Alpine fell-fields, open forest, high-elevation gravelly slopes
ELEVATION 8,000'–12,500'
SEASON Early July–mid-August
LOCATIONS Virginia Lakes Basin, Dana Plateau, north side of Pinchot Pass, Mt. Whitney Trail

LEAVES AND STEMS: This low-growing species, just 10–15 cm in height, has a cluster of stalks emerging from an underground stem. Gland-tipped hairs cover both the stems and linear leaves.

FLOWERS: The petal tube is contained within a bulbous calyx that narrows toward the top and is usually about 1 cm in length. Its sides are decorated with 10 purplish veins that form ribs. The white (occasionally pink) flower tube extends beyond the calyx and then opens into 5 lobes, each deeply notched once, and often with an extra little lobe to the outer sides. The petal lobes are only about 3 mm in length.

❖ *Stellaria calycantha* (northern starwort)
   FAMILY: Caryophyllaceae

DISTRIBUTION Common throughout, on both sides of the Sierra Crest, but often overlooked
HABITAT Seeps, mossy stream banks
ELEVATION 6,000'–12,300'
SEASON Early July–mid-August
LOCATIONS Dana Plateau, Rose Lake (north of Selden Pass), Bishop Pass Trail, Mt. Whitney Trail

LEAVES AND STEMS: The stems of this species mostly trail along the ground in wet mossy locations, reaching up to 25 cm in length. The shiny, smooth, oval-shaped leaves occur in pairs along the stem and are up to 2.5 cm long.

FLOWERS: The flowers are minute, with 5 sepals forming a star shape, in the center of which are 5 small white petals, only 1–2 mm in length—or rarely absent altogether. In the center of the flower is a (relatively) large, green, egg-shaped ovule, which will develop into the fruit. In this species, there are usually several flowers growing on each stem emerging from a leaf axil.

RELATED SPECIES: Other petite species of *Stellaria* look quite similar but almost always lack petals. *Stellaria crispa* (crisp starwort) has flowers that always occur singly, and its leaves have wavy margins. It mostly occurs between the Yosemite region and the Bishop Pass region, including on the Dana Plateau, near Merced Pass, and in the Bishop Creek drainage. *Stellaria umbellata* (umbrella starwort) has flowers that grow as an umbel. It occurs throughout the Sierra up to an elevation of 11,000 feet. Both species live in wet seeps and along mossy stream banks and are quite inconspicuous.

Stellaria crispa

❖ Rock Glacier Environments

The diversity of habitats—each with a quite different temperature, moisture availability, nutrient availability, and more—contributes to the high number of alpine and subalpine plants in the Sierra Nevada. Rock glaciers are one landform that creates a unique combination of conditions. At first glance, rock glaciers appear to be tongues of talus, but upon closer inspection you will note that they are shaped like glaciers, with relatively flat tops and steep fronts and sides. Like a glacier, ice is at the center, and they move slowly downslope. While an unusually cold pile of talus is a relatively inhospitable environment for plants, pockets of good soil formation can often be found on the rock glacier top. More important, wetlands are generally in front of rock glaciers—with a predictable and continuous water supply throughout the summer from the slowly melting ice. The assortment of plants inhabiting a rock glacier–derived wetland is similar to that of other wetlands, with one key difference: The cool environment created by rock glaciers provides these cold-loving species with a lower elevation home than they would usually inhabit. In addition, rock glaciers supply water throughout the summer, extending the growing season of wetland species in drier years. As global warming likely continues to increase growing season temperatures and decrease Sierra snowpack over the coming century, rock glaciers will provide a dependable, and therefore important, water source, creating a refuge for wetland alpine species. Some examples of species associated with the talus atop rock glaciers are *Ericameria suffruticosa*, *Erigeron compositus*, *Erigeron pygmaeus*, *Solidago multiradiata*, *Silene sargentii*, *Ribes cereum*, *Linanthus pungens*, *Phlox condensata*, and *Eriogonum incanum*. Species common in the rock glacier wetlands include *Antennaria corymbosa*, *Oreostemma alpigenum* var. *andersonii*, *Packera subnuda*, *Kalmia polifolia*, *Phyllodoce breweri*, *Gentiana newberryi*, *Epilobium oregonense*, *Mimulus primuloides*, *Castilleja lemmonii*, *Penstemon heterodoxus*, *Veronica wormskjoldii*, *Primula tetrandra*, *Potentilla flabellifolia*, *Salix orestera*, and *Sibbaldia procumbens*.

❖ *Stellaria longipes* subsp. *longipes* (longstalk starwort)
    FAMILY: Caryophyllaceae

> **DISTRIBUTION** Fairly common throughout, on both sides of the Sierra Crest
> **HABITAT** Wet meadows, seeps
> **ELEVATION** 3,300'–11,700'
> **SEASON** Late June–mid-August
> **LOCATIONS** Grass Lake (Rock Creek Basin), John Muir Trail south of Bear Ridge, Bubbs Creek

LEAVES AND STEMS: Rising between meadow grasses or along a seep, a single glossy stalk ranges from just 5 cm long up to about 30 cm. The leaves, narrow and elongate, occur in evenly spaced pairs along the stem.

(Continued)

(Continued)   **FLOWERS:** Extending well beyond the top leaves is the stalk that holds the flowers—often only one but sometimes a small cluster of blossoms, each on their own long stalks, as the name *longipes* indicates. The 5 white petals are notched nearly to their base, so at first glance, one assumes there are 10. At about 5 mm in length, they are slightly longer than the sepals and hide them. The pollen sacks at the tips of the stamens are a reddish-orange color, adding a decorative touch.

❖ *Comandra umbellata* subsp. *californica* (bastard toadflax)
    FAMILY: Comandraceae (Santalaceae)

DISTRIBUTION Occasional, mostly at montane elevations, in the western Sierra from the Yosemite region south through the San Joaquin drainage, becoming common in the Kings River drainage and extending into the eastern Sierra south of the Bishop Creek drainage
HABITAT Dry slopes
ELEVATION 1,000'–10,500'
SEASON Late June–early August
LOCATIONS Climb to Rancheria Mountain, slopes above Le Conte Canyon, Simpson Meadow, Kearsarge Pass Trail, Mineral King

LEAVES AND STEMS: This species is a subshrub, with stout stems that are 10–40 cm in length but woody only near the base. The stems range from burgundy to a pale green in color. The leaves are generally in the shape of elongate ovals and pointed at the tip. The foliage and stems both lack hairs or glands.

FLOWERS: The inflorescences occur at the ends of both the main stems and side branches, with heads of more than 20 flowers not uncommon. The individual cream-colored flowers are about 0.5 cm across and are composed of 5—or occasionally 4 or 6, as you can see in the photo—triangular petals fused to a central disk.

EXTRA TIDBITS: Members of the family Comandraceae are root parasites: Like all green plants, they photosynthesize to create their own sugars; however, unlike others, they top up by diverting sugars from the plants they parasitize.

❖ *Arctostaphylos nevadensis* subsp. *nevadensis*
    (pine-mat manzanita)   **FAMILY:** Ericaceae

DISTRIBUTION Common throughout on both sides of the Sierra Crest from the Yosemite region south to the Bishop Creek drainage; farther south, less common and restricted to the western Sierra
HABITAT Alongside rocks on dry slopes; open conifer forest
ELEVATION 6,000'–11,100'
SEASON Mid-June–mid-July
LOCATIONS Buena Vista Crest, North Fork San Joaquin River, Gem Lake (Rush Creek drainage), Mammoth Lakes Basin, Convict Creek drainage, French Canyon

LEAVES AND STEMS: True to its name, the pine-mat manzanita is a shrub with an elegantly prone growth form, spreading across the ground surface and over rocks. The branches usually reach upward just a few dozen centimeters, and like all manzanita stems, they are reddish, stiff, and rather scaly. The leathery leaves are oval shaped but sharp tipped. Short hairs densely cover the leaf stalks and young stems, but in contrast to the larger greenleaf manzanita, there are no glands present on the hairs.

FLOWERS: The white urn-shaped flowers open quite early, and by midsummer bunches of small berries replace the cluster of flowers near the end of branches. For most of the summer, the berries are greenish, reddening as the growing season comes to an end.

RELATED SPECIES: The greenleaf manzanita (*Arctostaphylos patula*) is a much larger shrub that often grows intermingled with pine-mat manzanita. It is often 1–1.5 m tall, sometimes even exceeding 2 m in height. Its leaves are a very bright green, and its flowers are pink. Its foliage can have glands or lack glands and simply be hairy. It is common on dry slopes and slabs up to an elevation of nearly 11,000 feet.

❖ *Cassiope mertensiana* (white mountain heather)
   FAMILY: Ericaceae

> **DISTRIBUTION** Common in the Yosemite region and fairly common south to Muir Pass but occurs sparingly south through the Kings River drainage; absent in the Kern River drainage
> **HABITAT** Moist slopes and forest floor, alongside rocks, and in small meadow patches in moist alpine locations
> **ELEVATION** 8,000'–12,000'
> **SEASON** Mid-June–mid-July
> **LOCATIONS** Twenty Lakes Basin, Donohue Pass, Shadow Lake, Duck Lake, Pioneer Basin

LEAVES AND STEMS: This subshrub can grow to 25 cm high, forming a thicket of short branches completely covered in densely overlapping, thick leaves, which are tiny and triangular and point upward.

FLOWERS: The flowers are round, downward-hanging white bells, just 0.5 cm wide. 5 slightly upturned petal tips extend beyond the floral tube. The flower stalk and 5 fused sepals are red—as if a tiny red star has been glued on the back of each flower. Each stalk holds only 1 flower. However, in a good season, stalks grow from the axils of many of the upper leaves, and the plants can be covered in the dainty blossoms, which were understandably one of John Muir's favorite flowers.

❖ *Orthilia secunda* (one-sided wintergreen)
   FAMILY: Ericaceae

> **DISTRIBUTION** Fairly common throughout, on both sides of the Sierra Crest
> **HABITAT** Shaded forest, often growing next to decaying logs, tree trunks, or small rocks
> **ELEVATION** 6,500'–10,500'
> **SEASON** Mid-July–late August
> **LOCATIONS** Shadow Lake, John Muir Trail south of Tully Hole, Rock Creek Trail, below Finger Lake (South Fork Big Pine Creek)

(Continued)

(Continued)   **LEAVES AND STEMS:** A single flowering stalk, up to 20 cm in length, emerges from a basal group of 2- to 5-cm-long shiny leaves that are oval shaped to nearly round. Most leaves are truly basal, but a few grow along the lower length of stem.

FLOWERS: White drop-shaped flowers formed by 5 overlapping petals hang from the underside of a single stem. Those near the base of the stem bloom first, and many stages of flowering and fruit may be visible simultaneously on the stem. The round greenish buds hang on the stems for several weeks before the flowers open. Early in flowering, the single style extends through a small opening in the petals, while the 5 stamens emerge only toward the end of flowering. The fruit is a small green capsule.

❖ *Pyrola minor* (lesser wintergreen)   **FAMILY:** Ericaceae

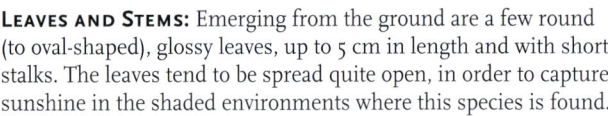

DISTRIBUTION Occasional in the eastern Sierra from the Yosemite area south through Big Pine Creek; rare in the western Sierra but distributed across the same latitudes
HABITAT Wet forests and stream banks
ELEVATION 7,000'–10,000'
SEASON Early July–early September
LOCATIONS Virginia Canyon at the Pacific Crest Trail junction, Dog Lake, Shadow Creek, Rock Creek Trail, Palisade Creek, Bishop Pass Trail (creek crossing beyond Treasure Lakes turn-off)

LEAVES AND STEMS: Emerging from the ground are a few round (to oval-shaped), glossy leaves, up to 5 cm in length and with short stalks. The leaves tend to be spread quite open, in order to capture sunshine in the shaded environments where this species is found.

FLOWERS: At the center of these leaves is the flowering stalk, generally 10–15 cm in length, occasionally a little taller. Small, white, nearly spherical flowers with red sepals dangle downward from the stem. Unlike other species of *Pyrola*, the style is not bent.

❖ *Pyrola picta* (white-veined wintergreen)   **FAMILY:** Ericaceae

DISTRIBUTION Common at montane elevations in the western Sierra, extending to the eastern Sierra in the Yosemite and Mammoth Lakes regions
HABITAT Dry, bare forest floor
ELEVATION 3,500'–10,000'
SEASON Late June–early August
LOCATIONS Lundy Canyon, Duck Pass Trail, Convict Creek drainage, Graveyard Meadows

LEAVES AND STEMS: The thick, dark-green leaves grow as a rosette. They are oval shaped, about 4–7 cm long, and mostly with distinctly white to pale-green veins. Note that a variant can often be found in the mixed conifer forest, where the leaves are hidden beneath the forest duff.

Flowers: The flowering stalks are 10–20 cm long, with the inflorescence along the top third of the stalk. The white 5-petal flowers form a downward-pointing bowl shape but are not fused together. Emerging from the center is a long, chunky, bent style. The variant of this species, which lacks visible leaves, often has much redder flowers.

❖ *Rhododendron columbianum (Ledum glandulosum)*
    (western Labrador tea)   **Family:** Ericaceae

Distribution Common throughout, on both sides of the Sierra Crest
Habitat Moist, shaded lakeshores, stream banks, and forest, especially prevalent under hemlock cover
Elevation 6,500'–11,200'
Season Mid-June–late July
Locations Dog Lake, Shadow Lake, John Muir Trail south of Tully Hole, and John Muir Trail south of Vidette Meadow

Leaves and Stems: This is a densely branched and leafy shrub up to 1 m tall—even occasionally 2 m. The notably dark-green, leathery, elongate, oval-shaped leaves are 2–8 cm long and 1.5–3 cm wide and can either extend straight out from the branch or tilt downward. Young leaves have very inrolled margins—they are nearly a cylinder—while older leaves can be flat to slightly inrolled. Plants often grow en masse near lakeshores, creating a fairly impenetrable patch.

Flowers: Each flower is composed of 5 petals, which lie nearly flat to slightly upturned. Emerging from the center of the flower are 10 long, white stamens that extend well beyond the petals, giving the flowers (and all rhododendrons) a showy appeal. Flowers, each with their own stalk, occur in clusters of up to 25, creating a large ball of white.

❖ *Trifolium monanthum* subsp. *monanthum*
    (carpet clover)   **Family:** Fabaceae

Distribution Fairly common throughout on both sides of the Sierra Crest
Habitat Seeps, wet meadows, stream banks
Elevation 4,000'–12,200'
Season Late June–early August
Locations Rock Creek Basin, Evolution Lake, Bishop Pass Trail

Leaves and Stems: As its name implies, this species of clover spreads across the ground, forming a soft carpet. Like all members of the genus, each leaf is divided into 3 leaflets—excepting that rare 4-leaf clover you might find. Each leaflet is at most 1 cm in length, rounded at the tip, and slightly toothed around the edge.

Flowers: The little flowers are just 7–12 mm long and occur singly, with broad banners poking up from the expanse of leaves. They are mostly white but with some pink to pale-purple streaks on the leaves, and the hidden keel is a more distinct purple color. (See also the illustration of a Fabaceae flower on page 15.)

❖ *Gentiana newberryi* var. *tiogana* (alpine gentian)   **FAMILY:** Gentianaceae

DISTRIBUTION Occurs throughout but becoming rarer south of the Palisades region
HABITAT Wet to drying meadows, moist alpine fell-fields
ELEVATION 7,000'–13,000'
SEASON Late July–mid-September
LOCATIONS Tuolumne Meadows, Rock Creek Basin, French Canyon, Rae Lakes Basin

LEAVES AND STEMS: The 1- to 4-cm-long leaves grow in small rosettes at ground level. They are thickish and oval-shaped, though often hidden in the tall, dense, grassy environments they prefer.

FLOWERS: No other flower in the Sierra looks quite like the alpine gentian: It is a large (2–5 cm), broad, white tube with 5 spreading petal tips at the top. The outside of the floral tube is decorated with 5 dark purple–green stripes, while the inside is covered with green dots. A frilly appendage adorns the area between the petal tips. Because this species and other gentians bloom in late summer, the flowers are especially obvious, because most other species have already faded.

❖ *Geranium richardsonii* (Richardson's geranium)   **FAMILY:** Geraniaceae

DISTRIBUTION Common at montane elevations throughout the western Sierra; common in the eastern Sierra from the Yosemite region south through the Bishop Creek drainage, occasionally reaching higher elevations in the eastern Sierra
HABITAT Wet sites, including stream banks, seeps, and wet meadows
ELEVATION 5,300'–10,500'
SEASON Late June–early August
LOCATIONS Warren Fork Lee Vining Creek, Agnew Meadows, Rock Creek Trail, Simpson Meadow, Bubbs Creek

LEAVES AND STEMS: The branched flowering stems can be as tall as 90 cm but rarely exceed 50 cm. The lower half of the stem is densely covered in large palmately lobed leaves; they are 4–10 cm in length and are deeply dissected into 5 (or 7) segments, each of which is further lobed near the tip.

FLOWERS: The flowers are located on stalks that rise well above the leaves. They have 5 broad petals, whitish in color and usually with light purple veins and white hairy bases adding beautiful detail. At the center are 10 stamens, their green bases tightly hugging the ovary, while their tops splay open.

❖ *Ribes inerme* var. *inerme* (white-stemmed gooseberry)   **FAMILY:** Grossulariaceae

DISTRIBUTION Occasional throughout
HABITAT Stream banks, dense forest
ELEVATION 5,000'–11,000'
SEASON Late June–early August
LOCATIONS Rock Creek Basin, Quail Meadows, Bear Creek, North Fork Big Pine Creek, Vidette Meadow, Cottonwood Lakes

LEAVES AND STEMS: This shrub can reach 3 m in height but is rarely more than half that. As indicated by its name, it has pale-gray to whitish stems that are thorny. The leaves are shiny and lack any hairs; they have 3 broad lobes and a coarsely toothed margin.

FLOWERS: The flowers have 5 short, white petals that stand upright, ringed by 5 much longer sepals that are bent back on themselves, adding a decorative touch to the flowers. The sepals also provide additional color; they are part purple or pink and shaded green elsewhere. The smooth berries are a burgundy to purple color and also lack any glands or hairs.

RELATED SPECIES: *Ribes nevadense,* the Sierra currant, is a shrub, usually 1–1.5 m in height. It lacks any thorns and has glossy, 3-lobed leaves that are very finely serrate along the leaf margin. The flowers are pale pink—the color provided by the calyx, because the petals are hidden inside and are much shorter and white. The fruits are small blue-colored berries dotted with small, gland-tipped hairs. See page 27 for a photo.

❖ *Stachys albens* (whitestem hedgenettle, cobwebby hedgenettle)
　　FAMILY: Lamiaceae

DISTRIBUTION Common throughout montane elevations in the western Sierra, especially from the San Joaquin drainage south; occasional throughout in the eastern Sierra
HABITAT Wet locations, including marshy meadows, seeps, and creek edges
ELEVATION 1,000'–8,200'
SEASON Late June–early August
LOCATIONS Yosemite Valley, Crane Flat, Reds Meadow, Whitney Portal

LEAVES AND STEMS: Ranging in height from 30 cm to 1.2 m, the thick, square stems are covered in dense, white, cob-webby hairs. The leaves, also covered in these hairs, occur in pairs. The elongate leaves are broad at their base, and along their margins are regularly spaced, rounded teeth. A further identifying characteristic is that they are slightly thick with distinct veins.

FLOWERS: While the overall length of the inflorescence is greater than 10 cm, much of that is bare stem. The flowers occur in single circles, called whorls, and between each whorl is a stretch of stem. The flowers themselves are white (or rose) with pink streaks. The 4 petals are fused to form distinct upper and lower lips. The 4 stamens stick far out of the floral tube.

❖ *Lewisia glandulosa* (Sierra lewisia, glandular lewisia)
　　FAMILY: Montiaceae (Portulacaceae)

DISTRIBUTION Occasional throughout, on both sides of the Sierra Crest
HABITAT Alpine fell-fields, where moist or along rocks
ELEVATION 9,800'–13,000'
SEASON Late June–early August
LOCATIONS Dana Plateau, Parker Pass, Bishop Pass, Diamond Mesa, Mt. Guyot

(Continued)

(Continued) **LEAVES AND STEMS:** The green to slightly purplish leaves grow as a very dense rosette of overlapping leaves. Each leaf is 2–5 cm long (occasionally longer), quite narrow, and fleshy. The leaves are slightly U shaped in cross section.

FLOWERS: The pink or white flowers, a little more than 1 cm in size, generally occur singly on stalks, but a rosette can have anywhere from a few to 50 flowers. The flowers have 6–8 long, narrow petals and 6 purple-tipped stamens in the center. The defining features for this species are the 2 gland-dotted sepals that surround the petals—the glands look like little purple (or black) rounded teeth along the rim of the otherwise green sepals.

RELATED SPECIES: *Lewisia kelloggii* (Kellogg's lewisia) is a very showy species that mostly occurs at slightly lower elevations in sandy granitic soils. It has 5–11 white petals that are 1–3 cm in length and a rosette of thick, oval-shaped leaves.

❖ *Lewisia nevadensis* (Nevada lewisia)
   FAMILY: Montiaceae (Portulacaceae)

DISTRIBUTION Fairly common throughout, on both sides of the Sierra Crest
HABITAT Wet meadows, moist sandy flats, moist forest floor, moist alpine fell-fields
ELEVATION 4,500'–11,800'
SEASON Mid-June–late July
LOCATIONS Tuolumne Meadows, Tioga Peak, Rae Lakes Basin, west side of Kearsarge Pass

LEAVES AND STEMS: This rosette species has a variable number of leaves, but it rarely has enough leaves to make the rosette look crowded. The fleshy leaves are long and narrow—from 3 to more than 10 cm in length—and have slightly upturned edges, giving them a U shape. Some leaves may lie flat on the ground surface, but more stick up into the air.

FLOWERS: Each rosette usually has many flowers, but they bloom over a period of time, and only a few decorate the plant at once. In contrast to *Lewisia pygmaea,* described on page 180, the flowers typically extend above the bed of leaves. The flowers have anywhere from 6 to 10 petals, often white, though they may have very bright-pink mid-veins, giving them a pinkish hue. Quite distinctive for this species, the petals are not all the same shape. Between 1 and 1.5 cm long, most taper near the tip, while 2 generally lie beneath the others and are opposite each other; these 2 have rather squared-off edges and are slightly broader than the others.

❖ *Lewisia triphylla* (three-leaved lewisia)
   FAMILY: Montiaceae (Portulacaceae)

DISTRIBUTION Fairly common west of the Sierra Crest; absent in the eastern Sierra except around Tioga Pass
HABITAT Moist sandy flats, open forest, meadows
ELEVATION 4,200'–10,500'
SEASON Late June–early August

LOCATIONS Tuolumne Meadows Campground, Murphy Creek Trail, west slope of Mt. Dana, King Creek (near Devils Postpile), Hutchinson Meadow

LEAVES AND STEMS: Growing to a height of 4–7 cm (or even less), this annual species is simply composed of a stem and 3 (or 2 or, very occasionally, up to 5) nearly cylindrical leaves that attach halfway up the stem. The leaves are 2.5–5 cm long and bright green. The stem may be branched or unbranched above the leaves. The leaves turn red as they wither.

FLOWERS: Plants range widely in the number of flowers, from 1 to more than 10. The white (or pale pink) flowers measure about 1 cm in diameter. They are composed of 5–9 narrow petals that are either rounded or pointed near the tip. The petals often have distinct pink veins.

❖ *Montia chamissoi* (toad lily)   **FAMILY:** Montiaceae (Portulacaceae)

DISTRIBUTION Fairly common throughout, on both sides of the Sierra Crest
HABITAT Seeps, stream banks, wet meadows
ELEVATION 4,000'–12,000'
SEASON Late June–late July
LOCATIONS Great Sierra Wagon Road, Tyee Lakes, Arrowhead Lake (Rae Lakes Basin), Cottonwood Lakes Basin

LEAVES AND STEMS: This spreading plant often seems to be mostly stem. The fleshy, oval-shaped, 1.5- to 5-cm-long leaves attach in opposite pairs along the stem. The creeping stems rise up to 15 cm tall and grow roots at stem junctions.

FLOWERS: The top of each stem has a small number of flowers, with more growing from the lower leaf nodes. The 5 white petals are just 0.5–0.9 cm long and tend to be yellowish toward the center. The flowers look similar to the three-leaved lewisia, but the stem and growth form are very different.

❖ Why Are So Many Plants Renamed?

This is one of the first Sierra plant guides to be published since the 2012 edition of the definitive book on California flora, *The Jepson Manual*. To the frustration of many wildflower enthusiasts, including at times myself, the new Jepson edition includes many, many name changes. New families, new genera, and even species and subspecies have been collapsed into one or split into many. Irritating as it may be to relearn plant names, the new names are assigned with good reason: to ensure that each name (whether at the family or subspecies level) refers   *(Continued)*

(Continued)   to a group of plants that have descended from a single population in the distant past, known as a monophyletic group. Moreover, the category must include all plants that have descended from the ancestral population. But do not despair: I have included the names from the 1994 *Jepson Manual* in both the index and in the species descriptions, as described on page 9.

Since 1735, when Carl Linnaeus established the current system for categorizing species (see "What Is a Scientific Name?" on page 79), plants have been divided into families, genera, and species based on visible traits, including petal number, stamen number, and fruit type, and also whether the petals are fused into a tube. This method, though mostly quite accurate, is imperfect. Over the last 25 years, researchers have begun to look at the similarity of plant DNA to determine relatedness; they have discovered many incorrect groupings that they are now reclassifying. Consider this example: Philadelphaceae, the family previously containing *Jamesia americana,* has disappeared because genetic work showed that it was embedded within a second family, Hydrangeaceae. In other words, the common ancestor for all members of Hydrangeaceae had descendants in both Hydrangeaceae and Philadelphaceae. In other cases, a family has been split, resulting in new family names: Portulacaceae is now divided into Montiaceae and Portulacaceae. The members of Portulacaceae are all descended from one common ancestor, while those in Montiaceae share a different common ancestor. Indeed, it turns out that the species now encompassed in Portulacaceae are more closely related to members of the cactus family, Cactaceae, than they are to those in Montiaceae. While an edition of *The Jepson Manual* in another 20 years' time is likely to include more name changes, the broad relationships between plant families have, we hope, now been correctly worked out. If you are curious about relationships between plant families, visit the Angiosperm Phylogeny Website, **mobot.org/mobot/research/apweb.**

❖ *Gayophytum diffusum* subsp. *parviflorum*
    (spreading groundsmoke)   **FAMILY:** Onagraceae

DISTRIBUTION Common throughout, on both sides of the Sierra Crest
HABITAT Open, gravelly slopes; scrubby locations; open forest
ELEVATION 3,500'–11,250'
SEASON Late June–mid-August
LOCATIONS Tuolumne Meadows, Rock Creek Basin, Fifth Lake (North Fork Big Pine Creek), Kearsarge Pass Trail, along Tyndall Creek near John Muir Trail

LEAVES AND STEMS: Though usually growing 20–50 cm in height, this species is easily overlooked, for the repeatedly branched stems are thin and wispy, and the stem leaves are only a few millimeters wide and are often bent up against the stem. In particular, they stand out poorly against the background on the bright, gravelly granite soils where they are often found.

FLOWERS: What might catch your eye are the numerous bright white 4-petal flowers, a little under 1 cm in diameter, making them much larger than other mid- to high-elevation species of *Gayophytum*. The petals open flat, resembling a saucer. As they finish blooming, the petals roll up, tinted pink on the outside.

RELATED SPECIES: *Gayophytum heterozygum* has flowers that look quite similar. It can be distinguished on the basis of its bumpy pods—bumpy because many of the seeds abort and remain small, with the remaining ones forming the bumps.

❖ *Gayophytum racemosum* (blackfoot groundsmoke)
　　FAMILY: Onagraceae

DISTRIBUTION Occasional throughout, often at high elevations
HABITAT Seasonally moist flats, meadows
ELEVATION 6,400'–12,000'
SEASON Late June–early September
LOCATIONS Twenty Lakes Basin, Minaret Lake, Saddlerock Lake (Bishop Pass Trail), Seventh Lake (North Fork Big Pine Creek), Baxter Lakes Basin, Bullfrog Lake

LEAVES AND STEMS: All species in this genus are annuals, with their abundance depending on the year's rainfall. This very branched species varies enormously in height, from a few to 40 cm. The leaves are narrow and tiny, slightly hairy, 1–2.5 cm long, and just a few millimeters in width.

FLOWERS: The white 4-petal flowers are truly small, with the petals measuring 1–2 mm in length. The petals fade to pink as they finish flowering. The narrow sepals are bent far back.

RELATED SPECIES: The related species *Gayophytum humile* has a similar range and looks very much like blackfoot groundsmoke, except this species tends to have no hairs and the petals do not fade reddish.

Gayophytum humile

❖ *Argemone munita* (prickly poppy, chicalote)
　　FAMILY: Papaveraceae

DISTRIBUTION Fairly common throughout montane elevations in the eastern Sierra; occasional at montane elevations in the western Sierra from the San Joaquin River drainage south
HABITAT Dry, sandy slopes, especially common in the years after a fire
ELEVATION 1,200'–9,000'
SEASON Late June–mid-August
LOCATIONS Virginia Lakes Basin, Onion Valley, Baxter Pass Trail, Shepherd Pass Trail, Cottonwood Creek

(Continued)

(Continued) **LEAVES AND STEMS:** The prickly poppy rarely occurs at the elevations included in this book, but it is too showy and memorable to omit, and many eastern Sierra trails pass through its range. Reaching from 60 cm to more than 1 m in height, the stems are densely covered with 5- to 15-cm-long, deeply lobed, toothed, and very prickly leaves—the leaf margins and the stem are densely covered in the prickles. Note that the leaf and stem are also hairy, shading them gray-green.

FLOWERS: Each plant has many large white flowers, 5–10 cm in diameter; their 5 petals have the look of crepe paper. At the center is a dense, spherical cluster of yellow stamens.

❖ *Parnassia palustris (Parnassia californica)* (marsh grass of Parnassus)
    FAMILY: Parnassiaceae (Saxifragaceae)

DISTRIBUTION Occasional throughout the western Sierra, extending east of the Sierra Crest in the northern Yosemite area
HABITAT Wet seeps, very wet meadows, stream banks
ELEVATION 6,200'–11,500'
SEASON Early August–mid-September
LOCATIONS John Muir Trail below the top of Nevada Falls, Bishop Pass Trailhead, Rosemarie Meadow (north of Selden Pass), west of Taboose Pass, Kearsarge Pass Trail

LEAVES AND STEMS: In midsummer, a cluster of 2- to 5-cm-long, oval-shaped leaves emerges from the root—some with a quite wide, flattish stalk and others nearly lacking a stem. They are a glossy light green, fairly thick, and with a distinct midvein. Because this species blooms so late, it often stands out as a patch of flowerless leaves, when nearby species are in full bloom.

FLOWERS: The 5 cream-colored petals are generally 1–1.5 cm long and have distinct translucent veins. The tips of the petals are slightly upturned—almost as if there isn't quite enough petal to lie flat. 5 stamens attach opposite the petals, and in between these lie 5 frilly staminodia—infertile structures decorated by threads topped with miniature round balls. See page 85 for a close-up photo.

RELATED SPECIES: In the Sierra, *Parnassia parviflora,* the small-flowered grass of Parnassus, is limited to the Convict Creek drainage, where it is very common in the meadows around Mildred Lake. Unlike its larger-flowered relative, this species grows among the meadow grasses, with its 1- to 2-cm-wide white flowers rising just above the grass blades.

❖ *Leptosiphon pachyphyllus (Linanthus pachyphyllus)* (Sierra linanthus)
    FAMILY: Polemoniaceae

DISTRIBUTION Occasional in the Yosemite area, becoming quite common in the Mono Recesses region and Bishop Creek drainage, and common just east of Mineral King, but otherwise quite rare
HABITAT Dry slopes and flats, forest openings, open talus slopes
ELEVATION 7,000'–11,500'

Season Early July–early August
Locations Convict Creek drainage, Pine Creek Pass Trail, Bear Lakes Basin, Lake Sabrina

Leaves and Stems: This species grows as a cluster of semiwoody stems, each 10–20 cm long. Sometimes the stems grow so close together that they look like a single dense shrub, while at other times there are just a few stems. The leaves are in pairs, and each is deeply divided into 5–6 lobes that are slightly broader than linear.

Flowers: The white, tubular, 5-petal flowers occur in small clusters. The calyx is about 1 cm long, while the flower tube is several millimeters longer. At the top of the tube, the petal lobes are bent back at approximate right angles, with some yellow coloring visible at the top of the tube. The stamens stick out slightly, and the yellow pollen is readily visible.

❖ Miscolored Plants on Calcitic Soils

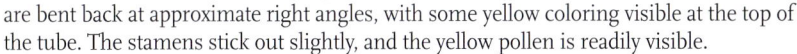

Are you staring at a rose-pink or even raspberry-colored plant that you are certain is typically white? Your eyes (or pink-tinted sunglasses) are not tricking you. I have found pink to purple variants of *Achillea millefolium, Leptosiphon pachyphyllus, Linanthus pungens,* and *Phlox condensata.* The plants usually grow near marble outcrops, and the soil in which they are growing, therefore, probably has a high pH (meaning the soil is alkaline). This phenomenon has never been investigated in Sierra species—nor anywhere on and off marble soils, as best as I can discover. However, it seems likely that an environmental trigger causes some plants on marble soils to produce anthocyanins, a class of chemicals that create blue to red pigments (see "A Rainbow of Flowers," page 95). The white color that is the norm in these species is likely created by one class of flavonoid pigments, but these species can also produce anthocyanins, a separate class of flavonoid pigments. The color change may occur because anthocyanin production increases in response to an environmental stress associated with the marble soils or because the soil pH has changed (the color of anthocyanins is sensitive to pH). The addition of magnesium to soil can cause anthocyanins to become more vibrant—and calcitic soils often have high magnesium concentrations. Whatever the exact mechanism, something about the marble soils affects the biochemical pathway that creates color pigments, resulting in a plant changing colors.

I have observed "miscolored" plants in the Convict Creek drainage, near Mt. Morgan in the Rock Creek Basin, near Chocolate Mountain on the Bishop Pass Trail, and on Mt. Perkins to the south of Pinchot Pass.

❖ *Linanthus pungens (Leptodactylon pungens)* (granite gilia, granite prickly phlox)
FAMILY: Polemoniaceae

DISTRIBUTION Very common throughout, on both sides of the Sierra Crest
HABITAT Rocky slopes, rocky flats, among talus, alongside boulders
ELEVATION 5,800'–12,200'
SEASON Mid-June–mid-July
LOCATIONS Mt. Dana Trail, Red Peak Pass, Selden Pass, Evolution Lake, Bishop Pass Trail, Kearsarge Pass Trail, Mt. Whitney Trail

LEAVES AND STEMS: A dense tangle of branches, this shrub can reach 30 cm in height, but at higher elevations it is frequently only half that, spreading out along the ground. Each leaf is divided into 3–7 needlelike lobes, the center one the longest, but each shaped like a very narrow triangle and ending in a sharp tip. Grabbing hold of one of these plants is a prickly prospect. The foliage is generally hairy, and the hairs are usually gland tipped.

FLOWERS: The tubular flowers start as tightly wound buds, sometimes tinged pink or purple on the outside. They unwind into 1.5- to 2-cm-diameter white flowers with overlapping petals. The 1- to 1.5-cm-long tube is pinkish-beige and broadens quite gradually, much like a funnel. Though the flowers are generally white, they may occasionally be pink, especially near calcitic rock.

❖ How Old Are Alpine Plants?

Alpine plants, including shrubby species, are short in stature; being large is a disadvantage for them because the insulating snowpack does not cover them and the biting winds do more damage to their branches. High-elevation species are not, however, young; they just grow very slowly. Tree ages have long been determined by counting the annual growth rings in their trunks; in a climate like the Sierra Nevada, with a distinct growing season, most trees show obvious annual growth rings. Recently, this method has been adapted to determine the age of small shrubs. With shrubs, growth rings in the root must be identified because individual stems die and are replaced, while the same root persists throughout a species' life. The roots are often 1 cm in diameter at most, making counting an eye-straining process done under a microscope. Using this method, a researcher sampled many of the woody species in a rock glacier community along the Duck Pass Trail. She determined that *Linanthus pungens* (granite gilia) can reach 120 years of age, and various high-elevation *Ribes* species (currants) can be more than 100 years old. Other notable examples include *Phlox diffusa* (spreading phlox) at 40 years, *Monardella odoratissima* (mountain monardella) at 45 years, and *Aquilegia pubescens* (Coville's columbine) at 25 years. Think about how old these plants are before you move a rock and expose their roots to desiccating winds.

❖ *Phlox condensata* (condensed phlox) **Family:** Polemoniaceae

Distribution Common close to the Sierra Crest from the Yosemite region south to the Bishop Creek drainage; absent farther south
Habitat Alpine fell-fields, gravel slopes
Elevation 6,000'–12,800'
Season Mid-June–mid-July
Locations Tioga Peak, Mono Pass (Rock Creek Basin), Coyote Ridge, Lamarck Col

Leaves and Stems: A classic cushion plant, this species prefers flat gravelly areas and is often found on passes and high plateaus. It hugs the ground, never rising more than a few centimeters above it. The leaves are diminutive—only a few millimeters long and somewhat triangular but slightly folded upward along the midrib. They tightly overlap on the short stalks, so you really see a carpet of prickly green points, not individual leaves.

Flowers: The 5-petal flowers are usually white but occasionally tinged purple or pink. During a "good" spring, the leaves can be completely covered beneath a sea of white petals. The rounded petal lobes are united into a short tube, but it goes unnoticed, for the flowers face upward and the petals open straight outward, doing their best to attract bumblebees in the windy alpine. The yellow pollen is just visible inside the narrow tube.

Related Species: *Phlox dispersa,* High Sierra phlox, occurs mainly around New Army Pass. Because its underground stem, or rhizome, is longer than that of *Phlox condensata,* its leaf clusters are more spread out and less cushionlike than *Phlox condensata.*

❖ *Phlox diffusa* (spreading phlox) **Family:** Polemoniaceae

Distribution Common on both sides of the Sierra Crest from the Yosemite region south through the Mono Recesses; farther south, common in the western Sierra, but absent in the eastern Sierra and on the Kern Plateau
Habitat Open slopes, among rocks
Elevation 4,000'–12,000'
Season Mid-June–mid-July
Locations Rancheria Mountain, Gaylor Lakes Trail, around Tioga Pass, Franklin Lakes

Leaves and Stems: As the common name suggests, the woody stems of this plant spread across the ground. They are much branched, and each branch ends in a dense tuft of leaves. The 1- to 1.5-cm-long leaves are very narrow—almost needlelike at times.

Flowers: Each stem ends in a single tubular flower that ranges from whitish to a brilliant bright pink, the latter more prevalent at lower elevations. The 5-petal lobes are much rounder than most other ground-hugging phlox species and, therefore, usually overlap slightly. The stamens with yellow pollen are visible inside the flower tube but do not stick out.

(Continued)

(Continued)   **RELATED SPECIES:** A related species, *Phlox pulvinata* (cushion phlox), has leaves that are longer and flat, rather than folded upward along the midrib, but are still very narrow. Its petals are narrow and come to a point at the tip. Cushion phlox is located in scattered locations close to the Sierra Crest from Yosemite south to the Kearsarge Pass area, including Gaylor Peak, the Dana Plateau, Coyote Ridge, and near Kearsarge Pass.

❖ *Eriogonum latens* (Inyo wild buckwheat)   **FAMILY:** Polygonaceae

Distribution Fairly common in the eastern Sierra from the Convict Creek drainage south; absent in the western Sierra
Habitat Dry, gravelly, or sandy slopes
Elevation 6,500'–11,100'
Season Late June–mid August
Locations Pass north of Lake Genevieve, south shore of Lake Mildred (Convict Creek drainage), Mt. Tom, Taboose Creek, Sawmill Canyon

LEAVES AND STEMS: Officially, this species has a rosette growth form, but most individuals have such an abundance of large leaves that they form a mound 10–20 cm in diameter and up to 10 cm in height. The somewhat elongate to spoon-shaped leaf blades are 1–2.5 cm in diameter and covered in short hairs.

FLOWERS: The white (to cream-colored) inflorescences are on long stalks, up to 40 cm in length. The many 6-petal flowers form a near-spherical inflorescence, 2–3 cm in diameter. At times they reach skyward, and at other times they lean out to the side.

❖ *Eriogonum lobbii* (Lobb's wild buckwheat)
        FAMILY: Polygonaceae

DISTRIBUTION Common throughout the eastern Sierra; common in the western Sierra in the Yosemite region but absent farther south
HABITAT Alpine fell-fields, sandy flats
ELEVATION 3,500'–12,300'
SEASON Late June–mid-August
LOCATIONS Virginia Lakes Basin, top of Clouds Rest, Dana Plateau, Mono Pass Trail (Rock Creek Basin), Coyote Ridge, east slope of Kearsarge Pass

LEAVES AND STEMS: This species grows as a spreading, often circular mat of many densely clustered rosettes, each of which can have a single flowering stalk. Each oval-shaped leaf is 1–4 cm long with a short stalk at its base. Both sides of the leaf are densely covered with white hairs, giving them a gray-green felty appearance.

FLOWERS: The most distinctive feature of this species is how the inflorescences lie flat on the ground beside the leaves, sometimes in a near circle around the leaves and other times concentrated to one side. The pale yellow to nearly white flowers form a dense head and color red as they age. The 6-petal flowers are fused at the base but spread quite open near the tips, and at least 3 of them have distinctly darker lines along their midribs.

❖ *Eriogonum nudum* var. *deductum* (reduced wild buckwheat, naked buckwheat)
  FAMILY: Polygonaceae

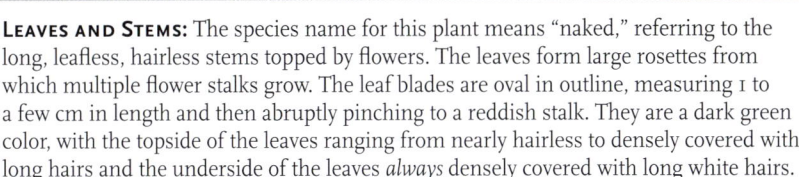

DISTRIBUTION Very common throughout, on both sides
of the Sierra Crest
HABITAT Dry, gravelly, or sandy flats or slopes
ELEVATION 3,500'–11,750'
SEASON Late June–mid-August
LOCATIONS Virginia Lakes Basin, Twenty Lakes Basin,
Thousand Island Lake, Bear Creek,
Rae Lakes Basin, east side of Kearsarge Pass

LEAVES AND STEMS: The species name for this plant means "naked," referring to the long, leafless, hairless stems topped by flowers. The leaves form large rosettes from which multiple flower stalks grow. The leaf blades are oval in outline, measuring 1 to a few cm in length and then abruptly pinching to a reddish stalk. They are a dark green color, with the topside of the leaves ranging from nearly hairless to densely covered with long hairs and the underside of the leaves *always* densely covered with long white hairs.

FLOWERS: The inflorescences measure about 2 cm in diameter and are a dense ball (or hemisphere) of white flowers. Emerging from the center of each flower are white stamens, tipped with burgundy-colored pollen. The colored pollen, in combination with the pinkish hue of the buds, often gives the inflorescences a pale-pink appearance.

RELATED SPECIES: A second very similar variety, *scapigerum,* occurs in the eastern Sierra up to 12,200 feet. The two subspecies are differentiated only by the number of tiny leaves at the base of the inflorescence, with a single leaf in var. *deductum* and 3–6 leaves in var. *scapigerum.* Note that additional varieties of the species occur at lower elevations in the Sierra.

*Eriogonum nudum
var. scapigerum*

❖ *Eriogonum ovalifolium* var. *nivale* (Sierra cushion wild buckwheat)
  FAMILY: Polygonaceae

DISTRIBUTION Common throughout, on both sides of the
Sierra Crest
HABITAT Alpine fell-fields, sandy or gravelly flats
ELEVATION 5,300'–13,000'
SEASON Late June–mid-August
LOCATIONS Twenty Lakes Basin, Dana Plateau, Bishop Pass,
Mt. Whitney Trail

LEAVES AND STEMS: The Sierra cushion wild buckwheat is one of the most characteristic species of high-elevation fell-fields, growing as a shallow mound called a cushion. The cushion is a dense collection of tiny, slightly fleshy leaves, each (usually) less than 1 cm in length, slightly folded along their midrib, and facing upward. They appear white due to the dense covering of small white hairs—this buckwheat species has the smallest, whitest leaves of all Sierra buckwheats.

FLOWERS: The flowering stalks are generally just 5–10 cm in length but can occasionally be longer. At the tip is a ball of tiny white to pale-pink 6-petal flowers that change to red or yellow as they fade. The petals have distinct, dark, longitudinal lines running down their middles.

❖ *Eriogonum spergulinum* var. *reddingianum*
(Redding's wild buckwheat)   **FAMILY:** Polygonaceae

DISTRIBUTION Common throughout, on both sides
of the Sierra Crest
HABITAT Sandy or gravelly flats
ELEVATION 5,000'–11,300'
SEASON Late June–mid-August
LOCATIONS Virginia Lakes Basin, San Joaquin Mountain, Mammoth Lakes Basin, Mono Creek, Ruby Lake
(Rock Creek Basin)

LEAVES AND STEMS: You will only find this species if
you go looking for it, but then you will discover that it is quite common. Ranging 5–40
cm in height, its stems are very fine, reddish, and much branched, so it often blends
into the dry, sandy substrate on which it typically grows. Its leaves are usually 1–3 cm
in length and narrow; many leaves grow near the base of the plant, but fewer develop
higher along the stem.

FLOWERS: In Redding's wild buckwheat, each flower is independently attached to a long
stalk, so the flowers are dispersed throughout the plant. Even smaller than most other
species in the genus *Eriogonum,* the tiny flowers are just 2 mm in diameter. The 6 petals are white to a very pale pink, with a dark line down the midrib, and are splayed wide
open. The midrib shows up distinctly in bud, giving the plants a pinkish appearance.

RELATED SPECIES: Two additional subspecies occur in the Sierra: Var. *spergulinum*
appears at somewhat lower elevations in the western Sierra and var. *pratense* is found in
the eastern Sierra from Mt. Whitney south.

❖ *Polygonum shastense* (Shasta knotweed)
        FAMILY: Polygonaceae

DISTRIBUTION Occasional in the western Sierra from the
Yosemite region south through the San Joaquin drainage;
rare to absent from the Kings River drainage south and
throughout the eastern Sierra
HABITAT Sandy to gravelly slopes, often alongside rocks
ELEVATION 8,200'–11,600'
SEASON Late June–early August
LOCATIONS Twenty Lakes Basin, Vogelsang Lake, Isberg
Pass, Garnet Lake, north side of Silver Pass, Martha Lake

LEAVES AND STEMS: Unlike most knotweeds, this is a
substantial plant—even a shrub. The wandering, woody stems are reddish and scaly-barked, up to 40 cm in length. The narrow 1- to 2-cm-long leaves are crowded on the
new growth toward the top of the stem. The small, oval-shaped leaves are thick and
leathery, appearing even thicker and narrower because their margins are rolled under.

FLOWERS: A white- to pink-petaled flower, about 5 mm in diameter, emerges from each
leaf node. Once the flowers push past the leaves, the petals open widely, revealing the
red pollen sacks, making the blossoms showy, albeit tiny.

❖ *Androsace septentrionalis* (pygmyflower rockjasmine)   **FAMILY:** Primulaceae

DISTRIBUTION Occasional throughout, always at high elevations
HABITAT Flattish, moist alpine fell-fields
ELEVATION 9,800'–13,500'
SEASON Early June–early July
LOCATIONS Mt. Dana Trail, Mono Pass (Rock Creek Basin), Coyote Ridge, Baxter Pass, headwaters of Tyndall Creek, Mt. Whitney Trail

LEAVES AND STEMS: This species is usually an annual, a rare life cycle for an alpine plant. However, it does not attempt to grow very large, reaching no more than 6 cm tall, and often only half that. The leaves, 0.5–2 cm long, form a rosette. Each leaf is almost diamond shaped: broad in the middle and quite pointed at both ends. The leaves turn red by the time the flowers set seed, and their wilted remains is often all you find.

FLOWERS: 1 to several flowering stems grow from the rosette's center, forming a tangled mass of very skinny red stems, each bearing a handful of tiny flowers. The calyx is greenish to reddish in color, with 5 distinctly sharp points. It encloses the miniature bulbous, tubular flower, just a few millimeters in diameter and with the final 2–4 mm of the 5 white petal lobes visible. This species blooms so early that you will often find just the collection of straggly red stems and red seed capsules—and only if you happen to stare straight down on one, for they really are very minuscule.

❖ *Actaea rubra* (western baneberry, red baneberry)
        FAMILY: Ranunculaceae

DISTRIBUTION Fairly common throughout, especially in the southern half of the High Sierra
HABITAT Streamsides; shaded slopes; often alongside rocks
ELEVATION 4,000'–11,000'
SEASON Early June–early July
LOCATIONS Lower stretches of Pine Creek Pass Trail, South Fork Big Pine Creek, above Long Lake (Bishop Pass Trail), Le Conte Canyon, trail from Milestone Basin to Tyndall Creek

LEAVES AND STEMS: Commonly reaching 30–70 cm tall, the branching plant has numerous bright-green stem leaves but lacks basal leaves. Each leaf is compound: It is divided into approximately oval-shaped, toothed leaflets, the topmost of which occurs in threes. Some of the side leaflets are divided into threes a second time. Each leaflet measures 3–9 cm in length.

FLOWERS: The flowers are densely clustered at the top of the stem. The numerous white (and greenish) stamens are the first thing you'll notice—the inflorescence looks almost like an elongate pom-pom. On closer inspection, you'll notice that each flower has many small white "petals," half of which are actual petals while the others are sepals. By mid-summer you will notice the berries—an intensely bright red and on a red stalk.

EXTRA TIDBITS: Beware: These berries are very toxic and can cause cardiac arrest.

❖ *Anemone drummondii* var. *drummondii* (Drummond's anemone)
   FAMILY: Ranunculaceae

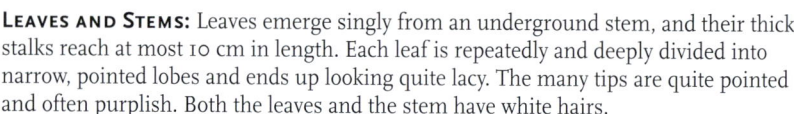

DISTRIBUTION Scattered populations throughout the
eastern Sierra and in the western Sierra from the
Yosemite region south to the Bishop Creek drainage,
with most western populations occurring in Yosemite
HABITAT Rocky slopes just below depressions that hold
snow until late in the season; almost always east- to
north-facing locations
ELEVATION 9,400'–11,700'
SEASON Mid-June–early July
LOCATIONS Crater Crest (north of Green Creek drainage),
above Red Lake (Virginia Lakes Basin), Bright Dot Lake (Convict Creek drainage),
Table Mountain (above Tyee Lakes)

LEAVES AND STEMS: Leaves emerge singly from an underground stem, and their thick
stalks reach at most 10 cm in length. Each leaf is repeatedly and deeply divided into
narrow, pointed lobes and ends up looking quite lacy. The many tips are quite pointed
and often purplish. Both the leaves and the stem have white hairs.

FLOWERS: The white flowers occur singly at the end of 10- to 25-cm-long stems. 5–
8 "petals" (actually sepals) surround a dense cluster of many yellow-tipped stamens.
The sepals are shaped like elongate ovals and are 1–2 cm long. The outer
side of the sepals can be quite purplish, especially in early bloom.

RELATED SPECIES: A second species, *Anemone occidentalis,* the western
anemone, occurs in sheltered east- and north-facing basins in the western
Sierra, including the northwest side of Red Top Mountain (southern Yosemite), the northwest ridge of Iron Mountain, and the north side of Deadman's
Pass. It has large white flowers with slightly pointier petals but becomes
much showier in seed, with long, featherlike styles forming a dense sphere.

*Anemone
occidentalis*

❖ *Aquilegia pubescens* (alpine columbine,
   Coville's columbine)   **FAMILY:** Ranunculaceae

DISTRIBUTION Common throughout, on both
sides of the Sierra Crest
HABITAT Rocky slopes, generally in the alpine zone
ELEVATION 7,000'–12,000'
SEASON Early July–mid-August
LOCATIONS Lake Helen outlet (Twenty Lakes
Basin), trail to Dana Plateau, above Long Lake
(Rock Creek Basin), Evolution Basin

LEAVES AND STEMS: One of the species that signals you are high
in the mountains, the alpine columbine can occur individually or
in large, spectacularly showy patches. The plants grow to 50 cm in
height and have a dense collection of leaves at their base. The basal
leaves are divided into 3 rounded leaflets, each of which is 1–2.5
cm long and deeply lobed. The stem leaves are simply 3-lobed. The
stems, at least toward the bottom, usually have gland-tipped hairs.

Flowers: These flowers point straight up, with 5 longer sepals and 5 shorter petals that open outward and 5 long spurs trailing behind—the entire flower is approximately 6 cm in length. Pure specimens are snow white. However, most flowers have some purplish or pinkish parts due to hybridization with the crimson columbine (see "A Tale of Two Columbines," below). A dense clump of yellow stamens emerges from the center of the flower.

❖ A Tale of Two Columbines

While only two columbines occur in the Sierra, *Aquilegia pubescens* (Coville's columbine) and *Aquilegia formosa* (crimson columbine), 25 exist within North America. This genus, with the two Sierra species as stereotypical examples, tells a wonderful story of plants undergoing rapid evolutionary change. Columbines all have nectar spurs, or long tubular structures with nectar in the inside tip. Variations in nectar spur characteristics seem to be the key to the creation of so many species, with species evolving different flower traits to match specific pollinators.

Aquilegia formosa (page 160) is red-flowered, has intermediate-length spurs that point upward, and is hummingbird pollinated. *Aquilegia pubescens* (opposite page) is white- to yellow-flowered, has much longer spurs that point downward, and is pollinated by hawk moths. Overall, in the columbine genus, the white individuals have long, downward-pointing spurs and are hawk moth pollinated; red individuals have shorter, upward-pointing spurs and are hummingbird pollinated; and blue to purple species have quite short, sideways-oriented spurs and are bumblebee pollinated (though none of these grow in the Sierra). The differences in flower color, spur length, and spur orientation help attract specific pollinators, yet they are likely caused by quite small mutations. Because these changes immediately affect which pollinators visit the species, populations with different traits will be visited by different pollinators and will not exchange pollen, rapidly leading to the creation of new species. This simple yet elegant story makes columbines a textbook example of a recent adaptive radiation—defined as a rapid increase in the number of closely related species because they evolve different traits. In this case, a change in nectar spur length, orientation, and color allowed these columbines to attract different pollinators. Yet another neat tidbit: Research has shown that flower color has evolved from blue to red to white but not the reverse. Researchers have also discovered that spur length increases but does not decrease.

But there is even more to the story. . . . These individual genetic mutations attract different pollinators to the species *most of the time*, but of course pollinators will try to sneak in a meal anywhere they can and will occasionally land on a different species of columbine and leave behind a bit of pollen from another species. Because the various columbine species diverged so recently, many of them can still interbreed and form fertile hybrids (see "Hybrids," page 233). In the Sierra, if you

(Continued)

(Continued)   are at an elevation around 10,000–11,000 feet, where both species frequently occur, you will notice that there is a rainbow of individuals, varying from red to many shades of light pink and purple to light yellow to white. And the spurs are variable in length and orientation. All the individuals that look like neither stereotypical parent are likely hybrids. For many reasons, the hybrids do not leave as many offspring as purebred parents do, so the two endpoints in the spectrum continue to survive.

❖ *Caltha leptosepala* (white marsh marigold)
   FAMILY: Ranunculaceae

photographed by Rebecca Wenk

DISTRIBUTION Common in the western Sierra, especially at montane elevations, but also frequently found in the subalpine zone; absent in the eastern Sierra south of Mono Lake
HABITAT Marshy areas, wet meadows
ELEVATION 6,000'–11,200'
SEASON Early June–early July
LOCATIONS Virginia Lakes Basin, Cathedral Lakes, Buena Vista Lake, Eagle Lake (near Mineral King)

LEAVES AND STEMS: Each plant has a cluster of 2- to 8-cm-long stalked leaves emerging from a single point. The round, rather thick, shiny green leaves often have wavy margins and are somewhat curved upward, giving them more dimension.

FLOWERS: Each plant has 1–4 white flowers. The flowers are 3–5 cm across and are comprised of white sepals (which look like petals). The flowers are often a little uneven in shape, and a dense cluster of long yellow stamens appears in the middle.

❖ *Ranunculus aquatilis* var. *diffusus* (water buttercup)
   FAMILY: Ranunculaceae

DISTRIBUTION Occasional throughout, on both sides of the Sierra Crest
HABITAT Shallow ponds and lakes, slow-moving water
ELEVATION 1,000'–11,100'
SEASON Mid-July–mid-August
LOCATIONS Reds Meadow, Blayney Meadows, Kenneth Lake (Rock Creek Basin), tarn below Chocolate Lake (near Bishop Pass Trail)

LEAVES AND STEMS: This aquatic plant often forms large mats of leaves and flowers. The leaves are dissected into multiple linear strands, but since they are submerged in shallow water, you simply note a mass of soggy linear leaves. A second type of leaves floats on the surface and is rounder in outline, with about 6 rounded lobes.

FLOWERS: Rising above the water are many white flowers, just more than 1 cm in diameter and featuring 5 upward-bent petals. In the center are many yellow stamens, and underneath the petals are 5 sepals, yellowish-white in color and somewhat bent back. Reddish stalks lift the flowers above the water.

❖ Too Much Light

Photosynthesis is a chemical process that occurs in the green leaves of plants. During the process, water and carbon dioxide combine to create sugars, and oxygen is released as a by-product. The energy provided by sunlight fuels this reaction. Chlorophyll, a biomolecule, captures the light energy, allowing it to be used for the photosynthetic reaction. If more light reaches the leaf surface than the chlorophyll can process, both the chlorophyll and other important biomolecules are damaged— and you can easily imagine that in a mountain range like the Sierra, alpine plants have an overabundance of sunlight. An added dilemma is that chemical reactions are slower at lower temperatures, so plants in cool, sunny alpine environments not only receive excess light, but they also process it slowly, leading to a greater surplus.

As a result, plants in alpine environments have evolved a number of mechanisms to counteract these problems. First, many species reduce the amount of light that hits their leaf surface by having hairy or waxy leaves, both mechanisms that reflect away some of the incoming light. Second, they adjust their photosynthetic system to match the cool, bright environment. Relative to plants in lower light environments, plants in the alpine and subalpine zones have photosynthetic systems that are able to process more incoming light before being overwhelmed. They also lower their optimal temperature, so their enzymes have better performance at cooler temperatures than lower elevation species do. Indeed, studies on *Caltha leptosepala,* a species that grows early in the season when temperatures are cooler, show that its photosynthetic machinery performs better under bright, low-temperature conditions than the photosynthetic systems of other species do. *Oxyria digyna* also adjusts its optimal temperature to match the environment. Another mechanism employed by alpine plants is to create chemical compounds that can remedy the damage caused by excess light. A range of antioxidant chemicals, including carotenoids and ascorbic acid, can perform this role, and many studies have shown high levels of antioxidants in high-elevation species.

❖ *Thalictrum sparsiflorum* (few flowered meadow rue)   **FAMILY:** Ranunculaceae

DISTRIBUTION Throughout, but more common once south of the Mammoth Lakes region
HABITAT Stream banks, marshy areas, often in willow thickets
ELEVATION 6,000'–11,000'
SEASON Late June–early August
LOCATIONS Rock Creek Lakes, Big Pine Lakes, Rae Lakes Basin, Bubbs Creek

LEAVES AND STEMS: The leaves of this species are nearly indistinguishable from Fendler's meadow rue. The stalks reach 30–120 cm in height, while long leaves (branches of leaflets) extend to the sides. Toward the base, these leaves approach 30 cm in length, while higher up the   *(Continued)*

(Continued)   stem, they are shorter than 10 cm. Each "leaf" is divided into 5–9 leaf-lets, which are generally further divided into 3 smaller leaflets, 1–2 cm wide and sparsely covered in hairs. The leaflets have a few shallow, rounded teeth.

FLOWERS: Look closely, and you will discover that the small flowers are eye-catching. A cluster of long white stamens and shorter green styles are in the middle, with whitish-green 3- to 4-mm-long sepals (which look like petals) surrounding them; each stalk can contain many flowers. Intriguing are the fruit pods, or achenes: As the flowers go to seed, each pistil develops into a greenish bowling pin–shaped fruit, and the flower is a sphere of these, with the tips pointed outward.

❖ *Ceanothus cordulatus* (mountain whitethorn)
          FAMILY: Rhamnaceae

DISTRIBUTION Common throughout on both sides of the Sierra Crest; mostly in the montane forest elevations but occasional extending higher
HABITAT Dry, sunny slopes; open forest; especially common following fire
ELEVATION 4,000'–9,700'
SEASON Late June–early August
LOCATIONS Smith Mountain, Agnew Meadows, Rainbow Falls, King Creek (near Devils Postpile), Onion Valley, Vidette Meadow

LEAVES AND STEMS: This species is best appreciated from the trail, for it grows as an impenetrable spiny thicket. This very stiff-branched shrub stands up to 1.5 m in height. The branches are a white-gray to pale-green color and end in a sharp point. The thick, oval-shaped leaves are generally 1–2 cm in length, with a finely sharp-toothed leaf margin. Unlike most high-elevation species, the leaves are retained during the winter.

FLOWERS: Dense clusters of the tiny white flowers are at the ends of stems. Each flower has a white stalk, above which is a ring of 5 triangular sepals and 5 petals, all white in color. At the center of the flower, where the petals and sepals merge, is a yellow ring surrounding a green bull's-eye, which is the ovary. The fruits are triangular capsules.

❖ *Ceanothus velutinus* (tobacco brush, snowbrush)
          FAMILY: Rhamnaceae

DISTRIBUTION Common in the eastern Sierra; rare in the western Sierra
HABITAT Dry slopes
ELEVATION 7,000'–10,000'
SEASON Early June–mid-July
LOCATIONS Convict Lake, Rock Creek Basin, Pine Creek Pass Trail, Lake Sabrina

LEAVES AND STEMS: Reaching anywhere from 1 to 6 m, this shrub has a very different feel compared to mountain whitethorn. It is still much branched and dense, but the twigs are green, flexible, and not spine-tipped, making for a much better encounter. In addition, the leaves are much larger (usually 4–7 cm), quite glossy, and aromatic, and they have a finely serrate margin. This species also has evergreen leaves.

FLOWERS: The individual flowers of this species are nearly indistinguishable from those of mountain whitethorn and also occur in dense clusters at the ends of branches; the inflorescence is 3–8 cm long. Each flower has 5 white triangular sepals, 5 white petals, and, at the center, a yellow ring and then green (the ovary).

❖ *Amelanchier utahensis* (Utah service-berry)
        FAMILY: Rosaceae

DISTRIBUTION Occasional throughout, on both sides of the Sierra Crest
HABITAT Dry to slightly moist slopes, often alongside rocks
ELEVATION 3,600'–11,200'
SEASON Late June–late July
LOCATIONS Trail to Bennettville, near Royal Arch Lake, near Garnet Lake, Ruby Lake outlet (Rock Creek Basin), Whitney Portal

LEAVES AND STEMS: This shrub reaches heights of 5 m, but rarely exceeds 2 m at the higher elevations. Its twigs range from grayish to a glossy reddish-brown at the tips. The leaves are generally 2–3 cm in both width and diameter but can be considerably smaller or larger. The lower half of the leaves is roundish, while the upper section is toothed.

FLOWERS: The 5 white petals are quite elongate, often bend in all directions, and are separated by gaps about as wide as the petals, giving the flower a sloppy appearance. The petals are connected to a central ring, to which at least 10 stamens are attached. Flowers occur in clusters of 3–6 at the end of branches. The blue berries are edible.

❖ *Cercocarpus ledifolius* var. *ledifolius* (curl-leaf mountain-mahogany)   **FAMILY:** Rosaceae

DISTRIBUTION Common in the eastern Sierra, occasional in the Kern River drainage, very rare elsewhere
HABITAT Dry, sandy slopes and flats
ELEVATION 5,000'–10,500'
SEASON Mid-May–late June
LOCATIONS Parker Lake Trail, Lake Sabrina, Shepherd Pass Trail, Mt. Whitney Trail

LEAVES AND STEMS: A tall shrub or small tree, curl-leaf mountain-mahogany has many tough, gray, smooth branches. Notably leathery leaves, usually just 1.5 cm long, grow in clusters on many short, stout side shoots. The margins of the leaves are inrolled, accentuating their thickness.

FLOWERS: It is not quite fair to list this species under white flowers because this plant has no petals. Instead, it features a whitish, steep-walled cup (called a hypanthium), inside of which are up to 25 stamens.   *(Continued)*

(Continued)   The ovary, which develops into the fruit, lies beneath the hypanthium. As the fruit forms, the style elongates into a long tail, which is covered with very long hairs. By August the entire shrub is covered with these beautiful tails (at the base of which are the seedpods); when the long hairs catch the sunlight, the entire plant seems to glow.

RELATED SPECIES: There are two varieties of the curl-leaf mountain-mahogany: var. *intermontanus* with a somewhat rounder leaf, and var. *ledifolius* with a quite narrow leaf. Both occur throughout the eastern Sierra, though *ledifolius* becomes more common farther south.

❖ *Chamaebatiaria millefolium* (fern bush)   **FAMILY:** Rosaceae

DISTRIBUTION Common throughout the eastern Sierra, from June Lake south; absent in the western Sierra
HABITAT Sandy or rocky slopes
ELEVATION 6,000'–11,000'
SEASON Mid-July–late August
LOCATIONS Pine Creek Pass Trail, western shore of Lake Sabrina, Shepherd Pass Trail, Mt. Whitney Trail

LEAVES AND STEMS: Reaching up to 2 m in height, the fern bush is taller than most other high-elevation shrubs. It appears particularly tall because both its relatively skinny branches and inflorescences extend straight upward. Its leaves are distinctive and resemble its namesake, a fern frond. They are pinnately branched, and those lobes are themselves pinnately divided into tiny, tiny leaflets, giving each leaf a very lacy look. The leaves are also rather thick and bend inward at the major veins—they are not flat!

FLOWERS: Inflorescences extend upward from the end of branches, each an elongate collection of many flowers. Like other members of the rose family, each flower is comprised of 5 white petals that are quite rounded in outline. The petals attach to a central cup, the hypanthium, the edge of which is decorated by many yellow-tipped stamens.

❖ *Drymocallis lactea* var. *lactea* (*Potentilla glandulosa* subsp. *nevadensis*)
    (Sierran woodbeauty)   **FAMILY:** Rosaceae

DISTRIBUTION Very common throughout, on both sides of the Sierra Crest
HABITAT Dry to moist forest floor, forest openings, meadows
ELEVATION 5,000'–12,000'
SEASON Mid-June–early August
LOCATIONS Tuolumne Meadows, below Waugh Lake, Devils Postpile, Piute Pass Trail, Kearsarge Pass Trail

LEAVES AND STEMS: Reaching 10–60 cm in height and often growing in large clumps, this species is hard to miss. The leaves are mostly clustered around the base of the stem and can reach up to 20 cm in length. They are pinnately compound leaves, with 7 or 9 lobed leaflets; the lobes can be either shallow or deep and are usually rounded. Though the flowering stems are usually only branched near the top, several stems can emerge from the center of each rosette of leaves.

FLOWERS: The flowers are stereotypical of the rose family, with 5 cream-colored petals surrounding a large yellow carpel and cluster of stamens. The stamens stand out, for they are broad and flat—almost paddle-shaped in outline. The flowers are 1–1.5 cm in diameter with a few flowers usually occurring on each stem.

❖ *Drymocallis pseudorupestris* var. *crumiana* (*Potentilla glandulosa* subsp. *pseudorupestris*) (Crum's woodbeauty) **FAMILY:** Rosaceae

DISTRIBUTION Occasional in the eastern Sierra from Convict Creek drainage south; common in the western Sierra in the Kings and Kern River drainages at higher elevations; absent elsewhere
HABITAT Alongside rocks in fell-fields, along outcrops, at meadow edges
ELEVATION 8,900'–12,600'
SEASON Late June–early August
LOCATIONS Mildred Lake, Rock Creek Basin, west side of Kearsarge Pass, Glen Pass, Lake South America, Nine Lakes Basin

LEAVES AND STEMS: A much shorter species than the Sierran woodbeauty, Crum's woodbeauty reaches at most 25 cm in height and is often just 10 cm. Its leaves are 6–9 cm in length and are pinnately compound, with 4 pairs of deeply lobed leaflets. In the more exposed locations, the leaflets tend to be slightly folded inward along their middle vein, while in sheltered locations they are flatter. The leaves are concentrated around the base of the plant, though a few grow along the flowering stem. Both the leaves and the stem have some glandular hairs.

FLOWERS: The 5-petal, cream-colored flowers measure a little more than a centimeter in diameter. The petals are fairly round in outline and just slightly overlap. At the center of the petals is the stout, yellow ovary surrounded by short yellow stamens.

❖ *Fragaria virginiana* (mountain strawberry) **FAMILY:** Rosaceae

DISTRIBUTION Occasional throughout, but there is less appropriate habitat east of the Sierra Crest
HABITAT Moist meadows, moist forest floor
ELEVATION 4,000'–11,000'
SEASON Mid-June–early August
LOCATIONS Virginia Canyon, Rock Creek Trail, John Muir Trail near Tully Hole, Vidette Meadow

LEAVES AND STEMS: The mountain strawberry looks very similar to its cultivated counterparts. This ground cover spreads over large areas, with 3- to 7-cm-long, smooth leaves that grow in threes and are rounded toward the base and toothed at the tip. There is no woody stalk; the aboveground portion of the plant—the leaves and 10- to 20-cm-long reddish, hairy stalks—dies back each year.

(Continued)

(Continued)   **FLOWERS:** The 5 bright-white petals are 5–7 mm wide and quite round in outline, arranged so they don't overlap. In the center is a yellow cone—what develops into the strawberry—to which are attached a great number of yellow pistils surrounded by a ring of stamens. The bright red strawberries are edible and delicious. And a piece of trivia: The little "seeds" that dot the outside of the red berry are actually the fruits, while the tasty red flesh is an enlarged receptacle—the plant part that supports the fruits.

❖ *Holodiscus discolor* var. *microphyllus (Holodiscus microphyllus* var. *microphyllus)* (small-leaf creambush, oceanspray)   **FAMILY:** Rosaceae

DISTRIBUTION Common throughout, on both sides of the Sierra Crest
HABITAT Dry, sandy slopes, often among rock outcrops
ELEVATION 5,000'–11,500'
SEASON Late June–late August
LOCATIONS Clouds Rest, below Squaw Lake (north side of Silver Pass), Bishop Pass Trail, Rae Lakes Basin, above Crabtree Meadow

LEAVES AND STEMS: Reaching a maximum height of 1 m, this shrub is a tangled mass of twigs. Immediately obvious are the shiny red ends to the branches—the new growth—while the older branches are duller. The oval-shaped, usually 1- to 2-cm-long leaf blades are toothed along their outer half. The veins running to each tooth are often depressed, so the leaves resemble a folded fan.

FLOWERS: At the end of most branches are inflorescences comprised of delicate light-pink stems with many small, white, 5-petal flowers, which have yellow centers. 15–20 yellow-tipped stamens emerge from the center of each flower and extend beyond the petals, giving the inflorescence a fuzzy outline.

RELATED SPECIES: Another variety, *Holodiscus discolor* var. *discolor,* occurs around the Yosemite and Mammoth Lakes regions. It is distinguished by having leaves with teeth that are themselves toothed—tiny serrations within the large serrations.

❖ *Ivesia santolinoides* (mousetail ivesia, Sierra ivesia)   **FAMILY:** Rosaceae

DISTRIBUTION Fairly common throughout, on both sides of the Sierra Crest
HABITAT Sandy flats with shallow soil, especially sandy patches among slabs
ELEVATION 5,000'–11,000'
SEASON July–August, even September
LOCATIONS Trail to Glen Aulin, Clouds Rest, John Muir Trail north of Lake Virginia, Kearsarge Pass Trail, Mt. Whitney Trail

LEAVES AND STEMS: Like the higher-elevation yellow-flowered ivesias, this is a rosette species, with a collection of leaves emerging directly from the root. Each leaf is divided into about 150 miniature leaflets, each densely covered in long hairs, giving the leaves the appearance of gray-green pipe cleaners—or mouse tails.

Flowers: The flowering stalks are much taller than the leaves and have many branches. While there are many 5-petal white flowers per stalk, they are widely dispersed on the long branches and bloom over a long period, so the inflorescence has a very open appearance. Each flower has 15 red-tipped stamens, adding a dainty decoration.

❖ *Prunus emarginata* (bitter cherry) **Family:** Rosaceae

Distribution Common throughout at montane elevations on both sides of the Sierra Crest, occasionally extending into the subalpine zone
Habitat Diverse habitats from dry, rocky slopes to beneath sparse forest cover
Elevation 4,000'–10,000'
Season Late May–early July
Locations Trail to Agnew Lake, Kaiser Pass, South Fork Big Pine Creek, slopes above Le Conte Canyon, Onion Valley

Leaves and Stems: Growing as either a shrub or a tree, bitter cherry commonly occurs as thickets. Like a domestic cherry, the wood is reddish and slightly scaly, and the branches are quite stout and stiff. The leaves occur in dense clusters and have the shape of elongate ovals. The leaf margins are finely lobed or toothed.

Flowers: The white 5-petal flowers are similar to many other species of shrubs in the rose family, for all have a round, slightly cupped petal shape. The petals attach in a broad ring, at the center of which are numerous white stamens, while the bulbous carpel attaches in the depression between the petals. The genus *Prunus* generally has fruits resembling the horticultural species in look if not in taste. The bitter cherry has small, bright red fruits that look remarkably like small cherries—they are unfortunately mostly seed with a coating of bitter flesh.

Related Species: The related western chokecherry, *Prunus virginiana* var. *demissa*, is a species common in the western Sierra at montane elevations, where it can form dense thickets.

❖ *Purshia tridentata* var. *tridentata* (antelope bitterbrush) **Family:** Rosaceae

Distribution Common throughout the eastern Sierra and on the Kern Plateau; var. *tridentata* dominant north of Bishop; var. *glandulosa* dominant south of Bishop
Habitat Dry, sandy slopes and flats, especially the dry shrubland areas of the eastern Sierra
Elevation 4,700'–11,000'
Season Early June–mid-July
Locations Tioga Pass, Gem Lake (Rush Creek drainage), Rock Creek Basin, North Fork Big Pine Creek

Leaves and Stems: This shrub is typically 0.5–1.5 m high, though it can occasionally reach twice that. The stiff,

(Continued)

(Continued)   red-brown branches form a dense tangle, with leaves growing in clusters on short side shoots. The 1- to 1.5-cm-long wedge-shaped leaves, as suggested by the species name, have three lobes; the outer lobe is rounded, and the middle lobe is rounded to sharp pointed. The quite thick leaves have long white hairs on both surfaces, though the top still appears glossy green while the underside is fuzzy white. Unlike some of the other flowering shrubs in the rose family, the leaves of this shrub do not have prominent veins.

FLOWERS: The 5-petal cream-colored flowers occur singly on little shoots emerging from the clumps of leaves. The teardrop-shaped petals and more than 20 yellow-tipped stamens attach to the edge of the hypanthium, the cup that houses the ovary.

RELATED SPECIES: There are two varieties of bitterbrush: var. *tridentata,* which is more common on the Kern Plateau and north of Bishop, and var. *glandulosa,* which is more common from Bishop south. Var. *tridentata,* unlike *glandulosa,* has hairier leaves and twigs without glands.

❖ *Sorbus californica* (California mountain ash)   **FAMILY:** Rosaceae

DISTRIBUTION Occasional throughout, on both sides of the Sierra Crest
HABITAT Shaded forest, stream banks, other moist locations
ELEVATION 5,300'–10,800'
SEASON Early June–mid-July
LOCATIONS Near Stubblefield Canyon, Slate Creek Fork Lee Vining Creek, Lyell Canyon, Garnet Lake, south side of Silver Pass, Bubbs Creek, Little Five Lakes

LEAVES AND STEMS: This shrub generally reaches 1–2 m in height, and the stocky gray stems are mainly leafy near their tips. The leaves are pinnately compound with a central axis and 3–4 pairs of leaflets plus one more at the tip. The leaflets are oval shaped, and the upper half of the leaf margins has minute, sharp teeth.

FLOWERS: The large inflorescences each have many white 5-petal flowers on elongate pinkish stems. The petals are tiny, quite round, and, together with the long white stamens, connected to a ring at the center of the flower. In the middle is the carpel. The bunches of fruits look like rose hips; they are the shape and approximate size of a small olive, turning from green to red as they ripen.

❖ *Micranthes aprica (Saxifraga aprica)* (Sierra saxifrage)
   FAMILY: Saxifragaceae

DISTRIBUTION Fairly common throughout
HABITAT Gravelly flats and alpine fell-fields that are moist early season
ELEVATION 5,500'–12,000'
SEASON Early June–early July

Locations Twenty Lakes Basin, Dana Plateau, east side Mono Pass (Rock Creek Basin), Kearsarge Lakes Basin, headwaters of Kern River

LEAVES AND STEMS: Clusters of 1- to 4-cm-long, oval-shaped leaves lie at ground level. The leaves are darkish green and identified by a reddish leaf margin (and sometimes underside) and often minute, sharp-pointed teeth along the top half of the leaf.

FLOWERS: A cluster of several to more than 20 flowers forms a ball at the top of a 5- to 10-cm-tall reddish stalk. The small flowers have a reddish cup-shaped calyx, and inside 5 straggly bright-white petals are attached. They are just 1.5–3 mm in length and shed quickly. Thereafter, the developing seedpods are actually very attractive—the brilliant burgundy-red, raindrop-shaped seedpods occur in pairs.

RELATED SPECIES: At first glance, *Micranthes nidifica* (previously *Saxifraga nidifica* var. *nidifica*; peak saxifrage) looks similar to *Micranthes aprica*. The most obvious difference is that the inflorescence in *Micranthes aprica* is a single, tight head at the end of the stem, while in *Micranthes nidifica*, multiple side branches have flowers. The leaves of peak saxifrage are also larger and more elongate, and the stems are less red. It too is an early bloomer, common in moist locations.

Micranthes nidifica

❖ *Micranthes bryophora (Saxifraga bryophora)* (bud saxifrage)
   FAMILY: Saxifragaceae

DISTRIBUTION Common throughout, on both sides of the Sierra Crest
HABITAT Seasonally moist flats, seeps
ELEVATION 5,700'–11,500'
SEASON Early June–early July
LOCATIONS Tioga Tarns, May Lake, Marie Lakes, Palisade Lakes, north side of Pinchot Pass, below Little Five Lakes

LEAVES AND STEMS: This diminutive saxifrage has a small rosette of 0.5- to 3-cm-long, oval-shaped, fleshy leaves. The leaves (and the flowering stems) are sparsely covered with gland-tipped hairs, giving the plants a shining appearance in the sun.

FLOWERS: The flowers are born on red flowering stalks, 5–15 cm in height and branched; the side branches are long and skinny, like gangly legs. Only a few flowers are in full bloom at a time—the rest appear to be buds dangling downward, but most are actually seedpods that look like inflated buds. There are 5 spade-shaped petals, white with 2 yellow dots near the base, and they are just 3–5 mm in length. 2 of the petals are sometimes narrower than the others and may lack the yellow dots—or all 5 petals may be identical. The pollen at the tips of the stamens is red, making the flowers even more decorative.

❖ *Micranthes odontoloma (Saxifraga odontoloma)*
(brook saxifrage)   **FAMILY:** Saxifragaceae

DISTRIBUTION Common throughout, on both sides of the Sierra Crest
HABITAT Banks of narrow, bubbling streams
ELEVATION 6,500'–11,200'
SEASON Mid-July–late August
LOCATIONS Lundy Canyon, Crater Meadow, Mildred Lake (Convict
Creek drainage), Bishop Pass Trail, John Muir Trail near Bench
Lake junction

LEAVES AND STEMS: The light-green leaves are nearly round in outline,
but their entire perimeter is decorated with very even, rounded teeth.
These leaves are often what you see at the edges of a creek, for
they are abundant long before the plant starts flowering. They vary
enormously in size, from just 4 cm to more than 20 cm in diameter.

FLOWERS: The flowering stalks are tall (20–50 cm) with long,
gangly branches sparsely covered with small flowers. The 1-cm-
wide flowers are complex, delicate, and beautiful though. 5 white
petals pinch in and connect to the base of the flower with just
a narrow thread. At the base of each petal are 2 yellow dots. The
10 paddle-shaped stamens are flattened and have red pollen when
they first open—positioned at the end like miniature pom-poms.
Emerging from the center of the flower is the red pistil, which elongates and splits
in two as it matures.

❖ *Micranthes tolmiei (Saxifraga tolmiei)* (Tolmie's saxifrage)
FAMILY: Saxifragaceae

DISTRIBUTION Occasional throughout the western Sierra
but absent in the eastern Sierra south of the Bishop Creek
drainage
HABITAT Gravel or talus patches surrounded by sand in
locations with long-lasting snow
ELEVATION 9,000'–12,000'
SEASON Mid-July–late August
LOCATIONS Above Cascade Lake (Twenty Lakes Basin),
north side of Silver Pass, Table Mountain (above Tyee
Lakes), north side of Glen Pass

LEAVES AND STEMS: This subshrub has slightly woody stem bases. A great abundance
of small (shorter than 1.5 cm), very narrow, and quite thick and fleshy leaves grows
en masse just above ground level in locations with late-melting snowbanks.

FLOWERS: An inflorescence with multiple flowers sits atop a 5- to 20-cm-tall red stem.
The small flowers are, at first glance, a busy combination of green and white: 5 green
sepals, 5 white petals (oval-shaped and occasionally split in two), and 10 white stamens
(so wide that they look like narrow petals with red tips). In the center are the double
cone–shaped green ovaries, which turn red as the fruits mature. When you find the
perfect patch of these plants, they are so completely covered in flowers that you can
barely see the leaves.

Related Species: *Saxifraga hyperborea* (previously *Saxifraga rivularis*; pygmy saxifrage) occurs throughout the Sierra but lives hidden in wet pockets beneath boulders and is so tiny that you will rarely see it. Its tiny leaves have three rounded lobes and lie flat against the ground. Above is a stalk that reaches just 1–10 cm, atop of which is a small flower, similar to those of other saxifrage species.

❖ What Is a Scientific Name?

The long Latinized names given to all living organisms can be cumbersome to learn (and remember). Carl Linnaeus established a hierarchical system in 1735 to categorize all living organisms. At the broadest level are kingdoms, which are split into phyla (called divisions in plants), and then successively into classes, orders, families, genera, and species. Within each of the seven groupings, all species within the category share a collection of common traits. Each subsequent level will have its own list of more specific commonalities. The Linnaean classification system was established long before modern concepts of evolution and species relatedness were known; at the time, species groupings were created to indicate physical similarities rather than relatedness. Today, species are being reassigned to different groups to better reflect their evolutionary history (see also "Why Are So Many Plants Renamed?" on page 55), but the same categories continue to be used.

Linnaean classification assigned names to each of the estimated 8.7 million species on Earth, including more than 300,000 plants. Relevant to this book, all plants are in the plant kingdom. Flowering plants are in one division, while cone-bearing trees are in a second division. The next two levels of hierarchy, the class and order, are rarely mentioned outside of botanical literature. The final three levels are family, genus, and species, and each is given for the species described in this book. Together, the genus and species form the scientific name and are italicized (or underlined when written). Members of a genus are generally recognizable as related—the shapes of the flowers are often very similar, while species can be distinguished by features such as woodiness, petal shape, flower color, or leaf shape. Genera within a family will (usually) share traits such as petal number, petal arrangement, stamen number, style arrangement and number, and fruit shape; in some cases these translate into immediately obvious differences and other times require careful study (and memorization). Two even more specific categories not part of Linnaeus's original scheme are subspecies and varieties. Both indicate populations of a species that are located in different geographic locations or have some distinguishing characteristic. However, as members of the same species, they can interbreed and produce fertile seeds if brought together. There is no clear distinction between the two terms, with some species divided into subspecies and others into varieties.

❖ *Valeriana californica* (California valerian)   **FAMILY:** Valerianaceae

DISTRIBUTION Occasional throughout montane elevations in the western Sierra; common in the eastern Sierra from the Yosemite region south to Mammoth Lakes, where it is more often found at high elevations
HABITAT Slightly moist meadows, moist gravelly to sandy slopes, moist forest
ELEVATION 7,100'–11,000'
SEASON Late June–mid-August
LOCATIONS East Lake (Green Creek Basin), Twenty Lakes Basin, Tioga Tarns, Clark Lakes (Agnew Pass), Kearsarge Pass Trail (east side)

LEAVES AND STEMS: When viewed from a distance, this species is easily mistaken for a member of Apiaceae because you first see a long stalk topped by a broad inflorescence of tiny white flowers. Its structure is quite different, however. The stems are 25–50 cm long, and the basal leaves are up to 13 cm long and are either simple elongate ovals or, more frequently, dissected into leaflets that can themselves be lobed.

FLOWERS: The inflorescence is composed of a dense collection of tiny, white, tubular flowers. The flower tube is much longer than it is wide, and 5 petal lobes are bent out at the tube's mouth. Unlike members of Apiaceae, the inflorescence is not an umbel, for the many side stalks with flowers do not radiate from a single point. Instead, clusters of flowers attach along the main stem at multiple points, but the stalks are different lengths, so the top of the inflorescence is flat-topped or domed. The white stamens and style both stick far out of the flower tube.

❖ *Viola macloskeyi* (Macloskey's violet, small white violet)
       FAMILY: Violaceae

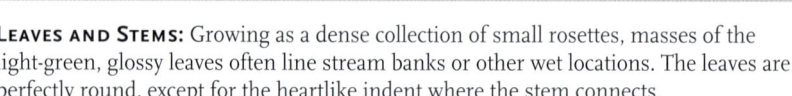

DISTRIBUTION Very common throughout, on both sides of the Sierra Crest
HABITAT Seeps, stream banks, edges of wet meadows
ELEVATION 3,300'–11,000'
SEASON Early June–mid-July
LOCATIONS Tenaya Lake, Ediza Lake, Rock Creek Basin, Rae Lakes Basin

LEAVES AND STEMS: Growing as a dense collection of small rosettes, masses of the light-green, glossy leaves often line stream banks or other wet locations. The leaves are perfectly round, except for the heartlike indent where the stem connects.

FLOWERS: The flowers are perfect little violets, white in color and about 1.5 cm across. As with all violets, they have 2 upper petals and 3 lower ones, the center of which bears purple streaks. The flowers occur singly on stalks, rarely exceeding 8 cm in height. While this species catches your attention early season, they bloom early, and soon only the leaves are left to identify them.

❖ *Allium obtusum* var. *obtusum* (red Sierra onion)
FAMILY: Alliaceae (Liliaceae)

DISTRIBUTION Fairly common around the Yosemite and Mammoth Lakes areas, becoming occasional farther south
HABITAT Sandy and gravelly flats and slopes
ELEVATION 5,400'–12,000'
SEASON Late June–early August
LOCATIONS North Dome, Tuolumne Meadows, near Tioga Lake, Buena Vista Lake, Dinkey Lakes, Glen Pass, Bighorn Plateau

LEAVES AND STEMS: This species is shorter than other high-elevation onions, reaching just 4–8 cm in height. It usually has only a single leaf, occasionally 2. The leaves are longer than the stem and quite variable in width, ranging 1–5 cm. The leaves are typically folded slightly inward, forming a U shape or channel.

FLOWERS: The flower is an umbel, with stalks that are generally shorter than 1 cm, making a tight inflorescence. The 3 sepals and 3 petals (all identical) are pale pink to white, with a brown-pink stripe down the center of each. This species blooms early but can carpet large areas approximately three weeks after the snow melts.

❖ *Calochortus leichtlinii* (Leichtlin's mariposa lily)
FAMILY: Liliaceae

DISTRIBUTION Common in the Yosemite area south through the Mono Recesses, becoming occasional farther south; much rarer throughout the eastern Sierra
HABITAT Dry flats, sandy and gravelly areas
ELEVATION 4,000'–10,500'
SEASON Mid-June–late July
LOCATIONS Trail to Glen Aulin, Dana Meadows, Minaret Summit, Bear Creek, Piute Creek, Vidette Meadow

LEAVES AND STEMS: Though it is the flowers you will notice—and that allow you to identify the species—there are leaves hidden behind the petals. The stems are 20–60 cm long, along which grow 1–2 small leaves. Longer leaves emerge from the ground, but they wither early.

FLOWERS: *Mariposa* is the Spanish word for "butterfly," and this species' petals indeed look like butterfly wings. They are shaped like a rounded triangle; the outer edges of the 3 petals are broad and showy—and usually 3–4 cm long. Most species of *Calochortus* have very showy patterning on their petals, though those of the Leichtlin's mariposa lily are mostly white with a purplish-brown triangular blotch and yellow stripe (covered with yellow hairs) toward the center of each petal. Nonetheless, I can easily imagine a butterfly fluttering by with a pair of wings made from these petals.

(Continued)

(Continued)   **RELATED SPECIES:** Occurring up to quite high elevations, especially in the eastern Sierra, *Calochortus bruneaunis* (Bruneau mariposa lily) is a showier mariposa lily. You will find it along many eastern Sierra trails, including Coyote Ridge, Birch Creek, Big Pine Creek, and the Baxter Pass Trail. Most of its petals are also white, while at the center is an elegant patterning of yellow and deep burgundy. The 6 stamens are a dark purple, and the three-forked style is pink.

Calochortus bruneaunis

❖ *Veratrum californicum* var. *californicum* (California corn lily)
     FAMILY: Melanthiaceae (Liliaceae)

DISTRIBUTION Common throughout on both sides of the Sierra Crest
HABITAT Wet meadows, stream banks, moist forest
ELEVATION 4,700'–10,500'
SEASON Early July–early August
LOCATIONS Dog Lake, Gaylor Lakes, Le Conte Canyon, Kearsarge Pass Trail (east side), Vidette Meadow

LEAVES AND STEMS: The corn lily is one of those rare species that manage to catch your attention all summer and into autumn. Soon after the snow melts, wet locations are dotted with the young stalks, looking very much like ears of corn, with many overlapping wide leaves. Later in the season they shoot upward, rapidly extending to 1–2 m in height. The very large (up to 40 cm long), oval-shaped leaves are now more spread out and no longer tightly clasp the stem, though they still mostly point upward. Also note that they have a distinctive ribbing pattern on them, adding dimension.

FLOWERS: In any given year, many of the stalks do not flower, instead growing until midsummer and then slowly dying back and storing up their energy for another year. In less ideal densely forested sites, very few individuals will flower. The remaining plants put out an abundance of white flowers. The inflorescence is usually 30–50 cm in length and includes flowers both along the main stem and along side branches, these also reaching up to 20 cm in length. All of these stem lengths are densely covered with the white-green 6-petal (actually 3 petals plus 3 sepals) flowers; the outer sections of the petals are white, possibly with a few green stripes, while the flower's center is a dark green.

EXTRA TIDBITS: This plant is very poisonous!

❖ *Platanthera dilatata* var. *leucostachys (Platanthera leucostachys)* (white-flowered bog orchid, Sierra bog orchid) **FAMILY:** Orchidaceae

DISTRIBUTION Very common throughout, on both sides of the Sierra Crest
HABITAT Seeps, stream banks, wet meadows
ELEVATION 4,000'–10,700'
SEASON Early July–mid-August
LOCATIONS Rock Creek Basin, French Canyon, east side of Piute Pass Trail, Evolution Valley

Leaves and Stems: The notably stout, slightly ribbed stalk of this tall orchid species is usually at least 30 cm in height and can top 1 m. The leaves near the base of the plant are up to 35 cm long and 1–3 cm in width, while the stem leaves are considerably smaller.

Flowers: The top length of the stem is covered with small white flowers, below each of which is a small, narrow, triangular leaf. Each flower has 3 petals and 3 sepals. The upper sepal forms the eponymous "hood," with the 2 upper petals flanking it. The other 2 sepals stick out sideways, while the lower petal forms the long, narrow "lip." The notably long (0.5–1.5 cm), narrow spur is a pouch that has formed at the back of the lip. Each flower is 1.5–2 cm in length, and up to 100 flowers can be on a single stalk, making a robust plant in full bloom an impressive sight.

❖ *Spiranthes romanzoffiana* (hooded ladies' tresses)
  Family: Orchidaceae

Distribution Occasional throughout, on both sides of the Sierra Crest
Habitat Seeps, wet meadows
Elevation 3,000'–10,700'
Season Mid-July–late August
Locations Virginia Canyon, Lyell Canyon, Devils Postpile, Glass Creek Meadow, trail to Mott Lake, John Muir Trail near Hilgard Branch Bear Creek

Leaves and Stems: This orchid is more common in the expansive wet meadows at montane elevations in the western Sierra, but it also occurs at higher elevations. It grows 10–30 cm in height and has a dense tuft of leaves near the base that are about one-third to one-half the length of the stem. The leaves are about 1 cm in width and sometimes slightly folded inward along the midrib.

Flowers: The inflorescence is immediately recognizable, for the squat, little white flowers truly spiral up the stem, as indicated by the genus name; each flower is only about 1 cm long and at most 5 mm wide. Though both the petals and sepals are short and mostly form a more tubular flower, they have the basic form of an orchid. Behind are 3 narrower sepals and in front are the 3 white petals; the bottom one, the lip, bends downward, while the other 2 are slightly broader and stick straight up. This is a late-blooming species, coloring seeps after other species have begun to fade.

❖ *Maianthemum stellatum (Smilacina stellata)* (starry false lily of the valley, false solomon's seal) **Family:** Ruscaceae (Liliaceae)

Distribution Common throughout the eastern Sierra, more occasional in western Sierra
Habitat Wet meadows, stream banks, shaded forest
Elevation 4,000'–10,600'
Season Early June–mid-July
Locations Lundy Canyon, Devils Postpile, French Canyon, Piute Pass Trail, North Fork Big Pine Creek

(Continued)

(Continued)   **LEAVES AND STEMS:** Growing in masses in moist, shaded areas, this plant has stems that generally reach 30–50 cm in height, occasionally higher. A good way to identify this species is by how its leaves attach to the stem—in a very even pattern from base to top, 1 leaf on the left, 1 on the right, and so on, and always the same distance apart. They are 5–17 cm in length and usually 1–1.5 cm wide.

FLOWERS: The open inflorescence is above the uppermost leaves and consists of 5–15 white flowers composed of 3 sepals and 3 petals about 5 mm in length. The flowers attach singly to the stem and spiral up the stem, albeit with a gap between each flower.

RELATED SPECIES: The broader leafed *Maianthemum racemosum* (previously called *Smilacina racemosa*; also given the common name false solomon's seal or feathery false lily of the valley) generally grows at lower elevations but is quite common in the western Sierra. Its leaves are 3–4 cm in width and attach in a similar pattern. Its inflorescences are much denser because they are racemes: The inflorescence has multiple side stalks, each with multiple flowers.

❖ *Triantha occidentalis* subsp. *occidentalis (Tofieldia occidentalis* subsp. *occidentalis)* (western false asphodel)   **FAMILY:** Tofieldiaceae (Liliaceae)

DISTRIBUTION Occasional throughout but more common in the western Sierra
HABITAT Wet meadows, seeps
ELEVATION 5,800'–11,000'
SEASON Early July–mid-August
LOCATIONS Pioneer Basin, French Canyon, John Muir Trail between Muir Pass and Le Conte Canyon, below Dusy Basin, Kearsarge Pass Trail

LEAVES AND STEMS: The leafless flowering stalk reaches 30–80 cm in height. Clustered around the base is a collection of fairly short (usually 5–10 cm, occasionally more), narrow (3–8 mm), thick leaves. The leaves are a notable bright green—if you manage to find them within the dense mats of grass where this species generally lives.

FLOWERS: The dense inflorescence at the top of the flowering stalk is composed of many white 6-petal flowers—often more than 15 flowers. The inflorescence is shaped either like a sphere or a domed cylinder. Upon close inspection, the "petals" are in two distinct sets of 3, one above the other: The inner 3 are actual petals, while the outer set are sepals, as is true for most lilies. Inside the petals are 6 stocky white stamens and the green ovaries, which turn to reddish-colored fruits as the flowers go to seed.

RELATED SPECIES: *Toxicoscordion venenosum*
var. *venenosum* (previously *Zigadenus venenosus*
var. *venenosus*; meadow death camas) is a quite
similar-looking species that occurs up to 10,000
feet, usually in quite wet meadows or alongside
seeps. Its long, narrow basal leaves likewise hide
among the meadow grasses, but unlike western
false asphodel, its flowering stalks also have
leaves. Its inflorescence of small white 6-petal
flowers is more elongate and open than that of
the western false asphodel, for the flowers are
attached with longer stalks. Note that the white
petals have a green splotch near the center, like
the flowers of the closely related corn lily; both
are in the family Melanthiaceae. However, I chose
to describe meadow death camas with western false asphodel because they have the same
stature and are easily mistaken for each other.

Toxicoscordion venenosum var. *venenosum*

Parnassia palustris (see page 58)

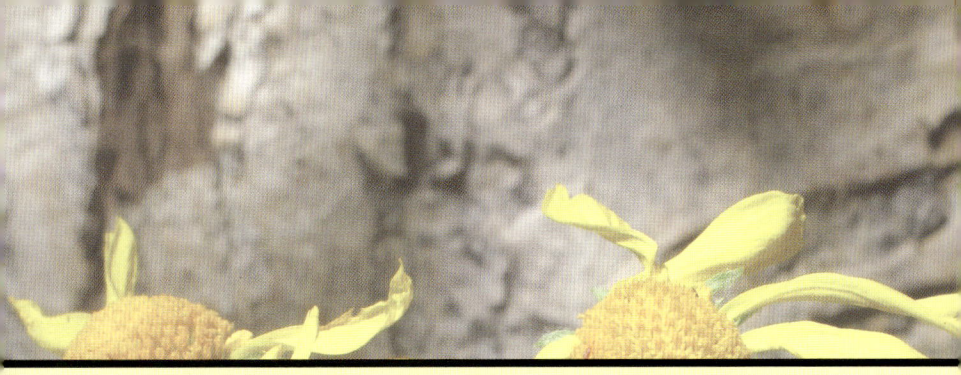

❖ Yellow and Orange Flowers

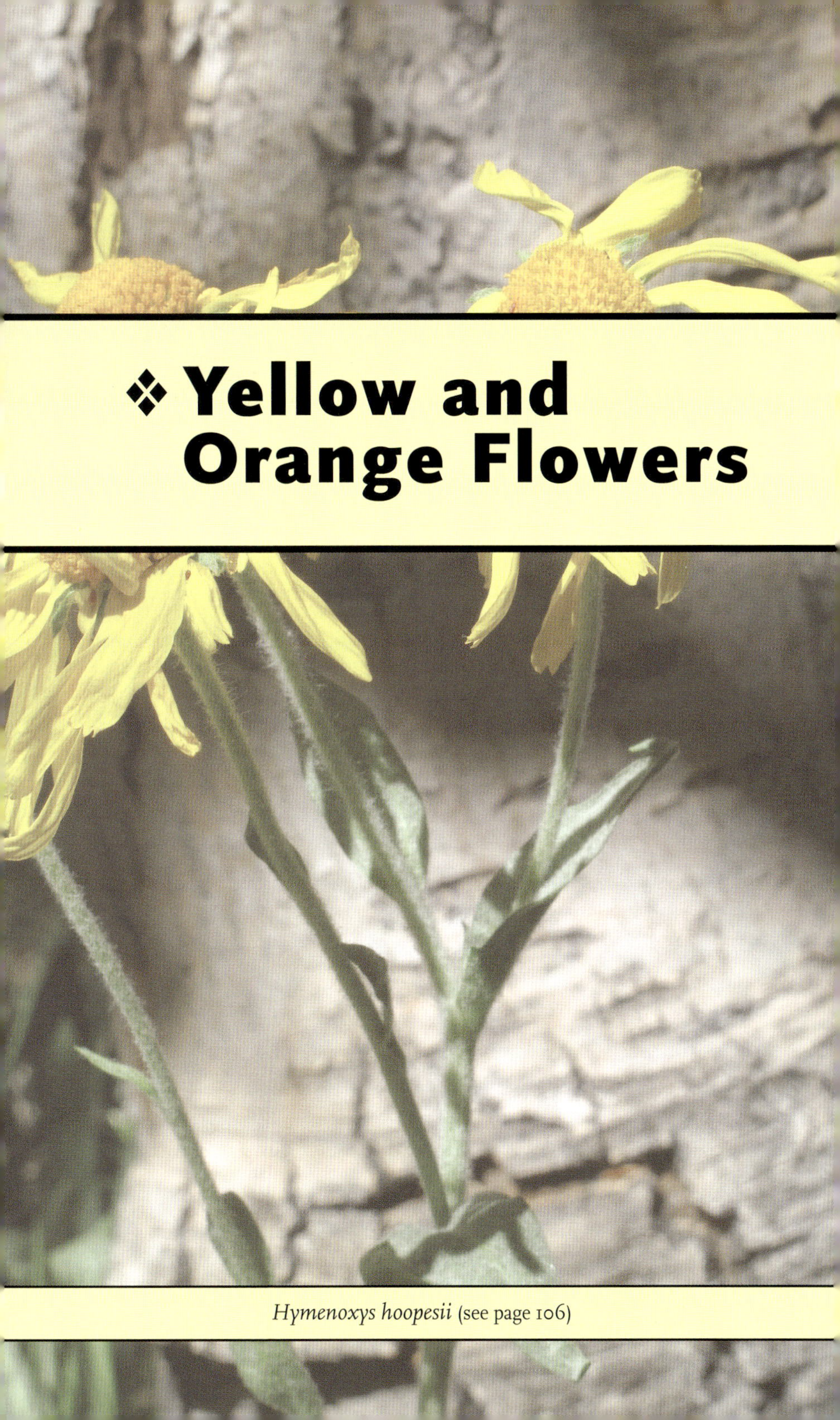

Hymenoxys hoopesii (see page 106)

❖ *Cymopterus terebinthinus* var. *californicus*
(turpentine cymopterus, pteryxia)   **FAMILY:** Apiaceae

Distribution Fairly common in the western Sierra; occasional in the eastern Sierra
Habitat Sandy to rocky flats and slopes, open forest
Elevation 4,000'–11,600'
Season Early June–mid-July
Locations Tuolumne Meadows, Red Cones (near Devils Postpile), French Canyon, west slope of Kearsarge Pass, headwaters of Kern River, Glacier Canyon Trail

LEAVES AND STEMS: This species has only basal leaves, which emerge from the taproot to form a tangled rosette: The leaves are pinnately dissected into leaflets, and each of those leaflets is further deeply dissected into yet smaller leaflets. The final leaflets are tiny, thick, and sharp pointed, and they tend to point upward. The total leaf length varies 2–16 cm.

FLOWERS: The inflorescences are at the end of 15- to 45-cm-long leafless stalks that trend diagonally, not rising far above the ground surface. The flowers occur as compound umbels, with a first series of branches that are 1–2 cm long and secondary umbel branches that are very short, creating a fairly flat-topped inflorescence of tiny, yellow, 5-petal flowers. The fruits of this species, and indeed all *Cymopterus,* are ribbed; imagine a piece of paper folded in, out, in, out, and so on, with the two ends glued together.

RELATED SPECIES: A second variety, *petraeus* (rock cymopterus), occurs in the eastern Sierra in the Yosemite region. Its leaves are much longer than they are broad.

❖ *Lomatium torreyi* (Torrey's lomatium, Sierra biscuitroot)
FAMILY: Apiaceae

DISTRIBUTION Fairly common throughout the western Sierra; fairly common in the eastern Sierra from the Yosemite area south to the Bishop Creek drainage
HABITAT Open forest, often alongside rocks
ELEVATION 4,800'–11,200'
SEASON Mid-June–early August
LOCATIONS Trail to Dana Plateau, Rock Creek Basin, French Canyon, near Muir Pass, below Lake Reflection

LEAVES AND STEMS: This small compact plant has flowering stems that are at most 30 cm long, but the leaves stick up, rather than hug the ground, as pteryxia (see profile above) does. The outline of the leaf blade can be anywhere from 2 to 15 cm—but it is dissected into leaflets, each of which is further dissected into smaller leaflets, and then yet again, known as a ternate-pinnately dissected leaf. The final segments are exceedingly narrow, and the leaf is almost fernlike in appearance.

FLOWERS: The yellow flowers are arranged in a compound umbel. The first stems to radiate outward are longer, and attached to the end of each of these longer stems is a second collection of very short stems that radiate outward. At the end of this second set of stems are the tiny 5-petaled yellow flowers. Unlike members of the genus *Cymopterus,* which have a similar inflorescence, the species in the genus *Lomatium* have fruits with only 2 protrusions (called wings), so they appear flattened.

❖ *Podistera nevadensis* (Sierra podistera)
FAMILY: Apiaceae

DISTRIBUTION Fairly common near the Sierra Crest in the Yosemite and Mammoth Lakes regions, generally on metamorphic rock; absent elsewhere
HABITAT Scree slopes, alpine fell-fields
ELEVATION 10,000'–12,500'
SEASON Early June–mid-July
LOCATIONS Tioga Crest, Dana Plateau, Mammoth Crest above Lake George

LEAVES AND STEMS: This species grows in just a few locations, but it is striking when seen. Growing as an expansive mat and rising just a few centimeters above the ground, the leaves are shiny, thick, sea-green in color, and sharp pointed. The leaves, including their stalk, are just a few centimeters long and are pinnately divided, with all the lobes pointing upward.

FLOWERS: The inflorescences are on stalks at most 5 cm in length and are generally nestled among the leaves. The tiny 5-petal flowers atop the flat-topped inflorescence are quite variable in color, ranging from yellow to white to purple. As they fade, they appear beige in color, the state you find the plant in by midsummer.

❖ *Agoseris aurantiaca* var. *aurantiaca* (orange agoseris)   **FAMILY:** Asteraceae

DISTRIBUTION Occasional throughout, on both sides of the Sierra Crest
HABITAT Meadows, vegetated slopes
ELEVATION 5,000'–11,500'
SEASON Early July–late August
LOCATIONS North of Garnet Lake, Chocolate Lakes (near Bishop Pass Trail), North Fork Big Pine Creek, north of Vidette Meadow

LEAVES AND STEMS: This classic dandelion has basal leaves that form a rosette. The leaves are 5–25 cm long, quite narrow, and taper to the tip. Their other characteristics are quite variable; sometimes they are sparsely hairy, and sometimes they have serrate edges.

FLOWERS: This species is most simply described as a burnt-orange dandelion. The inflorescence is at the tip of a 10- to 50-cm-long stalk and is composed of many overlapping long, narrow "petals" (ray flowers) that are often dark tipped. This species lacks disk flowers.

❖ From Rock Types to Soil Nutrients

You may view the Sierra as a sea of granite, but there is actually a diversity of rock types, and the chemistry of the various granitic rocks is quite variable. Not surprisingly, these rock types influence many of the soil characteristics that matter most to plants, including nutrient availability (of almost every nutrient), water availability, and temperature. One of the first things you might notice is that some of the Sierra's

(Continued)

(Continued)   lushest wildflower meadows are not on granite! Four of my favorite locations—the Virginia Lakes Basin, the Dana Plateau, Coyote Ridge, and the basin to the north of Pinchot Pass (though not very accessible)—are not on granite. The first three sites have soils (mostly) derived from metamorphosed sedimentary rocks, and the region around Pinchot Pass is a mixture of the metasedimentary rocks and some darker-than-usual granitic rocks. A few characteristics unite these soils: First, in comparison to granite, the rocks at these sites have higher concentrations of many chemical ions, including phosphates, meaning the soils have more nutrients. Second, compared to granite, they break down more rapidly from rock to sand- and silt-sized particles, forming deeper soils. In addition, the rocks decompose to form a fine-grained soil, which increases its ability to hold onto water. And finally, the soils tend to be darker in color, which means, at least at the surface, they are warmer. This combination of beneficial conditions allows these locations to have greater plant cover in comparison to similarly exposed locations on granite. How readily the different rocks break down can also determine the landforms; consider marble, a very rare rock within the Sierra. It is quite resistant to erosion, and you will almost always find it as a little point sticking out of a ridge or slope. (See "Plants of Calcareous Soils," page 99, to learn more about marble soils.)

❖ *Agoseris monticola* (*Agoseris glauca* var. *monticola*)
(mountain agoseris, pale agoseris)   **FAMILY:** Asteraceae

DISTRIBUTION Common throughout, on both sides of the Sierra Crest
HABITAT Gravelly or sandy flats, meadows, dry slopes
ELEVATION 6,500'–12,500'
SEASON Early July–late August
LOCATIONS Tuolumne Meadows, Dana Plateau, Marie Lake (north of Selden Pass), Rae Lakes Basin, Mt. Whitney Trail

LEAVES AND STEMS: The usually toothed or lobed leaves of this rosette species are 2–10 cm long. They are quite narrow, slightly widening in the middle and tapering to a point. Long, white hairs mostly cover the leaves and stems.

FLOWERS: The yellow inflorescences are at the end of 2- to 25-cm-long stalks and look like dandelions. Unlike most members of the sunflower family, they lack a central collection of disk flowers; instead, they have many layers of outward-pointing ray flowers, which look like long, narrow, yellow petals. The undersides of the ray flowers tend to be orangish.

RELATED SPECIES: *Agoseris parviflora,* or false dandelion, previously a subspecies of *Agoseris glauca,* is distinguished by having irregularly lobed leaves and lacking any glandular hairs. It occurs along Mono Creek, along Piute Pass Trail, and in the North Fork Big Pine Creek drainage. *Agoseris retrorsa,* spearleaf agoseris, is most common in upper montane fir forests but occasionally extends into the subalpine zone. Its leaves are lobed nearly to the midrib, with the sharp-pointed, narrow lobes pointing back toward the stem. Most showy is its large dandelion head of seeds, 2–5 cm

Agoseris parviflora

in diameter. It can be found on the trail west of Agnew Meadows, along Bear Creek, and at Vidette Meadow.

❖ Flowers in the Family Asteraceae

If you tear apart a flower in the family Asteraceae, you will quickly discover that the flowers are unique. This family, which includes daisies and sunflowers, has "flowers" that are actually the heads of many flowers, called an inflorescence. The ray flowers look like petals, while at the center, a dense cluster of disk flowers forms a circle. Each of the individual flowers is small, and its petals are fused into a tube at the base. In ray flowers, one side of the fused petals has elongated to form a "petal," while in the disk flowers, all the petals are usually very short. The calyx (fused sepals) is sometimes missing, and other times has become bristles or the fluffy, feathery material, called the pappus, that lets dandelion seeds be carried by the wind. The number of both ray and disk flowers in an inflorescence is variable between individuals, just as the number of flowers on any other plant can vary. In contrast, individual flowers, either those that comprise an Asteraceae inflorescence or ones in other families, generally have a constant number of petals. Though most species in the Asteraceae family have both ray and disk flowers, some species have only ray flowers (such as *Agoseris monticola* [mountain agoseris]), and others have only disk flowers (such as *Sphaeromeria cana* [gray chickensage]). Below the flowers is a collection of leaves, the phyllaries. As you read through the individual species descriptions, you will discover that the look of the phyllaries is often an identifying feature for a specific genus or even a species: Is there a single circle of them or multiple whorls? Are the tips flat or bent back? If you delve deeper into plant identification, you will find that, due to the vocabulary unique to this family, deciphering a key for Asteraceae is challenging. See also the sketch of an Asteraceae flower on page 15.

❖ *Arnica chamissonis* (Chamisso arnica)   **FAMILY:** Asteraceae

DISTRIBUTION Occasional throughout, on both sides of the Sierra Crest; very common on the Kern Plateau
HABITAT Moist meadows, open forest, stream banks
ELEVATION 6,000'–10,700'
SEASON Early July–mid-August
LOCATIONS Lyell Canyon, Devils Postpile area, Rock Creek Basin, Mono Creek, Seventh Lake (North Fork Big Pine Creek), Crabtree Meadows

LEAVES AND STEMS: Occurring in seasonally moist meadows, this species ranges 20–80 cm in height and is less leafy than the other tall arnicas. The long, narrow leaves occur in 4–10 pairs and have distinctly parallel veins running up them. The leaves appear gray-green due to the abundant long, white hairs on them; the leaves toward the top of the stem become much smaller. Though rosettes of leaves connected by rhizomes (underground stems) may spread across a meadow, they are never in dense patches, with soil visible between the individual tufts.

(Continued)

(Continued)   **FLOWERS:** The stems can have 1 to several inflorescences. Each inflorescence has 8–20 narrow, yellow ray flowers, as well as a central disk that is nearly as wide as the ray flowers are long.

EXTRA TIDBITS: This species generally reproduces asexually.

❖ *Arnica cordifolia* (heartleaf arnica)   **FAMILY:** Asteraceae

DISTRIBUTION Fairly common on both sides of the Sierra Crest, from the Yosemite area south through the Bishop Creek drainage, then rare to absent until the far southern Sierra
HABITAT Moist forest, damp meadows
ELEVATION 6,000'–11,000'
SEASON Late June–mid-August
LOCATIONS Gaylor Lakes, Mt. Dana, Tyee Lakes, Marie Louise Lakes (Bishop Creek drainage)

LEAVES AND STEMS: The scattered clusters of heart-shaped leaves are the best way to identify this *Arnica*. The leaves have slightly scalloped and subtly toothed margins, range 3–11 cm in length, occur along the stem in 2–4 pairs, and typically trend upward. Though multiple rosettes of leaves may grow together, this species does not form big mats of leaves. Also, not all rosettes produce flowering stalks in a given summer, and it is not uncommon to see straggly rosettes of leaves scattered across the ground.

FLOWERS: The 10- to 20-cm-long flowering stems tend to be unbranched to slightly branched, with each branch ending in a single outward-facing inflorescence. Each inflorescence has 6–14 relatively long, pointed ray flowers. And if you pull apart a head, you will see that the hairs on the underside of each flower are white; this is called the pappus, the fluff that helps seeds be dispersed by wind.

❖ *Arnica lanceolata* subsp. *prima (Arnica amplexicaulis)* (clasping arnica)
       FAMILY: Asteraceae

DISTRIBUTION Occasional on both sides of the Sierra Crest from the Yosemite region south through the San Joaquin and Bishop Creek drainages, becoming more common farther south
HABITAT Seeps, stream banks
ELEVATION 4,000'–11,000'
SEASON Mid-July–early September
LOCATIONS Long Lake (Rock Creek Basin), North Fork Big Pine Creek, Paradise Valley, Vidette Meadow, Farewell Gap

LEAVES AND STEMS: This arnica spreads extensively in wet areas. Patches can exceed 10 m in diameter; spearleaf arnica is the only other wet-site species to form such large patches. The plants reach 50–80 cm in height, and the stems have glands and long white hairs. There are 4–10 pairs of leaves, all about the same size, though they sometimes become larger partway up the stem. The leaves are finely toothed and generally lack hairs. This is the only broader-leaved arnica that appears glossy at times.

FLOWERS: The stems are usually branched toward the top, with multiple inflorescences per stem. Each head has 7–17 fairly broad yellow ray flowers that are 3-toothed at their tip.

RELATED SPECIES: *Arnica ovata* (previously *Arnica diversifolia*; sticky leaf arnica) is common only in the Yosemite region. It too prefers moist sites but is distinguished by sometimes lacking any hairs or glands. In addition, it has only 2–4 leaf pairs, with the largest leaves toward the middle of the stem.

Arnica ovata

❖ *Arnica longifolia* (spearleaf arnica, seep-spring arnica)   **FAMILY:** Asteraceae

DISTRIBUTION Occasional throughout the western Sierra; fairly common throughout the eastern Sierra
HABITAT Seeps, stream banks, wet meadows
ELEVATION 4,300'–11,100'
SEASON Late July–early September
LOCATIONS East shore of Saddlebag Lake, Sixth Lake (North Fork Big Pine Creek), Golden Trout Lake Trail (from Onion Valley)

LEAVES AND STEMS: Forming large clumps in wet locations, this species grows 30–60 cm in height. 5–7 pairs of stem leaves are shaped like long, skinny triangles: 5–12 cm long, broader at the base, pointed at the tip, and with a network of inset veins. The stems and leaves are typically thick, sticky, and inconsistently hairy; often, more hairs are located near the top of the plant.

FLOWERS: The stems have many branches, resulting in many inflorescences per stem and, overall, a large number of inflorescences per plant. Each inflorescence has 6–15 ray flowers, ranging in length 1–2 cm—neither long nor short for an arnica. The rays tend to point in a variety of directions, making for a slightly straggly inflorescence.

❖ *Arnica mollis* (hairy arnica)   **FAMILY:** Asteraceae

DISTRIBUTION Occasional throughout, on both sides of the Sierra Crest
HABITAT Damp areas, including meadows, stream banks, moist forest
ELEVATION 4,600'–12,000'
SEASON Early July–early September
LOCATIONS Cascade Lake (Twenty Lakes Basin), Chocolate Lakes (Bishop Pass Trail), Lake Sabrina Basin, Evolution Lake, Tyndall Creek

LEAVES AND STEMS: The stems are generally 20–30 cm in height but can be slightly shorter or much taller. Both the stems and the leaves tend to be sparsely covered with glands and long, white hairs, making the stem look a little prickly and the leaves a bit shaggy. There are 3–5 pairs of elongate (or occasionally ovate) leaves. Often, only a few individual rosettes are scattered across a meadow, while at other times they grow as a larger expanse.

FLOWERS: I use two floral features to identify a plant as *Arnica mollis*. First, the 12–18 yellow ray flowers are rather short in comparison to the quite wide central disk; indeed, the rays are usually shorter than the diameter of the disk. Second, the inflorescence is often described as hemispheric, indicating that the central disk bulges upward like half a sphere. 1 to a few inflorescences are at the ends of the stems.

❖ *Arnica nevadensis* (Sierra arnica)   **FAMILY:** Asteraceae

DISTRIBUTION Common throughout the Yosemite and Mammoth Lakes regions on both sides of the Sierra Crest; farther south, common only in the eastern Sierra
HABITAT Dry sites, often with scattered tree cover or in a forest
ELEVATION 6,000'–12,000'
SEASON Early July–late August
LOCATIONS Twenty Lakes Basin near Steelhead Lake, south of Garnet Lake, east of Purple Lake, Rock Creek Basin, Lamarck Lakes Trail

LEAVES AND STEMS: Sierra arnica is the most common arnica species in drier locations. Growing 10–50 cm in height, this plant often forms expansive mats on open, dry, forested slopes. Hairs and small glands cover both the stems and leaves. There are 2–3 pairs of ovate to elliptic leaves on flowering stalks, but the ground will also be scattered with clusters of leaves that lack a flowering stalk. Note that the leaves have a single main leaf vein; many other arnicas have several seemingly parallel veins radiating from the base of the leaf.

FLOWERS: The stems have few branches, with 1–3 inflorescences per branch. Each has 6–15 yellow rays surrounding a yellow disk, which is fewer ray flowers than several other arnica species. The rays tend to widen considerably toward the middle and base, giving them a slightly ovate shape. Unlike other arnica species, the individual ray flowers overlap slightly at the base. The rays are often 3-toothed at their tip.

❖ *Arnica parryi* (nodding arnica, Parry's arnica)
         FAMILY: Asteraceae

DISTRIBUTION Rare throughout west of the Sierra Crest; occasional throughout east of the Sierra Crest
HABITAT Wet meadows, open forest
ELEVATION 7,000'–11,100'
SEASON Early July–mid-August
LOCATIONS Garnet Lake, Green Lake (from South Lake), Fifth Lake (North Fork Big Pine Creek), Rae Lakes Basin

LEAVES AND STEMS: This is yet another species of spreading *Arnica* found in wet meadows. It does not, however, form dense clumps but, instead, scattered individuals that often look quite straggly. Usually reaching only 30 cm in height (but occasionally twice that), it is shorter than the other wet-site species and has only 3–4 leaf pairs. The leaves and stem are very gray-green due to the abundant hairs.

FLOWERS: The stems are branched, with a few inflorescences per branch. One notable feature: The buds droop, with the inflorescence stalks straightening up as the buds open. The inflorescences occasionally lack ray flowers but typically have between 5 and 10 short yellow rays that are fairly rectangular in outline.

❖ A Rainbow of Flowers

Three broad classes of pigments are responsible for all colors in flower petals—and indeed, all non-green plant parts. They are 1) carotenoids, which create yellow, orange, or red; 2) flavonoids (including anthocyanins), which create white, yellow, red, pink, purple, or blue; and 3) betalains, which create everything from yellow and orange to red and violet. If you have heard of these groups of pigments, it is probably because you have read about how important they are to our diet, rather than how they color plant petals. A diet rich in plant pigments is known to have health benefits, and the most colorful fruits and vegetables tend to have high concentrations of these pigments: Carrots are rich in carotenoids, beets are the best-known source of betalains, and blueberries are loaded with anthocyanins. But all of these pigments also exist in Sierra flowers. For instance, many of the bright-yellow and orange colors in members of the Asteraceae family, including the genera *Arnica* and *Agoseris,* are due to carotenoids, while the beautiful blue colors in the genus *Delphinium* and the many shades of pink and purple in the Polemoniaceae family are created by anthocyanins. While carotenoids and anthocyanins occur in most plant families, the only Sierra plants that contain betalains are those in the Montiaceae, Nyctaginaceae, and Polygonaceae families—and these species lack anthocyanins for reasons not completely understood. While there are only three groups of plant pigments, each encompasses many individual molecules, with slightly different chemical structures, leading to slightly different colors. Colors can become more intense due to a greater concentration of a given pigment or to a combination of multiple pigments; some intensely yellow flowers have both carotenoids and yellow flavonoids.

Petal color is clearly linked to pollinators (see "Pollinators," page 167), but it is also partially due to other uses for the pigment molecules in the plant. For example, carotenoids occur throughout the plant because they protect the plant's photosynthetic systems from excess light (see "Too Much Light," page 69); as a result, the petals will also be colored by the pigments. Meanwhile, anthocyanins help protect plants from UV radiation, and their production tends to increase under stressful conditions (see "UV Radiation," page 37).

❖ *Artemisia ludoviciana* subsp. *incompta* (mountain mugwort)
    FAMILY: Asteraceae

> **DISTRIBUTION** Common throughout, on both sides of the Sierra Crest
> **HABITAT** Dry locations, rocky slopes, often growing alongside rocks
> **ELEVATION** 4,000'–11,500'
> **SEASON** Late July–mid-September
> **LOCATIONS** Tuolumne Meadows, Blue Lake (Lake Sabrina Basin), North Fork Big Pine Creek, Mt. Whitney Trail

(Continued)

(Continued)   **LEAVES AND STEMS:** This is the most common species of herbaceous *Artemisia*. Generally shorter than wild tarragon, it reaches 20–80 cm in height. Hairs densely cover both the stem and the underside of the leaves, while the upper leaf surfaces have few to no hairs. The leaves are distinguished by their deeply incised, linear pinnate lobes (though they may not be lobed at all), and their margins are rolled under, a feature distinctly visible from underneath the leaves.

FLOWERS: The flowering stalks, each bearing inflorescences on side shoots as well as directly attached to the main stem itself, rise above most of the foliage. The inflorescences, 2.5–4 mm in diameter, have both very tiny, straggly ray flowers and disk flowers that vary in color from yellowish to reddish. The inflorescences point moderately downward but do not nod as much as wild tarragon and mountain sage.

❖ *Artemisia norvegica* subsp. *saxatilis* (mountain sage, boreal sagewort)
    FAMILY: Asteraceae

DISTRIBUTION Occasional throughout west of the Sierra Crest; rare east of the Sierra Crest
HABITAT Dry, sandy to rocky slopes but in fairly vegetated locations; often growing alongside rocks
ELEVATION 7,000'–12,000'
SEASON Late July–mid-September
LOCATIONS Virginia Canyon, Mt. Hoffman, west side of Pine Creek Pass, Evolution Basin near Sapphire Lake, Tyndall Creek

LEAVES AND STEMS: The mass of bright-green leaves, pinnately divided into many sharp-pointed linear lobes, at the base of this species immediately identifies it. Above these leaves reaches the 30- to 60-cm-tall stem, often reddish and covered in white hairs.

FLOWERS: Many nodding inflorescences decorate the upper part of the stem. In comparison to the other herbaceous *Artemisia* species, these heads are quite large, 7–11 mm in diameter. They are also notably bulbous. The phyllaries are few in number, quite broad, and green with a dark burgundy to black margin. It is difficult to distinguish between the ray and disk flowers, as the rays are minute. Both are yellowish in color, sometimes with a red tinge toward their base.

❖ *Artemisia rothrockii* (timberline sagebrush, Rothrock sagebrush)
    FAMILY: Asteraceae

DISTRIBUTION Occasional to common throughout most of the range but generally absent in Fresno County; quite common around Tioga Pass to the north and the Cottonwood Lakes area to the south
HABITAT Dry slopes
ELEVATION 6,000'–12,000'
SEASON Late July–mid-September
LOCATIONS Tioga Pass, Parker Pass, Crabtree Lakes, Cottonwood Lakes

LEAVES AND STEMS: This compact, woody shrub reaches 20–50 cm in height. The bark can be quite scaly, and tufts of leaves grow at the ends of short side branches. The leaves are often shaped like 3-lobed wedges but are sometimes long, narrow, and unlobed. The leaves are usually sticky with glands.

FLOWERS: Unlike the long stalks of inflorescences on many *Artemisia* species, this plant simply has short shoots with a small cluster of 3- to 5-mm-diameter heads. In addition, the inflorescences have only disk flowers; these are yellowish, with the reddish calyx adding more color.

❖ *Artemisia tridentata* subsp. *vaseyana* (mountain big sagebrush)
 FAMILY: Asteraceae

DISTRIBUTION Fairly common throughout
HABITAT Dry slopes
ELEVATION 4,000'–10,500'
SEASON Late July–mid-September
LOCATIONS Mt. Hoffman, Piute Pass, North Fork Big Pine Creek, Mt. Whitney Trail

LEAVES AND STEMS: Mountain big sagebrush is the classic woody sagebrush of the desert mountains—but also occurs in the Sierra. This high-elevation subspecies grows to 50–100 cm in height. The leaves are always a gray-green color due to the abundance of hairs covering both surfaces. The 1- to 3-cm-long leaves are wedge shaped, usually with 3 teeth at the tip.

FLOWERS: The inflorescences grow in long spikes up to 30 cm in length. Each is 1–3 mm in diameter, points upward, and tends to be yellowish. The inflorescences are discoid, meaning they lack ray flowers.

❖ *Chrysothamnus viscidiflorus* subsp. *viscidiflorus* (yellow rabbitbrush, sticky leaved rabbitbrush) **FAMILY:** Asteraceae

DISTRIBUTION Common throughout the eastern Sierra and on the Kern Plateau; absent elsewhere; other subspecies occur at lower elevations in the eastern Sierra
HABITAT Dry slopes, sagebrush scrub
ELEVATION 5,600'–12,000'
SEASON Late July–mid-September
LOCATIONS Virginia Lakes Basin, Convict Lake, Lake Sabrina, Coyote Flat

LEAVES AND STEMS: Extending to higher elevations than most rabbitbrushes, this shrub, with distinctly white wood, can reach 1.5 m, though the individuals at mid- to higher elevations rarely reach 1 m. The long, thickish, linear leaves are easily identified by their obvious twists and curl at the tip. Also note that the leaves are a distinctly bright green due to the lack of hairs.

(Continued)

(Continued)   **FLOWERS:** At the top of each branch is a dense cluster of inflorescences, each composed of 3–5 (and occasionally more) yellow disk flowers; there are no ray flowers. The styles stick far out, adding a decorative touch.

❖ Crepis acuminata (long leaved hawksbeard, tapertip hawksbeard)
FAMILY: Asteraceae

DISTRIBUTION Occasional throughout the western Sierra; fairly common throughout the eastern Sierra
HABITAT Dry slopes and flats
ELEVATION 5,500'–10,800'
SEASON Late June–early August
LOCATIONS Lundy Canyon, Minaret Summit, John Muir Trail at Piute Creek, Golden Staircase, east side of Baxter Pass, east side of Kearsarge Pass

LEAVES AND STEMS: At first glance, this rosette species, commonly reaching 20–50 cm in height, resembles a garden weed—indeed, many close relatives are invasive species. The 10- to 20-cm-long (or even longer), narrow leaves are deeply incised into long, narrow, triangular lobes, resembling dandelion leaves, albeit lighter in color due to the abundant hairs. Only the basal leaves are large, with the flowering stems having just a few smaller leaves.

FLOWERS: The flowering stems divide multiple times, with 30–70 small yellow inflorescences occurring on a plant; each inflorescence contains 5–10 ray flowers but lacks any disk flowers. The phyllaries form a narrow tube, while the ray flowers splay outward at the top.

RELATED SPECIES: *Crepis intermedia* (intermediate or limestone hawksbeard) occurs across the same elevation range and environments. A related species, it looks quite similar but has 8–16 phyllaries per inflorescence, while *Crepis acuminata* has 5–8 phyllaries.

❖ Crepis nana (dwarf alpine hawksbeard)   **FAMILY:** Asteraceae

DISTRIBUTION Occasional throughout, almost always near the Sierra Crest or other major crests
HABITAT Talus slopes, especially in metamorphic soils
ELEVATION 9,000'–13,000'
SEASON Early July–mid-August
LOCATIONS Red Lake (Virginia Lakes Basin), below Mildred Lake (Convict Creek drainage), Cardinal Mountain, south side of Glen Pass, Trail Crest

LEAVES AND STEMS: This short herb reaches just 2–10 cm in height. Its oval-shaped leaves are mostly basal. The leaves are up to 3 cm in length, lack hairs, and are often dull colored, with a bluish tinge.

FLOWERS: The small yellow flowers are never terribly showy—the ray flowers are tightly held within the narrow tube of purplish-green phyllaries and point upward, never opening much outward. As the petals wilt, the bright-white pappus (the hairs around the seed) is seen at the mouth of the phyllaries.

❖ Plants of Calcareous Soils

Calcite is a mineral composed primarily of the chemical compound calcium carbonate. Nearly pure sedimentary deposits of the mineral calcite are called limestone. When altered by high temperatures or pressures, it is transformed into marble, a metamorphic rock with much larger calcite crystals. Though calcitic rocks are rare in the Sierra, marble does occur in small outcrops along the Sierra Crest. These outcrops are derived from the remains of sea critters that lived more than 100 million years ago and are located within the layers of red metasedimentary rocks that overlie the granite near the Sierra Crest. Soils that form from marble are basic (have a high pH), leading to different nutrient availabilities than the more acidic granitic soils have. For instance, phosphorus may be very limited in basic soils. As a result of these differences, many species are restricted (or nearly restricted) to marble soils.

The largest region of marble in the Sierra is in and around Convict Creek drainage, approximately 5 miles south of Mammoth Lakes, and this canyon is home to both marble endemics and species with wider distributions that are rare in the Sierra. Elsewhere, there are also smaller patches of marble soils, including on Coyote Ridge and nearby Chocolate Mountain, near Bond Pass in northern Yosemite, and atop Cardinal Mountain and around Mt. Perkins. Though these regions are too small to host as distinctive a community as Convict Canyon, the species composition will always shift as soon as you step onto the marble—take a close look! And consider as well that a species may grow on many soil types outside the Sierra, but within the High Sierra, appropriate growing conditions may only be met on marble soils.

Species unique to marble soils, because of their restricted distributions, are not included in this book because they are not among the 400 species most commonly encountered on the trail. If you are headed to Convict Creek for a day of botanizing, look up the following species before beginning your walk: *Cymopterus cinerarius* (gray springparsley; occasional throughout the eastern Sierra but often associated with marble soil), *Dieteria canescens* var. *shastensis* (Shasta aster; in the High Sierra, only located in the Convict Creek drainage), *Draba cana* (canescent draba; mostly restricted to the Convict Creek drainage), *Draba lonchocarpa* (spear-fruited draba; common in the Convict Creek drainage and also occurs on Chocolate Peak along the Bishop Pass Trail), *Arctostaphylos uva-ursi* (bear-berry; in the High Sierra, restricted to the Convict Creek drainage, where it is very common), *Oxytropis parryi* (Parry's oxytrope; in the Sierra Nevada, found only on Coyote Ridge and near Taboose Pass), *Chamerion latifolium* (dwarf fireweed; in the High Sierra usually found on marble soils though occasionally found growing off it), *Oenothera cespitosa* subsp. *crinita* (cespitose evening-primrose; fairly common in the Convict Creek drainage

(Continued)

(Continued)   but otherwise absent in the Sierra), *Eriogonum microthecum* var.
laxiflorum (Great Basin wild buckwheat; common in the Convict
Creek drainage and on the east side of San Joaquin Mountain), *Salix brachycarpa*
var. *brachycarpa* (short-fruited willow; found only in the Convict Creek drainage),
Parnassia parviflora (small-flowered grass of Parnassus; in the High Sierra, limited
to the Convict Creek drainage, where it is abundant in Lake Mildred Meadow), and
Platanthera tescamnis (green flowered bog orchid; common in the Convict Creek
drainage area, with rare occurrences elsewhere in the eastern Sierra). Though they
occur both on and off marble soils, *Crepis nana* (dwarf alpine hawksbeard), *Eriogonum rosense* (Mount Rose buckwheat), and *Erigeron clokeyi* (Clokey's fleabane) are
three species in this book that are all very common on marble soils.

❖ *Ericameria bloomeri* (rabbitbush, Bloomer's goldenbush)   **FAMILY:** Asteraceae

DISTRIBUTION Fairly common in the western Sierra from
the Yosemite region south to the Bishop Creek drainage,
becoming occasional elsewhere
HABITAT Open forest, dry slopes
ELEVATION 5,000'–11,000'
SEASON Early August–mid-September
LOCATIONS Cathedral Fork of Echo Creek, east of
Tuolumne Meadows, top of Mammoth Mountain,
below Shadow Lake, Mono Creek

LEAVES AND STEMS: These small shrubs reach up to 60 cm
in height. A dense cluster of reddish, rarely woody stems
emerge from the base and are generally unbranched. The bright-green leaves are nearly
linear—up to 7 cm in length but only a few millimeters in width. Both the stems and
leaves often—but not always—have small glands that catch the sun.

FLOWERS: Many yellow inflorescences grow along the upper stretches of the stem,
each on a stalk 1–3 cm in length that grows from a leaf axil. The inflorescences are
rather straggly looking with only 4–14 disk flowers and 1–5 ray flowers, the latter often
unevenly distributed along one side of the disk.

RELATED SPECIES: The showy or rubber rabbitbrush, *Ericameria
nauseosa* var. *speciosa* (previously *Chrysothamnus nauseosus*), is a
much larger shrub, reaching 50–100 cm in height. Its flowering
stalks have numerous inflorescences. It is more common at lower
elevations but occasionally extends upward in the eastern Sierra.
Showy rabbitbrush has white-gray leaves due to matted hairs, and its
many inflorescences occur together at the tops of stems and alongside branches. *Ericameria parryi* var. *monocephala* (*Chrysothamnus
parryi* subsp. *monocephalus*; one-headed rabbitbrush) is occasional in

*Ericameria nauseosa
var. speciosa*

the eastern Sierra, just crossing into the western Sierra and occurring
up to an elevation of 12,100 feet. This species has far fewer inflorescences per flowering stalk. Like showy rabbitbrush, its inflorescences lack ray flowers, instead featuring
5–6 yellow disk flowers with tiny, narrow petals opening outward and the style sticking
skyward. The phyllaries are long, narrow, and felty, similar to the leaves. Both of these
species have many subspecies occurring at lower elevations in the Sierra.

❖ *Ericameria discoidea* (whitestem goldenbush) **FAMILY:** Asteraceae

DISTRIBUTION Occasional throughout the western Sierra;
common throughout the eastern Sierra
HABITAT Dry slopes, alpine fell-fields, open talus slopes
ELEVATION 7,600'–12,800'
SEASON Late July–early September
LOCATIONS Virginia Lakes Basin, Mt. Dana,
Mono Pass Trail (Rock Creek Basin), Piute Pass Trail,
Kearsarge Pass Trail

LEAVES AND STEMS: This spreading shrub reaches no more
than 40 cm in height. The stems—relatively stout and covered
with such a dense layer of white hairs that they appear white
and felty—are the most distinctive feature. The dark-green, oval-shaped leaves attach to
the stem without a stalk and are densely covered with small sticky glands.

FLOWERS: A cluster of narrow, stalkless inflorescences grows toward the top of each
stem. Each inflorescence is composed of 10–26 disk flowers but lacks ray flowers.
The styles extend far above the tops of the flowers, giving them a lacy look.

❖ *Ericameria suffruticosa* (alpine macronema, singlehead goldenbush)
    FAMILY: Asteraceae

DISTRIBUTION Fairly common throughout, on both sides of the Sierra Crest
HABITAT Open slopes, open forest
ELEVATION 8,100'–12,000'
SEASON Mid-July–late August
LOCATIONS Parker Pass, Rock Creek Basin, upper French
Canyon, west side of Piute Pass, above Evolution Valley

LEAVES AND STEMS: This species grows to 40 cm in height and
has reddish new growth, giving it a superficial resemblance to
Bloomer's goldenbush. However, this plant has quite woody
stems. The leaves are also different: This species has darker
green leaves, densely covered with sticky glands and distinctly
folded inward along the midrib. They are shaped like elongate
ovals, tapering where they attach to the stem.

FLOWERS: A single inflorescence (occasionally 2) grows from the end of a stem. The
inflorescence has 1–5 (or even 0) ray flowers and at least 15 disk flowers. As with other
goldenbush species, the style emerges far above the flower.

❖ *Erigeron compositus* (cut-leaf fleabane) see page 209

❖ *Eriophyllum lanatum* var. *integrifolium* (common woolly
    sunflower, Oregon sunshine) **FAMILY:** Asteraceae

DISTRIBUTION In the western Sierra, fairly common throughout from the Yosemite
region south through the Palisades area; very common in the eastern Sierra across
these same latitudes but rarely found farther south
HABITAT Dry slopes, open forest, alpine fell-fields
ELEVATION 6,900'–11,500'

(Continued)

(Continued)   **SEASON** Early July–early August
LOCATIONS Mono Pass (Yosemite), below
Agnew Meadows, below Longley Reservoir, Green Lake
(from South Lake)

LEAVES AND STEMS: The bases of the common woolly sunflower's stems are generally woody, making it a subshrub, but
the stems are mostly herbaceous and are rarely more than
20 cm tall. The leaves are gray-green due to a dense coating of
white hairs; they are also quite thick and vary enormously in
shape. The scattered stem leaves are often simply ovals, while
the basal leaves are divided into narrow lobes that cup inward and rarely lie flat.

FLOWERS: Both the disk and the (usually) 8 ray flowers are bright yellow. The rays are
relatively broad, so though there are relatively few rays, the gaps between them are small.

RELATED SPECIES: Several other subspecies occur at lower elevations or farther north or
south in the Sierra. These species look quite similar but can have 5–15 ray flowers and
may be taller.

❖ *Eucephalus breweri (Aster breweri)* (Brewer's aster)
    FAMILY: Asteraceae

DISTRIBUTION Common throughout the western Sierra;
occasional in the eastern Sierra
HABITAT Open forest, dry slopes
ELEVATION 4,000'–10,700'
SEASON Mid-July–early September
LOCATIONS Slate Creek Fork Lee Vining Creek, Sunrise
Lakes Trail, Ireland Lake, Convict Creek drainage, Golden
Staircase (John Muir Trail), Kearsarge Pass Trail

LEAVES AND STEMS: Usually reaching 20–60 cm in height, most of the stems on this
loosely branched herb are covered with small glands and sparse hairs that stick straight
out from the stem. The leaves are nearly oval but are slightly wider toward the base and
do not have a stalk; they vary greatly in hairiness but often have some hairs and glands.

FLOWERS: This species stands out from most of the other daisies by its lack of ray flowers. The main stem has many branches, and each branch ends in an inflorescence. The
yellow disk flowers extend beyond the phyllaries, with the white pappus (long hairs at
the base of the flower) visible below the yellow petals. The yellow styles and stigma stick
out even farther, altogether creating a long, narrow inflorescence.

❖ *Hazardia whitneyi* var. *whitneyi* (Whitney's goldenbush, Whitney's bristleweed)
    FAMILY: Asteraceae

DISTRIBUTION Occasional throughout the western Sierra; rare in the eastern Sierra
HABITAT Sunny locations alongside rocks or forest openings
ELEVATION 5,000'–10,200'
SEASON Late July–early September
LOCATIONS River Trail, west side of McGee Pass, Le Conte Canyon, Golden Staircase,
Farewell Gap

LEAVES AND STEMS: Many 20- to 50-cm-long branches diverge from a common point, sometimes pointing upward and other times more to the side. The bright-green, 2.5- to 5-cm-long, distinctly serrate, sharp-tipped leaves are attached along the entire length of the green to reddish stems. The stems and leaves can be glabrous—lacking hairs—or have scattered glandular hairs.

FLOWERS: The straggly, yellow inflorescences emerge from the leaf axils on the upper stretches of the stem. The small yellow disk is surrounded by 5–18 ray flowers, but these are narrow and trend upward, not outward, making them unobvious. More immediately striking are the narrow, sharp-tipped, often red-tipped phyllaries, some of which are distinctly higher or lower from others, or graduated.

❖ *Helenium bigelovii* (Bigelow's sneezeweed)   **FAMILY:** Asteraceae

DISTRIBUTION Occasional in the Yosemite and Mono Recesses regions, becoming common from the Bishop Creek drainage south (on both sides of the Sierra Crest)
HABITAT Moist locations, including stream banks, seeps, wet meadows
ELEVATION 4,000'–11,000'
SEASON Early July–mid-August
LOCATIONS Bishop Pass Trail, above Le Conte Canyon, below First Lake (North Fork Big Pine Creek), Kearsarge Pass Trail, Sandy Meadow

LEAVES AND STEMS: The great masses of shiny green leaves, sometimes exceeding 20 cm in length, can fill a meadow. Though rounded where they connect to the stem, the leaves have tips that end in a narrow point.

FLOWERS: The comical flowers are on stalks up to 1 m in length. The orange-brown disk flowers are arranged in a sphere, beneath which are attached the 14–20 yellow, downward-pointing, wedge-shaped ray flowers; the shape of the inflorescence has always reminded me of a badminton birdie.

❖ *Hieracium horridum* (prickly hawkweed, shaggy hawkweed)
     FAMILY: Asteraceae

DISTRIBUTION Common throughout, on both sides of the Sierra Crest, especially at high elevations
HABITAT Alongside rocks on dry slopes, sandy patches on talus fields
ELEVATION 4,800'–12,000'
SEASON Early July–mid-August
LOCATIONS Twenty Lakes Basin, Lamarck Lakes Trail, west side of Kearsarge Pass, Mt. Whitney Trail

LEAVES AND STEMS: The exceedingly long white hairs that cover the stems are the first feature to catch your eye on these 10- to 20-cm-tall plants. The elongate, oval-shaped leaves are concentrated near the base of the plant but occur sparingly along the length of the stems.   *(Continued)*

(Continued)   **FLOWERS:** The inflorescences are tiny but numerous, with many on each stalk; they are composed of 6–10 ray flowers and lack a central disk. The outer margins of the up-to-1-cm-long ray flowers are 4- to 5-toothed, and their styles extend beyond the end of the upward-pointing petals. The phyllaries are as densely covered in white hairs as the stems are, adding to the plants' shaggy appearance.

❖ *Hieracium triste (Hieracium gracile)* (slender hawkweed, woolly hawkweed)
FAMILY: Asteraceae

DISTRIBUTION Fairly common from the Yosemite region south through the Mono Recesses; occasional farther west and in the southwestern Sierra
HABITAT Meadows, moist forest
ELEVATION 7,200'–11,500'
SEASON Late July–late August
LOCATIONS Twenty Lakes Basin, Isberg Lake, Garnet Lake, Mono Creek, Nine Lakes Basin

LEAVES AND STEMS: This hawkweed frequently grows in tall grass, hiding the elongate leaves that form a basal rosette, but often only the 10- to 20-cm-tall stalk and tiny flowers are visible. The leaves typically lack hairs, though the upper stretches of the stems have small hairs.

FLOWERS: The stems have a few branches near the top, each ending in a small inflorescence of tiny, overlapping, yellow ray flowers, just 3–4 mm long; this genus has no disk flowers. Long, dark hairs cover the phyllaries and spread outward.

RELATED SPECIES: *Hieracium albiflorum,* or white hawkweed, is common in the lower and upper montane forests in the western Sierra but is rarely found higher than the red fir forests. The leaves are mostly basal, with the long stalk bearing lots of small white flowers. Like all hawkweeds, there are only ray flowers, and in this species, they open widely outward.

Hieracium albiflorum

❖ *Hulsea algida* (alpine gold, Pacific hulsea)   **FAMILY:** Asteraceae

DISTRIBUTION Common throughout, usually near the Sierra Crest or other high ridges
HABITAT Gravelly alpine slopes, alpine fell-fields, gravel in between talus
ELEVATION 9,500'–14,500'
SEASON Mid-June–mid-July
LOCATIONS Dana Plateau, Donohue Pass, Mt. Agassiz, summit of Mt. Whitney, New Army Pass

LEAVES AND STEMS: This rosette species is one of the largest plants at high elevations. The 5- to 10-cm-long, toothed leaves are mostly clustered near the base of the plant, though some grow along the stems; the leaves are usually partially folded along the midrib and are quite thick. The plants have a pungent aroma and are covered with glandular hairs, making them sticky to the touch.

FLOWERS: The bright-yellow flowering heads can reach 2.5 cm in diameter and are by far the largest yellow daisies at high elevations. Each inflorescence consists of a central disk surrounded by 25–60 very shiny and relatively narrow ray flowers.

❖ Glacial Refugia

The Pleistocene epoch, the geologic era that lasted from 2.6 million years ago until 11,700 years ago, was a time of repeated glaciations. At the start of the Pleistocene, the flora of the high-elevation Sierra would have been similar to what we see today. As snow and ice gradually covered the landscape, the plants—or at least their seeds—had to move. Some species migrated down the mountain, establishing at lower elevations, and then later migrated back to higher elevations as the glaciers retreated. Other Sierra species made an alternative escape: The glaciers in the Sierra were never thick enough to cover the tops of most mountains, so many summits and high plateaus rose above the ice fields. Classic examples include the Dana Plateau and the summit regions of many peaks in the Sierra, such as Mt. Lyell, Coyote Ridge, Mt. Darwin, Diamond Mesa, Mt. Whitney, and Table Mountain; flat to low-angle sand and talus fields atop ridges are generally a good indication that a location escaped glaciation. These so-called nunataks allowed many of the Sierra's alpine plants to persist at high elevations until the glaciers retreated. Two of the Sierra's most famous alpine species—alpine gold (*Hulsea algida*) and sky pilot (*Polemonium eximium*)—are today common in these high-elevation unglaciated landforms and likely spent the glacial periods sheltered there. Researchers hypothesize that populations of *Draba* species restricted to different nunataks for long periods may have diverged from one another, leading to the creation of new species and the diversity of *Draba* species in the Sierra with quite restricted distributions. Today, the large unglaciated plateaus are locations with particularly high plant diversity. See also "Sky Islands," page 228, for more about these landforms.

❖ *Hulsea brevifolia* (shortleaf alpinegold)
FAMILY: Asteraceae

DISTRIBUTION Fairly common throughout montane elevations in the western Sierra; absent in the eastern Sierra
HABITAT Open slopes, forest
ELEVATION 5,400'–9,000'
SEASON Early July–mid-August
LOCATIONS Porcupine Flat, east of Clouds Rest, Reds Meadow

LEAVES AND STEMS: Though this species is mostly restricted to montane, I included it because it is very common in the Devils Postpile area, so many people will see it along the John Muir Trail. This perennial has many stems, which reach 30–60 cm in height. Gland-tipped hairs densely cover the elongate leaves.

(Continued)

(Continued)   The lower leaves are toothed at the tips, while the leaves higher along the stems are narrowly oval shaped. All the leaves lack a stalk and tend to clasp—or surround—the stem.

FLOWERS: Each branch ends in an inflorescence with 10–23 yellow ray flowers surrounding a 1- to 1.5-cm-wide disk. The narrow rays are often distributed unevenly, so the inflorescences are not terribly symmetrical. Fading petals sometimes turn a burnt-orange color.

❖ *Hymenoxys hoopesii (Dugaldia hoopesii)* (owl's claws, orange sneezeweed)
    FAMILY: Asteraceae

DISTRIBUTION Common in certain locations throughout the Sierra but much rarer elsewhere; particularly common around Sonora Pass, Bishop Creek, near Mineral King, and the Kern River drainage
HABITAT Wet to dry meadows, open forest
ELEVATION 6,000'–11,700'
SEASON Mid-July–late August
LOCATIONS Virginia Lakes Basin, Dog Lake, Green Lake (from South Lake), Piute Pass Trail, John Muir Trail south of Bighorn Plateau, Cottonwood Lakes

LEAVES AND STEMS: This relative of sunflowers is generally 30–60 cm in height. The up to 30-cm-long, narrow, quite thick leaves are mostly basal, though ever-smaller leaves are found along the length of the stem. The stems and leaves can either have long white hairs or lack hairs and appear quite glossy.

FLOWERS: The tall flowering stems have many branches near the top, with each branch ending in a large inflorescence. The yellow disk flowers form a large dome shape surrounded by 2- to 4-cm-long yellow ray flowers that are notched at their ends. The ray flowers are often twisted and straggly, aiming in all directions when in full bloom and pointing increasingly downward as the flowers age.

❖ *Microseris nutans* (nodding microseris)
    FAMILY: Asteraceae

DISTRIBUTION Common in the western Sierra from the Yosemite region south through the San Joaquin drainage; rare to absent from the Kings River drainage south; also rare to absent in the eastern Sierra
HABITAT Many open habitats, including meadows and open forest
ELEVATION 4,000'–10,500'
SEASON Early June–early July
LOCATIONS Tuolumne Meadows Campground, Shadow Creek, Bear Creek, north of Evolution Lake

LEAVES AND STEMS: This common meadow species has flowering stems that are 10–70 cm in length, so the inflorescences stick above the grass blades. The leaves occur mainly as a basal rosette, with a few growing higher on the plant. The leaves are quite long and very narrow, with prominent triangular lobes protruding outward on the basal leaves.

FLOWERS: 1 to several yellow inflorescences, each on its own long stalk, are at the top of the plant. They are composed entirely of long, narrow, overlapping ray flowers that taper to a point; disk flowers are absent. The word *nodding* in the name refers to the buds, which noticeably droop.

❖ *Packera cana (Senecio canus)* (woolly groundsel)
   FAMILY: Asteraceae

> **DISTRIBUTION** Fairly common in the western Sierra, becoming very common in the eastern Sierra; occurs throughout the range
> **HABITAT** Among talus, dry scrubby or sandy slopes
> **ELEVATION** 6,000'–12,000'
> **SEASON** Early July–mid-August
> **LOCATIONS** Virginia Lakes Basin, Dana Plateau, Chocolate Lakes (near Bishop Pass Trail), John Muir Trail south of Charlotte Lake, John Muir Trail east of Crabtree Meadows

LEAVES AND STEMS: 1 or more flowering stalks, usually 10–30 cm tall, extend above a cluster of basal leaves; there are few leaves along the stem. The basal leaves are gray-green in color and felty in texture due to the abundant white hairs; in addition, the leaves are quite thick, with an oval-shaped blade at the end of a long, narrow base. The leaves tend to stick upward, not outward. While the base of the flowering stems can be quite hairy, the top tends to have fewer hairs.

FLOWERS: The flowering stems repeatedly branch, with dense clusters of inflorescences at the end of each stem. As with all groundsels, there is a single circle of phyllaries, all precisely the same length. The flowering head is a central disk of yellow flowers surrounded by no more than 10 straggly-looking yellow ray flowers.

❖ *Packera pauciflora (Senecio pauciflorus)* (alpine groundsel)
   FAMILY: Asteraceae

> **DISTRIBUTION** Occasional throughout, on both sides of the Sierra Crest, mostly at high elevations
> **HABITAT** Wet meadows, lakeshores
> **ELEVATION** 6,000'–11,500'
> **SEASON** Early July–late August
> **LOCATIONS** Dana Plateau, Rock Creek Basin, Long Lake (Bishop Pass Trail), Evolution Lake

LEAVES AND STEMS: Most of the leaves on this species are basal; they are oval to round shaped, often indented where the leaf blade attaches to the stem, and have tiny, even, rounded lobes around the leaf margins. Meanwhile, smaller stem leaves clasp the stem and are more elongate with deeper, less regular lobes. All leaves generally lack hairs.

FLOWERS: Inflorescences on alpine groundsel may or may not have ray flowers, and individuals with the two flowering patterns often grow together. The upper sections of the stems are branched with several inflorescences per stem. For both variants, the disk flowers are a deep yellow trending toward a burnt orange, while the relatively short ray flowers are yellow, and their tips are 3-lobed and broader than the bases. The phyllaries are long and smooth and range from green to reddish.

❖ *Packera werneriifolia (Senecio werneriifolius)* (hoary groundsel)
　　FAMILY: Asteraceae

DISTRIBUTION Common throughout on both sides of the Sierra Crest, usually at quite high elevations
HABITAT Among talus, alpine fell-fields
ELEVATION 10,000'–14,000'
SEASON Late June–early August
LOCATIONS Tioga Peak, Dana Plateau, Mono Pass (Rock Creek Basin), Kearsarge Pass, toward summit of Mt. Whitney

LEAVES AND STEMS: The 1.5- to 4-cm-long, quite leathery leaves form a dense rosette. They are a dark-green color, and the margins are slightly rolled under. The leaves are generally, but not always, covered in white hairs.

FLOWERS: Hoary groundsel can be densely covered with showy yellow inflorescences. The central disk flowers push upward to form a distinct mound, while the short, yellow ray flowers extend straight out and are sufficiently numerous and broad to fully ring the disk, leaving only small gaps between the rays. The phyllaries range from green to purplish and become bulbous once the flowers go to seed.

RELATED SPECIES: *Packera subnuda* var. *subnuda* (previously *Senecio cymbalarioides*; cleftleaf groundsel) occurs only at high elevations in the Yosemite region but is quite common in the Tioga Pass region. This meadow species features often solitary flowering stems (10–20 cm in height), surrounded by a rosette of glossy, toothed leaves.

Packera subnuda var. *subnuda*

❖ *Pyrrocoma apargioides* (alpine flames, alpine pyrrocoma)
　　FAMILY: Asteraceae

DISTRIBUTION Very common throughout, on both sides of the Sierra Crest
HABITAT Dry meadows, sandy slopes and flats
ELEVATION 6,000'–12,500'
SEASON Early July–mid-August
LOCATIONS Twenty Lakes Basin, Dana Plateau, Thousand Island Lake, Rock Creek Basin, Cottonwood Lakes

LEAVES AND STEMS: The narrow leaves form a rosette; each basal leaf is 4–10 cm long, slightly arched inward along the central vein, with long, sharp, irregular teeth extending outward.

FLOWERS: 1 to a few reddish-green, white-hairy stems extend upward (or outward), each topped by a single yellow inflorescence. 11–40 yellow ray flowers, relatively long compared to the disk, surround a small central disk. The outer part of the ray is bulbous, pinching in where it connects to the disk. Note that the co-occurring mountain dandelion lacks disk flowers.

❖ *Raillardella argentea* (silky raillardella)
   FAMILY: Asteraceae

DISTRIBUTION Fairly common throughout
on both sides of the Sierra Crest
HABITAT Dry, gravelly flats; alpine fell-fields
ELEVATION 8,100'–12,500'
SEASON Early July–mid-August
LOCATIONS Twenty Lakes Basin, Dana
Plateau, Humphreys Basin, Evolution Basin,
Upper Basin, Mt. Whitney Trail

LEAVES AND STEMS: The species name
argentea, or silver, is perfect because the
leaves are so densely covered in long, white
hairs that they appear silver. The quite thick
yet soft, 2- to 4-cm-long, elongate leaves
grow as rosettes.

FLOWERS: The flowering stalks and fused phyllaries are always reddish in color and
at times a deep burgundy shade. The species lacks ray flowers, but the small floral
tubes of the yellow disk flowers extend beyond the top of the long, narrow cylinder
of phyllaries, and the stamens reach even higher, giving these little flowers a quite
substantial profile.

❖ *Raillardella scaposa* (green leaved raillardella)   **FAMILY:** Asteraceae

DISTRIBUTION On both sides of the Sierra Crest,
common from the Yosemite region south through the
Bishop Creek drainage; farther south occasional in
the western Sierra and absent in the eastern Sierra
HABITAT Dry to moist flats and slopes, typically in
open areas
ELEVATION 6,500'–11,200'
SEASON Early July–mid-August
LOCATIONS Twenty Lakes Basin, Mono Pass
(Yosemite), Bear Lakes Basin, Lamarck Lakes Trail

LEAVES AND STEMS: The difference in stature between
the two species of raillardellas described in this book
is striking. This species sports narrow leaves that often
exceed 10 cm in length and a flowering stem that is
typically 15–30 cm long. The leaves are generally a
bright green, having few to no hairs. A single individual spreads across the landscape due to a branched
rhizome, or underground stem, from which the rosettes
of leaves grow.

FLOWERS: A single inflorescence tops each long flowering stalk. The green phyllaries are
fused into a long, narrow tube, from which the disk flowers emerge. Like silky raillardella,
the floral tubes extend above the phyllaries, and the stamens extend far above the petals.

❖ *Senecio fremontii* var. *occidentalis* (western dwarf mountain ragwort, western Fremont's groundsel)   **FAMILY:** Asteraceae

DISTRIBUTION Fairly common throughout on both sides of the Sierra Crest
HABITAT Among talus, sandy alpine slopes, often next to rocks
ELEVATION 7,000'–13,500'
SEASON Mid-July–late August
LOCATIONS Upper Lundy Canyon, Tamarack Bench (Rock Creek Basin), Kearsarge Pass Trail, Milestone Basin, west side of Mt. Whitney

LEAVES AND STEMS: Growing 10–20 cm in height, the leafy stems can occur in dense clusters—it is not uncommon for many stems to emerge alongside a boulder. Neither the leaves nor the stems have hairs, so they are shiny and bright green. The leaves are usually just 2 cm long, and they are serrate, with either rounded or pointed teeth. The stems and phyllary tips can be slightly reddish but less so than related species.

FLOWERS: Each stem has several bright-yellow flowering heads. 8 long ray flowers surround a small central disk; the rays are about twice as long as the diameter of the disk and are unevenly distributed around its edge.

❖ Treeline

When hiking in a mountain environment, you immediately notice when you get above the highest tree; suddenly there is no shade, less protection from the elements, and often a quite different collection of species growing underfoot. So what determines the treeline? Why can a whitebark pine grow upright in one spot but only grow as ground-hugging krummholz slightly higher? Research worldwide suggests that treeline is determined by the line where average daily temperatures of at least 43.7°F (6.5°C) occur at least 100 days during the growing season. The researchers who calculated this boundary refer to treeline as the highest elevation where trees grow upright, ignoring the krummholz that exists at the highest elevations. That the boundary is tightly linked with adequate growing conditions matches well with what is known about tree growth at higher elevations. Trees continue to photosynthesize at lower average temperatures but can no longer add enough height or girth each season to establish as trees; cell division becomes too slow at lower temperatures. This effect is reinforced as a tree grows because air temperatures are cooler farther from the ground surface, so the taller a tree becomes, the less hospitable its environment becomes. In other words, a seed can germinate and a seedling can establish, but it cannot become a "tree" at these lower temperatures.

Interestingly, the presence of trees just below the treeline makes the environment less hospitable to other species by shading the soil. The soils at locations above the last trees are comparatively warmer. Similarly, around treeline, trees are often quite widely dispersed, limiting soil shading; a few trees can persist at this elevation, though if they grew as a dense stand, it would be too cold for them.

In the Sierra, treeline ranges from about 9,500 feet in the northern Yosemite region to slightly above 11,000 feet in Sequoia National Park. While temperature is the primary factor determining treeline, water availability or topographic variation fine-tunes the pattern. As discussed in the introduction, a number of different trees, including the whitebark pine, the foxtail pine (found only south of Pinchot Pass), and the limber pine (generally in the eastern Sierra), are found at treeline elevations.

❖ *Senecio integerrimus* var. *exaltatus* (Columbia groundsel, mountain butterweed)
   FAMILY: Asteraceae

DISTRIBUTION Common throughout, on both sides of the Sierra Crest
HABITAT Dry slopes, dry meadows, open forest
ELEVATION 5,400'–11,200'
SEASON Early June–late July
LOCATIONS Slate Creek Fork Lee Vining Creek, Buena Vista Crest, Evolution Valley, Vidette Meadow, Kern Plateau

LEAVES AND STEMS: Individuals of this 20- to 50-cm-tall species tend to occur alone as a small rosette of leaves from which a single flowering stem emerges. Other plants may grow nearby, but they tend not to clump together, and not every plant sends out a flowering shoot each year. The leaves are usually 6–10 cm long but occasionally longer, with variable levels of hairiness. They are spindle shaped—elongate and very tapered at both the top and base. Also note that the leaves tend to die back quite early in summer.

FLOWERS: The flowering stalk branches many times near the tip, with each side stalk ending with a small yellow inflorescence. The inflorescences are straggly looking: Above the bright-green, black-tipped phyllaries is a small collection of disk flowers surrounded by up to 5 ray flowers (or occasionally more). The rays tend to fade quickly, and the phyllaries inflate as the plant goes to seed.

RELATED SPECIES: *Senecio integerrimus* var. *major* (lambstongue ragwort) is quite similar to var. *exaltatus* but has green, not black, phyllary tips. The phyllaries and upper stems can be densely hairy, even cobwebby in bud. The two species share the same habitat, geographic range, and elevation range, indicating that they will often co-occur, though var. *major* is more common at montane elevations and var. *exaltatus* is more common at higher elevations.

Senecio integerrimus var. major

❖ *Senecio scorzonella* (Sierra ragwort)
   FAMILY: Asteraceae

> **DISTRIBUTION** Common throughout, on both sides of
> the Sierra Crest
> **HABITAT** Meadows, lakeshores, open forest
> **ELEVATION** 6,200'–11,300'
> **SEASON** Mid-July–late August
> **LOCATIONS** Tuolumne Meadows, Lake Sabrina Basin,
> Upper Basin, Mt. Whitney Trail

LEAVES AND STEMS: Generally growing in dense clumps,
Sierra ragwort has basal leaves that are 6–12 cm long,
erect, and dark green; long, white hairs cover the leaves.
The flowering stalks can reach 40 cm in height. This
species is the only *Senecio* or *Packera* with tall, stout stalks
and large, oval-shaped to elongate leaves that have finely toothed to smooth margins.
The plants also have a few stem leaves, which are identical to, but smaller than, the
basal leaves.

FLOWERS: The very tips of the flowering stems branch repeatedly, with each stalk ter-
minating in a small inflorescence. The stalks, or peduncles, of the lower branches are
longer than those higher up, so all the flowering heads are at approximately the same
height. The individual flowering heads are only 1–1.5 cm across, with fewer than 10 ray
flowers (and occasionally none). The rays are bent backward and quite short, giving
the flowers a slightly bedraggled appearance.

❖ *Senecio triangularis* (arrowleaf ragwort)   **FAMILY:** Asteraceae

> **DISTRIBUTION** Very common throughout, on both sides of the Sierra Crest
> **HABITAT** Seeps, stream banks, wet forest, other moist to wet locations
> **ELEVATION** 4,000'–11,200'
> **SEASON** Early July–mid-August
> **LOCATIONS** Slate Creek Fork Lee Vining Creek, French
> Canyon, Piute Pass Trail, Evolution Valley, Mt. Whitney Trail

LEAVES AND STEMS: The tallest of the Sierra ragworts typically
exceeds 1 m in height and can reach twice that. These plants are all
the more obvious because they can occur in large clumps in wet
meadows or along streams. The leaf shape, as its name implies, is
a good identifying feature; leaves are shaped like 3- to 10-cm-long
acute triangles, long and skinny and rather straight where the
base of the leaf attaches to the petiole (leaf stalk). The entire stem
is leafy, though leaf size decreases higher up the plant. The leaf
margins can be finely serrate or more obviously toothed.

FLOWERS: The main stalk divides repeatedly near its top, and each
flowering branch holds several flower heads, creating a dense
clump of inflorescences at the top of the plant. Each inflorescence
is not particularly showy, though; the disks measure just 5 mm in
diameter and are unimposing because the margins of the approximately 8 ray flowers tend
to curl inward. And one final identification hint: The phyllary tips tend to be dark.

❖ Decisions Plants Make

Even before trying to identify the species you see, you will likely note that plants differ greatly in stature, leaf size and thickness, and number of flowers. Plants in different habitats generally have different characteristics. Consider the tall, leafy streamside vegetation; the small rosettes of alpine fell-fields; and the shrubs on a dry slope. The plants you notice in each of these situations grow there because their trait combinations allow them to survive under the constraints imposed by a particular habitat and its co-occurring species. Plant ecologists think of these suites of traits in terms of trade-offs, meaning that each trait comes with advantages and disadvantages. The trait combinations that ecologists find most interesting are those that suggest how plants can make a living in particular habitats.

Consider the following well-established trade-off, which exists across the entire globe: Plants that invest more resources in constructing robust leaves also have leaves that last longer. These better-constructed leaves give the plants more time to slowly, through photosynthesis, recoup the energy used in their construction. Consider the thin and flimsy leaves of the streamside vegetation versus the thick leathery leaves displayed by several of the subalpine zone's tallest shrubs, *Arctostaphylos nevadensis* var. *nevadensis* (pine-mat manzanita) and *Chrysolepis sempervirens* (bush chinquapin). These species have invested additional resources into constructing tough evergreen leaves that last for several seasons, while the streamside plants will die back to the root each winter.

Plants must also make a choice whether to invest more in growth or reproduction. Consider co-occurring annual and perennial plants: The annual species are shorter but produce abundant seeds (relative to their size), while the perennial species devote more of their yearly photosynthetic energy to growth (see also "Annual Plants at High Elevation," page 189).

❖ *Solidago multiradiata* (northern goldenrod)
    FAMILY: Asteraceae

DISTRIBUTION Common throughout, on both sides of the Sierra Crest
HABITAT Meadows, seeps, moister pockets in alpine fell-fields
ELEVATION 7,000'–13,500'
SEASON Early July–mid-August
LOCATIONS Twenty Lakes Basin, Rock Creek Basin, Evolution Lake, Rae Lakes Basin, Mt. Whitney Trail

LEAVES AND STEMS: Though this species is known to reach 50 cm in height, in the high-elevation Sierra, individuals are generally 10–30 cm tall. The leaves are longest near the base (about 4–8 cm long), becoming shorter up the length of the stem. They

(Continued)

(Continued)   are oval shaped (sometimes elongate), quite thick, and often slightly folded inward along the midrib.

FLOWERS: The flowering stems have many branches, but just near the tip, resulting in a dense cluster of small inflorescences. There are often 10 inflorescences—each a tiny yellow daisy—in a tight cluster, the only high-elevation species with this appearance. The yellow disk of each inflorescence is 4–8 mm across and ringed by 12–18 quite short (2–4 mm long), yellow ray flowers that curve slightly downward and pinch in where they connect to the disk.

RELATED SPECIES: A related species, *Solidago elongata* (previously *Solidago canadensis* subsp. *elongata*; west coast Canada goldenrod), is a much taller plant. It is usually more than 50 cm in height, with long, oval-shaped leaves along much of the stem length and side branches covered with inflorescences emerging from many leaf axils. The flowers of both species are very similar. It often grows in large patches, though only below 9,200 feet, becoming much more common around 7,000 feet.

❖ *Tetradymia canescens* (spineless horsebrush)
       FAMILY: Asteraceae

DISTRIBUTION Fairly common throughout the eastern Sierra; in the western Sierra, fairly common in the Kern River drainage but absent farther north
HABITAT Open forest, dry slopes
ELEVATION 5,600'–11,200'
SEASON Early August–mid-September
LOCATIONS Virginia Lakes Basin, Convict Creek drainage, east side of Baxter Pass, John Muir Trail near Wright Creek, Mt. Whitney Trail

LEAVES AND STEMS: This shrub reaches at most 80 cm in height but is often considerably shorter at high elevations. Dense hairs make its stems felted and white and its narrowly oval-shaped leaves a pale gray-green.

FLOWERS: The yellow inflorescences are clustered at the tops of the stems. There are generally 4 disk flowers per inflorescence and no ray flowers. The yellow disk flowers have unusually long and skinny petals that spread out above the phyllaries. The 4 long phyllaries, covered in long white hairs and all the same length, are a good distinguishing feature; most members of the family Asteraceae have more of them.

❖ *Tonestus peirsonii* (Peirson's tonestus, Peirson's serpentweed)
       FAMILY: Asteraceae

DISTRIBUTION Occasional in the eastern Sierra from the Rock Creek Basin south through the Kearsarge Pass area; nearly absent from the western Sierra
HABITAT Alongside rocky outcrops or boulders, often in locations with some nearby moisture
ELEVATION 9,200'–11,800'
SEASON Early July–mid-August
LOCATIONS Long Lake (Rock Creek Basin), Tamarack Lakes (Rock Creek Basin), Upper Lamarck Lake, Table Mountain (above Tyee Lakes), Sawmill Canyon

LEAVES AND STEMS: Emerging next to rocks, the stout, bright-green stems reach to about 20 cm in height and are densely covered with white hairs. The leaves are generally wedge shaped with a margin that is distinctly, but irregularly, toothed near the leaf's tip. Most leaves are basal, but small leaves also clasp the stem.

FLOWERS: The stems are often unbranched with a single inflorescence at the end. The inflorescence is about 1.5 cm in diameter, with a relatively broad yellow disk surrounded by short ray flowers. The phyllaries form a quite deep spherical cup, extending down more than 1.5 cm.

❖ *Wyethia mollis* (mountain mule ears, woolly mule ears)
FAMILY: Asteraceae

DISTRIBUTION Common on both sides of the Sierra Crest in the Yosemite and Mammoth Lakes regions, becoming occasional in the Mono Recesses; absent farther south
HABITAT Dry slopes, especially common on metamorphic and volcanic rock
ELEVATION 4,000'–10,400'
SEASON Mid-June–early August
LOCATIONS Rancheria Mountain, Virginia Lakes Basin, Twenty Lakes Basin, Thousand Island Lake, Heart Lake (Mammoth Lakes Basin), Pinnacles Creek (above French Canyon)

LEAVES AND STEMS: The stems of this species are usually 30–50 cm long—but despite the height of the stems, you are more likely to notice the leaves. They have similar dimensions and—not surprisingly, given the species name—are shaped like mule's ears. They are gray-green and feel like flannel, due to an abundance of short hairs covering the leaf surfaces.

FLOWERS: The flowers are like bright-yellow sunflowers, with 6–15 yellow ray flowers, each up to 4.5 cm long and widest in the middle. The disk flowers are a slightly darker yellow. Each plant can have many stalks, with 1 to a few flowers per stalk.

❖ Global Climate Change and Alpine Plants

It is well established that the globe is warming, and this will influence where each plant species will be able to live in the future. One question is how the distribution of high-elevation plants will change. The hypothesis, likely to be supported, is that warming temperatures will allow lower-elevation species to move up in elevation, displacing some of the current high-elevation specialists; high-elevation species are often very slow growing and do a poor job of competing with other species in "good" environments. Alpine plants can tolerate the growing conditions at high elevations better than lower-elevation species, but this balance of power may change as the alpine zone becomes warmer and a more hospitable place for other species to live. Moisture availability will also play a role in future

(Continued)

(Continued)   plant distributions. It is expected that the Sierra will have drier, warmer winters but potentially wetter springs in the future. We can expect that species will respond in unpredictable and individualistic ways. One recent study showed that increasing precipitation over the past 70 years in dry eastern Sierra communities allowed some Sierra Nevada species to move down in elevation (*Wyethia mollis* [mountain mule ears], *Purshia tridentata* [bitterbrush], *Cercocarpus ledifolius* [curl-leaf mountain mahogany]), while others (*Ribes roezlii* [Sierran gooseberry], *Chrysolepis sempervirens* [bush chinquapin]) expanded upward, possibly due to increasing temperature.

A long-term global monitoring experiment is underway to quantify these shifts at high elevations. Abbreviated GLORIA, the Global Observation Research Initiative in Alpine Environments includes study sites in the Sierra Nevada, the White Mountains to the east, and other mountain ranges worldwide. The sites are repeatedly censused to determine how species compositions shift at different elevations across time. Detailed climatic measurements are also collected. Data summaries from the Sierra are not yet available, but data from the nearby White Mountains have already shown that three species also present in the Sierra Nevada—*Phlox condensata* (condensed phlox), *Trifolium andersonii* (fiveleaf clover), and *Eriogonum ovalifolium* (cushion buckwheat)—have become less common at the lower elevations within their range over the last 50 years. And unfortunately, having the data does not mean that we will be able to prevent high-elevation species from disappearing.

❖ *Barbarea orthoceras* (American wintercress, American yellowrocket)
   FAMILY: Brassicaceae

DISTRIBUTION Common throughout, on both sides of the Sierra Crest
HABITAT Stream banks, shallow streams, wet meadows, seeps
ELEVATION 3,000'–12,000'
SEASON Early June–early August
LOCATIONS Dana Plateau, Slate Creek Fork Lee Vining Creek, Bear Creek, Upper Basin, west side of Kearsarge Pass, Guitar Lake, Cottonwood Lakes

LEAVES AND STEMS: This is one of the few high-elevation plants often found growing submerged in shallow water. The bright-green to dark purplish-green leaves form a dense rosette. The leaves are deeply lobed, especially near the base of the stem, where they are pinnately lobed nearly to the midrib, while the tip of the leaf is often a single broader lobe.

FLOWERS: Though the flowering stems can exceed 60 cm in length, the higher-elevation individuals are usually 30 cm tall at most. Small, yellow, 4-petal flowers densely cover the top of the flowering stalk. The seedpods are bright green and fairly round, and they stick nearly straight up.

❖ *Descurainia californica* (Sierra tansy mustard)
FAMILY: Brassicaceae

DISTRIBUTION Common throughout the eastern Sierra, occasionally crossing into the western Sierra, mostly from the Kings River drainage south
HABITAT Dry slopes and flats
ELEVATION 5,500'–11,300'
SEASON Mid-June–early August
LOCATIONS Dana Plateau, Tioga Crest, Devils Postpile, Heart Lake (Rock Creek Basin), above Second Lake (North Fork Big Pine Creek), Kearsarge Pass Trail

LEAVES AND STEMS: This branched herb is at least 20 cm tall and often reaches 50 cm in height. At first glance, it looks like a nonnative weed—and indeed, many related species are invasive. The leaves are deeply and irregularly lobed, often forming a compound leaf with 5–9 wavy-margined leaflets. Short hairs cover the stems and leaves.

FLOWERS: Like all members of the mustard family, the tiny yellow flowers have 4 petals and 6 stamens. There are many flowers on the plant, occurring in small clusters on stems that grow from just about every leaf axil. The seedpods, called siliques, are shorter than those of related species at 3–7 mm long and 1 mm wide and are pointed at both ends, making them somewhat spindle shaped. The seedpods point upward along the stem.

RELATED SPECIES: Several other species of tansy mustard can be found in the high Sierra. *Descurainia incana,* mountain tansy mustard, has seedpods that are 10–35 mm long and point away from the plant, while *Descurainia incisa* subsp. *incisa,* also called mountain tansy mustard, has siliques that are 6–12 mm long. Both have seedpods that are not particularly pointed at the tips.

❖ *Draba albertina* (slender draba) **FAMILY:** Brassicaceae

DISTRIBUTION Common throughout, on both sides of the Sierra Crest
HABITAT Moist meadows, woodland, moist sandy flats, disturbed or open soil
ELEVATION 5,900'–12,200'
SEASON Early June–mid-July
LOCATIONS Gaylor Lakes, Garnet Lake, Rock Creek Basin, Lake Sabrina Basin, Kearsarge Lakes, Cottonwood Lakes

LEAVES AND STEMS: Reaching 10–30 cm in height, this species is one of the Sierra's tallest drabas and the least compact of the high-elevation species. Though there is a dense rosette of basal leaves, the plant does not grow as a cushion, and the stems are usually branched. The oval-shaped, light-green leaves are decorated with sparse but long white hairs. There are few leaves along the stem.

FLOWERS: The yellow 4-petal flowers grow in clusters at the top of the stalks. The seedpods are a very elongate oval, pinched at both ends, and up to 1.5 cm long.

❖ *Draba densifolia* (denseleaf draba)   **FAMILY:** Brassicaceae

DISTRIBUTION On both sides of the Sierra Crest, fairly common in the Yosemite region, then becoming more occasional south through the Palisades and absent farther south; rare in the Rock Creek drainage
HABITAT Talus, alpine fell-fields
ELEVATION 8,600'–12,000'
SEASON Early June–late July
LOCATIONS Gaylor Lakes, Mt. Dana, Mammoth Crest east of Duck Pass, Coyote Ridge

LEAVES AND STEMS: This species of diminutive draba is readily identified by its leaves. The fleshy, bright-green leaves are generally quite narrow and pointed, though they may be rounded. The faces of the leaves are hairless, while the leaf margins have long hairs—a trait known as ciliate. Of course, because the leaves are densely clustered, they can be difficult to admire individually. The midvein is obvious along the back of the leaf.

FLOWERS: The flowering stems can reach 10 cm in height but are usually less than half that. The 4 yellow petals of this species are so small that they barely extend beyond the sepals—even when the species is in full bloom, you notice only a fringe of yellow among the mass of green leaves and sepals. The seedpods are oval shaped, not twisted, and densely covered in branched hairs.

RELATED SPECIES: *Draba cruciata* (Mineral King draba) is another species of *Draba* that has leaves without hairs on the broad leaf faces. It occurs in the southern Sierra, especially common in the Mineral King region, and grows as a taller rosette rather than as a cushion plant.

❖ *Draba lemmonii* (granite draba, Lemmon's draba)   **FAMILY:** Brassicaceae

DISTRIBUTION Common on both sides of the Sierra Crest from the Yosemite region south through the Bishop Creek drainage, then becoming much rarer
HABITAT Talus, alpine fell-fields, typically in locations where late-lasting snow provides some moisture
ELEVATION 9,500'–14,400'
SEASON Early June–late July
LOCATIONS Virginia Lakes Basin, Mt. Dana, Mono Pass (Rock Creek Basin), Chocolate Mountain (Bishop Pass Trail)

LEAVES AND STEMS: A common species, this draba looks quite similar to the other granite draba (*Draba longisquamosa*), which first occurs south of the Bishop area and becomes very common in the Kern River drainage. Until recently, the two were considered a single species but are now considered two distinct species. Both are quite short, occasionally extending to 10 cm in height. This species' oval-shaped leaves are bright green with few to no hairs on the leaf faces, but stiff, long hairs cover the leaf margins. In comparison to *Draba longisquamosa*, these hairs are less stiff and sometimes slightly curving. In addition, the leaf faces may have a few hairs on them (versus none, ever), and some of those hairs might be branched. The midvein is not obvious on the leaves of this species.

FLOWERS: The yellow, 5-mm-wide, 4-petal flowers can densely cover the top of the plant in early summer. By later in the season, the plants are covered with oval-shaped, twisted fruits with scattered, unbranched hairs. By the time the fruits are large, the petals and sepals will have shed.

❖ *Draba longisquamosa* (granite draba)
  FAMILY: Brassicaceae

DISTRIBUTION Occasional in the western Sierra in the far southern Kings River drainage; occasional in the eastern Sierra from the Kearsarge Pass area south, becoming very common in the Kern River drainage
HABITAT Shallow seasonal trickles, wet talus and alpine fell-field locations
ELEVATION 10,400'–14,300'
SEASON Early June–late July
LOCATIONS Lake South America, Diamond Mesa, east and west sides of Shepherd Pass

LEAVES AND STEMS: Small rosettes of dark-green to purplish-green leaves grow in very wet locations. The leaves are crowded at the base and generally measure 5–8 mm in diameter. The faces of the leaves lack hairs, while the margins are densely covered in very stiff, straight white hairs; this trait is known as ciliate.

FLOWERS: A single flowering stalk emerges from the rosette, with an open inflorescence of tiny yellow 4-petal flowers at the top. The seedpods are slightly twisted and hairy. Even after the seedpods are fully formed, the wilted petals and sepals are still firmly attached to the flowering stalk, an important identifying feature for this species.

❖ *Draba oligosperma* (few seeded draba)
  FAMILY: Brassicaceae

DISTRIBUTION Fairly common from the Yosemite region south through the Palisades, on both sides of the Sierra Crest, becoming much rarer farther south
HABITAT Alpine fell-fields; seasonally moist, sandy slopes
ELEVATION 10,500'–13,400'
SEASON Early June–mid-July
LOCATIONS Mt. Dana, Convict Creek drainage, Piute Pass, Coyote Ridge, Sawmill Pass

LEAVES AND STEMS: The leaves of this species are thick, very narrow, and relatively long—an odd description for a leaf that rarely exceeds 1 cm in length and is often only half that. Sometimes the miniature rosettes are so dense that the individual leaves are difficult to spot. The leaf faces are covered with pliant white hairs, giving them a shaggy appearance.

(Continued)

(Continued)   **FLOWERS:** The 4 petals are about 5 mm in length, twice as long as the sepals, and tend to stand upright. The squat, oval-shaped fruits are not twisted and are subtlety inflated near the base, with the stigma forming a distinct point at the tip. The fruits are covered in long white hairs that are simple or forked just once.

EXTRA TIDBITS: This species is known to almost always reproduce by apomixis—in other words, new seeds form without the addition of any pollen.

RELATED SPECIES: *Draba sierrae* (Sierra draba) is common only around the Rock Creek Basin, and its range extends just a bit to the south. It is 1–4 cm tall with yellow flowers, and its twisted, asymmetrical seedpods are covered with forked hairs.

❖ Apomixis

Pollinators are less abundant in the alpine zone—even with the Sierra's warm summer temperatures and pleasant weather, life is tough at high elevations, especially for insects. This has caused many high-elevation specialists to turn to apomixis, or asexual reproduction. Apomixis can occur via various mechanisms, but in each case, a seed genetically identical to the parent plant forms. Some species may always produce seeds by apomixis, while others may shift between apomixis and sexual reproduction depending on climatic conditions or the abundance of pollinators. The term *apomixis* also includes plants that create offspring vegetatively: through spreading stems, underground stems, or roots.

Apomixis is one mechanism that rapidly leads to new species because a mutation in a single plant will lead to it leaving behind different offspring than all other individuals; if the mutant has quite different floral or vegetative characteristics and succeeds in establishing a unique population, it may be considered a different species. It is likely that the great diversity of Sierra species in the genera *Antennaria, Boechera,* and *Draba* is partially due to apomixis because many members of these genera depend entirely on apomixis for reproduction. Apomixis is also common in the genus *Hieracium*. Overall, however, it is uncommon for the unique mutant offspring to survive and spread, or we would have many more species.

❖ *Erysimum perenne (Erysimum capitatum* var. *perenne)*
   (sanddune wallflower)   **FAMILY:** Brassicaceae

DISTRIBUTION Common throughout, especially at high elevations
HABITAT Alpine fell-fields, sandy slopes, talus, sparsely forested slopes
ELEVATION 4,700'–13,500'
SEASON Early June–mid-July
LOCATIONS Mt. Hoffman summit plateau, Mt. Dana, Mono Pass (Rock Creek Basin), Rae Lakes Basin, Mt. Whitney Trail, New Army Pass

LEAVES AND STEMS: The sanddune wallflower is a common constituent across a broad range of elevations. It is usually 15–30 cm in height but can be twice (or half) that. Though its leaves and stems have short, branched hairs, the hairs are sparse, and the foliage is a fairly bright green. The leaf shape ranges from an elongate oval to nearly linear, and the leaf margins are sparingly toothed and sometimes slightly lobed.

FLOWERS: Each of the many yellow flowers is 4-petaled, with the wedge-shaped petals splayed wide open. The upper 5–15 cm of the flower stalk is densely covered with these flowers, each attached singly to the stem with an approximately 1-cm-long stalk, creating a large cylindrical mass of flowers. As the flowers age, the stigmas and styles are pushed upward by the elongating fruits. By midsummer the petals have all been shed, and the stem is decorated with numerous long, skinny fruits, each ranging 4–10 cm in length.

RELATED SPECIES: The lower-elevation wallflower, *Erysimum capitatum* var. *capitatum* (western wallflower), is common at mid-elevations throughout the western Sierra and is unmistakable with bright-orange flowers. Other than flower color, the two species look very similar, though the western wallflower is generally taller.

❖ *Rorippa curvisiliqua* (curvepod yellowcress)   **FAMILY:** Brassicaceae

DISTRIBUTION Common throughout, on both sides of the Sierra Crest
HABITAT Drying mudflats from seasonal tarns or receding lakeshores
ELEVATION 3,000'–11,500'
SEASON Mid-July–late August
LOCATIONS Saddlebag Lake, east side of Red Peak Pass, Island Pass, Rock Creek Basin, upper stretches of Bubbs Creek

LEAVES AND STEMS: This annual species extends to quite high elevations, growing later in the season as waterlines recede and create the muddy flats it prefers. The leaves, up to 8 cm in length, form a straggly rosette, each pinnately notched nearly to the midrib, the lobes themselves irregularly toothed.

FLOWERS: Multiple reddish flowering stalks emerge from each rosette. They are branched near the tips and bear many small, yellow, 4-petal flowers. The petals are tiny—less than 2 mm in length—and mostly hidden within the slightly longer sepals.

❖ *Lonicera involucrata* var. *involucrata* (twinberry)
      FAMILY: Caprifoliaceae

DISTRIBUTION Occasional throughout the western Sierra; in the eastern Sierra, occasional in the Yosemite area but absent once south of Mammoth Lakes
HABITAT Wet meadows, stream banks
ELEVATION 6,500'–11,000'
SEASON Mid-June–mid-July
LOCATIONS Lundy Canyon, Tuolumne Meadows near Lembert Dome, John Muir Trail near Bear Creek Junction, Bubbs Creek Trail near Vidette Meadow

(Continued)

(Continued)   **LEAVES AND STEMS:** This shrub can grow to nearly 1 m in height, with oval-shaped leaves ranging 3–12 cm in length. The leaf's stalk transitions into a quite thick midvein that very obviously runs up the back of the leaf.

FLOWERS: The yellow to orange tubular flowers occur in pairs and are surrounded by a green, somewhat cupped, leaflike structure called an involucre. The involucre remains after the flowers are shed and becomes red colored, with 2 purple-black berries sitting on it as a tight pair. Because the species blooms early, the black berries outlined by red is the view I always associate with this plant.

RELATED SPECIES: *Lonicera cauriana,* or blue fly honeysuckle, is mostly restricted to montane elevations, though it occasionally occurs in the subalpine zone. It is found along stream banks and in wet meadows, in locations including the Lyell Fork of the Tuolumne River, Gem Lake, and Charlotte Lake. Like all honeysuckles, its flowers occur in pairs; they are pale yellow to cream colored and fuzzy due to a coating of fine hairs. The berries are blue to black—and the two flowers together form a single berry. The leaves occur in pairs and are sparsely covered in short, stiff, white hairs.

Lonicera cauriana

❖ *Sedum lanceolatum* (spearleaf stonecrop, lance leaf stonecrop)
   FAMILY: Crassulaceae

DISTRIBUTION Occasional throughout, on both sides of the Sierra Crest
HABITAT Flat granitic sands that are moist early season, moist fell-fields
ELEVATION 7,000'–12,000'
SEASON Early June–early August
LOCATIONS Mt. Dana, Mono Pass (Rock Creek Basin), Coyote Ridge, Kearsarge Pass Trail, Lake South America Trail

LEAVES AND STEMS: A cluster of 1 to a few red stems, up to 20 cm in height, emerges from the root, each densely covered in small, fleshy, often reddish leaves that are pointy tipped and somewhat inwardly cupped, making them appear nearly as thick as they are broad. The stem leaves wither early, often before the flowers open. This species, unlike the Sierra stonecrop, has basal leaves similarly narrow to the stem leaves.

FLOWERS: A cluster of many flowers tops each flowering stalk. The 5-petal flowers have wide-open, pointy-tipped petals, resembling bright stars. Each petal is slightly folded along the midrib and has a thick red line (vein) down its back that is very apparent in bud.

❖ *Sedum obtusatum* subsp. *obtusatum* (Sierra stonecrop)   **FAMILY:** Crassulaceae

DISTRIBUTION Common west of the Sierra Crest; nearly absent in the eastern Sierra, especially south of Mammoth Lakes
HABITAT Moist (or seasonally moist) cracks and seeps in granite outcrops
ELEVATION 5,000'–12,000'
SEASON Early June–early August
LOCATIONS Tioga Tarns, Tenaya Peak, Upper Ottoway Lake, Garnet Lake, Evolution Canyon

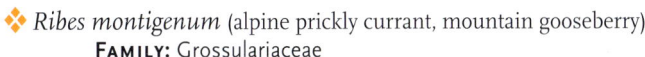

LEAVES AND STEMS: The leaves and flowering stems of this succulent emerge from cracks in granite outcrops in dense rosettes. The fleshy, slightly cupped, 0.5- to 3-cm-long leaves are broad, slightly reddish at the tip, and tapered at base. While there are many leaves at ground level, the red flowering stems are sparsely covered in narrower leaves, which wilt early.

FLOWERS: Each flowering stalk is comprised of 1 to a few branches, each with many flowers. The flowers have 5 yellow, 0.5- to 1-cm-long petals that are fairly blunt tipped with a distinct midvein that reddens with age. Unlike *Sedum lanceolatum,* the petals do not open as broadly; the flowers instead have a basal cup with just the petal tips bent wide open. The fruits, like all members of the genus *Sedum,* are a deep red and are shaped like miniature bowling pins.

❖ *Ribes montigenum* (alpine prickly currant, mountain gooseberry)
    FAMILY: Grossulariaceae

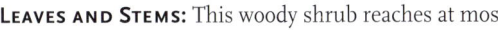

DISTRIBUTION Common throughout, on both sides of the Sierra Crest
HABITAT Open forest floor, especially under lodgepole pines; extending into the alpine zone in sheltered, slightly moist locations
ELEVATION 6,500'–12,500'
SEASON Early June–early July
LOCATIONS Cathedral Lakes, Rock Creek Basin, Evolution Valley, John Muir Trail north of Vidette Meadow

LEAVES AND STEMS: This woody shrub reaches at most 1 m in height but is often much shorter, spreading along the ground. The stems are best avoided: There are up to 5 thorns attached to the stem at each leaf node and many smaller ones in between! The leaves are shiny and dotted with glands. They are roundish, with 3–5 deep lobes cutting more than halfway to the center of the leaf and additional shallow indentations just a quarter of the way in.

FLOWERS: The flowers of this species generally grow in groups of 5. As with all currants, a showy calyx provides most of the flower color. In this species, pale, yellow-orange (to green, salmon-colored, or even red) sepal tips are splayed open in a bowl shape, while the center of the flower is a darker orange-red. The petals are minute red blades that emerge alternately from the base of the sepals. The ovary, which extends beneath the sepals, is bristly, a trait that remains as it develops into the quite small, red-orange fruits. They are generally quite seedy and dry, but edible.

❖ *Hypericum anagalloides* (tinker's penny, creeping St. John's wort)
    FAMILY: Hypericaceae

DISTRIBUTION Fairly common throughout, on both sides of the Sierra Crest
HABITAT Seeps, lakeshores, moist meadows
ELEVATION 4,000'–11,000'

(Continued)

(Continued)   **SEASON** Late June–early August
LOCATIONS Twenty Lakes Basin, Upper Ottoway Lake, Rock Creek Basin, Rae Lakes Basin

LEAVES AND STEMS: Growing as either a great mat of leaves or as a few trailing stems, this is quite a small plant. The stems range 3–30 cm in length but rarely rise above ground level, and the oval- to round-shaped leaves, which cover the entire stem, are usually less than 1.5 cm long. The leaf surfaces have small glands on them, making them a bit glittery in the sunlight.

FLOWERS: The small flowers are bright yellow. The 5 fused-together petals are 2–4 mm long and spread wide open. At the center of the flower, the green ovary is obvious and is surrounded by 15–25 stamens. Though the flowers grow singly, a mat of leaves may be decorated by many yellow dots.

RELATED SPECIES: The closely related *Hypericum scouleri* (previously *Hypericum formosum* var. *scouleri*; Scouler's St. John's wort) is a much larger plant, reaching 20–70 cm in height. Its flowers are bright yellow, measure 2 cm in diameter, and have a great cluster of long yellow stamens at the center, looking almost like a feather duster. This species is more common at lower elevations but occurs along Mono Creek and Palisade Creek along the John Muir Trail.

Hypericum scouleri

❖ *Mentzelia laevicaulis* (smoothstem blazing star)   **FAMILY:** Loasaceae

DISTRIBUTION Occasional throughout the eastern Sierra; mostly absent in the western Sierra
HABITAT Dry, sandy, open slopes
ELEVATION 4,000'–9,700'
SEASON Mid-July–late August
LOCATIONS Convict Lake, Pine Creek Trail, Tehipite Valley, Kern Plateau

LEAVES AND STEMS: This perennial can approach 1 m in height. Its stems are white and densely covered with minute hairs. The elongate, triangular leaves, which are deeply sharp toothed, clasp the stems, as they lack a stalk.

FLOWERS: Desert regions and the lower-elevation Sierra have many small members of the genus *Mentzelia*. The blazing star stands out because its vibrant, shiny yellow flowers are at least 8 cm in diameter. The 5 petals are shaped like narrow, pointed ovals and spread out in a very starlike pattern. At the center is a great cluster of stamens, adding an extra burst of energy to the stars. Because each stem has many branches, many of these flowers may be blooming simultaneously on a plant. The fruits, cylindrical in shape, form behind the petals.

❖ *Pedicularis semibarbata* (pine lousewort)
    FAMILY: Orobanchaceae (Scrophulariaceae)

DISTRIBUTION Common throughout the western Sierra; generally absent in the eastern Sierra
HABITAT Dry conifer forest
ELEVATION 4,600'–11,300'
SEASON Early June–mid-July
LOCATIONS Rancheria Mountain, Tuolumne Meadows, Bear Creek, Pear Lake

LEAVES AND STEMS: One of the few species to grow in bare soils in fir and lodgepole forests, this short species has an approximately 15-cm-tall stem and a spreading rosette of pinnately lobed leaves tinged a purplish-green with red-purple midribs. The 8- to 15-cm-long leaves are lobed nearly to the midrib, and each lobe is then toothed. In addition, there are stem leaves, much smaller than the leaves in the basal rosette and much less toothed.

FLOWERS: The tubular yellow flowers emerge from most leaf nodes on the stem, creating a dense, leafy inflorescence. The flowers are 1.5–2.5 cm long, but much of that length is often buried among the leaves, with only the tip emerging. The bottom 3 petals are a bright yellow, while the upper 2 petals form a yellow hood, sometimes of a much paler color.

❖ *Mimulus floribundus* (manyflowered monkeyflower)
    FAMILY: Phrymaceae (Scrophulariaceae)

DISTRIBUTION Common throughout montane elevations in the western Sierra, with scattered specimens occurring at quite high elevations; rare in the eastern Sierra
HABITAT Moist locations, often among rocks
ELEVATION 500'–11,000'
SEASON Mid-June–early August
LOCATIONS Mono Recesses, Evolution Valley, Rae Lakes Basin

LEAVES AND STEMS: An annual species, the manyflowered monkeyflower is quite variable in stature, sometimes a small unbranched plant rising less than 10 cm and other times with many sprawling branches and exceeding 30 cm in height. The oval-shaped leaves occur in pairs, and their margins are lobed or toothed.

FLOWERS: The yellow flowers are long and narrow, with a 3- to 8-mm-long calyx and a flower tube that sticks far beyond the calyx, reaching up to 15 mm in length. The floral tube is quite narrow and often has pale-red veins running along its length. The petal lobes are less asymmetrical than those in many other monkeyflowers, and there are red spots near the opening of the flower tube.

RELATED SPECIES: *Mimulus moschatus,* or musk monkeyflower, is a similar-looking perennial species common at montane elevations, occasionally occurring at higher elevations, including the head of Green Creek (Summit Lake) and at May Lake. The completely yellow flower has a long narrow tube and petal lobes that are nearly symmetrical. The oval-shaped leaves are covered in soft hairs and often a brilliant light green color, readily visible because this species often grows in large patches in wet locations.

Mimulus moschatus

❖ *Mimulus guttatus* (common yellow monkeyflower)
      FAMILY: Phrymaceae (Scrophulariaceae)

DISTRIBUTION Common throughout, on both sides of the Sierra Crest
HABITAT Stream banks, marshy areas
ELEVATION 500'–10,500'
SEASON Early July–early August
LOCATIONS Saddlebag Lake, Gem Lake, Reds Meadow, trail below Rock Creek Lake, North Lake trailhead, Rae Lakes Basin

LEAVES AND STEMS: This perennial species grows in dense patches along stream banks or seeps or singly along a creek. At montane elevations, the stems can approach 50 cm in length, while at higher elevations, they are typically shorter. The lower portions of the stems are well covered in green leaves that are nearly round to oval shaped and occur in pairs. The leaves lack a stalk, so they look a little like a figure eight with the main stem in the middle. The leaves usually, but not always, have teeth along their outer edge.

FLOWERS: The yellow tubular flowers, up to 4 cm in length, grow in pairs all the way up the stem, continuing to open at the top as they finish at the bottom. The calyx is red spotted and angular, and the flower tube is nearly twice as long as the calyx. The lobes of the 5 fused petals bend open and even downward, so the mouth of the tube is almost a raised platform, speckled with red dots and long yellow hairs.

EXTRA TIDBITS: The hair-covered lumps on the lower lip resemble an anther, perhaps enticing insects.

❖ *Mimulus nanus* var. *mephiticus* (skunky monkeyflower)

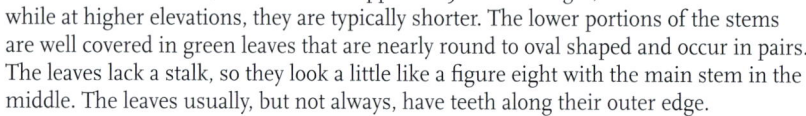

see page 191

❖ So Many Monkeyflowers

The genus *Mimulus* has 63 species in California and approximately double that in the western United States, with a few additional species occurring outside the country. Many of these species have evolved in the last million years, quite recently on the scale of species formation. Evolutionary biologists and ecologists are curious about how so many different species can arise so quickly. They also ponder how the species can then co-exist in the same location: Recently diverged species can usually still interbreed, so if they share a pollinator, the genes of such species are constantly mixed, or hybridized, blurring the distinction between the species (see "Hybrids," page 233). Even if the species cannot interbreed, pollinators may indiscriminately visit closely related species, constantly mixing pollen between the different species in a single location, wasting this precious resource. The monkeyflower species minimize hybridization or mis-pollination in numerous ways, a few of which have been carefully researched.

   One study looked at eight pairs of *Mimulus* species; in each pair, the two species were each other's closest relatives and lived in the same location. A careful analysis of flower dimensions showed that, in six of the eight pairs, one of the species had much smaller flowers than the other did, a difference that was not seen when closely related species live in different locations. Previous studies have shown that smaller flowers are more likely to be self-pollinated, meaning that the flowers pollinate their own stigmas, rather than receiving pollen from a different individual; this is a strategy to avoid mixing your pollen with close relatives, maintaining the divisions between species. Indeed, four of the small flowers had stamens that were taller than their carpels, an easy way to deposit pollen on your own stigma and minimize hybridization.

A second study compared *Mimulus guttatus* (common yellow monkeyflower) with *Mimulus bicolor* (yellow and white monkeyflower), an endemic to lower elevations in the Sierra. *Mimulus bicolor* has two forms: an all-yellow variant, which looks much like *Mimulus guttatus,* and a variant where only the two top petals are yellow. *Mimulus bicolor* that grows in patches together with *Mimulus guttatus* has more white-petaled variants, which results in less pollen mixing between the two species and greater seed production, likely because the two coloration patterns attract different pollinators. However, in areas without *Mimulus guttatus,* the *Mimulus bicolor* plants are mostly pure yellow because this variant produces more seeds when *Mimulus guttatus* is absent and there is no pollinator competition. Such studies show how pollinator preference for specific floral characteristics, as well as small differences in the number of seeds produced under various conditions, affect which flowers grow together—and makes me contemplate how many complex, but unseen, interactions occur in every location.

❖ *Mimulus primuloides* var. *primuloides* (primrose monkeyflower)
FAMILY: Phrymaceae (Scrophulariaceae)

DISTRIBUTION Common throughout, on both sides of the Sierra Crest
HABITAT Damp areas, including moist meadows, stream banks, seeps
ELEVATION 5,200'–12,000'
SEASON Early July–mid-August
LOCATIONS Lyell Canyon, John Muir Trail south of Red Cones, Rock Creek Basin, Evolution Basin

LEAVES AND STEMS: Rosettes of 1- to 2-cm-long, oval-shaped (to slightly more elongate) leaves carpet (or dot) the ground. The very light-green leaves are densely covered in long hairs, which hold the dew. I often first notice a patch of primrose monkeyflowers when my eye catches the glistening dew.

FLOWERS: From the center of each rosette rises a single red flowering stem, rarely more than 10 cm long. At its top is the upright flower: first, the narrow, red-striped, angular calyx and inside it the 1- to 1.5-cm-long yellow tube. The flower lobes are bent back at their tips, making the flowers especially showy as you stare down on the bright-yellow petals and yellow hairs at the mouth of the tube. 3 of the petals commonly have a single red spot (and maybe a few smaller speckles), while the other 2 are pure yellow.

❖ *Mimulus suksdorfii* (Suksdorf's monkeyflower)
    FAMILY: Phrymaceae (Scrophulariaceae)

DISTRIBUTION Common throughout, especially at higher elevations
HABITAT Moist, sunny locations with bare soil but prefers richer soils than other monkeyflowers
ELEVATION 5,500'–13,000'
SEASON Early July–early August
LOCATIONS West slope of Mt. Dana, west side of Long Lake (Rock Creek Basin), Palisade Basin, Rae Lakes Basin, John Muir Trail west of Center Peak, Cottonwood Lakes

LEAVES AND STEMS: This miniature annual is usually 1–6 cm in height. The leaves and stem are a dark reddish-green and covered with very short, glandular hairs that sparkle in the sun. Because the plant is so short, the leaves are densely clustered at ground level. It prefers well-developed soils and is more common at meadow edges than on sandy flats.

FLOWERS: The tiny yellow flowers are only 5–6 mm long, with the end of the flower tube opening into a distinctly 2-lipped form, with the front center petal considerably longer than the others. Each of the 5 petal lobes is slightly notched, and the opening to the flower tube is decorated with red splotches. The narrow, vibrant-red calyx features distinct ridges. A 2- to 8-mm-long stalk connects each flower to the main stem.

❖ *Mimulus tilingii* (Tiling's monkeyflower, larger mountain monkeyflower)
    FAMILY: Phrymaceae (Scrophulariaceae)

DISTRIBUTION Common throughout, on both sides of the Sierra Crest
HABITAT Seeps; stream banks; shallow, rocky streams
ELEVATION 4,700'–12,000'
SEASON Mid-July–early September
LOCATIONS Great Sierra Tunnel (near Bennettville), Ruby Lake (Rock Creek Basin), John Muir Trail south of Muir Pass, Rae Lakes Basin

LEAVES AND STEMS: This species commonly appears as a large mound or spreading mat of leaves and flowers, with individual stems rarely visible above the general mass of leaves. The leaves, which attach to the stem in pairs, are fairly oval shaped but a bit broader at the base. The leaves are quite thin, toothed around much of their perimeter, and may either be covered in sticky hairs or lack hairs altogether.

FLOWERS: The 3- to 4.5-cm-long yellow flowers have the characteristic monkeyflower look: A floral tube widens dramatically at the mouth, where 5 large petal lobes are bent back, providing a good view into the tube of a collection of red dots at its top. Like the common yellow monkeyflower, the lower petal lobes are bent dramatically downward, creating a platform at the tube's mouth. The red-spotted, angular calyx is about half as long as the flower tube. There are generally 1–5 flowers per stem, with just 1 flower joining at the uppermost leaf—this is an important feature to look for, as it distinguishes *Mimulus tilingii* from the closely related *Mimulus guttatus*.

❖ *Eriogonum incanum* (frosted wild buckwheat)
FAMILY: Polygonaceae

DISTRIBUTION Common throughout, on both sides
of the Sierra Crest, becoming very common at high
elevations
HABITAT Alpine fell-fields, sandy flats
ELEVATION 6,000'–13,100'
SEASON Late June–mid-August
LOCATIONS Twenty Lakes Basin, north side of Donohue
Pass, Evolution Basin, Bishop Lake, Kearsarge Lakes,
Mt. Whitney Trail

LEAVES AND STEMS: The wild buckwheat species are
notoriously difficult to distinguish among each other, but fortunately each of the
common species in the High Sierra has a unique look—and photos are generally all you
need to identify them. This species grows as a diffuse mat, with flower stems usually
extending upward 10–20 cm, but they can very occasionally be twice as tall or much
less, as seen in the photo. The leaves are spade shaped and up to 1.5 cm long, including
the stalk. They are so densely covered in long white hairs that they have a felted appearance, known as tomentose, on both the fronts and backs of the leaves.

FLOWERS: At the end of each flowering stalk is a dense spherical ball of yellow flowers,
an umbel. Each individual flower is just a few millimeters tall, with the petals fused at the
base and lobed at the tips. If you think that the flowers look quite variable in size, you are
correct; individuals sometimes have flowers with both stamens and pistils, while others
have just stamens or just pistils. The pistillate flowers can be 4–6 mm long, twice as big
as the plants with only stamens. Note that the female flowers turn red as they go to seed.
Note also that, though the inflorescences are usually compact, they can occasionally be
compound umbels, with stalks leading to several smaller, straggly umbels of flowers. This
arrangement becomes more obvious as the plants go to seed and elongate.

❖ *Eriogonum rosense* (Mount Rose wild buckwheat, rosy buckwheat)
FAMILY: Polygonaceae

DISTRIBUTION Occasional in the eastern Sierra from
the Yosemite region south to the Bishop Creek drainage;
absent in the western Sierra
HABITAT Sandy or gravelly flats, typically on
metamorphic rock
ELEVATION 7,000'–13,000'
SEASON Early July–late August
LOCATIONS North side of Lundy Pass, Dana Plateau,
Mono Pass (Yosemite), San Joaquin Mountain,
Coyote Ridge, Chocolate Peak

LEAVES AND STEMS: A specialist on non-granitic rocks, this species grows as a loose,
spreading mat; there are large stretches of sand or even other plants between the
clusters of leaves, but the dispersed rosettes are connected by underground stems. The
leaves are only 0.5–1.5 cm in length, shaped like elongate ovals and pointed upward.

(Continued)

(Continued)   The leaves are nearly as densely covered in long hairs as Sierra cushion wild buckwheat and frosted wild buckwheat are, but the color of the leaves is a little more green than white, especially on the backside of the leaves.

FLOWERS: The short flowering stems rarely reach more than 5 cm in height and are topped by a dense ball of brilliant light-yellow flowers, from which emerge yellow stamens; even the anthers at the tips are yellow. More so than any of the other matted buckwheat species, the flowering stems tend to point directly upward. Note that the flowers turn a reddish hue as they fade.

❖ *Eriogonum umbellatum* var. *covillei* (Coville's sulphur flower)
    FAMILY: Polygonaceae

DISTRIBUTION Common on the northern Kern Plateau and just into the Mt. Whitney area; also common on the east side of Sonora Pass; absent elsewhere; additional subspecies described below
HABITAT Among rocks or gravelly flats
ELEVATION 8,700'–11,600'
SEASON Early July–mid-August
LOCATIONS Bond Pass (Yosemite), Tyndall Creek, Crabtree Creek, New Army Pass

LEAVES AND STEMS: This is one of the few cases where a variety is given a separate description in this book, but when you see Coville's sulphur flower, you will be surprised that it is part of the same species as other varieties of *Eriogonum umbellatum*. The spreading mat of leaves, often expanding to more than 20 cm in diameter, rises just a few centimeters above the ground and is a collection of many individual rosettes of 0.5-cm-long, gray-green leaves.

FLOWERS: The flowering stalks are usually 3–6 cm in length and are often covered in long, white hairs. The stalks tend to lie sideways and sometimes even flat against the ground. There are many flowers per inflorescence, but this plant does not have a dense sphere like many of the other alpine species. The 6-petal yellow flowers are cup shaped when fully open, with the stamens extending outward. Both the buds and the wilting flowers have a reddish tone, so most inflorescences will have a few red blotches.

❖ *Eriogonum umbellatum* var. *nevadense* (Nevada sulphur flower)
    FAMILY: Polygonaceae

DISTRIBUTION Very common throughout the eastern Sierra; in the western Sierra, occasional throughout, becoming common in the Kern River drainage
HABITAT Sandy slopes
ELEVATION 4,500'–10,800'
SEASON Early July–mid-August
LOCATIONS Virginia Lakes Basin, Tioga Pass, Minaret Summit, Rock Creek Basin, east side of Piute Pass

LEAVES AND STEMS: This tall, slightly spreading subshrub can reach 50 cm in height and upward of 20 cm in diameter. The basal sections of the stems are quite leafy, with tufts of 1- to 2-cm-long, narrowly oval-shaped leaves. The underside of the leaves is usually hairy, and the top can sometimes be as well.

FLOWERS: To identify this species, consider its scientific name *umbellatum,* which indicates that the flowers look like those in the Umbelliferae family, the old name for Apiaceae, the carrot family. Like the Apiaceae, this species of buckwheat has inflorescences that are umbels, with multiple short stalks diverging from a central point and radiating outward; there are also several readily obvious leaves at this central point. At the end of each stout stalk is a tight cluster of small yellow flowers.

RELATED SPECIES: Another variety of this species, var. *furcosum,* occurs below 9,700 feet in the Sierra. It is distinguished by being a compound umbel, rather than a simple umbel: At the top of each of the radiating stalks, instead of a single flower, is another cluster of radiating stalks, each of these topped by a flower.

❖ *Ranunculus alismifolius* var. *alismellus* (water plantain buttercup, plantainleaf buttercup)   **FAMILY:** Ranunculaceae

DISTRIBUTION Common in the Yosemite area on both sides of the Sierra Crest, becoming rare to the south; absent from the eastern Sierra south of Mammoth Lakes
HABITAT Wet meadows
ELEVATION 6,000'–11,200'
SEASON Mid-June–late July
LOCATIONS Gaylor Lakes, Tuolumne Meadows, north side of Vogelsang Pass, Tyndall Creek

LEAVES AND STEMS: Many individuals tend to grow together, so the small rosettes are dispersed across the ground, sometimes in dense patches. A good identifying feature for this species is its pinched leaves: The blade is shaped like a narrow oval, 2–4 cm long, and is attached to a quite long stem. You will be most successful in finding this species in early summer because after the snow melts, buttercups are one of the first species to emerge. This species, unlike the lower-elevation creeping buttercup, does not sprout roots from nodes along the stem.

FLOWERS: The flowers are classic buttercups: 5 bright-yellow, quite round petals that glare in the sunlight. (Petal number can sometimes vary from 4 to 6.) At the center is the stout green carpel surrounded by a dense cluster of yellow stamens.

❖ Glossy Petals

After many years of photographing plants, I have a mental list of plants that are difficult to shoot—those where the petals will almost always have blotched color or white spots because they are so reflective in the sunshine. Some of the chief offenders on my list are buttercups (genus *Ranunculus*) and their relatives. The how and why of glossy buttercup petals is also of interest to researchers, who want to determine why many buttercups are glossy and how this might be beneficial for attracting pollinators—the whole reason for having petals in the first place. To solve this puzzle, researchers have looked at individual cell layers in the buttercup petal, both to determine how each layer reflects light and how this affects what color we will see.

(Continued)

(Continued)   First, a little physics background to understand the two ways light can be reflected: Light can be back reflected, like a beam of light shone on a mirror where all the light bounces back off in a single direction, or diffuse reflected, where it bounces off in all directions. Back reflection appears glossy, while diffuse reflection is matte. The white spots often seen on buttercups, especially on the upper half of the petals, is sunlight back reflected off the surface of the petal or the base of the translucent first cell layer, just like a mirror. Next comes a layer of yellow pigment molecules dissolved in oil; light is also back reflected off these, visible as a glossy yellow. However, much of the light travels to the next cell layer, starch-filled cells, from which it is diffuse reflected. Our eyes see this as the intense matte yellow behind the gloss. As for the why—it turns out that bees are most sensitive to this exact wavelength, presumably making the flowers more visible to pollinators. And maybe I shouldn't be ashamed about the white splotches on my photographs because they capture an important ecological trait of the buttercups.

❖ *Ranunculus eschscholtzii* var. *oxynotus* (Eschscholtz's buttercup)
FAMILY: Ranunculaceae

DISTRIBUTION Fairly common throughout, mostly at high elevations
HABITAT Slopes that contain late-melting snowbanks
ELEVATION 9,000'–12,500'
SEASON Early June–early July
LOCATIONS West slope of Mt. Dana, Kuna Crest, east side of Lamarck Col, north side of Pinchot Pass, Baxter Lakes, Farewell Gap

LEAVES AND STEMS: The leaves, up to 3 cm wide, emerge from an underground stem, usually within a week of snow-melt. They are fan shaped and have many lobes or are sometimes rounder in outline and more distinctly 3-lobed. The thickish leaves are always a glossy bright green.

FLOWERS: The flowers simply glow yellow. 5 bright-yellow, waxy petals reflect the sunlight, and in the center, a dense cluster of yellow stamens surrounds the cone-shaped receptacle to which the many carpels are attached. At the height of blooming, the leaves can be completely covered by the 1- to 2-cm-wide flowers.

❖ *Dasiphora fruticosa* (*Potentilla fruticosa*) (shrubby cinquefoil)
FAMILY: Rosaceae

DISTRIBUTION Fairly common in the eastern Sierra from the Yosemite region south to the Bishop Creek drainage; occasional in the eastern Sierra from the Yosemite region south to the Mono Recesses; a disjunct population also occurs on both sides of the Sierra Crest around Sawmill Pass; absent elsewhere
HABITAT Moist rocky areas, meadow perimeters, open slopes
ELEVATION 7,000'–12,000'
SEASON Mid-July–late August

LEAVES AND STEMS: This densely branched shrub rises to 1 m in height. Two immediately noticed features are the new growth's reddish-pink color and the red-brown sheen of the older branches' scaly bark. Leaves are divided into 5–7 narrow, 0.5- to 2-cm-long leaflets with under-curved margins. Long, white hairs cover the margins and parts of the upper surface of the leaves, and the veins are deeply inset.

FLOWERS: The flowers are 1.5–2 cm in diameter and grow individually or in small groups at the end of branches. The 5 yellow, quite round petals surround a burst of 20–25 yellow stamens. It is the only shrub with yellow roselike flowers that you will stumble across at high elevations.

❖ A Bee's-Eye View of a Flower

The sun's temperature determines the spectrum of wavelengths at which it emits radiation. The most radiation is emitted within the wavelengths that humans can see, between 400 and 760 nanometers (nm); we see 400 nm as purple or violet and detect 760 nm as red, with the rainbow of colors in between. Radiation between 300 and 400 nm is known as ultraviolet (UV) radiation; we cannot sense these wavelengths, though most insects and many other animals can. Indeed, a bee can see radiation between wavelengths of 300 and 650 nm, spanning from UVA to orange but excluding red. In particular, they have the highest sensitivity at 340 nm (UVA), 430 nm (purple), and 540 nm (green to yellow). Because most flowers are dependent on insects for pollination (see "Pollinators," page 167), flowers adapt to entice insects, not us. We can see that bee-pollinated species are often purple or yellow, two wavelengths at which bees are most sensitive. We cannot, however, see the often-showy UV patterns superimposed on the colored petals that match the UVA sensitivity peak.

There are two common UV patterns on flowers, both of which point the incoming insect toward the pollen at the center of the plant. The first is a bull's-eye where the center of the flower strongly absorbs UV light, luring the bee toward it. (An object's color, as we see it within the human visible spectrum, is determined by which wavelengths are *reflected* from the object, but when we discuss UV patterns on floral parts, we are describing patterns of UV *absorption*, with greater absorption appearing darker.) The second pattern to attract insects is nectar guides, lines that lead from the edge of the petal toward the middle, which the bee can walk along to reach the center of the plant. In some species, including many violets, members

(Continued)

(Continued)   of the family Polemoniaceae, and some lilies, purple nectar guides are visible to us, while in many other species, the nectar guides are in the UV spectrum and only UV-seeing insects can detect them. Note as well that most insects, including bees, have poor image resolution, instead depending on contrast to locate the nectar and pollen at the center of the flower. Nectar guides that contrast strongly against the surrounding petal are therefore particularly helpful to them. (If you have never looked at pictures of flowers from a bee's-eye view, search the Internet for images of "UV bee flowers" to see what you've been missing.)

❖ *Geum macrophyllum* var. *perincisum* (large-leaved avens)
   FAMILY: Rosaceae

DISTRIBUTION Rare to occasional throughout, on both sides of the Sierra Crest
HABITAT Stream banks; moist meadows and forest
ELEVATION 4,200'–10,800'
SEASON Mid-June–late July
LOCATIONS Sawmill Walk-In Campground (below Saddlebag Lake), Dana Meadows, Rock Creek Basin near Mosquito Flat and below Rock Creek Lake, Bubbs Creek

LEAVES AND STEMS: This species is commonly 20–60 cm in height but occasionally much taller. The basal leaves, which are not visible in the photo, are long and pinnately compound with 5–9 segments. The leaves along the stem are usually 3-lobed and 4–8 cm in length; the lobes themselves are deeply toothed. Fairly long, white hairs cover both the leaf and the stem.

FLOWERS: The flowers occur on side branches along the upper part of the stem. Each flower has 5 yellow petals encircling an enormous mound of tiny green stalks, the styles from the many pistils. Surrounding them is a ring of about 20 stamens. The plant becomes even more striking as it goes to seed, when the mound expands to a near sphere, completely covered in the now-longer reddish-colored styles.

❖ *Ivesia lycopodioides* var. *megalopetala* (club-moss ivesia)
   FAMILY: Rosaceae

DISTRIBUTION Common in the Yosemite area (on both sides of the Sierra Crest) and in the Rock Creek Basin; occasional around Piute Pass and Bishop Pass (also on both sides of the Sierra Crest) and in the Kern River drainage; absent elsewhere
HABITAT Diverse habitats, from moist meadows to rocky areas, often growing in cracks in rocks at high elevation
ELEVATION 7,500'–12,200'
SEASON Late June–mid-August
LOCATIONS West slope of Mt. Dana, Parker Pass, Ruby Lake (Rock Creek Basin), Lake Sabrina Basin, Wright Creek

LEAVES AND STEMS: This is a rosette species, often with a perfectly circular arrangement of leaves emerging directly from the ground. The leaf stalks are long and narrow, densely encircled with miniature green leaflets, each only a few millimeters long and divided into 3 minute parts. Each leaflet is individually visible only with close inspection, giving the long, narrow leaves the appearance of a pipe cleaner.

FLOWERS: The flowering stalks bear 3–15 yellow flowers, each with 5 small (2–5 mm), elongate to round petals, offset from and larger than the 5 sepals. Flowering stalks, generally 5–15 cm long, range from green to distinctly red.

RELATED SPECIES: A second variety, *lycopodioides,* is common in the eastern Sierra from Yosemite south to Bishop. Its petals and leaves are both slightly smaller than those of var. *megalopetala,* and it grows in drier locations. In addition, var. *scandularis* occurs in the eastern Sierra and is occasional in the western Sierra from the Kings River drainage south, often in rockier locations. It reaches at most 15 cm in height and has smaller leaf lobes but has flowers quite similar to var. *megalopetala.* The 10–20 flowers per inflorescence are arranged in a dense spherical head.

❖ *Ivesia muirii* (Muir's ivesia, granite mousetail)
   FAMILY: Rosaceae

DISTRIBUTION Common from the Yosemite region south through the Middle Fork of the Kings River, on both sides of the Sierra Crest, becoming more occasional once farther south
HABITAT Open, sandy, or rocky flats; rarely on metamorphic rock
ELEVATION 9,000'–12,500'
SEASON Early July–early August
LOCATIONS Mono Pass (Rock Creek Basin), Brown Lake (from South Lake), Evolution Basin above Sapphire Lake, Upper Basin

LEAVES AND STEMS: The plant has the appearance of a clump of green-gray mouse tails—each leaf is completely enveloped by almost 100 leaflets covered in long hairs. Each leaflet is less than 1 mm long and completely indistinguishable from another.

FLOWERS: A round clump of 10–20 flowers sits at the end of each flowering stalk. The flowers are not showy—the 5 pale-yellow petals, about 2 mm long and less than 1 mm wide, sit around the edge of a shallow bowl, yellowish in color. The small petals and sepals (covered in long hairs) give the flowers a quite straggly appearance.

❖ Some Famous Botanists

A plant's species name (the second half of its scientific name) or sometimes a genus name may be a Latinized derivative of the name of the botanist who first found it. In other cases, the person who discovers a plant will name it after another person. The collection of commemorative names attached to California plants provides a history of botanical exploration during the 70 years when most California plants were "found" by Western scientists, with a handful of more

(Continued)

(Continued)   recent additions. The greatest number of species—and also the
most common species—bear the name of the earliest explorers.
David Douglas, a Scottish botanist, was among the first Europeans to explore the
Western United States, with expeditions in 1824–27 and 1829–32. More than 80
species are named for him, including 6 in the Sierra Nevada: *Chaenactis douglasii*
var. *douglasii* (dusty maidens), *Silene douglasii* (Douglas' catchfly), *Cicuta douglasii*
(western water hemlock), *Artemisia douglasiana* (mugwort), *Polygonum douglasii*
(Douglas' knotweed), and *Carex douglasii* (Douglas' sedge).

However, Douglas's botanical collections focused on areas to the north of
the Sierra, and William Brewer's party was the first to systematically explore the
Sierra, between 1860 and 1864, and therefore collected more species restricted
to the Sierra. Brewer has 12 Sierra plants named after him, including *Angelica
breweri* (Brewer's angelica), *Eucephalus breweri* (Brewer's aster), *Erigeron breweri*
(Brewer's fleabane), *Draba breweri* (cushion draba), *Phyllodoce breweri* (purple
mountainheath), *Lupinus breweri* (Brewer's lupine), *Mimulus breweri* (Brewer's
monkeyflower), *Pectiantia breweri* (Brewer's miterwort), and *Potentilla breweri*
(Brewer's cinquefoil). While numerous common species had been collected by
the end of these early expeditions, many more years of searching were required
to find all the species inhabiting the Sierra Nevada; indeed, botanists continue to
occasionally find new species today. Botanists whose work began slightly later may
have fewer namesakes, but their work is no less important.

- Asa Gray was one of the most prominent American botanists during the second
  half of the 19th century. A professor at Harvard, he made two collecting trips
  to the American West and has Sierra species *Ligusticum grayi* (Gray's licorice
  root), *Potentilla grayi* (Gray's cinquefoil), and *Lupinus grayi* (Sierra lupine)
  named for him.

- John Muir is probably best known for his conversation efforts and geologic
  studies in the Sierra, but he was also an excellent botanist. Though not associated with either an academic institution or any of the big scientific expeditions,
  he was an astute observer and left valuable notes on Sierran plants. Asa Gray
  named two plants in his honor: *Carlquistia muirii* (Muir's tarplant) and *Ivesia
  muirii* (granite mousetail).

- Alice Eastwood, a self-taught botanist, became the curator of the California
  Academy of Sciences herbarium in 1890, at the age of just 31, and remained in
  that role until 1949. She voraciously explored California, collecting thousands
  of specimens for the herbarium. Of the 14 species named for her, just 1, *Salix
  eastwoodiae* (Sierra willow), grows in the Sierra.

- Frank W. Peirson, a Southern California botanist who worked extensively in the
  eastern Sierra in the 1920s and '30s, has *Tonestus peirsonii* (Peirson's tonestus),

Oreostemma peirsonii (previously *Aster peirsonii*; Peirson's aster), and *Castilleja peirsonii* (previously *Castilleja parviflora*; Peirson's paintbrush) named for him.

🐌 Mary Dedecker, who lived in the Owens Valley, was an amateur botanist of the highest caliber, continually exploring both the eastern Sierra and the desert ranges farther east until her death in 2000. In addition to the desert genus *Dedeckera*, the Sierra species *Trifolium macilentum* var. *dedeckerae* (Dedecker's clover) was named for her.

🐌 See also "Carl Sharsmith," page 214.

And if this article has piqued your curiosity, visit **calflora.net/botanicalnames** for an exhaustive list of the origin of California plant names.

❖ *Ivesia pygmaea* (dwarf ivesia, dwarf mousetail)
    FAMILY: Rosaceae

DISTRIBUTION Widespread on both sides of the Sierra Crest from the South Fork of the San Joaquin River south through the high peaks of the Kern River drainage
HABITAT Alpine fell-fields, cracks in slabs, generally on granite
ELEVATION 9,000'–14,000'
SEASON Early July–mid-August
LOCATIONS Evolution Basin, Glen Pass, Mt. Whitney Trail, New Army Pass, Farewell Gap

LEAVES AND STEMS: This species has an underground stem, known as a caudex, that branches, so many tufts of leaves will emerge at the ground's surface from a single rootstalk. The leaves are up to 10 cm in length—though each leaf will appear to be a stalk covered in 10–15 pairs of tiny leaflets. Each of these leaflets is further lobed, giving the stalk the appearance of a bottlebrush.

FLOWERS: The flowering stems are quite variable in length—anything 3–15 cm—and usually trail on or near the ground. At their end is the inflorescence, a cluster of 5–10 flowers, few enough that they are individually discernible. The yellow petals are 2–3 mm wide, larger than most *Ivesia* species. But the most important distinguishing characteristic: They have 10 stamens, not 5 like the other yellow *Ivesias*.

❖ Sierra Nevada Endemics

An endemic species is one that is restricted to a specific area; a plant endemic to the Sierra Nevada is not found outside the mountain range. Of the 570 species (or sub-species) that grow above 10,800 feet in the Sierra, 47 are endemic to the mountain range. If the entire Sierra Nevada flora, not just the high-elevation species, are considered, a somewhat greater percentage, 14%, of species are endemics. An endemic species has most likely evolved into its current form in the Sierra Nevada. Since it became a distinct species, it has failed to migrate to and establish in locations outside the Sierra. There are many possible hypotheses for the lack of range expansion,

(Continued)

(Continued)   among them that no comparable habitats are available in nearby high-elevation areas, that a plant has a relationship with a specific local pollinator, or simply that there has never been a continuous pathway of appropriate habitat along which the species could migrate. Many of the endemic species produce seeds or new plants asexually, known as apomixis (see "Apomixis," page 120); asexual reproduction can rapidly lead to a new species if a mutation occurs. Interestingly, at high elevations, there are more Sierra Nevada endemic species in dry habitats than wet habitats, supporting the hypotheses that there are currently no high-elevation dry corridors available for Sierra Nevada species to disperse along and that the high, dry environments most distinguish the Sierra Nevada from the Rocky Mountains and the moister mountain ranges to the north (see "Biogeography of High-Elevation Sierra Plants," page 157). Genera in which there are multiple Sierra endemics include *Lupinus, Castilleja, Draba, Ivesia, Eriogonum,* and *Mimulus.* Some showy Sierra endemics to seek out include *Polemonium eximium* (sky pilot), *Aquilegia pubescens* (Sierra columbine), and *Ivesia pygmaea* (dwarf ivesia).

❖ *Ivesia shockleyi* var. *shockleyi* (Shockley's ivesia, sky mousetail)
   FAMILY: Rosaceae

DISTRIBUTION Occasional in the eastern Sierra from the Yosemite area south through the Bishop Creek drainage; absent elsewhere
HABITAT Alpine fell-fields; dry, rocky flats
ELEVATION 9,200'–13,000'
SEASON Late June–early August
LOCATIONS Lee Vining Peak, Duck Pass and the Mammoth Crest, Green Lake (from South Lake)

LEAVES AND STEMS: This species of *Ivesia* is often found growing as a large mat because the underground stem, or caudex, is branched. It has fewer leaflets per stalk than many other species do, with only about 5–10 pairs of deeply dissected leaves—appearing as circles of tiny leaves enveloping the stem.

FLOWERS: Unlike most species of yellow-flowered alpine *Ivesia,* this plant has only a few flowers per head, each on their own short stalk. The petals are minute—about 2 mm long and less than 1 mm wide—and are opposite the larger, triangular sepals.

RELATED SPECIES: *Ivesia gordonii,* alpine ivesia, is fairly common in the Yosemite area but absent farther south. It has just 5 stamens, and its yellow petals are 2–3 mm in length but very narrow and considerably shorter than the large, triangular sepals that overshadow the petals. Flowers occur in dense heads of 10–20 blossoms. There are 10–15 pairs of leaflets per leaf, making them not as leafy as many other species of *Ivesia.* In var. *alpicola* the flowering stems stand upright and are not reddish, while in var. *ursinorum* they tend to lie on the ground and are reddish.

❖ *Potentilla breweri (Potentilla drummondii* subsp. *breweri)*
 (Brewer's cinquefoil) **FAMILY:** Rosaceae

> **DISTRIBUTION** Very common throughout, on both sides of
> the Sierra Crest; mostly at high elevations
> **HABITAT** Moist to drier meadows, alpine fell-fields
> **ELEVATION** 8,500'–11,800'
> **SEASON** Mid-June–late July
> **LOCATIONS** Mt. Dana, Humphreys Basin, Lake Sabrina
> Basin, Bullfrog Lake (Kearsarge Lakes Basin), Harrison
> Pass, Mt. Whitney Trail

LEAVES AND STEMS: The once diverse species *Potentilla
drummondii* was split into three separate species, this being
one of them. Many features unite it with *P. drummondii*
and *P. bruceae,* the other two high-elevation species that were divided off. All three have
mostly basal, pinnately compound leaves with oval-shaped leaflets that are wider near the
tip. This species has 3–7 leaflets per side, covered in white hairs and palmately toothed
more than halfway to the midvein; the related species do not have palmately lobed teeth.

FLOWERS: The 5-petal yellow flowers occur in inflorescences of 3–15, though there is often
only 1 flower open at a time. At the center of the flowers are many carpels attached to a
green mound (the receptacle) and surrounded by stamens with wide, flat pollen sacs.

RELATED SPECIES: The related species *Potentilla bruceae* (previously *Potentilla
drummondii* subsp. *bruceae;* Bruce's cinquefoil) has leaves with shaggy gray hairs,
and its leaflets are pinnately indented about halfway to the midvein. It is common throughout, mostly near the Sierra Crest, becoming rarer in the Kern River
drainage. Meanwhile, *Potentilla drummondii* (previously *Potentilla drummondii*
subsp. *drummondi;* Drummond's cinquefoil) has leaves that are sparsely hairy or
lack hairs. Its leaflets are also pinnately indented only halfway to the midvein. It
is common in the Tioga Pass region but mostly absent farther south.

*Potentilla
drummondii*

❖ *Potentilla flabellifolia* (fanleaf cinquefoil, high mountain cinquefoil)
  FAMILY: Rosaceae

> **DISTRIBUTION** Fairly common on both sides of the Sierra Crest from
> the Yosemite region south to the Bishop Creek drainage, becoming
> rarer farther south
> **HABITAT** Wet meadows; moist forest floor and forest openings
> **ELEVATION** 8,000'–12,000'
> **SEASON** Mid-June–late July
> **LOCATIONS** Twenty Lakes Basin, Slate Creek Fork Lee Vining Creek,
> Clark Lakes, Rock Creek Basin, Little Five Lakes area

LEAVES AND STEMS: This species has a dispersed rosette of long-
stalked leaves. Each of the bright, glossy-green leaves is divided into 3 fan-shaped
leaflets, which have shallow, rounded teeth around the top section of the leaf margin.

FLOWERS: Flowers occur singly or in small groups on 10- to 30-cm-long stalks. With a
diameter up to 2.5 cm, the yellow, 5-petal flowers are larger than many other cinquefoils
and a darker and more intense yellow.   *(Continued)*

(Continued)   **RELATED SPECIES:** *Potentilla grayi* (Gray's cinquefoil) is a quite similar species that also has 3 leaflets; indeed, the two species probably hybridize. It is distinguished by having fewer, deeper lobes on its central leaflet and having leaflets that are not fan shaped. It occurs at elevations below 10,000 feet and is quite common in the Yosemite area, becoming more occasional to the south, and is absent in the eastern Sierra once south of the Rock Creek drainage.

Potentilla grayi

❖ *Potentilla gracilis* var. *fastigiata* (slender cinquefoil)
FAMILY: Rosaceae

DISTRIBUTION Common throughout but especially west of the Sierra Crest
HABITAT Dry (to seasonally moist) meadows and flats; dry, open forest
ELEVATION 4,500'–11,000'
SEASON Late June–late July
LOCATIONS Tuolumne Meadows, Rock Creek Basin, south side of Selden Pass, John Muir Trail near Woods Creek crossing, headwaters of Tyndall Creek

LEAVES AND STEMS: The leaves of this herbaceous species generally lie close to the ground. There are 5–9 palmate lobes, each wedge shaped, with rounded (or pointed) teeth along the entire margin. The leaves are hairy, giving them a fuzzy appearance.

FLOWERS: Flowers occur toward the end of 20- to 50-cm-long flowering stalks. The 5 yellow petals are distinctly rose-petal shaped. The petals surround a cluster of yellow stamens with paddle-shaped pollen sacs and the central cone, the receptacle to which the many slender (but minute—1–2 mm) carpels are attached.

RELATED SPECIES: There are two varieties of this species. The common variety, *fastigiata,* has leaflets that are lobed less than halfway to the midrib, while a second variety, *elmeri* (Elmer's or combleaf cinquefoil), which is restricted to the eastern Sierra and much less common, has leaves that are lobed almost all the way to the leaf's midvein.

Potentilla gracilis var. *elmeri*

❖ *Potentilla pseudosericea* (Mono cinquefoil, silky cinquefoil)
FAMILY: Rosaceae

DISTRIBUTION Occasional throughout, mostly near the Sierra Crest
HABITAT Alpine fell-fields
ELEVATION 10,000'–13,200'
SEASON Late June–early August
LOCATIONS Mt. Dana, Mono Pass (Rock Creek Basin), Coyote Ridge, Sawmill Pass, New Army Pass

LEAVES AND STEMS: This diminutive plant has short leaf stalks, and its leaves barely rise above the ground. The 2- to 6-cm-long leaves are a pale green—the leaf blade hidden behind long white hairs. It is difficult to count the 5 deeply toothed leaflets that comprise each palmate leaf because the lobes fold inward.

FLOWERS: Clusters of 3–10 small flowers grow from rather short stems that often lie on the ground. The 5 yellow petals are narrower than those of many other cinquefoils, and the tips of the sepals, a paler shade of greenish-yellow, are visible between them.

❖ *Sibbaldia procumbens* (creeping sibbaldia)   **FAMILY:** Rosaceae

DISTRIBUTION Fairly common throughout, on both sides of the crest
HABITAT Alpine fell-fields; moist, gravelly areas
ELEVATION 8,500'–12,200'
SEASON Mid-June–late July
LOCATIONS Twenty Lakes Basin, Dana Plateau, Piute Pass, Evolution Basin, Kearsarge Pass

LEAVES AND STEMS: This ground cover species forms a low spreading mat. Its leaf is divided into 3 wedge-shaped leaflets, and each of these leaflets are 3-toothed and sparsely covered with glandular hairs. The leaflets range in size from 0.5 to 2.5 cm.

FLOWERS: The tiny flowers are at most 1 cm across—and even then are easily missed, because the 5 yellow petals are about 3 mm long and 1 mm wide, much smaller than the sepals that lie behind them. One's eyes are often more drawn to the reddish color of the closed sepals—once the flowers have finished.

❖ *Viola pinetorum* subsp. *pinetorum* (goosefoot yellow violet, pine violet)
    FAMILY: Violaceae

DISTRIBUTION Occasional throughout the western Sierra; occasional in the eastern Sierra from the Yosemite region south to the Bishop Creek drainage but rare farther south
HABITAT Open slopes, forest floor
ELEVATION 4,500'–11,000'
SEASON Mid-June–late July
LOCATIONS Twenty Lakes Basin, western base of Mt. Dana, Mammoth Crest, North Fork Big Pine Creek

LEAVES AND STEMS: A diffuse rosette of leaves with distinct veins grows from the root. The blade is 2–5 cm long, tapered to the tip, and connected to the base by a stout stalk. The leaf blade is more than twice as long as it is wide. Though the leaves are occasionally unlobed, their margins are often irregularly lobed with a rather jagged appearance.

FLOWERS: Like all violets, including cultivated ones, the flowers have 5 petals: 2 skinnier ones at the top, 2 sticking out sideways, and a broader one facing downward and decorated with purple veins. In this species, the petals at the top are quite narrow and point straight up. This violet has yellow petals, though their backs are a purplish-brown.

RELATED SPECIES: The subsp. *grisea* has gray-hairy leaves and occurs sparingly in the southern Sierra on both sides of the crest up to an elevation of 12,100 feet.

❖ *Viola purpurea* subsp. *purpurea* (mountain violet, goosefoot violet)
    FAMILY: Violaceae

DISTRIBUTION Common throughout montane forests on both sides of the Sierra Crest, occasionally extending to higher elevations
HABITAT Open slopes, forest floor
ELEVATION 2,000'–9,500'
SEASON Early June–mid-July
LOCATIONS Virginia Canyon, trail to Heart Lake (Mammoth Lakes Basin), King Creek (west of Devils Postpile), Rae Lakes Basin

LEAVES AND STEMS: A slightly spreading cluster of leaves grows from the ground. The leaves are triangular in outline and sometimes longer than they are wide. The leaf margins are wavy and toothed and have obvious veins all the way to the leaf margin.

FLOWERS: The 5 yellow petals of this violet have a distinctive arrangement. The upper 4 petals are all similarly oval shaped and only slightly longer than broad. Of these, the 2 upper petals point diagonally outward, and the next 2, with slightly purple veins, point straight outward. A single, much broader petal with purple veins points downward.

❖ *Lilium kelleyanum* (Kelley's lily)
    FAMILY: Liliaceae

DISTRIBUTION Common to occasional from the Mammoth Lakes region south to the Kern Plateau on both sides of the Sierra Crest; absent in the Yosemite region
HABITAT Moist forest, stream banks
ELEVATION 6,500'–10,700'
SEASON Early July–early August
LOCATIONS Sotcher Lake, Rock Creek Basin, Bear Creek, east side of Piute Pass, Evolution Valley, Vidette Meadow

LEAVES AND STEMS: One of the Sierra's tallest and showiest wildflowers, this plant has stems that can reach up to 2 m in height. The leaves are attached in circles around the stem, or whorled. Each of the 4–6 leaves per whorl is shaped like an elongate triangle and is up to 15 cm long. Several whorls of leaves are toward the bottom of the stem, while the flowers dominate the top.

FLOWERS: Though each plant typically has about 15 flowers, on occasion there are 30 of the showy 4- to 6-cm-wide flowers. The 6-petal flowers are a brilliant orange, usually with maroon spots. The flowers point downward, but the tip of each petal is curved backward, showcasing the inside of the flower: the petals and the downward-pointing style and stamens. Each flower is attached to the central stem by a 2- to 5-cm-long stalk.

❖ What Is a Petal?

The most memorable part of any flower is its colorful petals, right? If you looked at the sketches of plants in the Introduction or have a background in botany, you will know that a "standard" flower has four parts, or whorls: sepals, petals, stamens, and carpels. In most flowers, the sepals protect the flower bud, and they tend to be greenish because they can often photosynthesize. The petals, the showy flower parts, attract pollinators; the stamens, the male reproductive parts, produce pollen; and the carpels, the female reproductive parts, contain the ovules that develop into seeds. From an evolutionary perspective, all plant parts are derived from—and obviously quite modified from—leaves. Some flowers have all four parts, but there are many exceptions and species where a "petal" is not a petal.

Look first at a "normal" flower, such as a cinquefoil (*Potentilla*), where the sepals, petals, stamens, and carpel are all obviously unique and immediately identifiable structures. Now, look at a larkspur (*Delphinium*), and at first glance you will notice that the sepals are missing. Look again, and note that the true petals are the quite small structures in the center of the flower, while the long purple "petals" are actually the sepals; now you will also understand why *Delphinium* buds are purplish. Or consider a member of Asteraceae, where sepals have been modified into the fluffy pappus—each of the many ray and disk flowers lack any leaflike structure (see also "Flowers in the Family Asteraceae," page 91). In other species, the petals and sepals are indistinguishable, though you will notice that some petals lie in a circle atop the other "petals"; buckwheats (*Eriogonum*) and many lilies (such as *Lilium kelleyanum*, Kelley's lily) provide good examples of this. If you stare carefully at flowers, you will realize that they are built many different ways.

In all flowering plants, the same genes that were present in the most primitive flowers are still involved in the development of each flower part. However, as indicated by the many ways flowers are built, the components that are included are different among families and has changed many times over millions of years. For instance, in some plant families, including Rosaceae and Ranunculaceae, the petals are most likely derived from stamens, while in other families, including Portulaceae and Liliaceae, they are derived from sepals. Indeed, current research suggests that petals in modern-day plants have many independent origins, with the division between what to call a *petal* and a *sepal* quite arbitrary at times.

❖ *Lilium parvum* (Sierra tiger lily, alpine lily)   **FAMILY:** Liliaceae

DISTRIBUTION Common at montane elevations in the Yosemite and northern Mammoth Lakes regions on both sides of the Sierra Crest, occasionally extending into the subalpine zone; absent farther south
HABITAT Moist forest, stream banks, wet meadows
ELEVATION 4,600'–9,750'
SEASON Early July–early August
LOCATIONS Lundy Canyon, Cathedral Pass, Upper Ottoway Lake, Shadow Lake

(Continued)

(Continued)   **LEAVES AND STEMS:** Rising to about 1.5 m in height, this plant features stems and leaves similar to those of Kelley's lily (see page 142), with 4–6 long-triangular leaves encircling the stem in a whorl. There are multiple whorls of leaves, mainly along the lowest third of the stem. Above, smaller leaves attach singly to the stem.

FLOWERS: There are 5–25—or even more—flowers per plant, each attached to the central stem by a long stalk that emerges from a leaf axil. The 6 flower petals point upward from the base, forming the shape of a tube, though the petals are not fused. The lower half of the petals (forming the tube) is a maroon-spotted yellow to orange, while the outer tips are an intense orange-red. Unlike in Kelley's lily, only the very tips of the petals are bent open, with the stamens and style extending just to the mouth of the tube. The flowers of this species generally point outward or upward, rather than downward.

❖ *Triteleia ixioides* subsp. *anilina* (mountain pretty face)
     FAMILY: Themidaceae (Liliaceae)

DISTRIBUTION Common in the western Sierra from the Yosemite region south through the San Joaquin drainage; mostly absent elsewhere
HABITAT Dry forest, open flats
ELEVATION 500'–10,000'
SEASON Early June–mid-July
LOCATIONS Tuolumne Meadows, Lewis Creek, Devils Postpile, Tully Hole, Bear Creek

LEAVES AND STEMS: The leafless flowering stalk is 10–35 cm in height, while 1–2 long, narrow leaves arise from the base, though these fade before the plant is finished flowering.

FLOWERS: The inflorescence is an umbel, with 3–10 shorter stalks radiating from the top of the main stem. The flowers at the end of these stalks are comprised of 6 narrow, pale-yellow petals, each with a purplish-brown stripe up the center. At the center of the flower are so-called appendages, little forked protrusions that are the same color as the petals. And an important trait to note: The stamens are short (about the same length as the appendages) and slightly variable in length, and the pollen varies from a striking blue to cream color.

RELATED SPECIES: A much-lower-elevation subspecies, *scabra,*
has yellow pollen; how these two pollen colors influence the two
subspecies' natural history has not been studied. In addition, related
species *Triteleia montana* (mountain or Sierra triteleia) occurs in the
Yosemite area and farther north. Two features that distinguish it are
that its stamens are much longer (all the same length), and its petals
do not open as widely.

Triteleia montana

❖ Pollen Color

A flower's petals might be what first catches our attention, but
pollen grains also come in a variety of shades due to the same
pigment molecules that tint flower petals (see "A Rainbow of
Flowers," page 95). Pollen most commonly appears yellow to
orange, but many plants also have white pollen, with fewer exhibiting brown or
blue pollen. There have been insufficient studies on pollen-color variation to fully
understand why such a diversity of colors exists. Comparisons between closely
related species with different pollen colors indicate that certain colors may help
attract the best pollinators, could keep pollen sufficiently warm (or cool) depending on sun exposure, or might simply be due to the pollen having similar pigment
molecules as the petals.

Most insects do not prefer a certain pollen color but instead are attracted to
pollen with a high saturation or chroma, indicating the color lacks white or black
and is therefore very vivid. The vividness makes the pollen stand out against the
surrounding petals, helping direct the insect to it. In addition, the pigment in
bright-yellow pollen absorbs UV radiation, causing the anthers to appear as dark
dots to insects, another way to highlight the pollen for pollinators. These UV-
absorbing pigments also shield the genetic material at the center of the pollen
grain from mutation-causing UV radiation (see "UV Radiation," page 37).

Among Sierra species, pay special attention to the two subspecies of *Navarretia leptalea* and *Triteleia ixioides*; in each pair, one subspecies has yellow pollen
and the other blue. Many other members of the family Polemoniaceae also have
beautifully colored pollen.

❖ Red and Brown Flowers

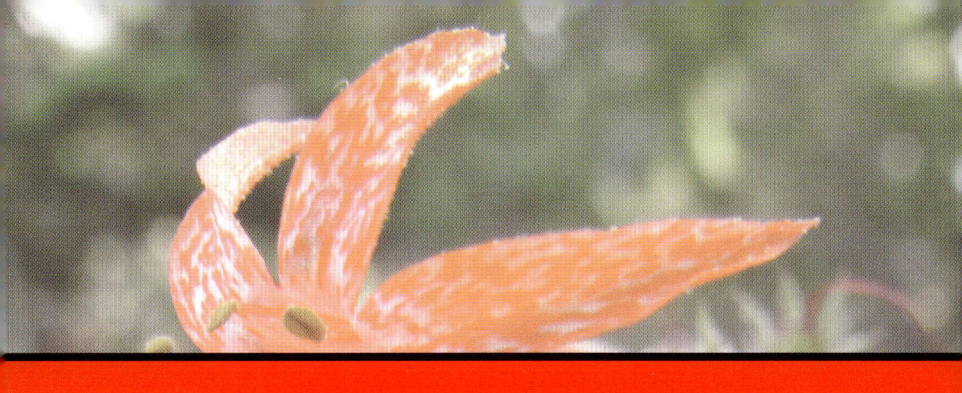

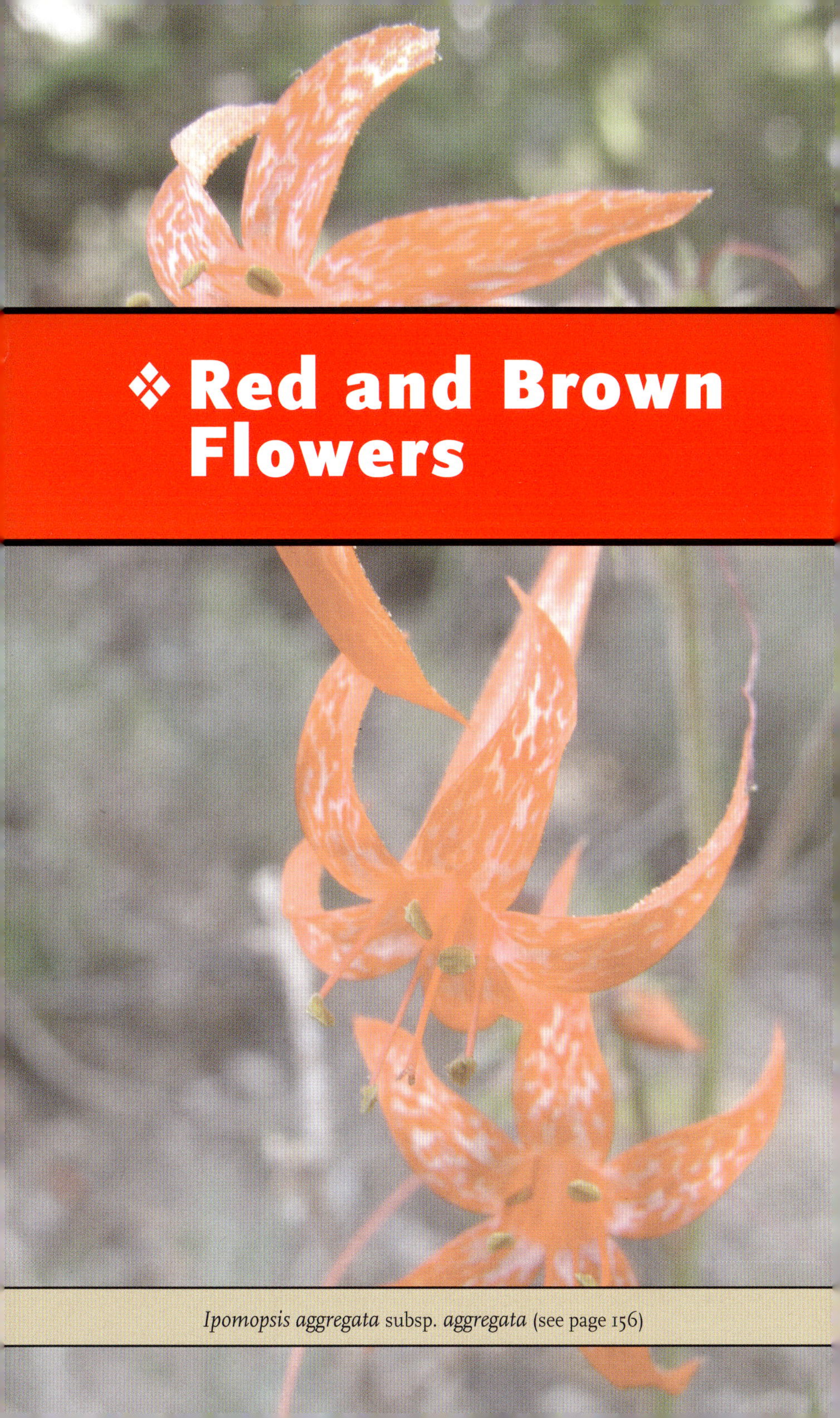

Ipomopsis aggregata subsp. *aggregata* (see page 156)

❖ *Artemisia dracunculus* (wild tarragon)
   FAMILY: Asteraceae

DISTRIBUTION Fairly common throughout the eastern Sierra; to the west of the Sierra Crest, rare in the Yosemite and Mammoth Lakes regions, becoming more common from Bishop south
HABITAT Dry slopes, flats, forest
ELEVATION 1,000'–12,000'
SEASON Late July–mid-September
LOCATIONS French Canyon, Coyote Ridge, Long Lake (Bishop Pass area), Taboose Pass, Vidette Meadow

LEAVES AND STEMS: Wild tarragon is a tall, herbaceous sagebrush, with its reddish, stiff stems reaching 50–150 cm in height. A defining characteristic of this species is the general lack of hairs on its stems and leaves. The long, narrow leaves may occasionally be divided into linear lobes.

FLOWERS: The many side branches are densely covered with tiny inflorescences, nearly spherical, usually reddish in color, and pointing downward. Like other *Artemisia* species, there are ray flowers, but the rays are so short that you'll barely note them. The green phyllaries have white membranous margins.

❖ *Cirsium andersonii* (rose thistle)
   FAMILY: Asteraceae

DISTRIBUTION Fairly common throughout, on both sides of the Sierra Crest
HABITAT Dry slopes, open forest
ELEVATION 2,500'–10,500'
SEASON Mid-July–early September
LOCATIONS Tuolumne Meadows, Thousand Island Lake, Devils Postpile, Rock Creek Lake, east side of Morgan Pass, east slope of Mt. Whitney

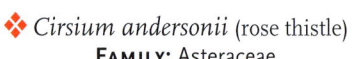

LEAVES AND STEMS: This beautiful thistle is hard to miss— it is usually 40–70 cm in height and very prickly. The leaves clasp the stem and vary from bright green to a duller color, depending on how many coarse white hairs they have. The leaves are deeply incised, somewhere between lobes and teeth, with the twisted lobes pointing in all directions and each ending in a long, white spine. The stout stems lack spines and are purplish-green in color—again often covered with white hairs.

FLOWERS: The flowers are a beautiful bright red to deep pink, with one inflorescence per stem and several stems per plant. Below the flowers themselves, the phyllaries form a bulbous shape; they too are spine tipped and often covered in cobwebby hairs. Above the 3- to 4-cm-tall disk flowers rise the long, pinkish styles, making the inflorescence stand a centimeter higher.

❖ *Rhodiola integrifolia* subsp. *integrifolia* (*Sedum roseum* subsp. *integrifolium*)
(ledge stonecrop, western roseroot)   **FAMILY:** Crassulaceae

DISTRIBUTION Common throughout, on both sides of the
Sierra Crest
HABITAT Alpine meadows, seeps, wet sand and talus,
slab edges, stream banks
ELEVATION 8,000'–13,000'
SEASON Late June–early August
LOCATIONS Twenty Lakes Basin, Rock Creek Basin,
John Muir Trail just north of Pinchot Pass

LEAVES AND STEMS: This species is easily identified by its
cluster of succulent stems, rising 10–20 cm above ground
level. Each stem is densely—and evenly—covered in flat,
fleshy, oval-shaped leaves that are truncated at the base and
often serrate at the tips. The stems and leaves turn a brilliant pink-red
in autumn, adding a splash of color to the drying meadows.

FLOWERS: The tips of many of the stems are covered in a dense cluster of flowers—
more than 30 is not uncommon. The buds are a deep purple, while both the petals and
the young fruits are a beautiful burgundy color—at first glance one mistakes the fruits
for flowers that are still in bloom. The flowers themselves have 4 (or 5) small petals and
usually 8 long stamens, while the fruits are bulbous and pointy tipped.

EXTRA TIDBITS: The roots of this species are fragrant, giving it the name *roseroot*.

❖ *Pterospora andromedea* (pinedrops)
    FAMILY: Ericaceae

DISTRIBUTION Common throughout the western Sierra;
occasional throughout the eastern Sierra
HABITAT Many different conifer forests, ranging from dry to
moister, open to dense
ELEVATION 4,000'–9,500'
SEASON Early July–early August
LOCATIONS White Wolf, Sunrise Creek, Devils Postpile
National Monument, lower stretches of Le Conte Canyon
and Palisade Creek

LEAVES AND STEMS: Pinedrops, like snow plants (see the next
page), are parasitic and obtain energy through fungal connections to nearby trees—not from sunlight (see "How Do Snow
Plants Get Their Carbon?" on the following page). The plant
parts you see comprise the flowering stalk, for the plant has
neither leaves nor a stem. From the time it emerges from the
ground, the stalk is elongate and skinny, rapidly expanding into
a pink to red stalk that can surpass a meter in length. Many stalks may emerge in
a small cluster from the same roots. The dead stalks from the previous year may be
in slightly different locations than the current year's flowers, indicating just how expansive the underground root network can be.

(Continued)

(Continued)   **FLOWERS:** Flowers densely cover the top one-fourth to one-third of the stalk length. The small cream to yellow flowers are dangling urns each topped by a red cap, the 5-tipped calyx, and a short red stalk. As the season progresses, they develop into small, round, red fruits called capsules, creating a very engaging decoration in the mid-elevation conifer forests. These stalks survive the milder winters and can be seen standing next to newly emerging flowering stalks the following season.

Allotropa virgata

RELATED SPECIES: *Allotropa virgata* (sugar stick) is a rare species, confined to fir forests with deep, rich soils. As its name implies, it looks like a candy cane, with red and white stripes spiraling up its stalk. Its stalk is notably pale and thick as it emerges. You may see it along the walk to Ostrander Lake or along the trail to North Dome from Tioga Road.

❖ *Sarcodes sanguinea* (snow plant)
    FAMILY: Ericaceae

DISTRIBUTION Common throughout the western Sierra; rare in the eastern Sierra
HABITAT Open to dense conifer forests
ELEVATION 4,000'–10,000'
SEASON Late May–late June
LOCATIONS Rancheria Mountain, Little Yosemite Valley, Ostrander Lake Trail, Devils Postpile National Monument, Quail Meadows

LEAVES AND STEMS: Like the related species pinedrops (see the preceding page), the snow plant is parasitic, obtaining energy from nearby trees, not from sunlight (see "How Do Snow Plants Get Their Carbon?" below). It has neither a true stem nor leaves—what emerges above the ground is a flowering stalk, or inflorescence. When the plants first emerge, they are entirely bright red due to the bracts (leaves that attach just below each flower in the inflorescence). The bracts tightly hug the stem, while the white stalk becomes visible as it elongates, eventually reaching up to 30 cm in height. The skinny red bracts are up to 3–6 cm long and often quite twisted or curled.

FLOWERS: The 5-petal flowers are the same color red as the bracts. The swollen urn-shaped flowers are 1–1.5 cm long with small petal lobes extending beyond the mouth of the flower tube. The flowers point straight out from the inflorescence stem. The fruits are round, red capsules (berry shaped).

❖ How Do Snow Plants Get Their Carbon?

Most plants create the energy needed to survive and grow through photosynthesis, a process that converts sunlight into sugars, a form of chemical energy that all living organisms can use. The green color in leaves, stems, and even buds is chlorophyll, the pigment that lets a plant capture the sun's energy for use in photosynthesis. There are, however, plants that lack green parts and the ability to photosynthesize, such as the snow plant (*Sarcodes sanguinea*) and close relatives, including pinedrops (*Pterospora andromedea*) and sugar stick (*Allotropa virgata*). These Sierra species, as well as orchids in the genus *Corallorhiza*, are known as myco-heterotrophs, with *heterotroph* indicating that they obtain their energy from another organism, not the sun, and *myco* telling us that the partner organism is a fungus. It is an elaborate relationship also involving nearby conifer trees, especially fir species. The tree's roots have one species of fungus growing on them, which helps the tree obtain nutrients and probably water from the soil, and the fungus receives sugars from the tree in return—a wonderful relationship that benefits both (see "Mycorrhizae," page 173). The relationship with the snow plant is a little less savory: The roots of the snow plant have a different species of fungus growing on them, which interacts with the tree's fungus, most likely in a parasitic manner, and co-opts the tree's sugars and nutrients. By a mechanism that is still being worked out, there is a flow of both sugars and nutrients through the second fungus into the snow plant. However, it is possible that the tree's fungal partner might become more abundant due to the snow plant's presence. As the story ends for now, the snow plant and its relatives can get away with being lazy, but beautiful bright red, plants.

❖ *Ribes roezlii* var. *roezlii* (Sierran gooseberry)
FAMILY: Grossulariaceae

DISTRIBUTION Common throughout montane elevations to the west of the Sierra Crest; absent in the eastern Sierra
HABITAT Various forest types, burnt slopes and openings
ELEVATION 1,500'–8,000'
SEASON Early June–early July
LOCATIONS Sunrise Creek, west of the Buena Vista Crest, Reds Meadow, Mono Creek

LEAVES AND STEMS: This shrub reaches up to 1.5 m in height. In comparison to other currants, the leaves are rather small (1.5–2.5 cm) and lack any glands or hairs. They are round in outline, with 3–5 rounded lobes that are indented approximately halfway to the center, with the 3 larger lobes each having 3 rounded teeth. There are 1–3 spines at each leaf node, but the plant is not overly spiny.

FLOWERS: The drooping tubular flowers present bright splashes of color—burgundy from the long, pointed, bent-back sepals and white from the narrow floral tube at the center. Emerging from the center of the petals are 5 stamens similar in color to the sepals. As with all currants, the base of the ovary is visible below the floral tube, and its bristles become increasingly obvious as it matures. The bristles are the precursors to the sharp prickles that will cover the bright-red 1.5-cm-wide fruits. Though difficult to obtain, the pulp from these berries is delicious—watching out for the prickles, cut one in half and suck out the insides.

❖ *Epilobium canum* subsp. *latifolium* (*Zauschneria californica*)
(California fuchsia, hummingbird trumpet)
FAMILY: Onagraceae

DISTRIBUTION Common throughout the western Sierra; occasional throughout the eastern Sierra, becoming more common south of Bishop
HABITAT Dry slopes, often alongside rocks
ELEVATION 800'–11,000'
SEASON Early August–late September
LOCATIONS John Muir Trail alongside Nevada Fall, Devils Postpile, Piute Canyon, trail to Golden Trout Lake (above Onion Valley), Farewell Gap

LEAVES AND STEMS: Though rare at upper elevations, this species is included because it is occasionally found there, and if you see the flower, you will certainly want to know what it is. Clusters of stems rise 10–40 cm in height, covered in opposite pairs of oval-shaped leaves that are a fuzzy soft gray-green due to a dense covering of hairs.

FLOWERS: The intensely red flowers grow from leaf axils near the tops of the stems. They have a long, narrow tube, and the 4 notched petal lobes then open broadly at the mouth—a stereotypical hummingbird-pollinated flower. The stamens and style are a similarly bright red.

❖ *Castilleja applegatei* subsp. *pallida* (wavyleaf paintbrush)
FAMILY: Orobanchaceae (Scrophulariaceae)

DISTRIBUTION Common throughout on both sides of the Sierra Crest, with different subspecies common in different regions
HABITAT Dry slopes, flats, forest openings
ELEVATION 1,200'–11,800'
SEASON Late June–mid-August
LOCATIONS Gardisky Lake Trail, Rock Creek Basin, Kearsarge Pass Trail, trail to Cottonwood Lakes

LEAVES AND STEMS: Ranging in height from 10 cm to more than 50 cm, the stems are generally purplish in color, mixed with patches of green. Though the stems are often unbranched, there are occasionally side branches—unlike most other paintbrushes. Most distinct are the green leaves, which bear sticky glands and have a leaf margin that undulates up and down—hence the name *wavyleaf*.

FLOWERS: The flowers form a dense head at the top of the stem and range in color from dark orange to an orangish-red. They provide less color than many paintbrushes, for the bottom half of the bracts (the leaves below each flower) and the calyx are often green, with only the tops vibrantly colored. While the calyx tube is 1.5–2.5 cm long, the petals form a narrow tube within the calyx that is about 1 cm longer, yellow on one side and red on the other, forming the narrow beaks you see extending from the mass of orange leaves.

❖ *Castilleja miniata* subsp. *miniata* (giant red paintbrush)
FAMILY: Orobanchaceae (Scrophulariaceae)

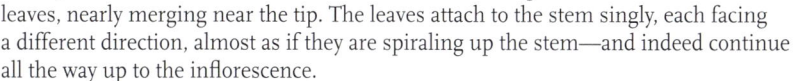

DISTRIBUTION Fairly common throughout, on both sides of the
Sierra Crest
HABITAT Stream banks, seeps, lakeshores, wet meadows
ELEVATION 4,000'–11,200'
SEASON Early July–mid-August
LOCATIONS Slate Creek Fork Lee Vining Creek,
Garnet Lake, Lamarck Lakes, Evolution Lake

LEAVES AND STEMS: The tallest of the Sierra paintbrushes, the
stout stems reach 40–80 cm in height. They are a bright green
and covered in soft hairs. The 3- to 6-cm-long leaves also have a
soft appearance and are broader and floppier than those of most
other paintbrushes. Three distinct inset veins run the length of the
leaves, nearly merging near the tip. The leaves attach to the stem singly, each facing
a different direction, almost as if they are spiraling up the stem—and indeed continue
all the way up to the inflorescence.

FLOWERS: This paintbrush comes loaded with reddish to orangish paint. Many of the
individual 2- to 4-cm-long flowers point more outward than upward, giving the paintbrush a broader stroke. Like all paintbrushes, the bright color comes from the calyx
and the bracts (the leaves below each flower), while the tube of petals is yellow, only
sometimes emerging beyond the calyx.

❖ The Paintbrushes' Dark Secret

When a plant lacks green parts, it is advertising itself as a carbon thief. Without
the ability to perform photosynthesis (the reaction that converts the sun's energy
into chemical energy in the form of sugars), the plant must get its carbohydrates
(sugars) from another organism. Some species, including the myco-heterotrophs
described in "How Do Snow Plants Get Their Carbon?" on page 150, are holopara-
sites, fully dependent on a host for carbon. There are also many thousands of partially parasitic species, called hemiparasites. Hemiparasites have green leaves and
are able to photosynthesize themselves but obtain at least some of their resources
from a host species; they generally attach themselves directly to their host's root to
steal nutrients, carbon, or even defense compounds. While it is difficult to assess
exactly what percentage of resources are self-created versus that taken from a host,
a study on *Castilleja miniata* (giant red paintbrush) parasitizing *Lupinus argenteus*
(silvery lupine) showed that *Castilleja* were acquiring alkaloid defense compounds
from the lupine, and possibly other resources. The paintbrushes that acquired these
compounds (versus those that were not allowed to be parasitic for the experiment)
were less damaged by insect herbivores and, as a result, were able to produce twice
as many seeds as nonparasitic individuals. (While both of these species grow in the
Sierra, this study was performed in the Colorado alpine.)

(Continued)

(Continued)   Another experiment, with *Castilleja* species that do not grow in the Sierra, showed that large quantities of water are lost to the atmosphere due to the mechanism the paintbrush species uses to pull carbon out of its host. This helped keep the paintbrush leaves cool under hot conditions but may deplete the surrounding soils of water, impacting other species. In addition to the genus *Castilleja*, most other genera in the family Orobanchaceae are hemiparasites (*Pedicularis*) or parasites (*Orobanche*). In the Sierra, the mistletoes (family Viscaceae) that grow at slightly lower elevations are also hemiparasites.

❖ *Castilleja peirsonii (Castilleja parviflora)* (Peirson's paintbrush)
   FAMILY: Orobanchaceae (Scrophulariaceae)

DISTRIBUTION Relatively common from the Yosemite area south through the Kings River drainage, but absent in the Kern drainage and the eastern Sierra south of the Palisades area
HABITAT Wet meadows
ELEVATION 6,500'–11,000'
SEASON Early July–mid-August
LOCATIONS Twenty Lakes Basin, Spiller Lake (near Bennettville), Thousand Island Lake, Lake Virginia, Rock Creek Basin

LEAVES AND STEMS: Generally growing as a small clump, this species can grow in abundance given the perfect marshy meadow— but otherwise is quite rare. The stems typically stand 15–30 cm tall, sometimes a little more. The color of the stems ranges from green to purplish, often grading from green at the base to purple at the tip. The leaves—also a mix of green and purple—are narrow triangles, covering the stem from the base to the flowers. They often, but not always, are covered in soft, white, glandular hairs that sparkle in the sun.

FLOWERS: Ranging in color from a reddish-orange to an orangish-pink, these beautiful paintbrushes have bracts and a tubular calyx that are the same color. While the calyx is 1.5–2 cm long, the narrow tube of yellow petals is at least 0.5 cm longer once the flower is fully open, and therefore extends beyond the calyx and gives the flowers a two-toned appearance. The large, dark-colored stigma emerges beyond the petals as well, adding a dot to the tip of each flower. This paintbrush can be distinguished from other species by the pinkish tinge to its petals, for both the wavyleaf paintbrush and the giant red paintbrush are purely red to orange.

❖ *Mimulus cardinalis* (scarlet monkeyflower)
   FAMILY: Phrymaceae (Scrophulariaceae)

DISTRIBUTION Occasional throughout, on both sides of the Sierra Crest
HABITAT Seeps and banks of shallow streams
ELEVATION 1,500'–8,500'
SEASON Mid-July–late August
LOCATIONS Pine Creek Pass Trail, Middle Fork Kings River, Taboose Pass Trail, Mt. Whitney Trail

LEAVES AND STEMS: It is common to see great masses of stems, up to 80 cm in height, of this perennial species. The stems and leaves are both densely covered in sticky glandular hairs. The light-green leaves, 3–8 cm long and oval shaped, attach to the stem in pairs. 3–5 deeply inset veins are obvious; they merge together at the leaf's base.

FLOWERS: The 5 cardinal-red, 4- to 5-cm-long petals are fused into a tube, most of which is hidden by the 2- to 3-cm-long calyx. What emerges is the very end of the tube and the lobed ends of the petals, 2 pointing upward and 3 flaring downward. The stamens and quite long style stick out from within. The flowers sit singly on short stalks that grow from the leaf nodes.

❖ *Keckiella rothrockii* var. *rothrockii* (Rothrock's keckiella)
   FAMILY: Plantaginaceae (Scrophulariaceae)

DISTRIBUTION Fairly common in the eastern Sierra from Bishop south; common in the southwestern Sierra south of Mineral King
HABITAT Pinyon-juniper woodland; dry, open slopes
ELEVATION 5,500'–9,600'
SEASON Mid-July–mid-August
LOCATIONS Coyote Creek, Taboose Creek, Onion Valley, Mt. Whitney Trail

LEAVES AND STEMS: The 30- to 60-cm-tall shrub is much branched, especially near the base, forming a thicket of stems. The leaves occur along the stem in pairs, occasionally triplets, and are covered in very short hairs but still appear a quite bright green. The thick leaves are quite small, mostly 1–1.5 cm in length—broader near the base and irregularly toothed around the margin.

FLOWERS: A close relative of penstemons (beardtongues), the flowers share a strong resemblance, but these blossoms are smaller and duller than penstemons and their tubes open wider. The 5 petals of this species also form a two-lipped tubular flower. They are reddish in bud and pale yellow with reddish-orange streaks once open.

RELATED SPECIES: *Keckiella breviflora* var. *glabrisepala,* the hairless gaping keckiella, is a fairly common shrub at montane elevations from the Yosemite area south through the Kings River drainage on both sides of the Sierra Crest. Its leaves lack any hairs, and its flowers, as the name suggests, look like a yawning mouth—the upper and lower flower lips are far apart, and the upper lip forms a hood. The flowers are mostly white (or pale pink) with darker stripes.

Keckiella breviflora var. *glabrisepala*

❖ *Penstemon rostriflorus* (Bridge's penstemon)
   FAMILY: Plantaginaceae (Scrophulariaceae)

DISTRIBUTION Occurs throughout, on both sides of the Sierra Crest, but more common in the eastern Sierra
HABITAT Dry, sandy slopes
ELEVATION 5,000'–10,700'
SEASON Late June–late July
LOCATIONS Lundy Canyon, descent from Lake Virginia to Tully Hole, Bishop Pass Trail, Baxter Pass Trail

(Continued)

(Continued) **LEAVES AND STEMS:** Though the bases of the stems are woody, they are hidden beneath a dense cluster of tall, leafy stems, usually 30–60 cm tall but occasionally reaching 1 m. The bright-green hairless leaves are 2–5 cm long, skinny (less than 1 cm), and quite thick. The leaves are folded along the midrib into a U shape. They usually attach to the stem in pairs but occasionally attach singly.

FLOWERS: 20—or more—bright-red, sparsely gland-dotted, tubular flowers attach to each flowering stalk. The blooms point straight out or slightly downward. The tube is 2–3 cm long and very narrow, comprised of 5 fused petals. The 2 upper petals are fused into a hood, while the lower 3 lobes are quite long and bent or curled back. Like other penstemons, the flowers on this species are especially obvious because the calyx is tiny, hiding little of the flower tube.

❖ Adapting to Hummingbirds

Hummingbirds seek out red, tubular flowers with an abundance of nectar. Some hummingbird-pollinated species in the Sierra are the scarlet penstemon (*Penstemon rostriflorus*), mountain pride penstemon (*Penstemon newberryi*), crimson columbine (*Aquilegia formosa*), scarlet monkeyflower (*Mimulus cardinalis*), and California fuchsia (*Epilobium canum*). In many of these genera, closely related species that are more purple or blue in color are pollinated by bees. Interestingly, in the columbine, penstemon, and monkeyflower genera, the hummingbird-pollinated characteristics have evolved more recently than the bee-pollinated coloration. Among other genetic changes, a mutation has occurred to create a redder color through the production of carotenoid pigments (see "A Rainbow of Flowers," page 95). Not only do hummingbirds like red, but bees are also less likely to visit flowers with a high carotenoid content because they cannot see wavelengths that appear red to us, and therefore red flowers do not stand out against the background (see "A Bee's-Eye View of a Flower," page 133). Studies have suggested that, due to the type of mutation, a conversion back to the bee-preferred colors is unlikely to occur, so if hummingbirds were to suddenly disappear, the red-flowered species would lose out.

❖ *Ipomopsis aggregata* subsp. *aggregata* (scarlet gilia)
   FAMILY: Polemoniaceae

DISTRIBUTION Occasional throughout the eastern Sierra; mostly absent west of the Sierra Crest
HABITAT Dry slopes and flats
ELEVATION 7,000'–11,500'
SEASON Late June–early August
LOCATIONS Virginia Lakes Basin, Minaret Summit, Coyote Ridge, North Fork Big Pine Creek, Shepherd Pass Trail

LEAVES AND STEMS: Usually standing 30–50 cm high, but occasionally nearly twice that, this species has a dense collection of basal leaves and more scattered stem leaves. The leaves are up to 5 cm long and deeply pinnately divided into very narrow lobes. They can be densely white-hairy—or not hairy at all.

FLOWERS: The bright-red flowers are striking—long, narrow tubes, with 5 wide-open, narrow, sharp-pointed petal lobes that form a star, at least 2 cm in diameter. The petals are often patterned with white blotches. The pollen at the end of the stamens is yellow, white, or occasionally pale blue.

RELATED SPECIES: *Ipomopsis aggregata* subsp. *bridgesii* is the more common subspecies in the western Sierra, found in locations including Rancheria Mountain, Devils Postpile, Kaiser Peak, and south of the Big Arroyo. It has bright-pink flowers with distinctly blue pollen and stamens that stick out of the flowering tube. A second related species, *Ipomopsis tenuituba,* occurs in the eastern Sierra, mostly at montane elevations. It has an even longer, narrower flower tube; lighter pink flowers; and stamens that are shorter than the flower tube (see photo on page 163).

Ipomopsis aggregata subsp. *bridgesii*

❖ *Oxyria digyna* (alpine mountain sorrel)
    FAMILY: Polygonaceae

DISTRIBUTION Common throughout, on both sides of the Sierra Crest, usually at high elevations
HABITAT Alongside rocks and outcrops, usually in locations with some moisture
ELEVATION 7,300'–13,500'
SEASON Early July–early August
LOCATIONS West side of Mt. Dana, Garnet Lake, Evolution Basin, Bishop Pass Trail, west side of Baxter Pass, Glen Pass

LEAVES AND STEMS: The glossy, green to reddish, heart- to kidney-shaped leaves grow from the base of the plant. The leaf blades vary greatly in size but are usually 2–4 cm in diameter. Below them is a stalk that is at least 3 times as long as the leaf.

FLOWERS: From the center of the leaf cluster emerges a single flowering stalk, usually reaching 10–30 cm in height. Most of the stalk length is densely covered with small, red, 4-petal flowers that droop downward. However, the flowers are equally showy once in seed, with small green fruits surrounded by a red, papery wing; the wing aids in seed dispersal, allowing them to float farther in the wind.

❖ Biogeography of High-Elevation Sierra Plants

Biogeography is the study of species' distributions, often referring to studies on a broad geographic scale. It considers where across the globe each species is found and categorizes the species into groups based on their distributions. If possible, biogeographers also try to determine in which location a species first evolved, versus locations it later dispersed to. For example, Sierra Nevada alpine plants are generally divided into 1) circumboreal species, those that are widely distributed in alpine and arctic habitats throughout the Northern Hemisphere (14% of species); 2) species common to the Sierra Nevada and the cordillera of western

(Continued)

(Continued)   North America, which includes the Rocky Mountains north into Canada (35%); 3) species common to only the Cascades and the Sierra (16%); 4) Sierra species that also occur in the Great Basin mountain ranges (20%); and finally, 5) species endemic to the Sierra Nevada or to the Sierra Nevada and other locations in California (15%). A plant endemic to the Sierra Nevada is one that does not exist outside the mountain range, while a California endemic occurs in both the Sierra Nevada and elsewhere in California.

Most Northern Hemisphere alpine floras contain a larger percentage of circumboreal species; the Sierra Nevada is unique because each of the different biogeographical categories contains a similar percentage of species. The explanation is that the Sierra Nevada is a drier mountain range, and many of the north-adapted species cannot tolerate the warm, dry, summer conditions, especially in the central and southern high-elevation Sierra, the regions included in this book. Quite a few circumboreal species have ranges that extend about as far as Tioga Pass (in Yosemite) but no farther south; this is the boundary where the climate is suddenly too hot and dry for them to survive. For example, one study showed that Sierra species whose ranges extend northward outside of the Sierra often only survive in wet locations in the Sierra; elsewhere, they would be too water-limited. In contrast, plants more common on drier sites are often those that also occur in mountain ranges to the east, where it is drier, or that are endemic to the Sierra Nevada. Indeed, there are more endemic species in the southern part of the High Sierra, with its drier climate, than to the north.

This knowledge of species distributions raises the question of where the species originated. For instance, many circumboreal species likely evolved into their current form in polar regions or northern Eurasia and then dispersed southward. Many species with North American cordilleran distributions or Cascade-Sierra affinities may likewise have originated afar and moved to the Sierra, but some may alternatively have evolved in the Sierra and then dispersed to other North American mountain ranges. Until the last decade, it was believed that the Sierra Nevada had been a high-elevation mountain range for only a few million years, and therefore, endemics aside, nearly all species had evolved elsewhere and moved to the Sierra; a few million years is insufficient time for such a diversity of species to evolve and then disperse throughout North America. We now know that there has been a high-elevation mountain range, the Ancestral Sierra, in this location for approximately 60 million years, and the Great Basin was a high plateau for much of this time. Moreover, the Sierra slightly predates the Cascade Mountains and is of similar age to the Rocky Mountains, indicating there is no reason to assume most species present in the Sierra originated elsewhere. Indeed, it is quite possible that some species, especially those preferring drier sites, originated in the Sierra and then dispersed elsewhere—this topic is in need of more research. The endemics most likely evolved into their current form in the Sierra or California because they occur nowhere else. See also "Sierra Nevada Endemics," page 137.

Some examples, classified by group, include:

Circumboreal: *Sagina saginoides, Gentianella amarella* subsp. *acuta, Epilobium anagallidifolium, Oxyria digyna, Potentilla pensylvanica*

Cordilleran: *Minuartia rubella, Cassiope mertensiana, Calyptridium umbellatum, Phlox condensata, Aconitum columbianum* subsp. *columbianum*

Cascades and Sierra: *Erigeron pygmaeus, Raillardella argentea, Silene sargentii, Pedicularis attollens, Eriogonum lobbii*

Great Basin and Sierra: *Podistera nevadensis, Lupinus argenteus* var. *meionanthus, Linum lewisii, Mimulus suksdorfii, Penstemon davidsonii*

California endemics: *Phyllodoce breweri, Lupinus breweri* var. *breweri, Lewisia glandulosa, Castilleja nana, Potentilla pseudosericea*

Sierra endemics: *Oreostemma peirsonii, Draba longisquamosa, Streptanthus gracilis, Polemonium eximium, Ivesia muirii*

❖ *Rumex californicus (Rumex salicifolius* var. *denticulatus)* (California dock)
   FAMILY: Polygonaceae

DISTRIBUTION Common throughout the eastern Sierra; occasional in the western Sierra
HABITAT Seeps and other moist locations, including on rocky slopes and on lakeshores
ELEVATION 5,800'–11,300'
SEASON Late June–early August
LOCATIONS Warren Fork Lee Vining Creek, trail to Dana Plateau, Seventh Lake (North Fork Big Pine Creek), Ladder Lake, Baxter Lakes Basin, Bullfrog Lake

LEAVES AND STEMS: This tall species (30–60 cm in height) grows in large clumps where there is sufficient moisture. The elongate leaves can be up to 10 cm in length, are narrow, and have a midrib that stands out distinctly on the back of the leaf—this last characteristic is easily noted because the leaves mostly extend upward.

FLOWERS: The inflorescences are similar to alpine sheep sorrel—a length of stem densely covered in tiny red to yellow flowers. However, these inflorescences are much longer, and the flowers have both stamens and carpels—the male and female parts occur on the same plant.

❖ *Rumex paucifolius* (alpine sheep sorrel)
    FAMILY: Polygonaceae

DISTRIBUTION Very common throughout the eastern Sierra and just west of the Sierra Crest; more occasional in the western Sierra but occurs throughout
HABITAT Alpine fell-fields, sandy or rocky flats or slopes
ELEVATION 3,500'–12,250'
SEASON Late June–early August
LOCATIONS Tioga Tarns, Garnet Lake, Humphreys Basin, Coyote Ridge, Evolution Basin, Tyndall Creek Basin

LEAVES AND STEMS: A short plant, ranging 10–40 cm in height, alpine sheep sorrel almost always grows in exposed locations. A basal cluster of 3- to 7-cm-long, narrow, somewhat fleshy leaves surrounds the stem, with a few smaller leaves higher up the stem. The leaves become gradually narrower and redder toward their bases. The stem itself, though narrow, is quite stiff.

FLOWERS: The inflorescences occur at the top of the main stem and possibly on a few side branches. Each is composed of many tiny (less than 4 mm wide) red flowers that droop downward. At first glance, all inflorescences look identical, but this species is dioecious, meaning that some plants have only female flowers (with carpels, but lacking stamens) and other plants have only male flowers (with stamens, but lacking carpels.) Only in the plants with female flowers do the flattened fruits form.

❖ *Aquilegia formosa* (crimson columbine)
    FAMILY: Ranunculaceae

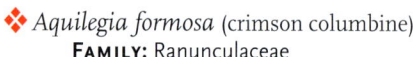

DISTRIBUTION Common throughout, on both sides of the Sierra Crest
HABITAT Moist to wet locations, including stream banks, seeps, meadow perimeters, moist forests, and wet talus slopes
ELEVATION 3,500'–11,000'
SEASON Early July–early August
LOCATIONS Mt. Hoffman Trail, Gaylor Lakes, Bishop Pass Trail above Long Lake, Birch Lake, Rae Lakes Basin

LEAVES AND STEMS: This species has a robust collection of leaves and often much-branched stems reaching 80 cm in height, though they are often much shorter. The basal leaves are divided into threes, and each of these stalked leaflets is again divided into 3 leaflets—or at least deep lobes—that are broad and rounded. The leaves higher up the stem tend to be 3-lobed a single time or even unlobed. The stems may lack hairs or have scattered gland-tipped hairs.

FLOWERS: Pointing downward from the tips of long branches, these beautiful flowers have 5 red sepals that extend sideways and 5 red (to orange) petals with spurs that extend skyward. The tips of the spurs are red and gradually transition through orange to yellow at the opening of each spur, while a thick cluster of long yellow-tipped stamens extend from the middle of the flower. The sepals and petals tend to have some gland-tipped hairs. If the flower you are admiring does not quite match this description, note that the crimson columbine and Coville's columbine frequently hybridize; see "A Tale of Two Columbines," page 67, for more information.

❖ *Scrophularia desertorum* (desert figwort)
   FAMILY: Scrophulariaceae

DISTRIBUTION Fairly common throughout the eastern Sierra and on the Kern Plateau; absent elsewhere
HABITAT Moist seeps or alongside rocks in sheltered locations
ELEVATION 6,000'–10,500'
SEASON Early June–early July
LOCATIONS Virginia Lakes Basin, South Fork Big Pine Creek, Kearsarge Pass Trail, Mt. Whitney Trail

LEAVES AND STEMS: Growing to 1 m in height and often much branched, the quite square-shaped, hairy stalk has many pairs of opposite leaves along the bottom third of the stem. The triangular leaves are 4–8 cm long and feature obvious veins; they are also jaggedly toothed.

FLOWERS: The tiny, two-toned, tubular flowers—a little under 1 cm in length and about as wide as they are long—are shaped like a small urn. The upper 2 petals, which jut skyward like a flag, are a beautiful red-burgundy. 2 small petals pointing sideways and 1 aimed downward are more greenish. The much-branched stem can be covered in dozens of these flowers. The flower tube is constricted just before the petal tips, giving it a roundish appearance.

❖ *Fritillaria atropurpurea* (spotted fritillary, purple fritillary)
   FAMILY: Liliaceae

DISTRIBUTION Occasional throughout, on both sides of the Sierra Crest, but plants often occur singly, making them easy to miss
HABITAT Open, usually dry forest
ELEVATION 5,600'–10,500'
SEASON Early June–early July
LOCATIONS North side of Hetch Hetchy Reservoir, western base of Mt. Dana, Tuolumne Meadows, Devils Postpile, Lake Sabrina

LEAVES AND STEMS: The narrow stems of the spotted fritillary reach 20–50 cm in height but are often missed because they have just a few very narrow leaves, and the flowers do not stand out. Each leaf is 4–12 cm long, becoming smaller higher up the stem.

photographed by Rebecca Wenk

FLOWERS: The 6-petal flowers are mottled maroon, yellow, and brown—quite pretty and also variable between individuals. The flowers nod downward, a good way to distinguish them from the related pine woods fritillary. Also note that the individual petals are quite narrow and taper at the tip. At the center is a column of 6 yellow stamens.

❖ *Fritillaria pinetorum* (pine woods fritillary)
   FAMILY: Liliaceae

DISTRIBUTION Occasional throughout, on both sides of the Sierra Crest
HABITAT Dry forest, open sandy slopes often around treeline
ELEVATION 5,600'–10,300'
SEASON Early June–mid-July
LOCATIONS West side of Mt. Dana, Dana Fork of the Tuolumne River, east of Vogelsang Lake, top of San Joaquin Ridge, South Fork Big Pine Creek

LEAVES AND STEMS: The entire length of the 10- to 40-cm-high stalk is covered in leaves, though they are denser near the base of the stem. The leaves are linear, 5–15 cm long, and cupped upward along the midrib. The tips of long leaves often end in curlicues. Both the leaves and the stems have a purplish hue to them.

FLOWERS: The petals of the pine woods fritillary are brownish-purple, making them quite inconspicuous. However, if you stumble upon one, look closely, for they are quite beautiful. The 6 petals are splayed wide open and patterned with maroon and yellow blotches and a slightly transparent margin. The petals are quite broad and rounded at the tip. The flowers may nod slightly but generally stick straight out.

❖ *Corallorhiza maculata* (spotted coralroot, summer coralroot)
   FAMILY: Orchidaceae

DISTRIBUTION Fairly common throughout the western Sierra but generally restricted to montane locations once south of the Mammoth Lakes region
HABITAT Moist forest, mostly beneath firs
ELEVATION 4,000'–9,000'
SEASON Mid-June–late July
LOCATIONS Porcupine Flat, near Lembert Dome, Yosemite Creek, Devils Postpile, above Lodgepole

LEAVES AND STEMS: This parasitic orchid lacks any green parts and is usually 20–30 cm in height. Instead the stem is very red to orangish—and there are no leaves; it is simply an inflorescence stalk. Why have leaves if you can't photosynthesize?

FLOWERS: About half the stem is covered with the dainty orchid flowers. Like all orchids, the flowers are bilaterally symmetrical. There are 3 petals: 2 burnt-red petals above and 1 large broad one at the bottom (white with pink to purple spots). Behind the flowers are 3 sepals, the same color as the upper petals; the upper 1 points forward and 2 stretch out to the side.

photographed by Rebecca Wenk

EXTRA TIDBITS: Coralroot orchids are parasites on nearby fir trees. You will most often find them in dark, undisturbed forests, where they have had many years to establish connections to the trees. This species is one of the most robust, reappearing quickly after disturbances, such as fire.

photographed by Rebecca Wenk

Ipomopsis tenuituba (see page 157)

❖ Pink Flowers

Phyllodoce breweri (see page 173)

❖ *Cymopterus cinerarius* (Gray's cymopterus, Gray's springparsley)
   FAMILY: Apiaceae

DISTRIBUTION Common in scattered sites in the eastern Sierra but otherwise rare; absent in the western Sierra
HABITAT Dry, rocky slopes; scree; often on metamorphic substrates
ELEVATION 6,800'–12,000'
SEASON Early June–early July
LOCATIONS Leavitt Peak, Convict Creek drainage, south of Taboose Pass (on Striped Mountain)

LEAVES AND STEMS: Each plant has a small number of basal leaves, but the flowering stalk is bare. The basal leaves are intricately dissected, and the individual narrow, pointed lobes tend to face upward. In comparison to the related species pteryxia (see page 88), this species has leaves that are considerably thicker, almost fleshy in appearance, and 3–5 cm in length.

FLOWERS: On almost all occasions you will find only the seed head because this species blooms early and quickly. The fruits are red and oval shaped, with distinct white ribs running along them. Each inflorescence will have several to many of these fruits, depending on how many flowers set fruit. And you may be lucky enough to see the flower, a dense ball of light-pink blossoms.

❖ *Oreonana clementis* (pygmy mountain parsley)   **FAMILY:** Apiaceae

DISTRIBUTION Fairly common at high elevations from Taboose Pass south to Olancha Peak; also in the far southwestern Sierra, south of Mineral King and on the Kern Plateau
HABITAT Dry, rocky to sandy slopes
ELEVATION 5,200'–13,000'
SEASON Mid-June–early August
LOCATIONS Summit of Kearsarge Pass, John Muir Trail south of Forester Pass, Mt. Whitney, New Army Pass

LEAVES AND STEMS: This species prefers gravelly soils, where a few small leaves—at most 7 cm in length, including the stalk—emerge. The leaves are twice pinnately dissected, but this may be difficult to ascertain because all the individual lobes are bent to face upward and are densely covered in stiff white hairs. Looking down on the leaf, you simply see a mass of quite short lobe tips pointing upward.

FLOWERS: From between the leaves grows the 3- to 8-cm-long flowering stem. The inflorescence is a dense sphere up to 3 cm in diameter. With close observation, you can discern the individual pale-pink flowers; they attach on the outside of the sphere like little stars. It takes a closer look to realize that beneath these flowers are short, very hairy, pale-pink stems; mostly you see only a single sphere of flowers. Once the petals are shed, the stems become more visible, and if you look at the geometry of the stems, you will realize this is a compound umbel. The oval-shaped fruits have several ribs and are sparsely to densely covered in long white hairs.

❖ *Apocynum androsaemifolium* (bitter dogbane)   **FAMILY:** Apocynaceae

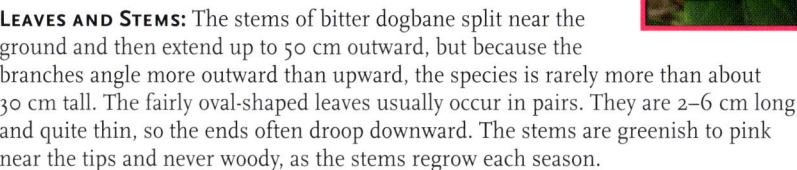

DISTRIBUTION Relatively common throughout the high-elevation eastern Sierra; in the western Sierra, common at montane elevations, with very scattered occurrences at higher elevations
HABITAT Open to somewhat vegetated slopes that are not exceedingly dry; very common at montane elevations after fire
ELEVATION 3,500'–10,500'
SEASON Early July–mid-August
LOCATIONS Rancheria Mountain, Virginia Lakes, Laurel Canyon, Convict Creek drainage, North Fork Big Pine Creek

LEAVES AND STEMS: The stems of bitter dogbane split near the ground and then extend up to 50 cm outward, but because the branches angle more outward than upward, the species is rarely more than about 30 cm tall. The fairly oval-shaped leaves usually occur in pairs. They are 2–6 cm long and quite thin, so the ends often droop downward. The stems are greenish to pink near the tips and never woody, as the stems regrow each season.

FLOWERS: The pink tubular flowers occur in clusters of about 20, each 4–8 mm in length. The bell-shaped floral tube opens up slightly at the end, with 5 short, triangular petal lobes that are rounded at the tip. The calyx is easily missed, as it is only a few millimeters in length, but if you need an extra identifying feature, it has 5 pinkish sharp-pointed tips that grasp the base of the floral tube. The seedpods are striking—exceedingly long, narrow pods reminiscent of daggers.

EXTRA TIDBITS: This butterfly-pollinated species has a very sticky pollen mixture. If smaller insects, such as flies, land in the flowers, they become permanently stuck.

❖ Pollinators

Most flowering plants require cross-pollination, a process in which pollen from one plant is deposited on the stigma of a second. Insects—especially bees, but also flies, wasps, ants, butterflies, and beetles—as well as other species, such as hummingbirds and bats, are important pollinators. Pollinators visit flowers to benefit themselves, and helping out the plant is incidental. Some insects consume the sugary nectar while others eat (or collect) the protein-rich pollen, and many flowering plants have fine-tuned their flower shape, flower color, and availability of pollen or nectar to attract specific pollinators. The collection of flower traits that attracts a particular group of pollinators is called a pollination syndrome. The differences between pollination syndromes are often indistinct, and of course, an animal will visit any plant from which it can gain some nourishment. Nonetheless, knowing what plant traits are most often preferred by various pollinators helps explain why there is such a diversity of floral shapes and colors:

(Continued)

(Continued)

🌸 Hummingbirds are attracted to red tubular flowers with abundant nectar. See "Adapting to Hummingbirds," page 156, for examples.

🌸 Butterflies prefer large, brightly colored flowers with abundant nectar that have a so-called landing platform where they can sit. They do not find strongly scented flowers appealing. Butterflies will visit a great diversity of species, including *Helenium bigelovii* (Bigelow's sneezeweed), *Monardella odoratissima* (coyote-mint), *Apocynum androsaemifolium* (bitter dogbane), and *Collomia linearis* (narrow-leaf mountain trumpet).

🌸 Hawk moths are nocturnal pollinators that head toward large, white, often tubular flowers that produce lots of nectar and often have an attractive scent. Examples include *Aquilegia pubescens* (Coville's columbine) and *Oenothera elata* subsp. *hirsutissima* (evening primrose), as well as the lower elevation *Asclepias fascicularis* (narrow-leaf milkweed) and *Lilium washingtonianum* (Washington lily).

🌸 Bees are a diverse group, with some species seeking more pollen and others nectar. Because bees can "see" ultraviolet light (see "A Bee's-Eye View of a Flower," page 133), bee-pollinated flowers often have ultraviolet patterns, called nectar guides, that point the bee toward the reproductive structures at the center of the flower. Bee-pollinated flowers are most often yellow, blue, or purple.

🌸 Fly pollination is particularly important at high elevations because flies are better able to cope with the cool alpine temperatures and high winds than many other insects are. Stereotypically, flowers adapted to fly pollination lack nectar, are usually dull (or dark) colored, and often have strong odors. Such fly-pollinated flowers do not occur in the high-elevation Sierra. But there are many different types of flies, with those that live in the high-elevation Sierra seeking out flowers with a great diversity of colors and forms, attracted to them in part by their warmth. In addition, flies' sensors are particularly attuned to yellow and white flowers, so they likely seek out these colored petals.

🌸 Beetles tend to pollinate species whose petals are wide open and produce abundant pollen, such as species in the genus *Claytonia*.

🌸 Mosquitoes are minor pollinators, instead usually identified as nectar thieves, indicating that they consume the flower's nectar without providing it with any pollination services. The only plant species known to benefit from mosquito pollination are some small-flowered orchids: A member of the genus *Platanthera* from the Pacific Northwest is known to be mosquito pollinated, but no studies have been done on Sierra species.

🌸 One last pollinator is the wind! Grasses and trees without showy flowers depend on the wind to disperse their pollen.

❖ *Ageratina occidentalis* (western snakeroot,
       western eupatorium)   **FAMILY:** Asteraceae

DISTRIBUTION Occurs throughout, on both sides of the
Sierra Crest, but especially common in the eastern Sierra
HABITAT Open slopes, often alongside rocks
ELEVATION 4,000'–11,200'
SEASON Mid-July–mid-September
LOCATIONS Around Tioga Pass, Piute Pass Trail, South Fork
Big Pine Creek, Golden Staircase, near Charlotte Lake

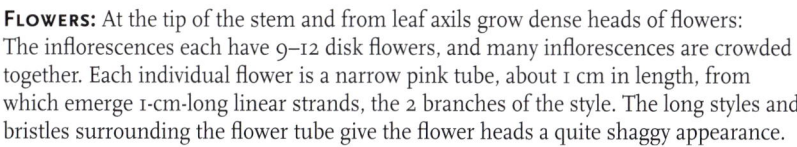

LEAVES AND STEMS: Though large and bushy, only the very
base of western snakeroot is woody, for the branches die to the
ground each winter. They regrow to reach 15–70 cm in height
by midsummer and are densely covered in 2- to 5-cm-long,
rather sloppy, fairly triangular leaves whose perimeter is sharply serrated.

FLOWERS: At the tip of the stem and from leaf axils grow dense heads of flowers:
The inflorescences each have 9–12 disk flowers, and many inflorescences are crowded
together. Each individual flower is a narrow pink tube, about 1 cm in length, from
which emerge 1-cm-long linear strands, the 2 branches of the style. The long styles and
bristles surrounding the flower tube give the flower heads a quite shaggy appearance.

❖ *Antennaria rosea* subsp. *confinis* (rosy pussytoes)   **FAMILY:** Asteraceae

DISTRIBUTION Fairly common throughout, on both sides
of the Sierra Crest
HABITAT Alpine fell-fields, dry meadows, open slopes;
often growing alongside rocks
ELEVATION 7,000'–12,300'
SEASON Late June–mid-July
LOCATIONS Dana Plateau, Rock Creek Basin,
Lamarck Lakes Trail, New Army Pass

LEAVES AND STEMS: Like other species of pussytoes, a mat of
oval- to wedge-shaped leaves spreads across the ground, with the
greenish to whitish leaf color determined by the density of white
hairs covering its surfaces; some leaves are so hairy that they
resemble felt.

FLOWERS: The flowers of this species are distinguished by the pinkish tinted, papery
phyllaries. Though these appear to be part of the "flower," they are actually leaves,
and the white fuzz at the center of each head are the disk flowers. Interestingly, all the
flowers typically lack stamens and therefore generally reproduce asexually via apomixis
(see page 120), where a plant produces genetically identical seeds without being
pollinated. They may also occasionally hybridize with other pussytoes.

RELATED SPECIES: *Antennaria umbrinella*, or brown pussytoes, is uncommon but occurs
throughout the Sierra, mostly at high elevations in dry flats or meadows. Its phyllaries
are white at the base and yellow to brown at the tip.

❖ *Stephanomeria tenuifolia* (narrow-leaved wire lettuce)   **FAMILY:** Asteraceae

DISTRIBUTION Fairly common throughout, on both sides of the Sierra Crest
HABITAT Various dry locations
ELEVATION 4,800'–11,200'
SEASON Early July–late August
LOCATIONS Mono Pass (Yosemite), Devils Postpile, Rock Creek Basin, Kearsarge Pass Trail, Crabtree Lake

LEAVES AND STEMS: The common name does a good job of summarizing the appearance of this species. Reaching 20–60 cm in height, the pale white-green (to green) stems always have the same diameter. The stems branch at all different angles and bend in a way that very much gives them the appearance of wire. The leaves are only toward the base of the plant, and these are long and very narrow—almost threadlike and often slightly curled at the tips.

FLOWERS: The pale-pink inflorescences extend from the branch ends. They have 3–5 ray flowers that open outward but lack disk flowers (as do their relatives, lettuce flowers). The style branches are similarly pink and reach skyward from the center of the flowers.

RELATED SPECIES: *Pleiacanthus spinosus* (previously *Stephanomeria spinosa*; thorny skeletonweed) is fairly common throughout the eastern Sierra but rarely extends to subalpine elevations. The shoots on which its flowers grow are short, stout, and spine tipped. Despite the differences, however, its long, wandering bluish-green stems and small pink inflorescences with few ray flowers look similar to those of narrow-leaved wire lettuce. You will come across this species along the South Fork Big Pine Creek and Taboose Creek.

Pleiacanthus spinosus

❖ *Hackelia mundula* (pink stickseed)
      FAMILY: Boraginaceae

DISTRIBUTION Common throughout montane elevations in the western Sierra, occasionally reaching into the subalpine zone; crossing to the eastern Sierra at Mammoth Lakes
HABITAT Dry slopes, open forest
ELEVATION 5,400'–9,500'
SEASON Mid-June–late July
LOCATIONS Rancheria Mountain, summit of Clouds Rest, Devils Postpile, Twin Lakes (Mammoth Lakes Basin), Kern Plateau

LEAVES AND STEMS: The stems, 40–80 cm in height, and leaves of pink stickseed are covered in long white hairs, sometimes densely so. The basal leaves are up to 30 cm in length and quite narrow, while the stem leaves are shorter and more oval shaped.

FLOWERS: This stickseed stands out by having pink flowers, ranging from bright to quite pale. As with other stickseeds, there are many flowers along the branched stems, opening sequentially from the bottom upward, and the 5 petals are splayed wide open, showing off the decorative so-called appendages at the center. The fruits are distinctly prickly.

❖ *Streptanthus gracilis* (alpine jewelflower)
FAMILY: Brassicaceae

DISTRIBUTION Fairly common at high elevations in the Kings River drainage and occurring occasionally in the Kern River drainage and in the eastern Sierra from Mammoth Lakes to Kearsarge Pass; absent elsewhere
HABITAT Sandy slopes, talus slopes
ELEVATION 8,800'–11,200'
SEASON Mid-June–early August
LOCATIONS Taboose Pass, Rae Lakes Basin, west side of Kearsarge Pass, Bullfrog Lake, Lake Reflection, Milestone Basin

LEAVES AND STEMS: This species is an annual, but it's one of the largest at high elevations. It is considered rare due to its rather restricted range but is quite common within parts of this range. The leaves are slightly fleshy, hairless, and smooth. The leaves are mostly a basal rosette, though some extend along the flowering stems. The leaves are often delicately lobed—the lobes perfectly rounded. The stem leaves clasp the stalk, and the basal leaves have short stalks.

FLOWERS: The flowering stems are also hairless and smooth, branching near the top to support many flowers. The 4 long, wedge-shaped, purple petals feature distinctly darker lines running along them. The sepals are likewise purple, adding to the flowers' color. The seedpods are very long and narrow.

❖ *Streptanthus tortuosus* (mountain jewelflower)
FAMILY: Brassicaceae

DISTRIBUTION Very common throughout the western Sierra; very common in the eastern Sierra from Sonora Pass south to Mammoth Lakes, becoming rare farther south
HABITAT Sandy slopes, talus slopes, under sparse tree cover
ELEVATION 700'–11,500'
SEASON Mid-June–early August
LOCATIONS Virginia Lakes Canyon, Shell Lake (above Bennettville), Duck Pass Trail, Hilgard Fork Trail of Bear Creek, Farewell Gap

LEAVES AND STEMS: The smooth, shiny leaves make this species immediately identifiable: They are circular to heart shaped in outline, clasping and completely encircling the stem. By late summer, the leaves begin to yellow but stay firmly attached to the stems. And the plant can be quite variable in height, ranging from just 10 cm to more than 1 m in sheltered locations.

(Continued)

(Continued)   **FLOWERS:** The blossoms for all jewelflowers look like little money bags—forming a pocket at the bottom and then pinching together, with the petals opening at their tips. For this species, the bases of the petals (forming the bag) are deep pink, while the tips are paler. The stamens and style poke out of the top, adding a decorative touch. The long, skinny fruits are shaded dark green to purple and curve into a broad arch.

RELATED SPECIES: *Streptanthus cordatus* var. *cordatus* (heartleaf jewel-flower) is an eastern Sierra perennial, most common at montane elevations but found as high as 11,100 feet. Most noteworthy is the bulbous, deep-purple calyx, from the mouth of which emerge 4 narrow, cream to purplish petals. The tall stalks are 30–90 cm in height.

Streptanthus cordatus var. *cordatus*

❖ *Symphoricarpos rotundifolius* var. *rotundifolius* (mountain snowberry)
　　FAMILY: Caprifoliaceae

DISTRIBUTION Occasional in the western Sierra and fairly common throughout the eastern Sierra
HABITAT Dry slopes
ELEVATION 6,500'–11,000'
SEASON Late June–late July
LOCATIONS West slope of Mt. Dana, Rock Creek Basin, Bishop Pass Trail, John Muir Trail along Bubbs Creek

LEAVES AND STEMS: This shrub is usually a little under 1 m in height. The branches are rather thin and distinctly bumpy wherever a leaf was once attached. The new pinkish growth is much smoother and often a bit velvety. The leaves have very obvious veins on their backs and are typically oval-shaped, though sometimes with irregular rounded lobes.

FLOWERS: 1 or 2 of the pink tubular flowers droop downward from each of the upper leaf axils—where the leaves attach to the stem. They are quite narrow, no more than 1 cm long, and have a very small purple calyx that sits on their base like a cap. In this family, the ovary, which develops into a fruit, is below the calyx; it is the purplish bulge below the flower. Most noteworthy are the bright white berries that develop by late summer. They are an elongate, oval shape, with quite blunt ends and a little pink decoration at their end—the calyx.

RELATED SPECIES: *Symphoricarpos rotundifolius* var. *parishii* (Parish's snowberry) has trailing stems. It is common in the eastern Sierra from Bishop south but rare in the Yosemite region. This variety also occurs on the Kern Plateau and toward the Mineral King area. *Symphoricarpos mollis,* or creeping snowberry, is a species common at montane elevations. Its leaves and flowers look very similar, but it is a vine, with long stems that trail along the ground.

Symphoricarpos mollis

❖ *Kalmia polifolia* (mountain laurel, swamp laurel)   **FAMILY:** Ericaceae

DISTRIBUTION Common throughout, on both sides of the Sierra Crest
HABITAT Boggy areas, meadows, moist lakeshores
ELEVATION 5,000'–12,000'

SEASON Early June–mid-July
LOCATIONS Twenty Lakes Basin, Duck Pass Trail, Rock Creek
Basin, Evolution Basin, Rae Lakes Basin

LEAVES AND STEMS: This subshrub, typically just 10 cm tall, forms mats. The leaves are less than 2 cm long and have an elongate oval shape. They are leathery, with slightly rolled under margins. The midvein is pale green to white.

FLOWERS: The flowers are an open, sideways-facing bowl, just a touch under 1 cm wide, comprised of 5 light-pink fused petals. Inside the bowl, the 10 dark-pink stamens readily stand out. From afar the stamens look like little dots on the petals, and indeed, they lie within indentations, giving the petals a flush appearance. When the flower is viewed from behind, the 10 pockets in the petals (in which the stamens sit) are visible as ridges on the petals. Flowers are attached to the stem singly, but many flowering stalks can emerge from leaf axils near the top of the stem.

EXTRA TIDBITS: When a bee lands on this flower, its weight triggers the stamens to pop out of their little pockets and whack the bee's back, depositing pollen.

❖ *Phyllodoce breweri* (purple mountainheath)
     FAMILY: Ericaceae

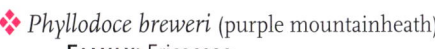

DISTRIBUTION Very common throughout, on both sides of the Sierra Crest
HABITAT Slightly moist to dry slopes, lakeshores, wet meadows, moist forest
ELEVATION 6,500'–13,200'
SEASON Mid-June–early August
LOCATIONS Saddlebag Lake, north side of Silver Pass, Rock Creek Basin, Kearsarge Pass Trail, near Guitar Lake

LEAVES AND STEMS: This ground cover shrub reaches at most 30 cm in height and covers large expanses. The stems are densely covered in leathery, needlelike leaves with inrolled margins.

FLOWERS: Brilliant-pink bowl-shaped flowers form in dense clusters at the tops of stems. 10 stamens and 1 style, all magenta, extend beyond the 5 petals, making the flowers especially festive.

❖ **Mycorrhizae**

The name *mycorrhizae* comes from Greek derivations for fungi (*myco-*) and root (*-rhiza*) and describes the relationship between a plant's roots and a fungus. Though there are many variations on how the fungus and the plant root connect, the connections lead to the transfer of sugars, mineral nutrients, and/or water between the two individuals. The vast majority of all plants, an estimated 90–95%, have a mycorrhizal partner. These relationships are generally beneficial to both the plant and the fungus, with the fungus obtaining sugars from the *(Continued)*

(Continued)   plant that it is unable to produce itself. In return, the plant obtains
nutrients or water from the fungus, as the fungus's much finer
roots are able to extract more nutrients from the soil—or directly from dead plant
matter—than a plant's roots can. In particular, fungi can absorb nitrogen that
is part of decaying material produced by a plant, animal, or microbe (known as
organic nitrogen), while most plants must wait for soil bacteria to convert nitrogen into nitrate or ammonium (two inorganic nitrogen forms). The prevalence of
mycorrhizal relationships suggests that they are essential for most species, and
indeed, most orchids could not even establish without a mycorrhizal partner.

Interestingly, the proportion of species with mycorrhizal partners decreases
at high elevations. One hypothesis is that fungi may be less able to survive in
the cool environments. Alternatively, it is possible that, because plants grow
less at high elevations, plants do not benefit as much from sharing their carbon
with fungi in return for additional nutrients, putting non-mycorrhizal families
at a relative advantage. In support of this, some families that lack (or mostly
lack) mycorrhizal relationships become more dominant at high elevations,
especially in dry locations; Brassicaceae, Caryophyllaceae, Crassulaceae, Cypera-
ceae, Gentianaceae, Juncaceae, Polygonaceae, and Saxifragaceae are all mostly
non-mycorrhizal. In contrast, species or families that are always mycorrhizal
may not be able to prevent mycorrhizae from establishing in their roots, and
they may find themselves at a disadvantage at the highest elevations. That said,
some dominant high-elevation families, including Asteraceae, Ericaceae, and
Polemoniaceae, are mostly mycorrhizal at both lower and higher elevations.

❖ *Pyrola asarifolia* subsp. *asarifolia* (bog wintergreen,
liverleaf wintergreen)   **FAMILY:** Ericaceae

DISTRIBUTION Occasional throughout the western Sierra;
fairly common in the eastern Sierra
HABITAT Wet forests and stream banks, occasionally along lakeshores
ELEVATION 4,000'–9,500'
SEASON Early July–early September
LOCATIONS Valentine Lake, Rock Creek Basin near Rock Creek Lodge,
above Willow Lake (South Fork Big Pine Creek)

LEAVES AND STEMS: The leaves are clustered near the ground and
are fairly round with a slight indentation at the base. The bright-
green, glossy leaves feature obvious veins that radiate from a central
stalk. The plant has no stem—only a flowering stalk.

FLOWERS: 5–20 flowers dangle along a leafless 20- to 40-cm-tall
stalk, with those near the bottom flowering first. The 5 petals are
generally a deep pink but vary from a quite faded pink to nearly red—and can be quite

mottled. They are bilaterally—not radially—symmetrical, for 1 petal is longer and less curled. The stocky style bends forward and lies along the longer petal.

❖ *Vaccinium cespitosum* (huckleberry, dwarf bilberry)   **FAMILY:** Ericaceae

DISTRIBUTION Very common throughout, on both sides of the Sierra Crest
HABITAT Moist conifer forest, lakeshores, meadows
ELEVATION 7,500'–11,500'
SEASON Early June–early July
LOCATIONS Tilden Lake, Cathedral Lakes, Rock Creek Basin, Lake Sabrina Basin, Baxter Lakes

LEAVES AND STEMS: This dwarf shrub typically forms a ground cover reaching at most 10 cm above the ground but occasionally rises higher. Older twigs are reddish-brown. The floppy leaves are oval shaped and very finely toothed at the tip.

FLOWERS: Flowers occur singly, emerging from the leaf axils. Most plants have only a few flowers, especially in shaded locations, but occasionally there are many. They are light pink and a roundish to sometimes elongate urn shape. Fruits are rarely produced and are generally quite small (5 mm), but when found the blue berries are delicious.

RELATED SPECIES: *Gaultheria humifusa,* alpine wintergreen, is a rather rare plant that inhabits wet, mossy meadows and seeps, typically alongside boulders. It has small, oval-shaped, leathery leaves. The 5-petal white flowers are shaped like little bells, with triangular red sepals surrounding the small petals. The fruits are small, somewhat hard berries, reminiscent of cranberries. It is most common in the Yosemite region, where it is found in locations including Twenty Lakes Basin and Upper Ottoway Lake, but is rarely found farther south in the Sierra Nevada.

Gaultheria humifusa

❖ *Vaccinium uliginosum* subsp. *occidentale* (western blueberry)
        FAMILY: Ericaceae

DISTRIBUTION Fairly common throughout the western Sierra; more occasional, but throughout, the eastern Sierra
HABITAT Wet meadows, wet lakeshores and stream banks, bogs
ELEVATION 6,500'–11,000'
SEASON Early June–early July
LOCATIONS West end of Tenaya Lake, Grass Lake (Lamarck Lakes Trail), Bear Creek, Evolution Valley, Le Conte Canyon

LEAVES AND STEMS: The larger of the Sierra's two blueberries, this shrub can be prostrate or reach upward of 50 cm in height. The plant is much branched and covered with small, oval-shaped leaves with completely untoothed edges. Mature leaves are generally a dark-green color with reddish margins, while newly expanding leaves are purplish. The twigs are whitish and quite brittle.

(Continued)

(Continued)   **FLOWERS:** Small (less than 1 cm long), narrowly urn-shaped, rose-pink flowers occur singly or in small groups. The petals are united together and fade quickly but remain attached even as the green fruits form. In August and September, you'll find the ripe fruits: tasty blueberries, about 5–7 mm in diameter. (And you're welcome to sample a few in national parks; just don't take them beyond the park boundaries.)

❖ *Astragalus whitneyi* var. *whitneyi* (balloonpod milkvetch, Whitney's milk vetch)
    FAMILY: Fabaceae

DISTRIBUTION Occasional in the eastern Sierra in the Yosemite and Mammoth Lakes regions; also present on Coyote Ridge and elsewhere in the Bishop Creek drainage
HABITAT Open, rocky areas, especially alpine fell-fields; typically found on metamorphic rock
ELEVATION 6,600'–12,000'
SEASON Mid-June–late July
LOCATIONS Tioga Crest, Dana Plateau, San Joaquin Mountain, Coyote Ridge, Chocolate Peak (Bishop Pass Trail)

LEAVES AND STEMS: Much larger than the other two milkvetch species included in this book, this species has much-branched, reddish stems that often exceed 20 cm in length. The long leaves look like branches themselves, for the 5–21 leaflets are widely separated. The slightly hairy leaflets are elongate ovals and tend to be folded inward along the midrib.

FLOWERS: The light-purple to pink flowers are about 1.5–2 cm in length and occur in dense, showy inflorescences at the ends of branches. Equally notable, as the name implies, are the inflated, semitranslucent seedpods, indeed resembling balloons. The pods are cream-colored with reddish-pink patterning, often with water droplets inside.

RELATED SPECIES: You may come across two other larger species of milkvetch in the Sierra. *Astragalus bolanderi,* Bolander's milkvetch, has slightly smaller, all-white flowers that occur in large clusters and is most readily found on the slope leading to Mt. Hoffman in Yosemite, but it is also present in sandy openings throughout the montane forests of the western Sierra. *Astragalus lentiginosus* var. *ineptus,* freckled milkvetch, is found in open rocky areas, including the Virginia Lakes Basin and the Convict Creek drainage. Its flowers are a creamier yellow offset against a red calyx, and its leaflets are strongly folded inward along the midrib. Both species also have inflated fruits.

Astragalus bolanderi

❖ *Ribes cereum* var. *inebrians* (mountain wax currant)
    FAMILY: Grossulariaceae

DISTRIBUTION Fairly common throughout but especially common in the drier eastern Sierra; this variety most common south of Bishop and in the southern Sierra
HABITAT Dry slopes, sandy slopes and flats, in small sandy patches on talus slopes
ELEVATION 3,000'–13,500'
SEASON Early June–mid-July

LOCATIONS West slope of Mt. Dana, Red Peak Pass, Lake Sabrina, Kearsarge Pass, Mt. Whitney Trail

LEAVES AND STEMS: This woody shrub can reach 1.5 m in height, though it often grows closer to the ground in windy locations. The leaves are roundish in outline, with 3–5 rounded lobes, generally cutting only one-fourth of the way to the center of the leaf. Leaves are usually densely hairy, often shiny, and, unlike var. *cereum,* rarely sticky to the touch. This species lacks spines at the leaf nodes. The leaves around the flower are narrow and untoothed.

FLOWERS: This species has up to 1-cm-long, very narrow, light-pink "floral tubes"—actually a colorful calyx—from which extend 5 splayed-open, quite short sepal tips. The petals are less than 1 mm long and visible inside the mouth of the tube. The flowers occur in groups of 3–7 and generally droop down. The fruits are 0.6-cm-wide, bright-red, edible berries often covered with small bumps, or glands. Unfortunately, they are rather seedy and bland compared with other currants.

RELATED SPECIES: A second variety, *cereum* (wax currant), occurs at lower elevations throughout the eastern Sierra. The leaves of var. *cereum* are covered with gland-tipped hairs, making them sticky, and the tiny leaves surrounding the flower have toothed lobes.

❖ *Ribes viscosissimum* (sticky currant)   **FAMILY:** Grossulariaceae

DISTRIBUTION Fairly common west of the Sierra Crest but quite rare in the eastern Sierra
HABITAT Moist forest, not-too-wet stream banks, occasionally in drier flats
ELEVATION 6,000'–10,000'
SEASON Early June–early July
LOCATIONS Near White Wolf Campground, King Creek (near Devils Postpile), Fish Creek

LEAVES AND STEMS: This shrub can reach 1.5 m in height and lacks spines. The leaf blade is notably thick, especially compared to other currants, and is covered with very sticky glands. The veins on the leaf blade are slightly depressed, giving the leaf a bit of a crunchy, crinkly feel. As for shape, the leaves are 3–8 cm in diameter (bigger than most other currant species) and have 3 rounded lobes, cut about one-third of the way to the leaf's center. The entire leaf margin is covered with small pointed teeth.

FLOWERS: The flowers, in clusters of 4–15, are white to pale pink, colored by the green-white to pink calyx, whose tips change from spreading outward to reflexed (bent back) as the flower ages. 5 small, white petals are attached near the mouth of the sepal tube and generally remain closed and overlapping. The 1-cm-wide black berries are quite glossy and edible.

❖ *Jamesia americana* var. *rosea* (rosy-petalled cliffbush)
FAMILY: Hydrangeaceae (Philadelphaceae)

DISTRIBUTION Relatively common in the eastern Sierra from the Rock Creek Basin south but absent farther north, excepting a disjunct population at Convict Lake; relatively common in the western Sierra from the Kings River drainage south
HABITAT Along outcrops and cliffs
ELEVATION 7,500'–12,500'
SEASON Early July–mid-August
LOCATIONS South shore of Convict Lake, Chocolate Lake junction (Bishop Pass Trail), below Loch Leven Lake (Piute Pass Trail), Birch Lake, Dollar Lake (Rae Lakes Basin)

LEAVES AND STEMS: This very branched shrub is less than 1 m in height and often grows as an espalier along outcrops—it seems to hug the rock. The bark has a distinct gray-white color, and individual branch segments are notably straight and stiff, and all have the same diameter. The 2- to 3-cm-long, fairly oval-shaped leaves are moderately hairy, with very distinct veins that are slightly depressed and a toothed margin.

FLOWERS: The 1- to 1.5-cm-wide flowers are attached singly or in small clusters at branch tips. The 5 petals are shaped like elongate rectangles with a rounded tip—they are nearly the same width throughout. Petal color varies from nearly white to light pink, with individual petals often graduating across these tones.

❖ *Sidalcea ranunculacea* (marsh checkerbloom)   **FAMILY:** Malvaceae

DISTRIBUTION Common throughout the Kaweah River drainage and in the western and southern Kern River drainage, including the Kern Plateau and southern Sierra but excluding the Mt. Whitney area; absent elsewhere
HABITAT Moist locations, including meadows and stream banks
ELEVATION 6,000'–10,000'
SEASON Late June–early August
LOCATIONS Elizabeth Pass, Lion Lake, Mineral King, Hockett Meadow, Lower Funston Meadow, just east of Kern Peak

LEAVES AND STEMS: This perennial herb reaches 20–50 cm in height. Stiff hairs densely cover both the stems and leaves. The leaves are mostly basal, though some occur along the stem. They are divided into 5–7 deep palmate lobes, nearly dividing the leaf to its base. Each lobe is further toothed or lobed.

FLOWERS: 5 quite stiff petals, fused at the base, make up the magenta flowers. The veins in the leaf petals are paler, even white, adding beautiful patterning. Like all members of the family Malvaceae, the numerous stamens are fused into a hollow tube, with the style pointing out through the center.

photographed by Debra Cook

❖ *Calyptridium monospermum* (one seeded pussypaws)
    FAMILY: Montiaceae (Portulacaceae)

DISTRIBUTION Common throughout, on both sides of the Sierra Crest
HABITAT Gravelly and sandy flats, forest floor, alpine fell-fields
ELEVATION 3,600'–12,000'
SEASON Mid-June–late July
LOCATIONS Cathedral Lakes, Dana Plateau, Kearsarge Pass, Cottonwood Lakes

LEAVES AND STEMS: The 1.5- to 4-cm-long, dark-green, fleshy leaves form a circular rosette of flat-lying leaves. They are shaped quite like spoons, with a broad, rounded top that pinches nearly to a point where they connect to the root. The leaf's veins are distinctly inset from the rest of the blade, giving them a rather bumpy look.

FLOWERS: The flowers range from pinkish to white and look like a ball of elaborately folded tissue paper from which bright-pink stamens emerge. The inflorescence is composed of many blossoms, each with 4 pink to white petals set inside a pocket of 2 white sepals, papery and nearly translucent; the latter remain when the petals shed. This species, in contrast to the closely related *Calyptridium umbellatum* (see below), has 2 or more inflorescences emerging from the same rosette of leaves. It is larger and more common at low elevations than the other species is.

❖ *Calyptridium umbellatum* (pussypaws)
    FAMILY: Montiaceae (Portulacaceae)

DISTRIBUTION Common throughout on both sides of the Sierra Crest, especially at high elevations
HABITAT Gravelly and sandy flats, forest floor, alpine fell-fields
ELEVATION 4,000'–13,500'
SEASON Late June–early August
LOCATIONS Mt. Dana, north side of Donohue Pass, Mono Pass (Rock Creek Basin), Trail Crest (Mt. Whitney Trail)

LEAVES AND STEMS: The leaves and general growth form are identical to one seeded pussypaws, a rosette of dark-green, 1.5- to 4-cm-long, spoon-shaped leaves that are fleshy and rather bumpy due to the veins. However, while one seeded pussypaws generally has a single rosette of leaves, *Calyptridium umbellatum* is typically comprised of several small rosettes, often with overlapping leaves.

FLOWERS: Each of the small rosettes has a single pink-stalked, ball-shaped inflorescence composed of many small pink to white flowers from which pink to red stamens emerge. The 2 pink to white sepals are thin, papery membranes, while there are 4 white, narrow, pointed petals. The inflorescence can be stalked or almost stalkless, nestled among the leaves. To distinguish this species from one seeded pussypaws, you must decide what constitutes a single rosette because one seeded pussypaws has multiple inflorescences per rosette, while this species has only a single inflorescence per rosette.

❖ *Claytonia nevadensis* (Sierra spring beauty)   **FAMILY:** Montiaceae (Portulacaceae)

DISTRIBUTION Fairly common around Tioga Pass and northern Yosemite but quite rare farther south
HABITAT Rocky seeps and very shallow streams, often on metamorphic rock
ELEVATION 9,500'–12,000'
SEASON Early July–mid-August
LOCATIONS Trail from Virginia Lakes to Summit Lake (west side of pass), northwest slope of Mt. Dana, Ionian Basin, Farewell Gap

LEAVES AND STEMS: While the long, branching underground stem is hidden from view, the trailing lines or large masses of leaves can be seen emerging from between rocks. The main leaf blade is 1–4 cm long and oval shaped but ends quite abruptly in a narrow stalk. The margin of the fleshy blade is often reddish.

FLOWERS: The flowers occur in groups of 2–8 but generally open one at a time and therefore seem to occur singly. 5 pale-pink (or white) petals, each decorated with some darker striped veins, emerge from between 2 green to reddish sepals. The narrow bases of the petals tend to be yellowish where they connect. 5 pink-tipped stamens also join at the base of the petals.

RELATED SPECIES: *Claytonia megarhiza,* alpine spring beauty, mostly occurs in Yosemite in locations with long-lasting snow, but there is also a population atop Silver Pass, far to the south. The fleshy leaves are reddish-green, approximately diamond shaped, and they lie flat against the ground, forming a dense, broad rosette. The small, pink, 5-petal flowers peek out from between individual leaves.

Claytonia megarhiza

❖ *Lewisia pygmaea* (alpine lewisia, dwarf lewisia)
       FAMILY: Montiaceae (Portulacaceae)

DISTRIBUTION Common throughout, on both sides of the Sierra Crest
HABITAT Wet meadows, moist sandy flats, moist alpine fell-fields, shallow rocky creeks
ELEVATION 7,500'–13,500'
SEASON Early July–early August
LOCATIONS Trail to Conness Lakes (Twenty Lakes Basin), Iron Lake, north side of Pinchot Pass, west side of Shepherd Pass, lakes east of New Army Pass

LEAVES AND STEMS: The leaves of this species form a small, tight rosette. The fleshy leaves are often just 2–4 cm long, though they can be twice that, and are very narrow. They point in all directions, some lying flat on the ground and others raised steeply upward.

FLOWERS: The rosette can be completely covered in the tiny white to pink flowers. With 5–9 petals that are 5–10 mm long and flowers that may be half buried within the mass of leaves, you need to look closely to appreciate these little gems. The petals are very slightly cup shaped, and they often finish in a narrower, rounded tip. The 2 sepals can be quite jagged at the tip but lack Sierra lewisia's dark-colored glands.

❖ *Chamerion angustifolium* subsp. *circumvagum (Epilobium angustifolium* subsp. *circumvagum)* (fireweed)   **FAMILY:** Onagraceae

DISTRIBUTION Common throughout the western Sierra; very common throughout the eastern Sierra
HABITAT Seeps, stream banks, moist to fairly dry slopes
ELEVATION 4,000'–11,500'
SEASON Mid-July–late August
LOCATIONS Lundy Canyon, Heart Lake (Rock Creek Basin), Evolution Lake, Le Conte Canyon, North Fork Big Pine Creek, Birch Creek

LEAVES AND STEMS: One of the tallest plants you will find at high elevations, fireweed can exceed 2 m in height. Along the stems are narrow, elongate leaves, most between 5 and 12 cm in length. Note that many stalks do not flower in a given year; they will grow to about 50 cm in height and are busily photosynthesizing and storing energy to bloom in a later year.

FLOWERS: Rising above the leaves is the inflorescence, with flowers attached directly to the central stem with short stalks. The showy flowers have narrow purple sepals, 4 broad light-purple petals that are 1.5–2 cm long, 8 purple stamens, and a white 4-part stigma at the end of a long style. Notice that behind the petals is a slightly swollen purplish tube; this is the ovary, called inferior because it is below the petals. It will eventually extend into a 4- to 10-cm-long fruits.

EXTRA TIDBITS: With such an elongate inflorescence, there are often flowers in different stages. You may notice that those at the top have stamens covered with pollen and a closed stigma, while older flowers no longer have pollen and have a stigma that is open.

RELATED SPECIES: *Chamerion latifolium,* dwarf fireweed, is a shorter species (up to 70 cm in height) that occurs on moist metamorphic talus in the eastern Sierra in locations including Lundy Canyon and the Convict Creek drainage. The leaves are broader, approaching oval shaped, but the flowers look quite similar to fireweed.

❖ *Epilobium anagallidifolium* (alpine willowherb)
    FAMILY: Onagraceae

DISTRIBUTION Common throughout, mostly at high elevations
HABITAT Meadows, stream banks, seeps, other moist locations
ELEVATION 7,000'–12,000'
SEASON Early July–mid-August
LOCATIONS Great Sierra Mine, Dana Plateau, Gem Lake (Rock Creek Basin), Humphreys Basin, Ionian Basin, Bullfrog Lake

(Continued)

(Continued)   **LEAVES AND STEMS:** This is the most common willowherb in high-elevation wet locations; at times you will come across just a few stalks, while elsewhere there will be large mats of stems in very shallow waterways. The stems, which can be upright or trailing, are at most 20 cm long and are often reddish. The stems tend to be distinctly curved or S shaped, a good distinguishing feature. Small oval-shaped leaves grow along the entire, often unbranched, stem and range from bright green to reddish in color. Glands cover both the stems and leaves.

FLOWERS: The small flowers grow at the ends of the stems; they are under 1 cm in length and have 4 pale-pink petals nestled inside the narrow, pointed sepals that are more than half the petal's length. Like all willowherbs, the seedpods are striking, a very narrow 2- to 4-cm-long pod that pops open in late summer; those of the alpine willowherb are distinctly arched. As they open, the 4 parts of the seedpod twist backward, releasing the white fluff-covered seeds and providing a new decorative touch to the plant.

❖ *Epilobium ciliatum* subsp. *glandulosum* (fringed willowherb, glandular willowherb)   **FAMILY:** Onagraceae

DISTRIBUTION Occasional in the Yosemite and Mammoth Lakes regions, becoming common in the eastern Sierra from Rock Creek drainage south and in the western Sierra from the southern San Joaquin River drainage south
HABITAT Seeps; wet, boggy meadows; stream banks
ELEVATION 4,000'–11,000'
SEASON Late June–late August
LOCATIONS Second Recess, Piute Pass Trail, North Fork Big Pine Creek, south end of Rae Lakes, Whitney Meadows

LEAVES AND STEMS: Of the many slender, small-flowered willowherbs, this is one of the tallest and most robust, ranging in height from 20 cm to more than 1 m. The entire stem is leafy, and the leaves are fairly oval shaped, though broader at the base, and have conspicuous veins. The upper leaves and stem often have glands, while those at the base of the plants generally lack them.

FLOWERS: Along the upper sections of the stem, flowers usually grow from each of the leaf axils. The flowers have 4 petals, each 4–14 mm long and prominently notched at the tip. Like other members of the family Onagraceae, the ovary is visible behind the petals and develops into a long, narrow pod.

EXTRA TIDBITS: Though you cannot see them, one of the distinguishing features of this subspecies are root nodules called turions, which are underground buds that will grow the following season.

RELATED SPECIES: A second subspecies, *ciliatum,* is a bit shorter, the petals are half as big, the leaves along the stem are much smaller, and it lacks turions. There are many additional species of similar willowherb, including the following three, which all have unbranched stems and petals that are about 5 mm long. *Epilobium hallianum* (Hall's willowherb) is 10–60 cm tall, has gland-tipped hairs on both its leaves and flowers, and—important to its identification—has

Epilobium hallianum

turions, or underground buds. It is common throughout, up to 12,000 feet. *Epilobium lactiflorum,* the white-flowered willowherb, is the only species to have purely white flowers. Its flowers also have gland-tipped hairs, but its leaves lack any hairs. Third, *Epilobium oregonense,* the slimstem (or Oregon) willowherb, is slightly shorter, reaching only up to 30 cm and having a more matted growth form. Its flowers are purple and with some glands, while its leaves lack hairs or glands. Distinguishing among these species is challenging without uprooting them—it is best to simply call all of these species willowherbs.

Epilobium oregonense

❖ *Epilobium glaberrimum* subsp. *fastigiatum* (glaucus willowherb, smooth willowherb) **FAMILY:** Onagraceae

DISTRIBUTION Common on both sides of the Sierra Crest from the Yosemite area south to the Kearsarge Pass area; also common farther west around Mineral King
HABITAT Moist areas, including gravelly stream banks, seeps, and disturbed soil
ELEVATION 7,500'–11,150'
SEASON Early July–early September
LOCATIONS May Lake, Slate Creek Fork Lee Vining Creek, south of Agnew Pass, Heart Lake (Rock Creek Basin), Hilgard Branch Bear Creek, Third Lake (North Fork Big Pine Creek), Charlotte Lake

LEAVES AND STEMS: At upper elevations this willowherb will generally be 10–40 cm tall, while robust lower-elevation individuals could be nearly twice as tall. Like many similar-looking willowherbs, the clumped stems are unbranched and quite leafy, with the leaves being elongate ovals that clasp the stem. The best distinguishing feature is that the bottom section of the stem is glaucous, meaning that it has a gray-waxy or powdery appearance and lacks glands or hairs; the upper stem and leaves may be gland-covered.

FLOWERS: The small flowering stalks grow from leaf axils toward the top of the stem. The 4-petaled flowers can be white, pink, or pale purple. There are generally several flowers per inflorescence.

RELATED SPECIES: A second subspecies, *glaberrimum,* occurs below 10,500 feet and is substantially larger with narrower leaves.

❖ *Epilobium obcordatum* (rockfringe) **FAMILY:** Onagraceae

DISTRIBUTION Common at high elevations on both sides of the Sierra Crest
HABITAT Dry slopes with scattered rocks, often growing alongside a rock
ELEVATION 7,500'–13,500'
SEASON Late July–mid-September
LOCATIONS Dana Plateau, west side of Red Peak Pass, north side of Silver Pass, Mono Pass (Rock Creek Basin), Mt. Whitney Trail, New Army Pass

(Continued)

(Continued)   **LEAVES AND STEMS:** There are no aboveground parts to indicate the location of this plant in early summer. Only later do the spreading stems emerge, usually next to a sheltering rock, and spread across the ground. The leaves densely line the short stems, with several pairs per centimeter. They are quite thick and toothed; they lack any glands or hairs and often have a slightly bluish tinge.

FLOWERS: Several large, showy magenta flowers top each of the unbranched stems. The 4 petals are once-notched and are 1–2.5 cm long. The 4-part stigma and the filaments—the stamen's stalks—are a similarly bright color, though the pollen is white. At times, all the leaves are hidden behind a mass of flowers, a very showy late-summer treat.

❖ *Castilleja lemmonii* (Lemmon's paintbrush)
    FAMILY: Orobanchaceae (Scrophulariaceae)

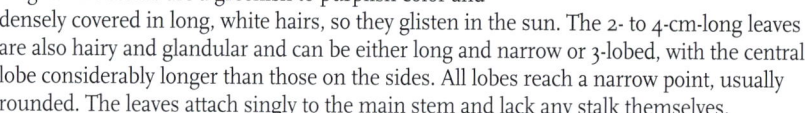

DISTRIBUTION Common throughout, on both sides of the Sierra Crest
HABITAT Moist to wet alpine meadows
ELEVATION 8,000'–12,000'
SEASON Early July–mid-August
LOCATIONS Twenty Lakes Basin, Lake Virginia, north side of Silver Pass, Bear Lakes Basin, Kearsarge Lakes

LEAVES AND STEMS: Growing in clusters—or even great masses—the unbranched stems reach 10–20 cm in height. The stems are a greenish to purplish color and densely covered in long, white hairs, so they glisten in the sun. The 2- to 4-cm-long leaves are also hairy and glandular and can be either long and narrow or 3-lobed, with the central lobe considerably longer than those on the sides. All lobes reach a narrow point, usually rounded. The leaves attach singly to the main stem and lack any stalk themselves.

FLOWERS: At the top of the stem is a single inflorescence composed of up to 20 flowers—though the single magenta mass is what will catch your eye. It really looks like a paintbrush, with the lobes of each flower representing the many individual bristles. If you look at a single flower, you will discover that it is the bracts—the leaves below each flower and the calyx, covered in long hairs—that are colorful. Inside is a much narrower, pale-yellow tube, the fused petals. The dark-colored and quite stout carpel is sometimes visible emerging from the top of a flower.

RELATED SPECIES: *Orthocarpus cuspidatus* subsp. *cryptanthus*, short flowered owl's clover, is occasional in the eastern Sierra in the Yosemite and Mammoth Lakes regions, where it generally occurs on metamorphic rock. Looking superficially like a paintbrush, small pinkish tubular flowers poke out from behind impressive bracts. These broad leaves beneath each flower are mostly green with a pinkish stripe near the tip—and are mostly what makes the inflorescence showy.

Orthocarpus cuspidatus subsp. cryptanthus

❖ Generalists and Specialists

As discussed on page 5, a plant's habitat is where it is able to grow. Some species are able to tolerate a wide range of conditions, so they can be thought of as habitat generalists, while others have a very narrow set of conditions under which they thrive; they are so-called specialists. Generalists are not necessarily one of the most common plants at any site; instead, *generalist* means the species are widespread across the landscape—you will stumble across a generalist in more diverse locations as you hike.

To identify whether a species is a generalist or a specialist, you must consider the occurrence of the species across the landscape together with various habitat characteristics. One study researched alpine landscapes between Yosemite and the Bishop region. Not surprisingly, it found that different species were common in drier versus wetter sites. Across all drier locations, three of the most widespread species were *Phlox condensata* (condensed phlox), *Castilleja nana* (dwarf alpine paintbrush), and *Erigeron pygmaeus* (pygmy fleabane); these are generalist species because they are able to tolerate a range of habitats. Many more specialist species inhabited only a subset of the dry sites studied. For instance, some species occur in sites with a diversity of exposures, slopes, and soil development but are restricted to certain rock types: *Eriogonum ovalifolium* var. *nivale* (cushion buckwheat) and *Silene sargentii* (Sargent's catchfly) avoid marble but occur on both granitic and non-marble metamorphic soils, while *Erigeron clokeyi* (Clokey's fleabane) and *Linum lewisii* (Lewis' flax) are mostly found on marble soils. The landscape can instead be divided by aspect (or exposure) and slope—one type of habitat is alpine fell-field, the fairly flat habitats at the tops of ridges or on plateaus. *Eremogone kingii* (King's sandwort) and *Packera werneriifolia* (hoary groundsel) are two species that can be considered fell-field habitat specialists but are not particular about soil type. Other species were designated as occurring only in very specialized habitats. For instance, *Ivesia lycopodioides* var. *lycopodioides* (club-moss ivesia) and *Lupinus lepidus* var. *lobbii* (Lobb's tiny lupine) prefer non-marble fell-field environments. Such studies are important to confirm what botanists note visually, as well as to provide a starting point for studies that investigate why certain species are (or aren't) restricted to certain habitats.

❖ *Castilleja linariifolia* (desert paintbrush, Wyoming
   paintbrush)   **FAMILY:** Orobanchaceae (Scrophulariaceae)

DISTRIBUTION Common in the eastern Sierra from the
Yosemite region south to around Kearsarge Pass
HABITAT Dry, sandy slopes and flats
ELEVATION 3,000'–10,500'
SEASON Early July–mid-August
LOCATIONS Virginia Lakes Basin, Rock Creek Basin, trail to
Longley Reservoir, Bishop Pass Trail

LEAVES AND STEMS: The 30- to 60-cm-tall stalks usually occur
singly or in small clumps. The stems are rarely
(Continued)

(Continued)   branched and graduate in color from an olive green near the base to
purple in the middle and pinkish at the tip. The leaves are also a showy
mix of green and purple. They may have 0–3 lobes but are always long and narrow—
indeed, linear as the scientific name indicates. They are curled along the midrib into
a U shape, giving them an even narrower appearance. The leaves are clustered near the
base of the plant, with the upper stem typically having fewer and much shorter, smaller
leaves. The stems and leaves generally lack both hairs and glands and often appear shiny.

FLOWERS: Like all members of this genus, the inflorescence at the top of the stem looks
like a paintbrush, in this case full of a bright-pink paint. The head is usually made up
of 10–20 individual tubular flowers, each 2–3.5 cm long, quite narrow, and extending
beyond the calyx tube. The colorful part is actually the calyx, the fused sepals, and the
bracts (the leaves below each flower), while the yellow-greenish petals lie within. They
too form a tube that extends beyond the calyx as the flowers age, giving the older plants
a two-toned appearance.

❖ *Castilleja nana* (dwarf alpine paintbrush)
　　　FAMILY: Orobanchaceae (Scrophulariaceae)

DISTRIBUTION Common throughout on both sides
of the Sierra Crest
HABITAT Alpine fell-fields; dry, rocky flats and
slopes; low-angle talus slopes
ELEVATION 7,000'–13,000'
SEASON Early July–mid-August
LOCATIONS Dana Plateau, Lower Ottoway Lake,
Mono Pass (Rock Creek Basin), Evolution Basin,
headwaters of the Kern River

LEAVES AND STEMS: Usually reaching 10–15 cm in height, but occasionally as high as
25 cm or as short as 5 cm, this is the smallest of the High Sierra paintbrushes. Its stem is
never branched, though a tuft of multiple stems emerges from the root. The leaves range
from mint green to a deep purplish green, generally with pale leaf margins. Because the
leaves are quite thick and folded up along the midrib, the different-colored margins are
quite obvious. The leaves can have up to 5 narrow, pointed lobes or lack lobes. The 3-lobed
leaves below each flower (bracts) tend to be about the same color as the stem leaves.

FLOWERS: Like all paintbrushes, the inflorescence is at the top of the stem. The flowers
of the dwarf alpine paintbrush are quite variable in color, ranging from nearly white
to various shades of pink, green, and sometimes nearly purple. The dominant color is
provided by the bracts (the leaves below each flower) and the calyx, while the petals form
a narrow tube that is mostly hidden inside the 1- to 2-cm-long calyx. The pale-yellow
petals and black-tipped pistil usually emerge at the end of the calyx. Individuals
growing in alpine fell-fields tend to be a more intensely pinkish-gray color, while lower
elevation individuals are paler.

RELATED SPECIES: *Castilleja pilosa*, parrothead paintbrush, is a rarer high-elevation paintbrush that looks quite similar. The most obvious difference is that the bracts, the leaves
below each flower, have rounded tips, while the dwarf alpine paintbrush has pointed
bracts. The parrothead paintbrush also tends to have a greener, rather than pinkish, color.

❖ *Orobanche fasciculata* (clustered broomrape)
     FAMILY: Orobanchaceae

DISTRIBUTION Occasional throughout the eastern Sierra; rarer in the western Sierra but present throughout the range
HABITAT Dry slopes with patches of bare soil; usually associated with *Artemisia* or *Eriogonum* species in the high-elevation Sierra
ELEVATION 1,000'–11,400'
SEASON Early June–early July
LOCATIONS San Joaquin Ridge, Devils Postpile, Heart Lake Meadow (Rock Creek Basin), west shore of Lake Sabrina, Baxter Pass Trail

LEAVES AND STEMS: This parasitic plant lacks any green leaves. Instead, it obtains its energy via connections to the roots of nearby plants. In the high-elevation Sierra, members of the genera *Artemisia* and *Eriogonum* are the most likely hosts.

FLOWERS: The clustered flowering stalks are pink to gray-pink and rise 5–15 cm above the ground. Sometimes there are a few taller stalks and other times a dense cluster of 20 short stems, emerging almost like a ball of flowers. At the top of each stalk is the elongate pinkish-orange tubular flower, with 2 petal lobes pointing upward and 3 downward.

❖ *Pedicularis attollens* (little elephant's head)
     FAMILY: Orobanchaceae (Scrophulariaceae)

DISTRIBUTION Common throughout, on both sides of the Sierra Crest
HABITAT Moister to drier meadows and lakeshores
ELEVATION 5,500'–13,000'
SEASON Late June–early August
LOCATIONS Virginia Lakes Basin, Rock Creek Basin, Lake Sabrina Basin, Kearsarge Lakes

LEAVES AND STEMS: A rosette of 10- to 15-cm-long leaves encircles the base of the flowering stem, while farther up the stem, the leaves rapidly become quite small and then disappear. The leaves are pinnately lobed all the way to the midrib, with the sharp-pointed lobes often a distinct purplish color (and otherwise green), while the midrib is green.

FLOWERS: The tiny (5–7 mm long) pink flowers cover the top section of a 10- to 30-cm-long—and occasionally longer—flowering stem. Each looks like a tiny elephant head, albeit with a very short trunk. 2 fused petals at the top form the quite twisted trunk. The edges of the petals are a brighter pink (or light purple), while the center is white with purple veins. The flowering stalk can be exceedingly white-hairy—even fuzzy looking—especially early in the season.

❖ *Pedicularis groenlandica* (elephant's head)
FAMILY: Orobanchaceae (Scrophulariaceae)

DISTRIBUTION Common throughout, on both sides of the Sierra Crest in the Yosemite and Mammoth Lakes regions, becoming occasional in the eastern Sierra south of the Bishop Creek drainage but continued common to the west
HABITAT Wet meadows and lakeshores
ELEVATION 7,000'–11,500'
SEASON Mid-June–late July
LOCATIONS Twenty Lakes Basin, Rock Creek Basin, Rae Lakes Basin, lakes to the east of Kearsarge Pass

LEAVES AND STEMS: The leaves grow both as a basal rosette and along the lower reaches of the 30- to 60-cm-long stem, though they become much smaller toward the top of the stem. The leaves, up to 20 cm long, are pinnately lobed, with the sharp, narrow lobes extending to the midrib and large gaps between each of the lobes. The leaves can be either green or tinged purplish, especially early season, and lack any hairs.

FLOWERS: The inflorescence is up to 10 cm long and is composed of approximately 1-cm-long, bright-magenta flowers that bear a distinct resemblance to an elephant head. The upper petal forms a hood that is curved downward and ends in a tip—the elephant's trunk—while 2 petals extending to the sides are the floppy ears.

❖ *Dicentra uniflora* (steer's head)　**FAMILY:** Papaveraceae

DISTRIBUTION Fairly common in the Yosemite area on both sides of the Sierra Crest; occasional south through the Mono Recesses and again in the far southwestern Sierra; absent elsewhere
HABITAT Forest, gravelly flats
ELEVATION 7,500'–11,200'
SEASON Mid-May–early July
LOCATIONS Tilden Lake, Lundy Canyon, northern edge of Tuolumne Meadows, Cathedral Fork Echo Creek, Kern River drainage south of Mountain Home State Forest

LEAVES AND STEMS: 1–3 leaves emerge directly from the ground, often within days of the snow melting. The 4- to 6-cm blue-green leaves are much divided into rounded lobed leaflets—and are often what first catches your eye.

FLOWERS: Near each set of leaves emerges just 1, or occasionally up to 3, light-pink flowers, each about 1.5 cm long and on its own short pinkish stalk. The 2 central petals are pushed flat against each other (the steer's nose), while the side petals are bent back on themselves (the ears), giving a good impersonation of a miniature bull. Only the astute hiker is treated to seeing this species—not only does this species bloom very early in the season, but the flowers blend in remarkably well. I usually only notice the plants as I step over them; they never show up in the distance.

❖ *Mimulus breweri* (Brewer's monkeyflower)
   FAMILY: Phrymaceae (Scrophulariaceae)

DISTRIBUTION Very common throughout, on both sides of the Sierra Crest
HABITAT Moist to seasonally dry areas, especially in locations with bare or disturbed soil
ELEVATION 3,400'–11,200'
SEASON Mid-June–early August
LOCATIONS Virginia Lakes Basin, Gaylor Lakes, Mono Creek, Rock Creek Basin, Evolution Basin

LEAVES AND STEMS: Like so many annuals, this species can occur in large patches in wetter years and be nearly absent following dry winters. The reddish stems are more elongate than the skunky or slender monkeyflower, rising 3–21 cm; they are typically unbranched. The leaves are usually 1–2 cm in length and quite narrow. The leaves have untoothed margins and are densely covered in gland-tipped hairs; they occur in pairs, slightly more crowded toward the top of the stem.

FLOWERS: These tiny flowers are pink; the flower tube is just a few millimeters wide and slightly under 1 cm in length. The 5 petal lobes are not particularly bent open, but if you peer into the throat, you will note it has 2 yellow ridges. The pedicel, the stalk connecting the flower to the stem, can range 2–15 mm in length. The fact that this stalk is usually longer than the calyx is a key feature for identifying this monkeyflower.

❖ Annual Plants at High Elevation

An annual species is one that germinates, grows, produces seed, and dies in a single growing season. A perennial plant's life cycle spans multiple years, and it almost always spends multiple years growing before it begins flowering. (Biennials are an intermediate case. They live for two years: In the first year they simply grow, while in the second season, they begin by growing but then produce flowers and fruits, after which they die.)

At low elevations there are many annuals: Consider all the beautiful grassland flowers in coastal California. They germinate in February and March and have flowered and set seed by the end of May, if not much earlier. These are warm, pleasant months at lower elevations, and the plants can grow fast and be confident that they will have abundant pollinators. However, perennial species become more and more dominant at higher elevations—the growing season is short, growth is limited, and pollinators are scarce. Only 1 in 8 species occurring above 10,000 feet is an annual. Once you reach 12,000 feet, only 1 in 20 species is an annual, mainly a few species of tiny *Mimulus*, *Gayophytum*, and *Polygonum*. But this is still a much higher percentage of annual species than what exists in cooler, wetter alpine areas, such as the

(Continued)

(Continued)   European Alps, where only 1% of alpine species are annuals. One
benefit annual species have is that the seeds can remain dormant
until conditions are ideal. During drought years, very few individuals will germinate,
while in seasons with abundant moisture, the ground may be covered with showy
little flowers. Because annual species invest little energy in deep roots or sturdy
stems, they can instead focus on growing fast and producing lots of small seeds.

❖ *Mimulus leptaleus* (slender monkeyflower)
    FAMILY: Phrymaceae (Scrophulariaceae)

DISTRIBUTION Occasional from the Yosemite region
south through the Mono Recesses, becoming rarer farther
south; absent in the eastern Sierra south of Rock Creek
HABITAT Sandy flats, disturbed or open dry soils
ELEVATION 4,000'–11,300'
SEASON Mid-June–early August
LOCATIONS Tenaya Lake, Thousand Island Lake, Mono
Recesses, Sallie Keyes Lakes, Rock Creek Basin, Bench Lake

LEAVES AND STEMS: This annual has stems that are 1–14 cm
tall, with most of the narrow leaves near the top of the stem.
Gland-tipped hairs cover the leaves and stem.

FLOWERS: One of the smaller monkeyflowers, this one has a pink flower tube that is only
5–10 mm in length and very narrow. The flower lobes at the top of the tube are very short,
and each has a darker magenta line down the middle. There are 2 yellow ridges inside
the flower's throat. Unlike Brewer's monkeyflower, another very small monkeyflower, the
stalk connecting the flower to the main stem is absent or very short. At times, because the
stalks are so short, many flowers can emerge next to each other, creating a crowded head.

❖ *Mimulus lewisii* (Lewis' monkeyflower)   **FAMILY:** Phrymaceae (Scrophulariaceae)

DISTRIBUTION Occurs throughout on both sides of the
Sierra Crest; common in the Yosemite region, becoming rarer
to the south
HABITAT Moist slopes, seeps, stream banks
ELEVATION 3,800'–10,200'
SEASON Early July–mid-August
LOCATIONS Green Creek, Shadow Lake, Agnew Meadows,
Middle Fork Kings River, Rambaud Creek

LEAVES AND STEMS: A species most common at montane
elevations, it also occurs in wet locations in the subalpine zone,
where you may find great expanses of the quite tall stems (up to
80 cm). Like the closely related scarlet monkeyflower, the stems
and leaves are sticky due to a covering of glandular hairs. This
species has narrower leaves, but they are still a vibrant light
green, occur in pairs, and have 3–5 distinct veins that merge at the base of the leaf.

FLOWERS: The flowers vary in color from a light pink to an intense rose pink. The petal lobes that emerge from the long flower tube are so beautifully showy that you barely realize that much of the 3- to 5-cm-long flower tube is hidden within the green calyx. The lobes are almost rectangular in outline, up to 2 cm in length, and bent wide open, showing off the long yellow hairs and yellow coloring in the flower's throat. Flowers occur individually on long stalks emerging from leaf nodes.

❖ *Mimulus montioides* (montia like monkeyflower)
    FAMILY: Phrymaceae (Scrophulariaceae)

DISTRIBUTION Occasional from the San Joaquin River drainage south through the Kern Plateau, becoming abundant in a few regions, including Cottonwood Lakes, the area southeast of Cedar Grove, and around Huntington Lake
HABITAT Seasonally moist sandy flats, especially with granitic soils
ELEVATION 3,000'–11,000'
SEASON Late May–early July
LOCATIONS Huntington Lake, Mitchell Peak, Cottonwood Lakes, Timosea Peak, Pacific Crest Trail north of Olancha Peak

LEAVES AND STEMS: While most individuals rise just a few centimeters above the ground, this annual has known ranges of 3–18 cm in height. The very narrow leaves occur in pairs, and gland-tipped hairs densely cover both the leaves and the stems.

FLOWERS: The flowers can be either pure yellow or a combination of yellow and purple, with the upper 2 petals a deep magenta purple and the lower 3 yellow with red patterning at the mouth of the flower tube. The petals are notched about a third of the way to the floral tube. The pedicel, the stem connecting the flower to the leaf node, is moderately long.

❖ *Mimulus nanus* var. *mephiticus (Mimulus mephiticus)* (skunky monkeyflower)
    FAMILY: Phrymaceae (Scrophulariaceae)

DISTRIBUTION Common in the Yosemite region and south of Mt. Whitney but more occasional in between; occurs on both sides of the Sierra Crest
HABITAT Dry to seasonally moist gravelly slopes and flats
ELEVATION 5,000'–12,100'
SEASON Mid-June–late July
LOCATIONS Clouds Rest, summit of Mt. Warren, San Joaquin Mountain, Dragon's Back Trail on Mammoth Mountain, Shepherd Pass Trail, Mt. Whitney Trail

LEAVES AND STEMS: This annual is especially abundant in wet years, but you will always find a few scattered individuals. It generally grows only a few centimeters above the ground, though you will occasionally see plants exceeding 10 cm. Because the stem is so short, the leaf blades are quite crowded along it, giving the plant a bushy look. The stem leaves have a narrow oval shape, and their margins are densely

(Continued)

(Continued)　covered with gland-tipped hairs, with slightly
fewer hairs occurring on the leaf blades. The
leaves and stem have a strong odor—a good way to identify
this species.

FLOWERS: These monkeyflowers can be either yellow or
magenta, though a given patch will typically be a single color.
Like all monkeyflowers, the petals are fused into a long tube
that widens at the top. The 5 petal lobes spread wide open,
creating a flower approximately 1 cm in diameter; the petal
lobes are fairly rectangular in outline and less asymmetrical
than some monkeyflowers. In both colors of flowers, the throat
is hairy and yellow with pink spots. The pedicels, the stalks connecting the flower
to the stem, are quite short for a monkeyflower—always well under a centimeter—
contributing to the crowded look of the inflorescence.

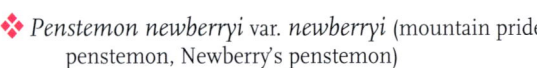

❖ *Penstemon newberryi* var. *newberryi* (mountain pride
　　　penstemon, Newberry's penstemon)
　　　　FAMILY: Plantaginaceae (Scrophulariaceae)

DISTRIBUTION Very common throughout, on both sides
of the Sierra Crest
HABITAT Alongside boulders in open forest and on
open slopes
ELEVATION 3,500'–10,500'
SEASON Early June–mid-July
LOCATIONS Almost everywhere, including Clouds Rest,
Bennettville, Duck Pass Trail, Bishop Pass Trail,
Goddard Canyon, Rae Lakes Basin

LEAVES AND STEMS: This woody shrub reaches up to 30 cm
in height, and the many stalks are densely covered in pairs
of 1- to 3-cm-long, oval-shaped, minutely toothed leaves. The
older leaves have an almost bluish hue, while the younger ones are a vibrant green.

FLOWERS: The tubular magenta flowers are 2–3 cm long and widen only slightly toward
the mouth. Quite apparent are the upper and lower lips at the tube ending, with both
the 2 upper lobes and 3 lower lobes bent entirely open to showcase the white hairs on
the lower part of the tube. The 5 lobes of the glandular, rose- to green-colored calyx tube
are narrow and sharply pointed.

❖ To Sweat or Not to Sweat

When we get too hot, our bodies sweat, and as the sweat evaporates, our skin is
cooled. The more we sweat, the cooler we stay, but also the more we need to drink
to replace the lost water. Now imagine you are a plant basking in the sun; even at
high elevations, plant leaves can become too hot, causing damage to the bio-
molecules inside (see also "Too Much Light," page 69). Like us, plants can cool
themselves through evaporative water loss; they do so through small holes called

stomata, which are mostly located on the underside of their leaves and which they can open and close. But they also face a dilemma: If they lose water at a rate faster than it can be replaced by their roots, they risk becoming too water stressed, leading first to wilting and potentially to death. In dry soils they simply cannot afford to lose water all day. To further complicate the choice these plants must make, the stomata are also the entry point for carbon dioxide, the gas that is converted to sugars during photosynthesis; to grow, plants must keep their stomata open for at least part of the day.

Plants therefore face a delicate balance. In bright environments, most species deflect some incoming radiation (both visible light and other wavelengths) by having a reflective leaf surface—hairs or a waxy coating are the two most common adaptations. Hairs have a second advantage in locations with dry air; they create a thicker layer of still and humid air around the leaf. This envelope of air leads to less water being lost to evaporation when the stomata are open to take in carbon dioxide. It is also one way that plants in dry environments can decrease the amount of water lost while photosynthesizing. Plants also vary in the amount of water loss they can tolerate before wilting.

Studies on Sierran species provide some examples of the strategies plants use. For example, *Penstemon davidsonii* (Davidson's penstemon), which inhabits moister soils, loses more water while photosynthesizing than does *Penstemon newberryi* (mountain pride penstemon), which lives in slightly drier soils. In another study, *Eremogone kingii* (King's sandwort), common in many dry alpine fell-field environments, becomes increasingly water stressed throughout the day without suffering any long-term ill effects. In other words, over the course of the day, it can lose water through its stomata at a much faster rate than it can replenish it from the soil without wilting, and then re-equilibrate overnight when its stomata are closed. Several co-occurring species are unable to tolerate the same degree of water stress and are absent or uncommon on the driest sites. See "Decisions Plants Make," page 113, to learn more about the trade-offs plants face.

❖ *Collomia linearis* (narrow-leaf mountain trumpet)
   FAMILY: Polemoniaceae

DISTRIBUTION Common in the Yosemite region and the San Joaquin drainage, on both sides of the Sierra Crest; fairly common in the Kern River drainage but nearly absent in the Kings River drainage
HABITAT Moist meadows, damp forest openings
ELEVATION 4,000'–10,500'
SEASON Late June–early August
LOCATIONS Tuolumne Meadows, west slope of Mt. Dana, Agnew Meadows, Rock Creek Lake, Cottonwood Lakes

(Continued)

(Continued)   **LEAVES AND STEMS:** This species is one of the tallest annuals extending into the subalpine zone; the plants can exceed 30 cm in height.
The stems are leafy throughout, and the leaves are usually shaped like exceedingly long, skinny triangles, for they narrow little where they attach to the stem. At least some of the stems and the leaves tend to be gland-covered.

FLOWERS: The flowers cluster in one or more dense inflorescences toward the top of the plant. The flowers, pale pink to purplish in color, are a narrow tube with 5 bent-open petal lobes at the top. The inside of the flower tube tends to be yellowish. As the petals fall off, the tuft of tubular, gland-covered sepals remains.

❖ *Leptosiphon ciliatus (Linanthus ciliatus)* (whiskerbrush)
     FAMILY: Polemoniaceae

DISTRIBUTION Common throughout, on both sides of the Sierra Crest
HABITAT Forest opens, flats, meadow edges
ELEVATION 1,000'–10,500'
SEASON Early June–early July
LOCATIONS Tuolumne Meadows, Mammoth Trail, Mono Pass Trail (Yosemite), East Lake (south of Bubbs Creek), Mineral King area

LEAVES AND STEMS: This annual species varies from having a single 2-cm stem up to a branched 30-cm-tall plant, though plants toward the lower end of the height spectrum are more common. At regular intervals along the reddish, hairy stem (or sometimes just once) is a dense tuft of needlelike "leaves" covered in long white hairs—these are actually the many linear lobes of a pair of leaves. I'm not sure if the leaves or their hairs are the *whiskers* referred to in the plant's name.

FLOWERS: Emerging from the top tuft of white, bristly "leaves" (bracts, in this case) is 1 to a few tubular pink flowers, a little under 1 cm in diameter. The tube is quite narrow and elongate (1–2.5 cm), ending with the bent-open petal lobes. The petal lobes are pink on the outer edges with a dark pink dot toward the middle and yellow coloring the throat. Though each plant is small, they can often grow in enormous masses, providing a sheet of pink color.

❖ *Bistorta bistortoides (Polygonum bistortoides)* (American bistort)
     FAMILY: Polygonaceae

DISTRIBUTION Fairly common throughout the western Sierra; crossing to the eastern Sierra around Tioga Pass
HABITAT Wet meadows, grassy stream banks
ELEVATION 4,500'–10,300'
SEASON Late June–early August
LOCATIONS Virginia Lakes Basin, Gaylor Lakes, Isberg Lakes, south of Silver Pass, Alta Meadow, Hockett Meadow

LEAVES AND STEMS: Reaching up to 50 cm in height—or even a little higher—American bistort can occur in large masses in wet meadows or seeps. Dense clusters of the narrow, elongate leaf blades, generally 10–20 cm in length, stick upward among many reddish-colored stems. The stem leaves are much smaller but similarly elongate.

FLOWERS: At the top of the stalk are the tiny white to pale-pink flowers, forming a tight, dense, quite cylindrical inflorescence. Each flower, should you wish to pull them apart, is 4–5 mm long with 5 petals.

❖ *Eriogonum wrightii* var. *subscaposum* (short-stemmed bastard-sage)
        FAMILY: Polygonaceae

DISTRIBUTION Common throughout, on both sides of the Sierra Crest
HABITAT Sandy to gravelly slopes; alongside rocks
ELEVATION 4,000'–10,600'
SEASON Early July–mid-August
LOCATIONS North of Garnet Lake, French Canyon, below Dusy Basin, Kearsarge Pass Trail, Mt. Whitney Trail

LEAVES AND STEMS: This common species is a subshrub (or occasionally a shrub), indicating that the lower branches are woody while the upper sections tend to be green; it grows to no more than 40 cm in height and often much less as it hugs the ground or a nearby rock. The bark has a distinct reddish hue and is quite flaky. The leaves may be gray-green if covered with dense white hairs (what is most common) but may also lack hairs. The leaves grow in small clusters along the basal sections of the branches.

FLOWERS: The flowering stalks, notably stout and straight, lack hairs and are a vibrant green. The flowers grow as tufts along the length of the stalk and especially at the tip. The petals are white, but the flowers appear a pale pink due to the pinkish-brown midveins down the center of each petal and pink shading on the back of wilted petals.

RELATED SPECIES: A second variety, *olanchense,* grows along the western slopes of Olancha Peak and has a more compact growth form.

❖ *Polygonum minimum* (little mountain knotweed, broadleaf knotweed)
        FAMILY: Polygonaceae

DISTRIBUTION Fairly common throughout, especially at high elevations
HABITAT Unvegetated soil, especially disturbed locations; meadows
ELEVATION 4,600'–11,500'
SEASON Early July–mid-August
LOCATIONS North end of Saddlebag Lake, Garnet Lake, Evolution Valley, Kearsarge Pass Trail

LEAVES AND STEMS: These tiny annuals sometimes appear in unlikely locations, such as the damp mudbanks that

(Continued)

(Continued)   form as lake waters retreat during the summer. Generally measuring less than 10 cm in height, the stems tend to be reddish. The oval-shaped leaves are crowded at the top of the stems.

FLOWERS: The tiny flowers, less than 5 mm across, are composed of 5 narrow, white or pale-pink petals, the very bases of which are fused together. Each plant has only a few flowers, attached individually at the leaf axils.

❖ *Polygonum polygaloides* subsp. *kelloggii* (milkwort knotweed, Kellogg's knotweed)
     FAMILY: Polygonaceae

DISTRIBUTION Common throughout, on both sides of the Sierra Crest
HABITAT Meadows, seeps, moist disturbed soil
ELEVATION 4,500'–11,300'
SEASON Late June–early August
LOCATIONS Tuolumne Meadows, Tioga Peak, Ruby Lake (Rock Creek Basin), Evolution Lake, Rae Lakes Basin, Cottonwood Lakes

LEAVES AND STEMS: Like the little mountain knotweed, this species is small, with the stem reaching less than 10 cm (with rare exceptions). Here the similarities end because this species' entire stem is densely covered with tiny, narrow, quite thick leaves with under-rolled leaf margins.

FLOWERS: At each leaf node is a minute pink to white flower, mostly hidden behind the leaf itself and just appearing as a pink dot unless you have a good magnifying glass. The flowers, like all members of the genus *Polygonum,* are 5-petaled.

❖ *Primula fragrans (Dodecatheon redolens)* (scented shootingstar)
     FAMILY: Primulaceae

DISTRIBUTION Common from the Bishop Creek drainage south to the Whitney area on both sides of the Sierra Crest; absent farther north
HABITAT Moist meadows; moist slopes, including sandy and rocky areas; alpine stream banks
ELEVATION 6,500'–12,200'
SEASON Early July–mid-August
LOCATIONS Lake Sabrina Basin, Evolution Lake, North Fork Big Pine Creek, Rae Lakes Basin, Guitar Lake

LEAVES AND STEMS: The 20- to 40-cm-long, narrow leaves form a rosette—maybe better visualized as a tuft of leaves, as they tend to point both upward and outward. The leaves, stem, and flowers are all densely covered in gland-tipped hairs, but the hairs are so tiny that the plants simply look fuzzy without close inspection.

FLOWERS: Like all shootingstars, this species has stocky stamens that form a point and long bent-back petals. In contrast to the Sierra shootingstar, this species always has 5, not 4, petals, and at the base of the petals is only a yellow ring—no red one. The petals form a little bulge as they bend back, so the yellow circle is shaped like an inner tube. Each flowering stalk holds 5–10 flowers.

❖ *Primula jeffreyi (Dodecatheon jeffreyi)* (Sierra shootingstar)
      FAMILY: Primulaceae

DISTRIBUTION Common throughout, on both sides of the Sierra Crest
HABITAT Moist meadows, other quite moist locations, stream banks
ELEVATION 4,500'–11,500'
SEASON Early July–early August
LOCATIONS Lukens Lake, outlet to Dollar Lake (Rae Lakes Basin), below Trail Camp (Mt. Whitney Trail), Sky Blue Lake

LEAVES AND STEMS: The plants have quite large (10–60 cm in length) and rather narrow leaves that lack glands or hairs. The leaves form a large rosette, with leaves generally pointing upward.

FLOWERS: These pinkish-purple flowers are difficult to miss: A single stalk, commonly 30 cm tall (but at times twice that), is topped with up to 18 flowers, each on a stalk that is about 3–5 cm long. Many of these stalks bend over, but some remain upright, so the flowers shoot in all directions. The tubular flowers have 4 (or occasionally 5) bent-back petal lobes, each skinny and 1–1.5 cm long. At the center of the tube are an outer yellow ring and inner reddish ring, and then, pointing opposite the lobes, are 4 dark reddish-brown stamens and a single skinny style, the point of the shootingstar. At first glance, this species may be confused with the scented shootingstar, which always has 5 petals; also note that in locations where they co-occur, the scented shootingstar tends to grow at higher elevations.

❖ Buzz Pollination

A bumblebee's buzz is more than a passing sound. The sound we immediately recognize is part of a carefully choreographed procedure that the bee uses to extract pollen from certain flowers. Here is the setup: To prevent pollen thieves and to encourage pollinators to visit their flowers many times, some plant species do not prominently display pollen on the tips of stamens. Instead of the pollen-containing sacs at the top of the stamens (the anthers) being fully open, the anthers have only narrow slits through which the pollen can exit.

    A process known as sonication is used to extract this well-guarded pollen. A bumblebee grabs hold of the flowers and curls her body around the pollen sacs. She then vibrates her body (that is, buzzes), which causes the flower to vibrate and release the pollen grains. This cunning mechanism ensures *(Continued)*

(Continued)   that non-buzzing bees and other insects cannot obtain the pollen.

In addition, to increase cross-pollination between individuals, a single visit releases only some of the pollen, encouraging repeat visits. Each time a bumblebee buzzes a flower, some of the pollen grains she is already carrying from other individuals might land on the stigma, leading to cross-pollination.

While honeybees buzz for other purposes, they do not buzz pollinate; this is the domain of bumblebees—as well as many other species of bees and one species of fly. In the Sierra, the most common buzz-pollinated flowers are shooting-stars (genus *Primula*), louseworts and elephant's heads (genus *Pedicularis*), and some of the wintergreens (genus *Pyrola*). In buzz-pollinated species, the stamens are generally grouped together and surround the stigma closely, providing a landing platform for the bumblebees. Buzz-pollinated species tend to have many pollen grains, a good source of nutrition for bumblebees, and lack nectar.

❖ *Primula suffrutescens* (Sierra primrose)   **FAMILY:** Primulaceae

DISTRIBUTION Common in the Mammoth Lakes region and then from Bishop south on both sides of the Sierra Crest; more occasional in Yosemite and the Mono Recesses
HABITAT Seasonally moist to fairly dry, sandy to gravelly locations alongside rocks
ELEVATION 8,500'–13,500'
SEASON Mid-June–late July
LOCATIONS Clouds Rest, Dragon's Back Trail on Mammoth Mountain, west side of Duck Pass, Mather Pass, east side of Kearsarge Pass, east side of New Army Pass

LEAVES AND STEMS: The woody base is hidden behind a continuous cover of small rosettes. The leaves are 1.5–3.5 cm long, with a wedge shape that tapers sharply near the base. They are quite thick and distinctly toothed or serrated along the upper margin.

FLOWERS: A single unbranched flowering stalk rises from each rosette on which 2–12 flowers rest. The blooms are an intensely bright magenta—occasionally paler—making them easy to remember. 5 fairly round petals attach into a short tube, the center of which is yellow.

❖ *Primula tetrandra (Dodecatheon alpinum)*
    (alpine shootingstar)   **FAMILY:** Primulaceae

DISTRIBUTION Common throughout, on both sides of the Sierra Crest
HABITAT Moist meadows, other quite moist locations
ELEVATION 6,500'–12,000'
SEASON Early June–mid-July
LOCATIONS Twenty Lakes Basin, Rock Creek Basin, Evolution Lake, Upper Basin

LEAVES AND STEMS: This small, dainty shootingstar graces almost every meadow in the alpine and subalpine zones. It is also one of the first species to begin blooming. The (usually) 4- to 10-cm-long leaves are quite narrow and almost fleshy; they lack hairs and grow as a rosette.

FLOWERS: A single flowering stalk grows from the rosette. On this stalk, up to 10 flowers grow, each connected to the end of the stalk by reddish stems that are several centimeters long and tend to bend over, making the flowers point down. The flowers themselves are an exquisite shape, mimicking their name beautifully. A dark tip—actually 4 stamens with the style at the end—and 4 bent-back light-purple petals dangle behind. The smallest of the Sierra's shootingstars, it could only be confused with the lower elevation subalpine shootingstar, which has 5 petals and is quite bumpy and wrinkled at the base of the stamens.

❖ *Horkelia fusca* var. *parviflora* (dusky horkelia, tawny horkelia)　**FAMILY:** Rosaceae

> **DISTRIBUTION** Fairly common throughout montane elevations in the western Sierra, becoming especially common in the Yosemite region; mostly absent in the eastern Sierra south of the Mammoth Lakes region
> **HABITAT** Dry to wet meadows
> **ELEVATION** 5,500'–10,800'
> **SEASON** Late June–early August
> **LOCATIONS** Virginia Lakes Basin, Tioga Lake, Rafferty Creek, Devils Postpile

LEAVES AND STEMS: Clumps of leaves may either appear singly or as part of a larger mat. The quite bright-green leaves are narrow and divided pinnately into many leaflets, each of these pinnately notched. Though the leaves may be either basal or attached to the lower sections of the flowering stalks, they appear as a layer close to the ground.

FLOWERS: Flowering stalks usually exceeding 20 cm in length emerge from the basal leaves and are topped by a head of 5–20 flowers. The petals are narrowly wedge shaped and generally white with pink-maroon veins—the veins often give the entire petals a pinkish hue. Equally obvious are the bright maroon to pink, hairy, triangular sepals that sit opposite the petals.

❖ *Rosa woodsii* subsp. *gratissima* (Mojave rose)　　**FAMILY:** Rosaceae

> **DISTRIBUTION** Common throughout the eastern Sierra; occasional west of the Sierra Crest
> **HABITAT** Creek banks, lakeshores, wet slopes, seeps
> **ELEVATION** 3,500'–10,500'
> **SEASON** Late May–early July
> **LOCATIONS** Rush Creek Trail, Convict Lake, Pine Creek Trail, Birch Creek, Mt. Whitney Trail

(Continued)

(Continued) **LEAVES AND STEMS:** These roses grow as massive thickets wherever water is available, often forming a 3-m wall of infinite thorns. Indeed, they have prickles along all branch lengths. The thin leaves are comprised of 5–7 oval-shaped, 2- to 4-cm-long leaflets that are toothed along much of the margin.

FLOWERS: The 5-petal flowers are generally 4 cm across and range from a light pink to a deep magenta. The petal shape is unmistakably that of a rose, and like a domesticated rose, the petals are large and overlapping, hiding the sepals underneath. In the center are a large number of yellow stamens. Flowers occur singly or in small groups, throughout the thicket of branches. The oval-shaped red fruits form in late summer.

RELATED SPECIES: A second subspecies, *ultramontana,* occurs only in the eastern Sierra and is somewhat less common. It has fewer prickles, and no prickles on the inflorescence, and the stem prickles it does have are slimmer and shorter than those of Mojave rose.

❖ *Spiraea splendens (Spiraea densiflora)* (rock spiraea, rose meadowsweet)   **FAMILY:** Rosaceae

DISTRIBUTION Common west of the Sierra Crest south through the Kings River drainage, as well as along the Marble Fork of the Kaweah River; in the eastern Sierra, common from the Yosemite region south to the Palisades
HABITAT Alongside rocks in moist to fairly dry, usually open locations, including cracks in slabs and sandy slopes
ELEVATION 4,000'–11,000'
SEASON Early July–mid-August
LOCATIONS Twenty Lakes Basin, Lembert Dome, Rock Creek Basin, Bear Lakes Basin, Piute Pass Trail, Alta Peak

LEAVES AND STEMS: Typically reaching just 0.5 m in height, this densely branched shrub has thin, dull-colored, oval-shaped leaves that may or may not have toothed margins. The branches are rather thin and often have a reddish tone.

FLOWERS: The inflorescences rise straight above the leaves on long shoots and consist of masses of quite small (about 0.5 cm), brilliant magenta flowers. Should you look closely at the flowers, you will see that each has 5 petals and many equally pink stamens that extend beyond the petals, making the heads of flowers appear even larger. The inflorescence stems range from pinkish to green.

❖ *Galium hypotrichium* subsp. *hypotrichium* (alpine bedstraw)   **FAMILY:** Rubiaceae

DISTRIBUTION Common in the eastern Sierra from the Yosemite region south to the Bishop Creek drainage; farther south, replaced by two similar-looking subspecies
HABITAT Dry, rocky slopes
ELEVATION 6,000'–12,200'
SEASON Mid-June–early August
LOCATIONS Virginia Lakes Basin, Convict Creek drainage, Mono Pass Trail (Rock Creek Basin), Coyote Ridge, Chocolate Mountain

LEAVES AND STEMS: Though common throughout the eastern and southern Sierra, this species is easily overlooked. The flowers are tiny and dull, and the stems and leaves are so small that they simply appear as a tangled thicket from afar. Take a closer look and you will see a dense cluster of stems, up to 12 cm in length. The leaves are less than 1 cm long and attach to the stem in sets of 4. The plant is generally hairy, though the exact pattern of hairs varies by subspecies.

FLOWERS: The 4-petal flowers are just a few millimeters in diameter and have a pinkish hue. When in full bloom, the 4 bright-yellow stamens look quite large in comparison to the tiny petals. However, you are more likely to notice the fruits, densely covered in long, white hairs; though still only 5 mm in diameter, the fruits are abundant enough that the plant appears to be well-decorated with tiny pom-poms.

RELATED SPECIES: There are three subspecies of alpine bedstraw that you might see. The most common is subsp. *hypotrichium,* which is often described as being velvety due to its abundant short hairs; it is the only species to grow north of Bishop. Subsp. *subalpinum* is hairy but not velvety, and subsp. *inyoense* is the only one to have woody stems. Subsp. *subalpinum* and *inyoense* are both restricted to regions south of Bishop and occur on both sides of the Sierra Crest.

❖ *Kelloggia galioides* (milk kelloggia)   **FAMILY:** Rubiaceae

DISTRIBUTION Common throughout the western Sierra; common in the eastern Sierra from the Yosemite region south to Bishop
HABITAT Open forest floor
ELEVATION 4,000'–10,500'
SEASON Early June–late July
LOCATIONS Virginia Lakes Basin, Slate Creek Fork Lee Vining Creek, Mammoth Lakes Basin, Rock Creek Lake, Woods Creek crossing, Vidette Meadow

LEAVES AND STEMS: This herb has skinny, branched stems and reaches 15–40 cm in height. It is more common at montane elevations but occurs sparingly up higher. The narrow leaves occur in pairs, are quite glossy, and lack hairs. The stem is slightly angled at each leaf node, giving the plant a very jointed appearance.

FLOWERS: The tubular 4-petal flowers occur at the ends of branches. The narrow white tube is just 3 mm long, with pink petal lobes extending another 3 mm outward. Noteworthy is the ovary, located below the flower tube. It is bulbous and bristly while in flower and expands slightly more as it develops into a fruit.

❖ *Heuchera rubescens* (pink alumroot)
    FAMILY: Saxifragaceae

> **DISTRIBUTION** Common throughout, on both sides of the Sierra Crest
> **HABITAT** Alongside boulders and outcrops, in sheltered, usually moist locations
> **ELEVATION** 3,600'–13,400'
> **SEASON** Mid-June–late July
> **LOCATIONS** South of Garnet Lake, Convict Lake, Lamarck Lakes Trail, Evolution Basin, Milestone Basin, near Trail Camp (Mt. Whitney Trail)

LEAVES AND STEMS: A great profusion of 1- to 6-cm-wide leaves often emerges from a crack in a rock or damp soil next to a rock, forming a mound of bright green. The leaves are approximately round in outline but are palmately lobed, and the lobes are typically sharp-toothed.

FLOWERS: Light-pink flowering stalks, usually 20–30 cm in length, grow upward. The inflorescences have many side branches, each with up to 7 small flowers, resulting in a long, open inflorescence. The pale-pink to white flower tubes are the calyx, while 5 skinny, 3-mm-long white petal lobes emerge from the tube and flop in arbitrary directions. 5 white stamens tipped with red pollen sacks also stick out of the tube.

❖ *Lithophragma glabrum* (rock star, bulbous woodland star)
    FAMILY: Saxifragaceae

> **DISTRIBUTION** Occasional throughout
> **HABITAT** Seasonally wet gravel flats, forest openings, seeps
> **ELEVATION** 5,500'–12,000'
> **SEASON** Early June–early July
> **LOCATIONS** Upper McCabe Lake, below Gardisky Lake, Mt. Dana Trail, top of Taboose Pass, Bubbs Creek headwaters

LEAVES AND STEMS: A small cluster of palmately lobed, 1- to 3-cm-wide leaves appears at the ground surface; the 3–5 lobes extend nearly to the leaf's center and may be rounded or pointy tipped. Early season they have a reddish hue along the margins, and the entire leaf turns red-orange midsummer. Smaller leaves with the same shape grow along the flower stalks.

FLOWERS: A 10- to 25-cm-tall, quite red stalk supports 1–7 dainty little flowers. Each of the 5 light-link petals is divided into 5 sharp-tipped nodes, creating a beautiful—albeit small—star shape. This species blooms early and is a delightful early summer treat.

RELATED SPECIES: *Lithophragma bolanderi,* Sierra star, is fairly common in the mixed conifer and upper montane fir forests. Its 5 white petals are unnotched, its leaf lobes are round and broad, and its stems

Lithophragma bolanderi

are green, not reddish. It can be found along the Merced River Canyon, at Sallie Keyes Lakes, and along Mono Creek.

❖ *Allium bisceptrum* (twincrest onion, aspen onion)   **FAMILY:** Alliaceae (Liliaceae)

DISTRIBUTION Common throughout the eastern Sierra; generally absent in the western Sierra
HABITAT Open forest, especially under aspens; meadows
ELEVATION 6,000'–10,200'
SEASON Early June–late July
LOCATIONS Lundy Canyon, Convict Lake, Rock Creek Trail, North Fork Big Pine Creek Trail

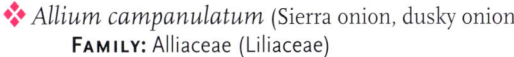

LEAVES AND STEMS: This wild onion has a central stem reaching 10–35 cm in length, as well as 2 (or sometimes more) long, linear leaves emerging from the bulb.

FLOWERS: The inflorescence is clustered at the top of the stalk, growing as an umbel. Each of the many pinkish-purple 6-petal flowers is on its own 1- to 2-cm-long stalk. The petals are spread wide open, and the stamens are topped with vibrant pink pollen and are about the same length as the petals. The petals are a single color with a darker stripe down the center—in contrast to the more ornate patterning on the related Sierra onion, which grows in the western Sierra.

❖ *Allium campanulatum* (Sierra onion, dusky onion)
      FAMILY: Alliaceae (Liliaceae)

DISTRIBUTION Occasional in the Yosemite and Mammoth Lakes regions (on both sides of the Sierra Crest); farther south, restricted to montane elevations in the western Sierra, extending eastward again on the Kern Plateau
HABITAT Dry slopes, flats, meadows
ELEVATION 3,500'–10,250'
SEASON Early June–mid-July
LOCATIONS Tuolumne Meadows, Slate Creek Fork Lee Vining Creek, Glass Creek Meadow, Sotcher Lake, Monache Meadow

LEAVES AND STEMS: Just 2 leaves emerge from the ground. They are 10–30 cm long, very skinny, and folded inward along the midrib. The leaves wither by the time the onion is in bloom.

FLOWERS: The inflorescence is at the end of a 10- to 20-cm-long stem and is an umbel of 10–50 flowers, each at the end of a 1- to 2-cm-long stalk. The pink flowers have 6 petals, with a distinct reddish, jagged band toward the base of the petals.

❖ *Allium validum* (swamp onion, Pacific onion)
   FAMILY: Alliaceae (Liliaceae)

DISTRIBUTION Common throughout, on both sides of the Sierra Crest
HABITAT Wet meadows, seeps
ELEVATION 6,500'–11,200'
SEASON Mid-July–mid-August
LOCATIONS Gardisky Lake Trail, Rock Creek Basin, French Canyon, Evolution Valley, East Lake (south of Bubbs Creek)

LEAVES AND STEMS: The tallest of the Sierra's wild onions, the swamp onion is generally about 30–70 cm tall but can reach 1 m. The round, thick stem is surrounded by approximately 6 long, flattish leaves. Both the leaves and stalk have a distinct onion taste.

FLOWERS: Like all onions, many flowers grow from the end of the main stem. In this species each flower is just 6–10 mm long, but there are 20–50 flowers growing as an umbel, creating a dense inflorescence. Unlike many other species of *Allium*, this umbel is not spherical; instead, it is cupped by 3 large, papery leaves, called bracts, that push the flower stalks skyward. As for the flowers, the petals face upward, forming a flower that looks almost tubular. The stamens and styles extend far beyond the petals, giving the entire flower a furry appearance.

Hackelia mundula (see page 170)

❖ Blue and Purple Flowers

Polemonium eximium (see page 240)

❖ *Dieteria canescens* var. *canescens* (*Machaeranthera canescens* var. *canescens*) (hoary aster)   **FAMILY:** Asteraceae

DISTRIBUTION Common throughout the eastern Sierra; occasional in the western Sierra
HABITAT Dry, sandy slopes
ELEVATION 5,000'–11,500'
SEASON Mid-July–early September
LOCATIONS Virginia Lakes Basin, below Agnew Lake, Rock Creek Basin above Mosquito Flat, North Fork Big Pine Creek

LEAVES AND STEMS: A tuft of stems emerges from the root, colored gray-green due to the abundance of short hairs that cover the vegetation. The 3- to 8-cm-long, narrow leaves tend to be slightly folded inward along the midrib and are distinctly toothed.

FLOWERS: Though most stems have only a single inflorescence, some side branches may have flowers. The inflorescences are little purple daisies with yellow centers; the ray flowers are a darker purple than many other daisies. Because the rays are few and narrow, there are often gaps between them, giving the flowers a slightly straggly feel. Most notable are the rather pointed, strongly bent-back (recurved) phyllaries; they resemble well-armored spheres.

❖ *Erigeron algidus* (stalked fleabane, Sierra fleabane)
     FAMILY: Asteraceae

DISTRIBUTION Common throughout, on both sides of the Sierra Crest
HABITAT Alpine fell-fields, meadows
ELEVATION 7,900'–13,500'
SEASON Early July–mid-August
LOCATIONS Twenty Lakes Basin, south side of Muir Pass, Rae Lakes Basin, Mt. Whitney Trail

LEAVES AND STEMS: A dense rosette of narrow leaves emerges from the root. The leaves are usually covered in hairs, shading them a green-gray. The leaves are very densely clustered, with the somewhat spoon-shaped, partially folded leaves facing upward and pinching to a narrow petiole (leaf stalk) at the base.

FLOWERS: On this stereotypical daisy, flowers occur singly on purplish stalks, but many 2- to 20-cm-long flowering stalks can emerge from the central tuft of leaves, leading to a showy display. The large yellow disk is surrounded by a dense ring of light-purple to nearly white ray flowers. The ray flowers usually number 50–150—so many that they distinctly overlap and overlay one another despite being very narrow.

❖ *Erigeron breweri* var. *breweri* (Brewer's fleabane)   **FAMILY:** Asteraceae

DISTRIBUTION Common throughout, on both sides of the Sierra Crest
HABITAT Dry rocky slopes, dry forest openings
ELEVATION 4,000'–11,000'
SEASON Early July–mid-August
LOCATIONS Rancheria Mountain, Lyell Canyon, Morgan Lakes, Lamarck Lakes Trail, Vidette Meadow

LEAVES AND STEMS: This species is the gangliest of the high-elevation fleabane daisies, with skinny, upright to partially reclined stems that are typically 20–40 cm in length. The short, stalkless leaves are attached along the entire length of the stem, but nowhere is the stem densely leafy; both the leaves and stem are covered in short, stiff hairs that are slightly bent backward.

FLOWERS: With an inflorescence 1–1.5 cm in diameter, these daisies are smaller than many others. There are usually 15–30 light-purple ray flowers but occasionally as many as 45. There are 1–5 flowering heads on each stem and many clustered stems per plant.

RELATED SPECIES: A related species *Erigeron elmeri* (Elmer's fleabane) has a quite similar growth form, but its stems have just a few short stiff hairs that lay flat against the stem and the stems tend to be unbranched. This species grows at similar elevations, but mostly in the western Sierra from the Yosemite region south through the San Joaquin drainage.

❖ *Erigeron compositus* (cut-leaf fleabane)
    FAMILY: Asteraceae

DISTRIBUTION Common throughout, mostly at high elevations
HABITAT Dry, sandy to rocky slopes; among talus
ELEVATION 8,000'–14,000'
SEASON Early July–early August
LOCATIONS Mt. Dana, San Joaquin Mountain, Lamarck Col, east of Long Lake (Bishop Pass Trail), Mt. Whitney Trail

LEAVES AND STEMS: This compact cushion plant is readily recognizable by its leaves: Each leaf is divided into 3 lobes, and each lobe is divided into 3 additional lobes, creating an intricately notched leaf that reminds me of a coral because it is folded rather than flat. White hairs cover both the leaves and stem.

FLOWERS: A curious feature of this daisy is that the flowers can occur with or without rays, though the rayless species are more common. In these, there are simply 1- to 1.5-cm-wide yellow circles of disk flowers attached singly to stout stems, while other individuals have 30–60 short, pale-purple rays surrounding the disk.

RELATED SPECIES: *Erigeron vagus*, rambling fleabane, is quite similar but has leaves that are just once divided into 3 lobes, and the inflorescences always have ray flowers. It is much rarer, occurring only in alpine fell-fields and usually only on metamorphic rock. You can find it on Excelsior Mountain and the south side of Mt. Dana.

Erigeron vagus

❖ *Erigeron glacialis* var. *glacialis* (*Erigeron peregrinus* var. *callianthemus*)
(wandering fleabane, subalpine fleabane)   **FAMILY:** Asteraceae

DISTRIBUTION Common throughout, but especially in
the western Sierra
HABITAT Forest openings, meadows, moist forest
ELEVATION 4,800'–11,500'
SEASON Early July–mid-August
LOCATIONS Cathedral Pass, Evolution Valley, Kearsarge
Pass Trail, Vidette Meadow

LEAVES AND STEMS: The common name *wandering fleabane* is perfect for this species, as clusters of these plants,
connected by underground stems, spread across forest openings or meadows. The stems
are usually 15–30 cm but occasionally taller, and the bright-green, fairly narrow basal
leaves often reach 15 cm in length. The plants rarely form dense mats; instead, you see a
great collection of rosettes dispersed across the forest floor with soil between them.

FLOWERS: While most flowering stalks have a single inflorescence, some have several.
The disk is small in comparison to the length of the light-purple ray flowers; there are
always more than 30 8- to 15-mm-long rays, and they densely overlap each other.

RELATED SPECIES: Var. *hirsutus* is also common in the Yosemite area but rare farther
south. The feature that distinguishes these varieties might be difficult to discern: The
stalk leading to the inflorescence has long, soft hairs in var. *hirsutus,* while that in var.
glacialis is covered with short, stiff hairs.

❖ *Erigeron pygmaeus* (pygmy fleabane)
   FAMILY: Asteraceae

DISTRIBUTION Common throughout, on both sides of
the Sierra Crest
HABITAT Sandy patches among talus, alpine fell-fields
ELEVATION 9,500'–13,000'
SEASON Early July–early August
LOCATIONS Mt. Dana, Garnet Lake, Rock Creek Basin,
Piute Pass, Bishop Pass, Mt. Whitney Trail

LEAVES AND STEMS: This small, compact plant of high
elevations usually has several (to many) dense rosettes
of small, spoon-shaped leaves; these leaves are densely
covered with short, white hairs and are partially folded along the midrib.

FLOWERS: The central disk of the pygmy fleabane is not particularly large, but it stands
taller than other daisies, both because the light-purple ray flowers tend to be slightly
folded downward and because the disk flowers have exceedingly long
stamens. In early summer, these rise above the disk like the points of
a crown, as the outer disk flowers are the first to open.

RELATED SPECIES: *Erigeron clokeyi* var. *pinzliae* (Clokey's fleabane)
is another fell-field species, but is mostly restricted to metamorphic
rocks, occurring in the Virginia Lakes Basin, on Tioga Peak, at Mono

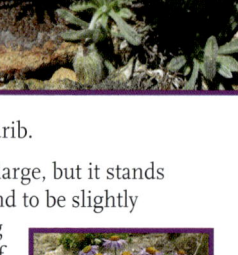

Erigeron clokeyi var.
pinzliae

Pass (Yosemite), in the Convict Creek drainage, and on Coyote Ridge. Reaching up to 20 cm in height, it is slightly taller with almost gangly stems and long, skinny, very gray-hairy leaves that are folded along the middle. It too has long stamens.

❖ *Eurybia integrifolia (Aster integrifolius)* (thickstem aster)
   FAMILY: Asteraceae

> **DISTRIBUTION** Occasional throughout the western Sierra, only crossing to the eastern Sierra at Tioga Pass and the Mammoth Lakes region; south of Mammoth Lakes, occurs mainly far to the west of the Sierra Crest
> **HABITAT** Dry meadows, open forest
> **ELEVATION** 5,200'–10,100'
> **SEASON** Mid-July–early September
> **LOCATIONS** Slate Creek Fork Lee Vining Creek, Gardisky Lake Trail, Mono Pass (Yosemite), High Trail above Agnew Meadows, Mono Creek

LEAVES AND STEMS: The thickstem aster is usually 15–40 cm tall but is occasionally taller. As the name implies, the stems are quite stout and often tinged slightly red. The upper reaches of the stem can have a slight zigzag to them, changing direction at the leaf nodes. Gland-tipped hairs densely cover both the stems and slightly thick leaves. The leaves are elongate triangles that clasp the stem and have a very distinct midrib.

FLOWERS: The purple daisylike flowers are generally composed of 10–15 ray flowers, though a plant may have 8–27. The rays are not always evenly distributed around the plant, leading to a straggly appearance. The disk flowers are yellow. The most obvious feature is the phyllaries, which are thick and bent back; this gives the buds the appearance of a rolled-up hedgehog. Like the stems, they range in color from green to reddish.

❖ *Oreostemma alpigenum* var. *andersonii (Aster alpigenus* var. *andersonii)*
   (tundra aster)   **FAMILY:** Asteraceae

> **DISTRIBUTION** Very common throughout, on both sides of the Sierra Crest
> **HABITAT** Meadows, lakeshores, grassy forest openings
> **ELEVATION** 6,500'–12,000'
> **SEASON** Early July–early September
> **LOCATIONS** Twenty Lakes Basin, Garnet Lake, Rock Creek Basin, Evolution Lake, Guitar Lake

LEAVES AND STEMS: This is one of the most common species in high-elevation meadows. Its leaves are all basal—and therefore usually well hidden among the meadow vegetation. They can exceed 10 cm in length but are less than 5 mm in diameter and folded inward along the midrib, making them look even narrower. There are usually small teeth around the leaf margin.

FLOWERS: A single reddish flowering stalk grows from the middle of the rosette, usually reaching no more than 20 cm in height. On it is a single inflorescence with pale-purple

(Continued)

(Continued)   ray flowers, 10–16 mm in length, and yellow disk flowers. One good feature to identify this species is that the rays are curled into a quite narrow U shape where they attach to the inflorescence disk.

❖ *Oreostemma peirsonii (Aster peirsonii)* (Peirson's aster)
   FAMILY: Asteraceae

DISTRIBUTION Occasional from the Kearsarge Pass area south to New Army Pass; mostly west of the Sierra Crest and always east of the main Kern River drainage
HABITAT Alpine fell-fields, dry meadows
ELEVATION 9,500'–12,250'
SEASON Mid-July–early September
LOCATIONS Kearsarge Lakes, headwaters of Tyndall Creek, Crabtree Lakes, Mt. Whitney Trail

LEAVES AND STEMS: Though this species has a very restricted distribution, it is a common member of the alpine fell-field community where it occurs. Because this species prefers dry, rocky environments, the rosettes of leaves are readily visible: Leaves are about 1–2.5 cm long, very narrow, and folded inward, creating a U shape. A branched underground stem, or caudex, results in many tufts of leaves belonging to a single individual.

FLOWERS: Like the tundra aster, the other member of this genus described in this book, Peirson's aster has a single flowering stem. It also shares the feature that the purple ray flowers pinch to a narrow notch where they attach to the disk. However, there are usually fewer than 15 ray flowers, and the flowering stem trails along the ground.

❖ *Symphyotrichum spathulatum* var. *spathulatum (Aster occidentalis* var. *occidentalis)* (western mountain aster)   **FAMILY:** Asteraceae

DISTRIBUTION Occasional in the Yosemite and Mammoth Lakes regions on both sides of the Sierra Crest, becoming rarer from the Mono Recesses south
HABITAT Wet to dry meadows
ELEVATION 1,500'–11,150'
SEASON Mid-July–early September
LOCATIONS Virginia Lakes Basin, Saddlebag Lake, Devils Postpile, Mono Creek, Ruby Lake (Rock Creek Basin), Piute Pass Trail

LEAVES AND STEMS: Growing to a height of 60 cm, this species spreads readily across meadows or moist forest floors. The basal leaves are oval shaped and have a long stalk, while the stem leaves generally lack stalks and may clasp the stem. Though this species can be hairy, it is less hairy than many other species that were previously included in the genus *Aster*; as a result, the leaves are a brighter green. The stems can be either green or a darker shade, bordering on burgundy.

FLOWERS: This is another species of daisy with purple ray flowers and yellow disk flowers. The stems are somewhat branched, with between 1 and 10 inflorescences per plant. There are 15–40 ray flowers that are about 1 cm long and, as with many asters, are a much darker purple in bud. The phyllaries are red-margined (or not) and slightly splayed open, but not bent backward, and are much daintier than those of the thickstem aster.

RELATED SPECIES: *Symphyotrichum ascendens* (western aster) is another mid-elevation species that occasionally extends to higher elevations. Three features that distinguish it from *Symphyotrichum spathulatum* are that its phyllaries are not purple-tipped and have many different lengths (in other words, the phyllaries are graduated), and its leaves are smaller and quite narrow.

❖ *Hackelia micrantha* (small-flowered stickseed, Jessica's stickseed)
    FAMILY: Boraginaceae

DISTRIBUTION Common throughout the eastern Sierra; fairly common throughout the western Sierra
HABITAT Meadows; open, dry forest
ELEVATION 6,200'–11,500'
SEASON Mid-June–early August
LOCATIONS Virginia Lakes Basin, Gardisky Lake, Dana Gardens (western base of Mt. Dana), Convict Creek drainage, Rock Creek Basin

LEAVES AND STEMS: Always exceeding 30 cm in height and occasionally much taller, this plant has stout stems and leaves that bear long white hairs. The basal leaves are elongate and narrow, usually 6–20 cm in length, while the leaves on the stem are much shorter.

FLOWERS: Though the common name for the genus *Hackelia* is stickseed, these species closely resemble—and are closely related to—forget-me-nots, with a bright-blue flower with 5 fused petals. At the center of the flower are white appendages forming a narrow ring. The upper stretch of the stem is dotted with these little flowers, sometimes quite dispersed along the stem and other times in denser heads. The flowers at the bottom of the stalk open first, and by midsummer there will be flowers at the branch tips, and the aptly named prickle-covered fruits lower down.

RELATED SPECIES: *Hackelia velutina*, velvet stickseed, is common in openings in the montane forests and occasionally extends higher. The tall plant has larger flowers, as well as larger appendages at the center of the flower, than the small-flowered stickseed has. The floral tube is pinker and sticks out from the calyx, but the petals are a similar blue. The name *velvet* refers to the leaves, which are densely covered in short, soft hairs. This species is found in many locations, including Rancheria Mountain, Devils Postpile, and Kaiser Ridge.

Hackelia velutina

❖ *Hackelia sharsmithii* (Sharsmith's stickseed)
   FAMILY: Boraginaceae

DISTRIBUTION Occasional near the Sierra Crest from a little north of Kearsarge Pass south to New Army Pass
HABITAT Alongside outcrops and under boulders, often toward valley bottoms, near lakes, or other sheltered, shaded locations
ELEVATION 10,300'–12,100'
SEASON Mid-July–mid-August
LOCATIONS Dragon Lake, Kearsarge Peak, Shepherd Pass Trail at the Pothole, Trail Camp (Mt. Whitney Trail), Rock Creek (west of New Army Pass)

LEAVES AND STEMS: This is listed as a rare species in California and will be seen by only a few lucky hikers. It is included because it is quite showy and reasonably common within its limited range. Growing alongside rocks, it reaches 10–30 cm in height. The stems are reddish, and the rather thin, broad leaves are oval shaped and clasp the stem, lacking any stalk.

FLOWERS: The flowers look like other stickseeds, though the 5 fused petals are a paler periwinkle-blue, sometimes appearing nearly white with just the edges of the petals colored blue. The petals are also larger than other Sierra stickseeds. Dense to sparse clusters of flowers occur on branched inflorescences at the top of the stems.

❖ Carl Sharsmith

Carl Sharsmith is a name closely linked with the history of Sierra Nevada botany, especially relating to the Tuolumne Meadows region of Yosemite. Born in 1903, he first explored Yosemite as a seasonal ranger in 1930. He was captivated by the alpine flora and noticed that many species had very specific habitat preferences. He soon began to ponder about the history of the diverse collection of plants he found: which species grew only in the Sierra (endemics), which had ranges expanding into the North American deserts, and which grew throughout the Northern Hemisphere (see also "Biogeography of High-Elevation Plants," page 157, and "Sierra Nevada Endemics," page 137). These interests took him back for another degree, and in 1940 he obtained a PhD from the University of California, Berkeley for a thesis titled "A Contribution to the History of the Alpine Flora of the Sierra Nevada." In the following years he split his time between being a university professor and, during summers, a ranger in Tuolumne. Sharsmith enjoyed exploring every corner of the Yosemite high country and sharing his knowledge with visitors. Mt. Dana and the Dana Plateau were particularly favored locations that he visited again and again. He continued to spend time in Tuolumne until his death in 1994. Two species bear Sharsmith's name: *Hackelia sharsmithii* (Sharsmith's stickseed) and *Draba sharsmithii* (Mount Whitney or Sharsmith's draba), both of which he discovered in August 1937 while collecting plants in the eastern Sierra. Though it appears from herbarium records that others may have found the *Draba* slightly ahead of him, his name has stuck.

❖ *Mertensia ciliata* var. *stomatechoides* (streamside bluebell, tall fringed bluebell)   **Family:** Boraginaceae

> **Distribution** Fairly common at montane elevations throughout the western Sierra, occasionally extending into the subalpine zone; absent from the eastern Sierra
> **Habitat** Stream banks, seeps, wet meadows
> **Elevation** 5,000'–10,300'
> **Season** Mid-June–late July
> **Locations** Yosemite Creek, Kaiser Crest, Bubbs Creek, Farewell Gap

Leaves and Stems: A tall plant, 40 cm to more than 1 m in height, the streamside bluebell occurs in dense masses in moist locations. It is more common in wet locations in montane forests but is found in the subalpine zone along sufficiently moist, sheltered stream banks. The stems and leaves lack hairs and sometimes have a gray-green powdery appearance, called glaucous. The basal leaves can exceed 30 cm in length, are quite thin, and are fairly oval shaped, while the stem leaves are broader and clasp the stem.

Flowers: The top of each tall stem has several side branches, each generally drooping under the weight of a large cluster of narrow, bell-shaped flowers. The beautiful periwinkle-blue flowers are composed of 5 fused petals that form a 1- to 1.5-cm-long tube with small lobes at the ends.

❖ *Phacelia eisenii* (Eisen's phacelia)
       Family: Boraginaceae (Hydrophyllaceae)

> **Distribution** Fairly common throughout the western Sierra; mostly absent in the eastern Sierra
> **Habitat** Sandy soils
> **Elevation** 5,000'–11,000'
> **Season** Mid-June–late July
> **Locations** Lower Gaylor Lake, May Lake, Bear Creek, Sallie Keyes Lakes

Leaves and Stems: This tiny annual reaches just 2–10 cm tall. The stems are usually reddish tinted, unbranched, and densely covered with stiff white hairs and small glands. The leaves are oval shaped with long reddish stalks. Note that because it is an annual, it will only germinate in large numbers in years with sufficient moisture.

Flowers: Many 2- to 5-mm-wide flowers grow along the top half of the stems. The 5 pale-purple petals are fused at the base. Beneath the petals are 5 distinctly red and very narrow sepals; these too are fused at the base.

❖ *Phacelia hastata* var. *compacta* (timberline phacelia, compact phacelia)
    FAMILY: Boraginaceae (Hydrophyllaceae)

DISTRIBUTION Common throughout, on both sides of the Sierra Crest, from the Yosemite region south to Bishop Pass, becoming more occasional to the south
HABITAT Dry sandy slopes, talus slopes
ELEVATION 6,900'–13,000'
SEASON Early July–mid-August
LOCATIONS Tioga Peak, Dana Plateau, Mono Pass (Rock Creek Basin), Bishop Pass, Kearsarge Pass, Mt. Whitney Trail

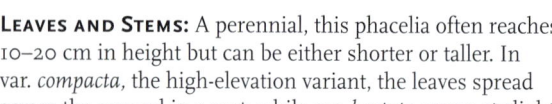

LEAVES AND STEMS: A perennial, this phacelia often reaches 10–20 cm in height but can be either shorter or taller. In var. *compacta,* the high-elevation variant, the leaves spread across the ground in a mat, while var. *hastata* grows at slightly lower elevations and has erect, taller stems. Both have narrow, oval-shaped leaves that are rather thick and furry due to the abundance of long hairs; the midrib and veins branching from the midrib are distinctly indented in the leaf blade.

FLOWERS: The inflorescences are densely coiled, with the flowers opening sequentially from the base to the top. Once fully open, there is a dense ball of flowers. The flowers themselves are pale purple to whitish, with 5 petals that are fused together and long white styles that extend far beyond the petals.

❖ *Phacelia hydrophylloides* (waterleaf phacelia)
    FAMILY: Boraginaceae (Hydrophyllaceae)

DISTRIBUTION Very common throughout the montane forests of the western Sierra, rarely extending into the subalpine zone
HABITAT Open forest, edges of forest openings
ELEVATION 6,500'–10,000'
SEASON Mid-June–late July
LOCATIONS Jack Main Canyon, Mammoth Pass, Kaiser Pass, Dinkey Lakes, Alta Meadows

LEAVES AND STEMS: This perennial species reaches 10–30 cm in height, often growing as a cluster of quite leafy stems. The soft, hairy leaves are broad and irregularly lobed; some lobes are rounded and others toothed; some lobes extend to the midrib, and others are very shallow. The leaves are mostly along the stems, not basal.

FLOWERS: The inflorescences are dense, spherical heads 2–3 cm in diameter. The many tubular, purple, 5-petal flowers are quite showy, with curled-back petal lobes and stamens that stick far beyond the petals.

❖ *Phacelia mutabilis* (changeable phacelia)
    FAMILY: Boraginaceae (Hydrophyllaceae)

DISTRIBUTION Very common at montane elevations in the western Sierra, crossing to the eastern Sierra around Mammoth Lakes and occasionally elsewhere
HABITAT Open forest, flats
ELEVATION 3,700'–11,500'
SEASON Early July–early August
LOCATIONS Sotcher Lake, Rae Lakes Basin, East Lake (south of Bubbs Creek), Olancha Pass

LEAVES AND STEMS: True to its name, this species is a little difficult to describe, as its height and leaf form are quite variable. The stems reach 10–60 cm in height, and the stem-leaf shape varies from compound to dissected to oval. Distinguishing the species from the timberline phacelia, the basal leaves are usually pinnately compound or lobed, and the leaf veins are less indented on the lower stem leaves. Both the leaves and stems are covered in stiff, white hairs.

FLOWERS: As described on the previous page for the timberline phacelia, the flowers occur in a coiled cyme, with the basal flowers opening first and the inflorescences slowly uncurling as the flowers mature. The 5 dark- (to pale-) purple petals form a closed cup, from the center of which emerge the long white styles.

RELATED SPECIES: *Phacelia ramosissima* (branching phacelia) has very branched stems that "wander" over nearby plants. The leaves are deeply pinnately lobed—or even form leaflets. The petal lobes on the flowers open outward in a flat disk with the stamens pointing skyward. This species occurs throughout to an elevation of 10,000 feet.

❖ *Boechera davidsonii (Arabis davidsonii)* (Davidson's rockcress)
    FAMILY: Brassicaceae

DISTRIBUTION Occasional in the Yosemite region, the Kings and Kern River drainages, and the eastern Sierra from the Bishop Creek drainage south; rare to absent elsewhere
HABITAT Cracks in rocky outcrops, alongside shaded rocks
ELEVATION 4,000'–11,500'
SEASON Mid-June–early August
LOCATIONS Top of Half Dome, west of Sixth Lake (North Fork Big Pine Creek), Palisades Lakes, Bench Lake, Hamilton Lakes

LEAVES AND STEMS: This species is fairly rare but stands out from other rockcress species because of its habitat—it seeks out sheltered, moist, rocky locations—and because its leaves are hairless and shiny. 1 or a few stems, up to 20 cm in length, will emerge from the basal rosette of elongate leaves that are pointed at their tips.

FLOWERS: The 4 petals are white to pale purple and are just under 1 cm in length. The seedpods are flat, point outward, and can be either straight or slightly curved.

❖ *Boechera howellii (Arabis platysperma* var. *howellii)* (Howell's rockcress)
   FAMILY: Brassicaceae

DISTRIBUTION Common throughout, on both sides of the Sierra Crest, generally at high elevations
HABITAT Dry slopes, talus slopes, alpine fell-fields; especially at high elevations
ELEVATION 5,600'–12,750'
SEASON Mid-June–late July
LOCATIONS Twenty Lakes Basin, Garnet Lake, Mono Recesses, south slope of Mt. Gould, Junction Pass (from Center Basin), Crabtree Meadow, Nine Lakes Basin

LEAVES AND STEMS: Rising to just 20 cm in height, this short high-elevation species of *Boechera* has leaves growing as a rosette. The stems and leaf blades lack hairs, often appearing nearly glossy, while the margins of the leaves can be densely hairy.

FLOWERS: The 4-petal flowers range from white to lavender. The pods are erect—or at least nearly erect—and most easily distinguished from other species by their width: They are 2.5–6.5 cm long and 3–7 mm wide, quite a bit wider than any other high-elevation species.

❖ *Boechera lemmonii (Arabis lemmonii* var. *lemmonii)* (Lemmon's rockcress)   **FAMILY:** Brassicaceae

DISTRIBUTION Very common throughout the eastern Sierra; occasional throughout the western Sierra
HABITAT Alpine fell-fields, sandy soil, talus slopes
ELEVATION 6,500'–13,500'
SEASON Mid-June–late July
LOCATIONS Mt. Dana, Mono Pass (Rock Creek Basin), south slope of Mt. Gould, New Army Pass

LEAVES AND STEMS: One of the most common species of rockcress at high elevations, these plants reach no more than 25 cm in height. As with other rockcress, this species has both a rosette of basal leaves and stem leaves. The leaves and stems are mostly hairy, with the hairs not very dense but quite short and branched, giving the foliage a slightly felted look.

FLOWERS: The 4-petal flowers range from lavender to purple; unlike other rockcress species, they are never white. The seedpods stick out from the stem or rise slightly upward. They tend to be attached only on one side of the stem, an excellent identifying feature.

RELATED SPECIES: *Boechera depauperata* (previously *Arabis lemmonii* var. *depauperata*; soldier rockcress) is a shorter species, with stems never reaching 15 cm. Its seedpods point outward, are straight to slightly curved, and are not one-sided.

❖ *Boechera lyallii (Arabis lyallii)* (Lyall's rockcress)
   FAMILY: Brassicaceae

DISTRIBUTION Fairly common in the eastern Sierra from the Yosemite region south to the Kearsarge Pass area; occasional throughout the western Sierra
HABITAT Dry slopes, talus slopes, gravelly to sandy locations, especially in subalpine to alpine zones
ELEVATION 7,000'–12,200'
SEASON Mid-June–late July
LOCATIONS Dana Plateau, Gaylor Lakes, Rock Creek Basin, Bishop Pass, Rae Lakes Basin, Guyot Flat, Farewell Gap

LEAVES AND STEMS: Two features distinguish Lyall's rockcress from all other species: It reaches no more than 15 cm in height and is hairless (or nearly hairless) throughout. The stems tend to be glaucous—covered with a white, slightly powdery coating. Most of the leaves of this species are located at the base, though a few small stem leaves occur as well. In contrast to the small-flowered rockcress (*Boechera paupercula*), its leaves are fairly oval shaped and rounded at the tips.

FLOWERS: The 4-petal flowers are lavender to purple. The seedpods are quite broad (1.5–2.5 mm) in comparison to the tiny plants and stick straight upward.

❖ *Boechera paupercula (Arabis lyallii* var. *nubigena)*
   (small-flowered rockcress)   **FAMILY:** Brassicaceae

DISTRIBUTION Fairly common in the eastern Sierra from northern Yosemite south to Big Pine Creek, becoming rare farther south; rare in the western Sierra; especially common around Tioga Pass
HABITAT Dry slopes, talus slopes, alpine fell-fields
ELEVATION 9,500'–12,000'
SEASON Mid-June–late July
LOCATIONS Dana Plateau, Slate Creek Fork Lee Vining Creek, San Joaquin Ridge, Box Lake (Rock Creek Basin), Lake Sabrina Basin

LEAVES AND STEMS: This species is quite similar in stature to Lyall's rockcress, reaching no more than 15 cm in height and mostly having basal leaves. However, it is hairy on at least some of its leaves and stem, with either branched or unbranched hairs. In addition, its leaves are narrower and pointier.

(Continued)

(Continued)   **FLOWERS:** The small flowers range from lavender to purple. The seedpods stick straight up
and are 2.5–5.5 cm long and up to 2 mm wide.

RELATED SPECIES: *Boechera inyoensis* (Inyo rockcress), see photo
at right, is fairly common in the eastern Sierra from quite low to
12,000 feet. Its seedpods trend outward or somewhat upward and
are straight. The stem leaves are hairy and clasp the main stem.

Boechera inyoensis

❖ *Boechera retrofracta (Arabis holboellii* var. *retrofracta)* (reflexed rockcress)
    FAMILY: Brassicaceae

DISTRIBUTION Occasional throughout, on both sides of the
Sierra Crest
HABITAT Rocky slopes, gravelly and sandy areas,
open conifer forest
ELEVATION 1,500'–11,750'
SEASON Early June–late July
LOCATIONS Tioga Crest, Garnet Lake, Trail Lake (Mono Creek
drainage), Rock Creek Basin, Evolution Basin

LEAVES AND STEMS: One of the taller species of rockcress, this
plant has stalks that can reach 15–100 cm in height. The bottom
reaches of the stem are covered in short, arrow-shaped, clasping
leaves, while the upper stretch has few leaves. Branched hairs
densely cover the entire stem and leaves.

FLOWERS: The small 4-petal flowers range from white to
lavender. The relatively long, skinny seedpods hang downward,
pressing tightly against the stem.

RELATED SPECIES: The closely related *Boechera pendulocarpa* (previously *Arabis holboellii* var. *pendulocarpa*; dropseed rockcress) also has fruits that hang
downward, but they are less closely pressed against the stem. Another related species,
Boechera pinetorum (previously *Arabis holboellii* var. *pinetorum*; woodland rockcress), has
slightly curved seedpods.

❖ *Boechera stricta (Arabis drummondii)*
    (Drummond's rockcress)   **FAMILY:** Brassicaceae

DISTRIBUTION Common throughout the eastern Sierra
and around Tioga Pass; rarer in most of the western Sierra,
becoming more common in the Kern River drainage
HABITAT Open forest, meadows, rocky slopes with
considerable vegetation cover
ELEVATION 7,000'–11,200'
SEASON Mid-June–late July
LOCATIONS Gaylor Lakes, Ruby Lake (Rock Creek Basin),
Evolution Lake, Rae Lakes Basin, John Muir Trail along
Bubbs Creek, Wallace Creek near John Muir Trail

LEAVES AND STEMS: One of the most common rockcress species in the eastern Sierra, it is also one of the tallest, with stems always extending beyond 15 cm in height and sometimes reaching to 1 m. There is both a rosette of basal leaves and leaves extending upward along the stem. Though the stems may have a few hairs, the leaves are generally hairless and are a fairly bright green. The stem leaves range from distinctly triangular to arrow shaped and clasp the stem.

FLOWERS: The 4-petal flowers are generally white but occasionally trend toward pale lavender. The sepals are hairless and hence, like the leaves, a bright green. The quite narrow seedpods are erect, sticking straight upward. Because there can be many flowers per plant, a robust plant may have a dense cluster of seedpods at their tips.

❖ *Lonicera conjugialis* (double honeysuckle, purpleflower honeysuckle)   **FAMILY:** Caprifoliaceae

> **DISTRIBUTION** Common in the western Sierra, becoming restricted to more westerly locations once south of the Mono Recesses; in the eastern Sierra, restricted to the area around the Rock Creek Basin
> **HABITAT** Stream banks, moist forest
> **ELEVATION** 4,000'–10,800'
> **SEASON** Mid-June–late July
> **LOCATIONS** Grand Canyon of the Tuolumne, Lyell Canyon, King Creek (near Devils Postpile), west side of Farewell Gap

LEAVES AND STEMS: This shrub usually reaches 60–100 cm in height but occasionally grows taller. The bright-green leaf blades are approximately oval shaped, and the young foliage can be quite purplish. The leaf margins have a fringe of stiff hairs, with a few hairs also occurring on the leaf blades.

FLOWERS: Both the flowers and the fruits are distinctive—like all honeysuckles and twinberries, they occur in pairs. This species has flowers that are a rich deep color bordering on purple and burgundy, with the petals forming a distinctly 2-lipped flower. From the center emerge 5 long stamens, also burgundy colored, with dense packets of yellow pollen at the ends. The fruits are 2 bright-red berries, joined together along one edge to form an approximate figure eight.

❖ *Astragalus kentrophyta* var. *danaus* (Sweetwater Mountains milkvetch)   **FAMILY:** Fabaceae

> **DISTRIBUTION** Common in the Yosemite region, then occasional south to Mt. Whitney; always at high elevations
> **HABITAT** Alpine fell-fields where there is sand and no large rocks; usually on metamorphic rock
> **ELEVATION** 9,500'–13,000'
> **SEASON** Late June–late July
> **LOCATIONS** Tioga Crest, Dana Plateau, west slope of Mt. Dana, west slope of Mt. Tom, Sawmill Pass, Baxter Pass

(Continued)

(Continued)   **LEAVES AND STEMS:** A matted perennial, this milkvetch epitomizes
the cushion plant growth form, albeit in quite a prickly way. Rising
a few centimeters above the ground surface is a mound of tiny, narrow, sharp-pointed
leaflets, just 3–7 mm in length and covered with long white hairs. There are usually
3 but occasionally 5 leaflets per leaf.

FLOWERS: The tiny purple-and-white flowers that peep out from among the leaves
are like any flower in the pea family, with a broad petal called a banner at the back, the
pointed keel at the front, and 2 petals known as wings partially covering the keel.

❖ *Astragalus purshii* var. *lectulus* (woollypod milkvetch, Pursh's milkvetch)
    FAMILY: Fabaceae

DISTRIBUTION Fairly common in specific areas,
usually near the Sierra Crest, but absent elsewhere
HABITAT Open, rocky areas, especially alpine fell-fields;
typically found on metamorphic rock
ELEVATION 3,500'–12,500'
SEASON Early June–early July
LOCATIONS Tioga Crest, Dana Plateau, Convict Creek
drainage, Green Lake (from South Lake)

LEAVES AND STEMS: The white, densely hairy leaves often lie
flat against the gravel substrates they prefer, making them
easy to overlook, as the leaves blend in with the rocks. Each leaf is subdivided into
3–11 leaflets, which are 2–10 mm in length and gray in color due to the hairs.

FLOWERS: The small purple flowers have the classic shape of all flowers in Fabaceae,
diagrammed on page 15, with 2 broad petals known as the banner rising at the back and
the pointy keel facing forward and flanked by 2 wings. The seedpods are about 1 cm in
length and are so densely covered in long white hairs that they appear furry—this is the
photo shown, for the plants bloom early and quickly.

❖ *Lupinus argenteus* var. *heteranthus* (silvery lupine)
    FAMILY: Fabaceae

DISTRIBUTION Common in the eastern Sierra
from the Yosemite region south to Big Pine
Creek, occurring occasionally as far south as
Sawmill Pass; absent elsewhere
HABITAT Dry slopes
ELEVATION 5,500'–10,000'
SEASON Early July–mid-August
LOCATIONS Virginia Lakes Basin, Convict Creek
drainage, Lake Sabrina, Coyote Ridge

LEAVES AND STEMS: Reaching 20–50 cm in height, the silvery lupine lives up to its
name; its leaves and stems are so densely covered in long hairs that they appear silvery.
This is especially noticeable because these plants have a lot of leaves—both at the base of
the plant and along the stem, unlike many lupines that mostly have stem leaves. There
are 5–9 elongate, narrow leaflets per leaf.

FLOWERS: If you look at a lupine flower, you will immediately see that it is a member of the pea family, with the stereotypical flowers shown on page 15. The large, broad petals at the back are called the banner, while 2 broad wings are at the bottom. If you pull the wings apart, you will see the final petal, the pointier keel, which is generally hidden from view in the lupines. The shape and hairiness of the keel are important identifying features for lupines. This species has a straight keel with hairs along its upper margin. The seeds are in long, hairy pods.

❖ *Lupinus breweri* var. *breweri* (Brewer's lupine)
   FAMILY: Fabaceae

DISTRIBUTION Fairly common in the Yosemite region, becoming more occasional from the San Joaquin drainage south
HABITAT Forest, meadows, alpine fell-fields
ELEVATION 4,500'–11,600'
SEASON Early July–mid-August
LOCATIONS Virginia Lakes Basin, Dog Lake, Isberg Pass, Kaiser Peak

LEAVES AND STEMS: This species is the lowest growing lupine in the Sierra, and this is the variety common north of the Kern River drainage. Growing as an open mat, the rosettes of leaves surround the flowering stems. Each leaf is composed of 7–10 leaflets that are silvery-hairy. Compared with other mat-forming lupines, the leaves are a bit broader and have rounder tips. The combination of plant height and leaflet number makes this plant easy to identify.

FLOWERS: The flowers occur in dense inflorescences that rise above the leaves. They are purplish, though the center of the banner is white and quite round. In this species, the keel is straight and lacks hairs. (See page 15 for a labeled diagram of a lupine flower.)

❖ *Lupinus breweri* var. *bryoides* (matted Brewer's lupine)
   FAMILY: Fabaceae

DISTRIBUTION Common in the Kern and Kaweah River drainages, especially at high elevations
HABITAT Forest, meadows, alpine fell-fields
ELEVATION 7,500'–13,500'
SEASON Early July–mid-August
LOCATIONS Bighorn Plateau, Cottonwood Lakes, New Army Pass, Olancha Peak, Kern Peak

LEAVES AND STEMS: This variety of Brewer's lupine occurs mostly in the Kern River drainage. It is much shorter and more matted than the more northerly variant, crawling along the ground with its leaflets, just 3–5 mm long, covered in long hairs.

FLOWERS: The purple flowers occur in dense inflorescences and rise just a little above the white, hairy carpet of leaves. The banners are notably broad and white. (See page 15 for a labeled diagram of a lupine flower.)

❖ *Lupinus covillei* (shaggy lupine)   **FAMILY:** Fabaceae

DISTRIBUTION Fairly common in the western Sierra
in the Yosemite region, becoming occasional farther south;
generally absent in the eastern Sierra
HABITAT Meadows, moist flats, small forest openings
ELEVATION 7,300'–10,800'
SEASON Early July–mid-August
LOCATIONS Budd Lake, Mono Pass Trail (Yosemite),
Kaiser Peak, Darwin Lakes, Hamilton Lakes, Farewell Gap

LEAVES AND STEMS: This tall herb often exceeds 60 cm in
height, but note that like most high-elevation lupines, it lacks woody stems and completely vanishes during the winter. Its leaves are all along the stem—there are no basal leaves—and they are densely covered in soft, shaggy hairs. There are generally 7–8 leaflets per leaf, each 3–11 cm in length and very narrow with pointed tips.

FLOWERS: There are long inflorescences of purple flowers. While the long, white, hairy leaflets are the best identifying feature for this species, two flower features to remember are that the keel is very slightly curved upward and the inflorescences are not dense, with a small gap between the individual whorls (circles) of flowers. (See page 15 for a labeled diagram of a lupine flower.)

❖ *Lupinus latifolius* var. *columbianus* (Columbia lupine, broad-leaved lupine)
        FAMILY: Fabaceae

DISTRIBUTION Common throughout at montane elevations in the western Sierra, extending to higher elevations in the Yosemite and Mammoth Lakes regions
HABITAT Stream banks, moist forest, meadows
ELEVATION 3,500'–11,000'
SEASON Early July–mid-August
LOCATIONS Tenaya Lake, Dana Gardens (western base of Mt. Dana), Devils Postpile, Farewell Gap

LEAVES AND STEMS: One of two very large lupine species in the Sierra, the plants are generally 60–120 cm in height and occasionally even taller (or shorter). The leaves are mostly along the stems, with 6–9 leaflets per leaf, each 4–10 cm in length. The bottoms of the leaves are mostly hairy, while the tops are hairless to hairy. The leaflets are a bit broader than in many other species, with an especially broad, blunt tip.

FLOWERS: The inflorescences are long and not particularly dense, with space between the circles of flowers—much like the shaggy lupine described above. To distinguish this species from the similarly tall large-leaved lupine, you have to pull apart the flower and look at the keel, the pointed petal at the bottom of the flower that is hidden from view. In this species the upper edge of the keel is ciliate, meaning that it is covered with long, stiff hairs, and the keel is sharply turned upward toward the end, with a long, narrow, pointed tip. (See page 15 for a labeled diagram of a lupine flower.)

❖ *Lupinus lepidus* var. *lobbii* (Lobb's lupine)
    FAMILY: Fabaceae

DISTRIBUTION Very common on both sides of the Sierra Crest in the Yosemite and Mammoth Lakes regions, becoming more occasional to the south
HABITAT Dry slopes and flats, meadows
ELEVATION 8,000'–12,500'
SEASON Early July–mid-August
LOCATIONS Twenty Lakes Basin, Mono Pass (Yosemite), Garnet Lake, Humphreys Basin, Taboose Pass

LEAVES AND STEMS: This and Brewer's lupine are the only low-growing species in the Sierra. Unlike the mats formed by Brewer's lupine, this species has a discrete rosette growth form, with a circle of leaves surrounding a stem and no leaves along the length of the stem. The stems are less than 10 cm in length, and both stems and leaves are hairy—sometimes quite hairy. Two important identifying characteristics are that each leaf is composed of only 5–8 leaflets—and often just 5 or 6 leaflets—and the leaflets are quite pointed.

FLOWERS: The inflorescence is usually quite dense, with the flowers crowded along the stem. Each flower has a mostly white banner and purple wings and keel; the keel is ciliate. (See page 15 for a labeled diagram of a lupine flower.)

RELATED SPECIES: Two other varieties of Lobb's lupine, both of which are a bit taller, are common at high elevations throughout the Sierra. Var. *ramosus* is 10–30 cm in height and has at most 7 whorls of flowers, while var. *confertus* is 25–60 cm in height and has more than 7 whorls of flowers, making for a tall, dense inflorescence. Both have leaves composed of relatively few pointy-tipped leaflets.

❖ *Lupinus polyphyllus* var. *burkei* (large-leaved lupine, meadow lupine) **FAMILY:** Fabaceae

DISTRIBUTION Common in both the western and eastern Sierra in the Yosemite and Mammoth Lakes regions; farther south, common in the western Sierra but rare to absent in the eastern Sierra
HABITAT Wet meadows, seeps, stream banks
ELEVATION 4,600'–10,700'
SEASON Early July–mid-August
LOCATIONS Virginia Lakes Basin, trail to Bennettville, Dana Gardens (western base of Mt. Dana), Shadow Lake, North Lake, Paradise Valley, Mineral King

LEAVES AND STEMS: Another tall species of lupine, the large-leaved lupine stands 50–100 cm tall and is easily confused with the broad-leaved lupine. Each leaf has 5–11 leaflets that are 4–15 cm in length; they are generally less hairy than the broad-leaved lupine,

(Continued)

(Continued)   with the top lacking hairs and the bottom sparsely hairy. Also note that the leaves are quite broad but pointed at the tip.

FLOWERS: The tall inflorescence of purple flowers looks similar to many lupines. Like the broad-leaved lupine, the keel is turned upward, but the most important distinguishing feature is that the keel lacks hairs along its upper margin. Remember, the keel is hidden from view in the flower, and you have to pull apart the 2 petals known as wings to see the keel. (See page 15 for a labeled diagram of a lupine flower.)

RELATED SPECIES: *Lupinus andersonii* (Anderson's lupine), 20–90 cm in height and with few leaves, occurs occasionally throughout the Sierra. It has 6–9 leaflets, each 2–6 cm in length. Most of the leaves are along the stem, and the leaves have few enough hairs to appear green. The inflorescences are not dense, and the keel is not ciliate, meaning it lacks a row of stiff hairs.

Lupinus andersonii

❖ *Lupinus pratensis* var. *pratensis* (Inyo meadow lupine)
    FAMILY: Fabaceae

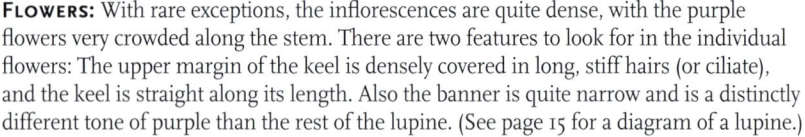

DISTRIBUTION Fairly common in the eastern Sierra from Rock Creek Basin south to Mt. Whitney, becoming very common on Coyote Ridge; occasionally crossing into the western Sierra
HABITAT Wet to dry meadows, grassy patches on sandy flats
ELEVATION 6,300'–11,100'
SEASON Mid-July–mid-August
LOCATIONS Mosquito Flat (Rock Creek Basin), Piute Pass Trail, Coyote Ridge, above Palisade Lakes, Kearsarge Pass Trail

LEAVES AND STEMS: A midsize lupine that reaches 30–70 cm in height, this species can cover vast expanses in high-elevation meadows. There are 5–10 leaflets per leaf, each 3–8 cm in length, quite narrow, and distinctly pointed. They have fine, flat-lying hairs on both sides but are still green in color.

FLOWERS: With rare exceptions, the inflorescences are quite dense, with the purple flowers very crowded along the stem. There are two features to look for in the individual flowers: The upper margin of the keel is densely covered in long, stiff hairs (or ciliate), and the keel is straight along its length. Also the banner is quite narrow and is a distinctly different tone of purple than the rest of the lupine. (See page 15 for a diagram of a lupine.)

RELATED SPECIES: There are two varieties of Inyo meadow lupine. Var. *eriostachyus* has hairs on the back of its banner, the petal at the top of the flower, while the more common var. *pratensis* lacks hairs on its banner.

❖ N-Fixation

A plant needs a very basic set of resources to survive: sunlight, carbon dioxide, water, and essential elements (nutrients). The nutrients come from the soil, mostly in the form of inorganic ions, such as nitrate, ammonium, and phosphate. Plants must extract 14 elements from the soil. Greater amounts of macronutrients— nitrogen, phosphorus, potassium, calcium, sulfur, and magnesium—are required, while only very small amounts of micronutrients—boron, chlorine, manganese, iron, zinc, copper, molybdenum, and nickel—are necessary. Plants are mostly at the mercy of the environment, with the availability of the ions varying with soil chemistry, soil moisture, and time of year. In many environments, the most limiting resource is nitrogen, the mineral organisms require in the highest amounts— especially because plants are competing with other plant roots, fungi, and soil microbes for access to nitrogen. Some microbes, however, can convert nitrogen gas, which is abundant in the atmosphere, into ammonium, one of the inorganic forms that plants can use; this energy-intensive process is called nitrogen fixation. Many plants in the pea family, Fabaceae, form root nodules (little spheres) in which one type of nitrogen-fixing bacteria, rhizobia, can live. The bacteria obtain energy and an oxygen-free habitat (the nodule) from the host plant and, in return, provide it with abundant nitrogen. As a result, plants in Fabaceae generally have leaves with much higher nitrogen concentrations than other plants growing nearby have. Nitrogen fixation continues to be important for species in Fabaceae at high elevations, with a study in the Rockies showing that more than 70% of a plant's nitrogen comes from nitrogen fixation. Studies in other mountain ranges have yielded similar results. The entire community gains from this relationship, for both dead leaves and dead plants add nitrogen to the soil, where they benefit nearby plants. So next time you pass a big patch of lupines, look around and see if the surrounding plants seem larger and happier. And also appreciate that this is probably part of the reason many lupines are so big and leafy.

Some genera in other Sierra families also have species that form relationships with bacteria able to fix nitrogen. These include *Alnus* (Betulaceae), *Ceanothus* (Rhamnaceae), *Cercocarpus* (Rosaceae), *Chamaebatia* (Rosaceae), and *Purshia* (Rosaceae); they are called actinorhizal, and a different nitrogen-fixing bacteria, *Frankia*, lives within root nodules they form.

❖ *Gentiana calycosa* (Rainier pleated gentian, explorers' gentian)
    FAMILY: Gentianaceae

DISTRIBUTION Occurs throughout but in very limited locations
HABITAT Wet slopes, meadows, seeps, forests
ELEVATION 7,000'–10,500'
SEASON Late July–mid-September
LOCATIONS Agnew Lake outlet, east end of Garnet Lake, Shadow Lake outlet, trail to Farewell Gap (Mineral King)

LEAVES AND STEMS: This species has matted, sprawling stems with fairly densely spaced pairs of opposite leaves, but it lacks the cluster of basal leaves present in most gentians. The leaves are 1–3 cm long, oval to round, and notably thin. Both the leaves and stems are quite glossy.

FLOWERS: The flower is a large (2–5 cm), somewhat open, deep-purple tube topped with 5 barely spreading petal tips. The insides of the petals have quite obvious dots, and

(Continued)

(Continued)   there are so-called appendages, a narrow, triangular lobe between the petal lobes. The calyx is just 1 cm long, very short compared with most High Sierra gentians.

❖ *Gentianella amarella* subsp. *acuta* (autumn dwarf gentian, northern gentian)   **FAMILY:** Gentianaceae

DISTRIBUTION Fairly common throughout, on both sides of the Sierra Crest
HABITAT Wet meadows, seeps
ELEVATION 6,000'–11,500'
SEASON Mid-July–early September
LOCATIONS Virginia Lakes Basin, Soda Springs (Tuolumne Meadows), Gardisky Lake, Rock Creek Basin, Tyee Lakes

LEAVES AND STEMS: This species typically reaches 20–30 cm in height but is occasionally twice that tall. In contrast to so many high-elevation species, it lacks hairs; instead, it has bright-green, shiny stems and opposite pairs of narrow, pointed leaves, sometimes with purplish tips.

FLOWERS: The plant is often branched, with the upper stretches of all branches with dense clusters of 1- to 1.5-cm-long, narrow, tubular lilac flowers; these are much smaller than other gentians. Their 4 or 5 petal tips extend above the greenish tube base, and a fringe of hairs is present near the top of the floral tube.

RELATED SPECIES: *Comastoma tenellum* (previously *Gentianella tenella* subsp. *tenella*; Samiland gentian or Dane's dwarf gentian) is a quite rare species occurring in wet meadows and seeps, including on the Dana Plateau, at Heart Lake (Rock Creek Basin), and at Mirror Lake (Mt. Whitney Trail). Previously part of the same genus as the northern gentian and similar in appearance, it has small flowers, but its long, narrow flowers are 4-petaled and occur singly at the end of narrow, purplish stalks, easily hidden among tall grasses.

❖ Sky Islands

Many of the Sierra's mountaintops and high alpine ridges and plateaus are remnants of the low-angle Ancestral Sierra that formed 50 million years ago. Unlike the valleys and steeper escarpments, these locations were not covered with glaciers during the Pleistocene epoch's repeated glaciations. Consequently, alpine plant populations could persist in these locations while the lower slopes and valleys were filled with ice (see "Glacial Refugia," page 105). The existence of stable habitats such as these, across geologic time, is thought to be one of the main reasons for the enormous diversity of plant species in the Sierra—and throughout California. Today, these so-called sky islands represent unique alpine habitats; the absence of glacial scouring means they tend to have deeper soil profiles and are generally drier, both because they have a shallower winter snowpack and are mostly west- to south-facing.

A recent study of Yosemite National Park's sky islands documents not only what plant species occur in these locations but also the variation in habitats across 12 of the park's unglaciated plateaus. To determine the diversity of environments on each plateau, many individual plots—including sites with different soil moisture, aspect (or exposure), and rock type—were sampled. Overall, 255 species were recorded across the sites. As predicted, plateaus with a greater assortment of habitats contained a greater number of species. Rarer species were associated with uncommon habitats, such as meadows or seeps perched high on a ridge; some of these "rare" species are common in wetlands at lower elevations, while for others, these isolated islands may be their main pockets of habitat.

Sixteen species were designated as widespread signature species that existed almost everywhere. These habitat generalists (see also "Generalists and Specialists," page 184) include two sedges (*Carex*), three different grass species, and *Selaginella watsoni* (Watson's spikemoss), a primitive plant. The other species are *Antennaria corymbosa* (flat-top pussytoes), *Antennaria pulchella* (beautiful pussytoes), *Boechera paupercula* (small-flowered rockcress), *Calyptridium umbellatum* (pussypaws), *Castilleja nana* (dwarf alpine paintbrush), *Draba breweri* (cushion draba), *Ivesia lycopodioides* (clubmoss ivesia), *Lupinus lepidus* (Lobb's lupine), *Packera werneriifolia* (hoary groundsel), and *Solidago multiradiata* (northern goldenrod). *Comastoma tenellum* (Samiland gentian) was one of the rarest species, growing only in moist, grassy locations. Such sites occur only on the subset of sky islands where a topographic drainage forms high on the slope, as is observed on the saddle between Mt. Dana and Mt. Gibbs. *Erigeron vagus* (rambling fleabane) is another rare species; it was encountered on Excelsior Mountain (above the Virginia Lakes Basin), Mt. Dana, Mt. Gibbs, Mt. Lewis, and Kuna Peak, all locations with metamorphic rock. Knowing which species inhabit the sky islands is an essential first step to ensure the survival of the Sierra's diverse flora as increasing temperatures and changing rainfall patterns impact the mountain range.

❖ *Gentianopsis holopetala* (Sierra gentian, Sierra fringed gentian) **FAMILY:** Gentianaceae

DISTRIBUTION Common throughout, on both sides of the Sierra Crest
HABITAT Moist to wet meadows
ELEVATION 6,500'–12,000'
SEASON Mid-July–early September
LOCATIONS Gaylor Lakes, Lyell Canyon, Rock Creek Basin, Lake Sabrina Basin, Rae Lakes Basin, Bighorn Plateau

(Continued)

(Continued)   **LEAVES AND STEMS:** A single 5- to 25-cm-tall green-purple flowering
stem arises from a group of basal leaves. The leaves are often hidden
among blades of grass, but if you poke around, you will find the bright-green, elongate
blades that are folded slightly inward from the middle. (Note that in lower-elevation
meadows, this species can be considerably taller, with longer leaves.)

FLOWERS: A single 2- to 4-cm-long, narrow, tubular, purple flower sits atop each
flowering stalk. 4 petal tips flare open from the tube's top. If you admire the plant from
the side, you will see that darker purple veins run the length of the purple petals. The
4 sepals are also fused into a tube with long, pointed tips and distinctly angled and
dark-colored corners at the midpoint of each sepal.

EXTRA TIDBITS: The Sierra gentian can sometimes be an annual—sprouting from
a seed in spring and completing its life cycle in a single year.

❖ *Swertia perennis* (felwort, star swertia)   **FAMILY:** Gentianaceae

DISTRIBUTION Occasional south of Pinchot Pass on both sides of
the Sierra Crest; absent farther north
HABITAT Wet slopes and meadows; always in moist locations
ELEVATION 7,500'–11,500'
SEASON Mid-July–early September
LOCATIONS South end of Rae Lakes Basin, west side of Kearsarge
Pass, Center Basin, Mirror Lake (Mt. Whitney Trail), Mineral King

LEAVES AND STEMS: The tall, glossy stems reach 10–50 cm in height
and are sometimes purple tinted. The stem leaves are long and narrow
with pointed tips, while basal leaves are broader.

FLOWERS: Flowers grow from many of the leaf axils along the stem:
The 5 intensely periwinkle petals are splayed wide open, with darker veins striping
the petals. Standing taller than many co-occurring species, they are dainty stars rising
above the vegetation.

❖ *Agastache urticifolia* (horsemint, nettle leaf giant hyssop)
   FAMILY: Lamiaceae

DISTRIBUTION Common in the Yosemite and Mammoth Lakes
regions on both sides of the Sierra Crest; occasional in the Kings
and Kaweah River drainages; absent elsewhere
HABITAT Meadow edges, dry to moist flats, not-too-wet stream
banks, mostly at montane elevations
ELEVATION 3,500'–10,000'
SEASON Mid-June–early August
LOCATIONS Agnew Meadows, lower Le Conte Canyon
and Palisade Creek, Paradise Valley

LEAVES AND STEMS: These tall plants have stout stems that often
top 1 m in height and can reach 1.5 m. Like all members of the
mint family, the stems are square. The leaves occur in pairs along the length of the
stem, have an approximate oval shape (but with a pointed tip), are quite fragrant, are

covered with small glands, and have a partially serrate margin. The plants often grow in dense clusters in wet areas.

FLOWERS: An inflorescence 3–10 cm in length graces the top of each stem. The many tiny flowers, mostly recessed in the tubular calyx, are pale purple, rose, or white in color and have a large lower lip. 2 pairs of stamens extend out of flowers, the lower pair much longer than the upper pair. The individual flowers are short-lived, but the sepal tips are light purple and continue to give the inflorescence color after the petals are gone.

❖ *Monardella odoratissima* subsp. *pallida* (mountain monardella, pennyroyal)
   FAMILY: Lamiaceae

DISTRIBUTION Common throughout the western Sierra and in the eastern Sierra from the Yosemite region south through the Palisades, becoming more occasional to the south
HABITAT Dry, sandy slopes and flats; forest openings
ELEVATION 5,200'–11,600'
SEASON Early July–mid-August
LOCATIONS Twenty Lakes Basin, Garnet Lake, Selden Pass, Rock Creek Basin, Farewell Gap

LEAVES AND STEMS: Considered a subshrub because its stems are woody only at the base, the plants are typically 20–30 cm tall but occasionally grow taller. The cluster of many stems can spread across 30 cm—or farther. The stiff, square stems are sparsely covered with opposite pairs of small (1.5–3 cm long), narrow, leathery, hairy leaves. Your nose might be the first sense organ to alert you that a patch of mountain monardella is near, for the leaves are very aromatic.

FLOWERS: This is one of the most colorful plants on dry slopes. At the top of the stems are dense, rounded heads comprised of 30–50 flowers. The flowers are lilac (to white) and, like other mints, are a 2-lipped tube, formed from the 5 petals, with 4 stamens extending well beyond the floral tube. 4 rose-colored bracts (leaves beneath the flowering head) color the buds.

EXTRA TIDBITS: The leaves can be used to make tea.

RELATED SPECIES: This species is divided into 2 subspecies, subsp. *pallida* and subsp. *glauca*. Subsp. *pallida* has purple flowers and leaves less than 1 cm long beneath the flowering heads, while subsp. *glauca* has white flowers and larger leaves beneath each flowering head. Both varieties occur throughout the Sierra.

❖ *Linum lewisii* var. *lewisii* (western blue flax, Lewis' flax)
   FAMILY: Linaceae

DISTRIBUTION On both sides of the Sierra Crest but occurs only in scattered locations
HABITAT Dry slopes, often on metamorphic rock
ELEVATION 7,000'–11,800'
SEASON Early June–mid-July
LOCATIONS Virginia Lakes Basin, Mt. Dana, Island Pass, Convict Creek drainage, Diamond Mesa (Shepherd Pass area), Guitar Lake

(Continued)

(Continued) **LEAVES AND STEMS:** Many stiff stems emerge from the ground, each usually reaching 10–40 cm in height. 1- to 2-cm-long, narrow, oval-shaped leaves occur along the entire length of the stem and are a pale sea-green. Both the leaves and stem are hairless.

FLOWERS: The flowers are easily identified by their vibrant periwinkle color; though rare, you cannot miss the 5-petal flowers, quite large, at 1–3 cm in diameter. Each stem bears a few to many flowers, though typically only 1–2 are open at once. The petals are readily shed, and you will often see flowers lacking 1 or more petals.

❖ *Collinsia parviflora* (small-flowered blue-eyed Mary)
    FAMILY: Plantaginaceae (Scrophulariaceae)

DISTRIBUTION Fairly common throughout, on both sides of the Sierra Crest
HABITAT Moist forest
ELEVATION 2,700'–11,700'
SEASON Early June–mid-July
LOCATIONS Tuolumne Meadows, Rock Creek Basin, North Fork Big Pine Creek, Bubbs Creek, Colby Meadows

LEAVES AND STEMS: These annuals can be as short as 3 cm or (very rarely) as tall as 40 cm. Both the purplish stems and the short, narrow leaves are dotted with glands, and the leaves may have margins that are rolled under.

FLOWERS: These tiny flowers are 4–8 cm long and very narrow. Like other *Collinsias,* they are 4-petal lobes that spread open at the top of the narrow flower tube. The upper 2 petals are white, while the lower ones are blue-purple and slightly longer. This species can be distinguished from the common *Collinsia torreyi* by its elongate, sharp-pointed sepal lobes; the sepal tube is purplish with green tips.

❖ *Collinsia torreyi* var. *wrightii* (Wright's blue-eyed Mary)
    FAMILY: Plantaginaceae (Scrophulariaceae)

DISTRIBUTION Common throughout the western Sierra; much rarer in the eastern Sierra
HABITAT Dry forest openings on coarse granite soil, open disturbed soil
ELEVATION 5,500'–11,000'
SEASON Mid-June–mid-July
LOCATIONS Tuolumne Meadows Campground, Dana Gardens (western base of Mt. Dana), Minaret Lake Trail, Cottonwood Lakes

LEAVES AND STEMS: Generally only 10 cm high but occasionally reaching 25 cm, this annual species has a single stem that is often branched where the first leaves connect. The stem and leaves are both gland-dotted—the little dots glisten in the sun. Leaves, up to 4 cm in length, occur in pairs and are at least 5 times longer than wide and especially narrow toward the tip. There are often only a few leaf pairs on the main stem, with the lower reaches of the stem completely bare.

FLOWERS: Each plant can have anywhere from a few up to 30 flowers. The diminutive flowers, always less than 1 cm in length, occur both on side branches and toward the top of the main stalk, either in pairs or with multiple flowers encircling the stem. The petals are fused into a tube, but the tube is mostly hidden in the gland-covered calyx, and you notice only the 4 petal lobes that open flat and stare straight at you—the 2 upper are white, and the lower ones are purple and nearly twice as long.

RELATED SPECIES: Several additional varieties occur at upper and lower montane elevations in the western Sierra, including *Collinsia torreyi* var. *brevicarinata* and *Collinsia torreyi* var. *torreyi*.

❖ *Penstemon azureus* var. *azureus* (azure penstemon)
  FAMILY: Plantaginaceae (Scrophulariaceae)

DISTRIBUTION Fairly common in the San Joaquin River drainage; rare in the Kings River drainage; generally absent elsewhere
HABITAT Sunny, sandy, and gravelly slopes and flats
ELEVATION 5,000'–8,700'
SEASON Early July–mid-August
LOCATIONS West of Agnew Meadows, between Pocket Meadow and Mono Creek, Lake Thomas A. Edison, Florence Lake

LEAVES AND STEMS: This species is considered a subshrub because the very bases of the stems are woody. Long green branches extend above the base and reach 20–70 cm in height. The narrow, elongate leaves reach anywhere from 1 to 6.5 cm in length, attach to the stem in pairs, and often have a slight blue tinge to them. Both the stems and leaves lack hairs or glands.

FLOWERS: Above the last leaves is the long inflorescence of showy purple to deep-blue—azure—flowers. Though the flowers are not dense on the stalk, they immediately catch your attention, for they are 2–3.5 cm in length and generally face upward on the stem. The tube is quite bulbous, flaring slightly toward the mouth to reveal the curved white stamens. Note that the base of the floral tube often tends to a more magenta color, while the top is bluer.

RELATED SPECIES: Occurring predominantly in the Bishop Creek and Big Pine Creek drainages, *Penstemon papillatus,* Inyo beardtongue, is a subshrub that reaches 20–40 cm in height. Look for the following three features to identify it: 1) a narrow floral tube 2.5–3.5 cm in length and purple to purplish-blue in color; 2) a staminodium, the infertile stamen inside the floral tube that lacks any hairs; and 3) leaves that occur along the entire length of the stem.

❖ Hybrids

If you are trying to identify a plant and keep getting stumped because the individual looks a bit like each of two different species, you may have found a hybrid. A hybrid has parents that are two different species. Very few animals can form successful hybrids—that is, a hybrid that can produce its own fertile offspring—but hybridization is much more common in plants. For biologists, one of the biggest questions about hybrids is,

(Continued)

(Continued)   "If these two species can interbreed, why don't all the individuals hybridize, eventually resulting in a single species?" The answer: The differences in habitat or pollinator choices that distinguish the two species tend to ensure that the parent species are more successful—they leave more offspring. Hybrids tend to be intermediate in terms of traits and therefore are not perfectly suited to either parent's habitat or chief pollinators. Thus, hybrids will not grow as well or be visited by as many pollinators, together leading to fewer seeds.

The hybrid individuals will have characteristics of both parents, usually including intermediate petal color and shape. Finding hybrid individuals can be very frustrating because you—and I—want to be able to call each plant a specific species. When no species description is a good match, I always assume that I have misread the species description and only after much time realize that I have found a hybrid. Two of the showiest examples of hybridization you will see in the Sierra are between *Penstemon davidsonii* (Davidson's penstemon) and *Penstemon newberryi* (mountain pride penstemon) and between *Aquilegia pubescens* (Coville's columbine) and *Aquilegia formosa* (crimson columbine) (see also "A Tale of Two Columbines," page 67). Some species within the monkeyflowers (*Mimulus*), pussytoes (*Antennaria*), and rockcress (*Boechera*) genera are also known to hybridize. And there are certainly many additional examples that have not yet been studied thoroughly. A population of *Penstemon* growing at the southeastern corner of Steelhead Lake (in the Twenty Lakes Basin) clearly has hybrids as well as purebred parents; plants with a diversity of petal colors and flower tube shapes grow together here. Because these are long-lived individuals, they are likely to still be there if you want to have a look.

❖ *Penstemon davidsonii* var. *davidsonii* (Davidson's penstemon, alpine penstemon)   **FAMILY:** Plantaginaceae (Scrophulariaceae)

DISTRIBUTION Fairly common throughout, on both sides of the Sierra Crest
HABITAT Patches of soil on otherwise rocky slopes and flats
ELEVATION 9,400'–12,500'
SEASON Early July–mid-August
LOCATIONS Twenty Lakes Basin, Piute Pass, Evolution Basin, Glen Pass, Kearsarge Pass

LEAVES AND STEMS: This high-elevation species forms a low-growing mat of woody stems, and up to 2-cm-long, thick, hairless, oval- to round-shaped leaves sprawl across sandy openings between rocks. The stalks are usually less than 5 cm long but are densely covered in pairs of leaves, usually smaller toward the tip.

FLOWERS: Each stalk has 1–5 of the light-purple, tubular flowers, each 2–3 cm long. In comparison to the quite robust-looking stems and leaves, the petals are remarkably thin and delicate but large. The broad, bulbous floral tube is quite flared at the opening, with 2 petal lobes on top and 3 at the bottom, providing a good view of its white-hairy interior. At the base of each floral tube is the calyx, colored a mixture of green and purple and covered in gland-tipped hairs.

❖ *Penstemon heterodoxus* var. *heterodoxus* (Sierra penstemon)
　　FAMILY: Plantaginaceae (Scrophulariaceae)

DISTRIBUTION Very common throughout, on both sides of the Sierra Crest
HABITAT Dry to moist meadows, forest openings, dry slopes, alongside rocks
ELEVATION 6,500'–11,500'
SEASON Early July–mid-August
LOCATIONS Twenty Lakes Basin, Rock Creek Basin, Bishop Pass Trail, Kearsarge Pass Trail

LEAVES AND STEMS: This species' rosettes of leaves can form sprawling mats, covering the ground with 1- to 4-cm-long leaves, while at other times there may be just a few small tufts of leaves. The elongate, unlobed, thick leaves are often partially folded along the midrib. Leaves on the flowering stem occur in pairs and look identical to the basal leaves.

FLOWERS: Flowering stems rarely exceed 40 cm and are usually only half that, with flowers encircling the stem in 1 or more circles, called whorls, each composed of 10–25 flowers. Each of the dark purplish-blue, tubular flowers is 1–1.5 cm long and glandular (and therefore shiny in sunlight). The flowers are wider at the mouth of the tube than the base and stick straight out sideways from the stem.

RELATED SPECIES: Two subspecies co-occur across the area: var. *heterodoxus,* with plants less than 20 cm tall and flowers in 1–2 clusters, and var. *cephalophorus,* with plants more than 20 cm tall and flowers in 2–6 whorls. Though both occur throughout, var. *cephalophorus* is rare north of Mammoth Lakes.

❖ *Penstemon procerus* var. *formosus* (western small flowered penstemon)
　　FAMILY: Plantaginaceae (Scrophulariaceae)

DISTRIBUTION Occasional in the Yosemite area, becoming rare farther south but occurring sporadically throughout
HABITAT Alpine fell-fields, meadows
ELEVATION 7,000'–11,600'
SEASON Early July–early August
LOCATIONS Gardisky Lake, Dana Plateau, Lake Sabrina Basin, Mt. Whitney Trail

LEAVES AND STEMS: Generally found at high elevations, this penstemon tends to grow as a mat or small clump, with stems reaching 15 cm in height at most. The leaves are mostly at the base of the plant and are long, narrow, quite leathery, and folded inward along their midrib.

(Continued)

(Continued)   **FLOWERS:** At first glance, the flowers are easily confused with *Penstemon heterodoxus,* but a number of features distinguish these two species. First, these flowers are much smaller (just 6–10 mm), point downward (not outward), and lack glands. Also, there are far more flowers per inflorescence. This last feature is only apparent on particularly healthy individuals, but these plants can have 40 of the small flowers crowded together.

❖ Red Versus Blue Penstemons

Penstemons are a very diverse genus, with 250 species in North America, including 23 in the Sierra Nevada; 10 have been included in this book. Their flower color, which ranges from red to pink to purple to blue, is created by anthocyanin molecules (see "A Rainbow of Flowers," page 95). Slight chemical changes to the pigment molecules cause different colors to be reflected (and therefore seen by us), leading to a transition from purple, violet, or dark blue (the pigment delphinidin) to blue or magenta (cyanidin) to red or orange (pelargonidin). Researchers have determined that the "original" (most primitive) penstemons had blue-purple flowers, while red flowers are the result of more recent mutations. The transition from blue to red has occurred at least eight times within the genus; meanwhile, due to the type of mutation, there has never been a switch from red back to blue. Pollinators are likely the force behind this change: All red-colored penstemons are hummingbird pollinated, while blue-flowered species are fly or bee pollinated (though certain bee species forage from the red-flowered species too). In the high-elevation Sierra, *Penstemon rostriflorus* (Bridge penstemon) and *Penstemon newberryi* (mountain pride penstemon) are hummingbird pollinated. If hummingbirds were to disappear, these species would be losers, unable to shift their color back toward blue to attract a different group of pollinators. See also "Adapting to Hummingbirds," page 156, and "A Tale of Two Columbines," page 67, for additional examples of shifts in flower color within a genus.

❖ *Penstemon rydbergii* var. *oreocharis* (meadow penstemon)
FAMILY: Plantaginaceae (Scrophulariaceae)

DISTRIBUTION Very common in the western Sierra from the Yosemite region south through the San Joaquin drainage, becoming occasional farther south; common in the eastern Sierra from the Yosemite region south through the Kearsarge Pass area
HABITAT Mountain meadows, ranging from wetter to drier locations
ELEVATION 4,900'–12,000'
SEASON Late June–early August
LOCATIONS Slate Creek Fork Lee Vining Creek, Lyell Canyon, Agnew Meadows, South Fork Big Pine Creek

LEAVES AND STEMS: Occurring either in small clumps or spreading masses, this penstemon has 2.5- to 7-cm-long, rather narrow, quite pointed, thinnish leaves. The leaves are densely clustered at the ground surface and become somewhat sparser up the flowering stems. Note that the leaves have no glands or hairs.

FLOWERS: The top sections of 20- to 40-cm-tall (or even taller) flowering stalks are encircled by 1 or more whorls of 10–30 purple, tubular flowers, with bare stretches of stem between the whorls. Each flower is 1–1.5 cm in length, is somewhat flared at the mouth, and has a white-hairy interior. The outside of the tubes lack glands and hairs, a key feature to distinguish it from the Sierra beardtongue.

❖ Nectar Replenishment

Plants produce nectar, or sugar water, to attract pollinators. Though some pollinators seek the protein-rich pollen (see also "Pollinators," page 167), many species—including hummingbirds, butterflies, many wasps, bees, and ants—are in search of sugary nectar to consume. A nectary is the small gland that exudes nectar; it can be located in a flower or on a leaf or stem. Inside some flowers, nectar fills a small reservoir, while in other cases, just a drop is released at a time. If a plant wants to continuously entice nectar-seeking pollinators to its flowers, it needs to provide a nonstop supply of nectar. A study comparing several *Penstemon* species in the far southern Sierra showed that bee-pollinated species provided small quantities of more-sugary nectar and replenished their nectar quickly, while hummingbird-pollinated species had a larger reservoir of more-dilute nectar and took moderately longer to replenish the reservoir. These patterns match visitation rates: Bee-pollinated plants are visited up to 100 times per day, while hummingbird-pollinated species are visited less frequently, but the hummingbirds consume more nectar per visit. In a second part of the study, *Penstemon speciosus* (royal or showy penstemon), a bumblebee-pollinated species, produced far more nectar when nectar was continually removed than it did in an untouched flower, showing that the flower was responding to pollinator demand. Next time you walk by a penstemon, consider how fine-tuned these plants are at appealing to pollinators. Pollinators are equally aware of how fast nectar is replenished and revisit the flowers at optimal intervals.

❖ *Penstemon speciosus* (showy penstemon, royal penstemon)
    FAMILY: Plantaginaceae (Scrophulariaceae)

DISTRIBUTION Common in the eastern Sierra from the Yosemite region south through the Bishop Creek drainage; also common in the Kern River drainage once south of Mt. Whitney; absent elsewhere
HABITAT Open, dry slopes, often growing among sagebrush
ELEVATION 5,000'–11,500'
SEASON Late June–mid-August
LOCATIONS Virginia Lakes Basin, Gardisky Lake Trail, San Joaquin Ridge, Brown Lake (from South Lake)

(Continued)

(Continued)   **LEAVES AND STEMS:** The leafy stems typically grow 10–20 cm high but are occasionally more than twice as tall. The leaves are up to 9 cm long, narrow, and often folded upward along the midrib and curved backward toward the tip. The thick leaves, which generally attach to the stem in pairs, lack hairs and are often a pale mint-green color.

FLOWERS: This species earns its title of showy penstemon both because of the beautiful bright-blue color of the petals and because the flowers are so densely crowded on the flowering stem. The large tubular flowers are narrow at the base and then bulge abruptly, flaring still wider at the mouth.

❖ *Veronica americana* (American brooklime, American speedwell)
     FAMILY: Plantaginaceae (Scrophulariaceae)

DISTRIBUTION Common throughout montane elevations on both sides of the Sierra Crest, occasionally reaching higher elevations
HABITAT Seeps, stream banks, other moist locations
ELEVATION 4,000'–10,500'
SEASON Early June–late July
LOCATIONS Sotcher Lake, Rock Creek Trail, Bishop Pass Trail, Third Lake (North Fork Big Pine Creek)

LEAVES AND STEMS: This sprawling plant covers large expanses because the stems can form roots at leaf nodes. The stems can reach more than 50 cm in length but never rise much above ground level. The leaves and stems both lack hairs and can indeed be quite shiny. The leaves are elongate-oval shaped, with a fine-toothed, and often reddish, margin.

FLOWERS: The tiny periwinkle-colored flowers are dispersed along the upper length of the stem. They are racemes, indicating that flowers open in progression from lower to higher along the stem, and indeed those toward the bottom have gone to seed by the time the top ones are opening, with only a few flowers open at a time. As with other species of *Veronica,* the 4 petals are fused, with the asymmetrical lobes opening outward and 2 stamens extending beyond the shallow flower tube. Unlike the several smaller species of high-elevation *Veronica,* this plant has inflorescences that grow from leaf nodes, not at the top of the main stem.

❖ *Veronica wormskjoldii* (American alpine speedwell)
     FAMILY: Plantaginaceae (Scrophulariaceae)

DISTRIBUTION Common throughout
HABITAT Moist meadows, stream banks, seeps, lakeshores
ELEVATION 5,000'–11,500'
SEASON Late June–mid-August
LOCATIONS Twenty Lakes Basin, Humphreys Basin, Upper Palisade Lake, west side of Taboose Pass, Cottonwood Lakes

LEAVES AND STEMS: This short, often spreading herb can form extensive clumps in wet alpine locations; its stems usually reach 10–15 cm in height but occasionally grow a little taller. Unlike the stems of other species of *Veronica,* these rise straight upward. Both the stems and the small, elongate, oval-shaped leaves are a bright green. The leaves are largest at the base of the plant, up to 4 cm, and become much shorter along the stem. The stems and leaf margins are covered in long, white hairs.

FLOWERS: The 4-lobed, tubular flowers are a beautiful dark-periwinkle color. They are subtly bilaterally symmetrical, with the upward-facing petal slightly larger and more bulbous. A characteristic of all *Veronicas,* there are only 2 stamens that stick out from the flower tube. The flowers are clustered, often densely, toward the top of the stems, each attached to the main stem with a short stalk.

RELATED SPECIES: *Veronica serpyllifolia* subsp. *humifusa,* thyme-leaved or brightblue speedwell, occurs throughout montane elevations in the western Sierra and in the eastern Sierra north of the Mammoth Lakes region, occasionally reaching higher elevations. The petals are rounder than those of American alpine speedwell, and the stems tend to crawl along the ground.

Veronica serpyllifolia subsp. *humifusa*

❖ *Gilia cana* subsp. *cana* (showy gilia, desert gilia)
    FAMILY: Polemoniaceae

DISTRIBUTION Common in the eastern Sierra from the Bishop Creek drainage south; absent elsewhere
HABITAT Dry, sandy slopes
ELEVATION 5,200'–10,000'
SEASON Mid-April–mid-June
LOCATIONS North Fork Big Pine Creek, Kearsarge Pass Trail, Mt. Whitney Trail

LEAVES AND STEMS: Of the many annual *Gilia* species growing in the low- to mid-elevation eastern Sierra, this one extends to the highest elevations. The reddish stems, with many branches, reach up to 30 cm in height, though in most years, they reach only half that height. The toothed leaves, densely covered with long hairs, are concentrated near the base of the plant—while the leaves are mostly green, the sharp teeth have a reddish hue.

FLOWERS: The flowers are a beautiful reddish-purplish color, setting off the equally showy periwinkle-colored pollen at the tips of the stamens. The 5 petals are fused into a shallow yellow tube but then open widely above, so that the flower is about 1.5 cm in diameter.

❖ *Navarretia leptalea* subsp. *bicolor* (*Gilia leptalea* subsp. *bicolor*) (Bridges' gilia)
    FAMILY: Polemoniaceae

DISTRIBUTION Fairly common in the Yosemite region, on both sides of the Sierra Crest; absent to the south
HABITAT Moist to dry sandy flats, meadows, small patches of disturbed soil
ELEVATION 5,500'–10,000'
SEASON Mid-June–late July
LOCATIONS Near White Wolf Campground, Dog Lake, Slate Creek Fork Lee Vining Creek, Johnson Lake

(Continued)

(Continued)   **LEAVES AND STEMS:** A close relative of the genus *Gilia,* this species looks superficially similar to showy gilia, though the two do not overlap in range. It too is an annual with many branches and grows 10–20 cm in height. However, it has long, narrow leaves that occur throughout the plant.

FLOWERS: Many tubular, 5-petal, purplish flowers decorate the plant with 1 to several flowers at each node. The tube is quite narrow at the base, widening considerably at the top. If you peer in, you will notice that the top of the tube is white, while lower down, it is yellow. The 5 stamens are a pale purple, topped with vibrant periwinkle-colored pollen. A second, lower-elevation subspecies, *leptalea,* has larger flowers with a purple tube.

❖ *Polemonium californicum* (California polemonium, moving polemonium)
      FAMILY: Polemoniaceae

DISTRIBUTION Common in the Yosemite area and occasional at montane elevations in the western Sierra south to Courtright Reservoir; absent elsewhere
HABITAT Dry slopes, open forest
ELEVATION 7,000'–9,700'
SEASON Mid-June–late July
LOCATIONS Rancheria Mountain, May Lake Trail, Tenaya Peak, Kaiser Pass

LEAVES AND STEMS: The stems of this species reach only 10–20 cm in height, but the plants often grow in masses, spreading across the ground via a rhizome, an underground stem. Nearly all the leaves are at the base of the plant and are each pinnately divided into 11–23 oval-shaped leaflets, with the top 3 leaflets always fused together. Gland-tipped hairs cover the stems and leaves.

FLOWERS: The flowers are in open clusters at the top of a nearly leafless stalk. Though the 1-cm-diameter flowers are tubular, the tube is short, and the dark-purple petal lobes overlap to form a bowl shape. The center of the "bowl" is yellow, with white pollen sacks and long white pistils visible inside.

❖ *Polemonium eximium* (sky pilot)
      FAMILY: Polemoniaceae

DISTRIBUTION Common nearly throughout but almost always near the Sierra Crest; absent in the Mammoth Lakes region and rare along the Great Western Divide
HABITAT Talus slopes, cliffs
ELEVATION 10,500'–14,000'
SEASON Early June–mid-July
LOCATIONS Summit of Mt. Dana, top of Kearsarge Pass, north side of Forester Pass, toward Mt. Whitney summit

LEAVES AND STEMS: Dense clusters of leaves grow from underground stems and usually reach 6–10 cm in length. Each leaf is divided into 20–35 leaflets, but as the leaflets are themselves deeply lobed, the stalk simply appears to be encircled in miniature leaflets. The leaves and stems are covered in sticky glands and have a very strong smell—you often know in advance that you are approaching a big patch of plants!

FLOWERS: These flowering heads are the alpine Sierra's showiest: a 4-cm-wide ball of vibrant purple, and at the highest of elevations. The ball is composed of many individual tubular flowers, each a little under 1 cm wide at the mouth. The petal lobes are broad and wide open, overlapping just a little. And as a finishing touch, white pollen on the tips of the stamens is just visible inside the tube. As this species rarely grows below 12,000 feet, only determined hikers will get to enjoy them.

EXTRA TIDBITS: The flowers have a strong scent to attract pollinators.

❖ Pika Diets

At high elevations, especially when walking near talus piles, you may come across small heaps of drying leaves that appear intentionally placed. And so they are, for these are winter stockpiles for a small relative of rabbits, the North American pika. Unlike most high-elevation mammals, pikas do not hibernate in winter. Instead, they subsist on stockpiles of leaves, carefully dried and then stored beneath rocks. While pikas occasionally live at much lower elevations, they are generally associated with alpine and subalpine environments where temperatures are lower; pikas maintain a high body temperature and metabolism and do poorly in warm locations. Pikas are not, however, fussy eaters, instead consuming any available plant species, including mosses; if you find a pika stash, look at the leaves and try to compare them with nearby vegetation to determine what is being eaten. You are especially likely to find pikas in the vicinity of rock glaciers (see "Rock Glacier Environments," page 47) because these locations have a cooler environment and dense vegetation. At the highest elevations, *Hulsea algida* (Pacific hulsea) and *Polemonium eximium* (sky pilot) are popular dinner choices for pikas probably because the plants have such large leaves.

❖ *Polemonium occidentale* subsp. *occidentale* (western polemonium)
　　FAMILY: Polemoniaceae

DISTRIBUTION Rare to occasional throughout, on both sides of the Sierra Crest
HABITAT Wet meadows, stream banks
ELEVATION 7,000'–10,900'
SEASON Late June–early August
LOCATIONS Gardisky Lake, trail from Minaret Summit to Starkweather Lake, below Ruby Lake (Rock Creek Basin), North Lake trailhead, below Green Lake (from South Lake)

LEAVES AND STEMS: The only tall polemonium species, this plant has stalks that are commonly 40–60 cm high but occasionally taller. The base of the plant is densely leafy, while the flowering stalks have only a few leaves. Each leaf is quite long (up to 40 cm) and divided into many elongate, oval-shaped leaflets that line the leaf stalk in pairs. Unlike other species, the western polemonium's leaves lack sticky glands or hairs.

(Continued)

(Continued)   **FLOWERS:** The flowers occur in clusters at the tops of flowering stalks. The 2-cm-wide purple flowers are larger and less crowded on the flowering stalk than other polemoniums, such that you admire them individually. Also, the petals tend to splay open more widely and are narrowed at the tips. The yellow stamens and notably long, purple-tipped, 3-pronged pistil stick out of the tube.

❖ *Polemonium pulcherrimum* var. *pulcherrimum* (sky pilot, Jacob's-ladder)
    FAMILY: Polemoniaceae

DISTRIBUTION Common near the Sierra Crest in the Yosemite region; absent elsewhere
HABITAT Scree slopes, talus slopes, alongside outcrops
ELEVATION 9,800'–12,100'
SEASON Early June–mid-July
LOCATIONS Pass at head of Virginia Lakes Basin, Tioga Peak, western slopes of Mt. Dana

LEAVES AND STEMS: A small cluster of leaves grows directly from the underground rhizome and rarely exceeds 6 cm in length. Each leaf is divided into leaflets covered with gland-tipped hairs. In shaded environments the leaves can reach 1 cm in length and tend to be oval shaped, while in the alpine zone, they are thicker, smaller, and rounder.

FLOWERS: A few flowers grow together at the end of a flowering stalk, though they open sequentially within an inflorescence, so the plants often appear sparsely flowered. In particularly windy locations, the stalk is frequently nestled among leaves, while it will stretch upward in more sheltered locations. The flowers are approximately bell shaped, with a yellow tube opening up into small pale- to dark-purple petal lobes; the yellow center is quite vibrant in this species.

❖ *Aconitum columbianum* subsp. *columbianum*
    (Columbian monkshood)   **FAMILY:** Ranunculaceae

DISTRIBUTION Fairly common throughout the western Sierra; common throughout the eastern Sierra
HABITAT Streamsides, moist meadows, willow thickets
ELEVATION 6,500'–10,500'
SEASON Early July–mid-August
LOCATIONS Lundy Canyon, Heart Lake (Rock Creek Basin), Mono Creek, Bubbs Creek at Junction Meadow

LEAVES AND STEMS: This tall plant commonly grows to more than 1 m in height—if not 1.5 or even 2 m. The stems are stout with leaves on the bottom half. The leaves are 5–15 cm wide, with 3–5 deep palmate lobes. Each lobe is further toothed.

FLOWERS: The flowers, sometimes widely spaced and other times closer together, adorn the top sections of the stem. Each flower looks very much like its namesake, a monkshood. Like the larkspurs, the showy plant parts are the sepals, not the petals. The

inset photographed by Rebecca Wenk

uppermost of the 5 sepals is shaped like a pointed hood. Below are 2 sepals that are quite broad and rounded, while 2 narrower sepals point down. In the center are 2 barely visible petals and a cluster of stamens.

EXTRA TIDBITS: Note that all parts of this plant are very toxic.

❖ *Delphinium depauperatum* (dwarf larkspur, few-flowered larkspur, blue mountain larkspur)   **FAMILY:** Ranunculaceae

DISTRIBUTION Common from the Yosemite region south through the San Joaquin River drainage, on both sides of the Sierra Crest, becoming much rarer farther south
HABITAT Moist to dry forest floor; open slopes
ELEVATION 4,000'–10,500'
SEASON Mid-June–late July
LOCATIONS Yosemite Creek Trail, High Trail above Agnew Meadows, Mono Creek

LEAVES AND STEMS: The shortest of the delphiniums, this species reaches just 10–40 cm high and is at most slightly branched. The small number of leaves are concentrated toward the bottom half of the stem and mostly shed before the flowers start. They are deeply palmately lobed into 5–10 narrow segments. Note that the stems are not hairy.

FLOWERS: Each stalk has 4–22 flowers. Like all delphiniums, the long "petals" are sepals, while the much smaller white and blue petals are located to the inside. The spur is often a lighter color than the sepal lobes. The sepal lobes spread wide open, often even slightly folded back. The lobes are distinctly tapered and pointed, creating a starlike outline. Like the similar-looking meadow larkspur, the sepals have little round dark indents on them. The upper 2 petals, located in the very center of the flower, are white and folded along their center, while the lower 3 are purple and folded back on themselves.

❖ *Delphinium glaucum* (glaucus larkspur, Sierra larkspur)
    FAMILY: Ranunculaceae

DISTRIBUTION Common in the Yosemite and Mammoth Lakes regions on both sides of the Sierra Crest; very rare farther south
HABITAT Wet meadows, stream banks
ELEVATION 6,000'–10,700'
SEASON Early July–mid-August
LOCATIONS Lundy Canyon, Dana Gardens (western base of Mt. Dana), Sotcher Lake (near Reds Meadow)

LEAVES AND STEMS: The tallest of the high-elevation delphiniums reaches heights of 80–150 cm. The stems are notably stout and are usually a pale green, as the stem is covered with a whitish powder (called glaucous, hence the species' name). The large leaves—8–15 cm across—have 5–7 lobes, with the lobes nearly reaching to the leaf's center. Each of the lobes is intricately toothed, with the teeth all forming narrow points.

(Continued)

(Continued)   **FLOWERS:** More than 50 blue-purple flowers adorn each of the tall stalks. The spur and all the sepals are the same color, while the petals—just visible in the center—are slightly lighter. The spur tends to be quite wrinkled and slightly upturned at the tip or rounded along its entire length. The sepal lobes are relatively narrow and long and face forward, in contrast to the turned-back look of the dwarf larkspur.

❖ Albinism

Have you ever walked past a patch of flowers and noted a lone white representative interspersed with its purple compatriots? Or kept trying to find a picture that matched the white flower you found, only to give up in frustration—and later find a look-alike in pink? If so, you may have seen an example of albinism, a lack of pigment in a plant part that is usually colored. If all the flowers on a plant are white, the albinism is probably caused by a mutation, or change, in the individual's genes that occurred when it first formed as a seed, and the mutation affects the flowers on the entire plant. In other cases, a mutation occurs in one shoot as the plant grows, and a single branch will exhibit albino flowers.

In plants, we almost always note albinism in petals. Albino leaves would have no chlorophyll, and such a plant would be unable to photosynthesize and would quickly die. The "correct" petal color is also important to plants; the color normally observed is that which attracts the most pollinators (see "Pollinators," page 167). We can therefore assume that albino plants will probably have lower success at attracting pollinators and setting seed compared with surrounding individuals—though in one non-Sierran species studied, it made no difference.

Over the years I have found albino variants of *Primula tetrandra* (also known as *Dodecatheon alpinum*; alpine shootingstar), *Penstemon heterodoxus* (Sierra beardtongue), *Delphinium glaucum* (Sierra or giant larkspur) (see photo), *Veronica wormskjoldii* (American alpine speedwell), *Lupinus albicaulis* (sickelkeel lupine), and *Pedicularis attollens* (little elephant's head). However, I am sure there are many other species to add to this list, for almost every horticultural species is known to occasionally produce albino mutants!

❖ *Delphinium nuttallianum* (meadow larkspur, Nuttall's larkspur)
     FAMILY: Ranunculaceae

DISTRIBUTION Common in the Yosemite and Mammoth Lakes regions, becoming much rarer to the south
HABITAT Open forest, meadow edges, stream banks
ELEVATION 5,500'–10,500'
SEASON Mid-June–late July
LOCATIONS Tuolumne Meadows, Gaylor Lakes Trail, Reds Meadow, base of Mt. Silliman

LEAVES AND STEMS: A smallish larkspur, the meadow larkspur reaches 5–50 cm in height and has only a few leaves, which are on the lower stem. The leaves are divided into narrow lobes that extend most of the way to the stalk—though the leaf is round in outline, it is mostly a few "spokes" with air in between. Unlike the closely related dwarf larkspur, the stem of this species is sometimes hairy.

FLOWERS: Each plant has only 2–12 flowers that range in color from a bright blue, through various purples, and occasionally almost to pink. The spur is long, narrow, and straight, while the sepal lobes are quite broad—they taper only at the very end and are otherwise the same width throughout. At the middle of each lobe is a round indent or pockmark that is darker than the surrounding sepal. The tiny petals are visible in the middle of the flower. The upper petals are usually whitish and are not folded in half. The sepals all tend to open straight outward, not upward.

RELATED SPECIES: A closely related species, *Delphinium gracilentum,* slender or pine forest larkspur, mainly grows below 8,000 feet in elevation. It is distinguished by having fewer leaf lobes (and broader lobes, so there is more leaf). It also has more flowers (8–20 per stalk), though the flowers look quite similar to those of meadow larkspur.

Delphinium gracilentum

❖ *Delphinium polycladon* (high mountain larkspur, mountain marsh larkspur)   **FAMILY:** Ranunculaceae

DISTRIBUTION Common throughout, on both sides of the Sierra Crest; most common larkspur south of the Mammoth Lakes region
HABITAT Any moist to wet locations: meadows, stream banks, seeps
ELEVATION 6,000'–11,500'
SEASON Early July–mid-August
LOCATIONS Dana Gardens (western base of Mt. Dana), Thousand Island Lake, Rock Creek Basin, Bishop Pass Trail, Junction Meadow (on John Muir Trail)

LEAVES AND STEMS: Reaching heights of 80–130 cm tall, this species can grow in large clumps. The round leaves are rather shallowly lobed and have large teeth. The teeth form points, but not terribly narrow ones.

FLOWERS: The inflorescences can be sparse or showy, with 3–35 flowers attached to each stalk. The spur is straight and a bit shorter than other species. Meanwhile, the sepal lobes are broader and more rounded, nearly forming a bowl-like shape. A hairy patch is often visible in the very center of the flower. The middle of the top sepal is pinched into a little tuck.

EXTRA TIDBITS: In all larkspurs, the spur is formed from the uppermost sepal. Inside it are the nectar-filled spurs that form at the back of the two upper petals.

❖ *Solanum xanti* (chaparral nightshade, purple nightshade)
FAMILY: Solanaceae

DISTRIBUTION Occasional throughout on both sides of the Sierra Crest; mostly restricted to montane forest elevations
HABITAT Dry, sandy slopes; open forest; especially common after fires
ELEVATION 1,000'–8,300'   *(Continued)*

(Continued)

SEASON Early June–late July
LOCATIONS Barney Lake (Robinson Creek drainage), Yosemite Creek, Gem Lake (Rush Creek drainage), Shadow Lake Trail

LEAVES AND STEMS: This species almost never extends to sub-alpine elevations but is included because it is so distinctly different from any plant included in the book. The branched stems can exceed 50 cm in length but generally are not upright. The leaves are oval shaped with distinct veins.

FLOWERS: The light-purple flowers are comprised of 5 fused petals, forming a broad bowl with a distinct pentagonal shape. On some individuals, the ends of the petals are pointed, while other times they are smooth. At the center of the flower are 5 chunky, yellow stamens. This species, a relative of tomatoes, has small green—and poisonous—berries.

❖ *Viola adunca* subsp. *adunca* (western dog violet, early blue violet)
   FAMILY: Violaceae

DISTRIBUTION Fairly common throughout the western Sierra at montane elevations but occasionally extending to higher elevations; rare to absent in the eastern Sierra
HABITAT Wet locations, including seeps, stream banks, moist forest
ELEVATION 3,300'–11,500'
SEASON Late May–mid-July
LOCATIONS Near White Wolf Campground, Soda Springs (Tuolumne Meadows), Lyell Canyon, Center Basin, Cotton-wood Lakes Basin

LEAVES AND STEMS: The leaves grow mostly as a rosette at the base of the plant, but some extend up the short flowering stems. The round- to oval-shaped leaves are up to 6 cm in length (though often much smaller) and are raised upward by a long stalk. They are a fairly bright green and have a smooth margin.

FLOWERS: Each rosette of leaves can have 1 to several flowering stems, usually shorter than the leaves but occasionally exceeding 20 cm in length. A purple-flowered violet, this species is easily identified by its shape: It has a quite long, narrow form, especially notable when viewed from the side. The 5 petals in all violets are fused at the base, forming a tube that juts out to the side of the sepals, called a spur—and in this species, the spur is long and often curved at the tip.

❖ *Iris missouriensis* (western blue flag, Rocky Mountain iris)
   FAMILY: Iridaceae

DISTRIBUTION Common throughout the eastern Sierra; much rarer and typically at lower elevations in the western Sierra
HABITAT Moist meadows and seeps
ELEVATION 3,000'–10,700'
SEASON Early June–mid-July
LOCATIONS Virginia Lakes Basin, Tuolumne Meadows, Glass Creek Meadow, Piute Pass Trail below Loch Leven Lake, North Fork Big Pine Creek

LEAVES AND STEMS: This tall species is the only high-elevation iris, with the stems and leaves both reaching up to 50 cm in height. Like all members of the iris family, the stems are flattened—a perfect identifying characteristic. The leaves are long, narrow, and very tough and thick. They mostly grow from the base of the plant, though the stems can also be leafy.

FLOWERS: Resembling a large horticultural iris, the flowers are 4–7 cm in diameter. There are 2 sets of 3 "petals": the inner true petals are a more pure purple and extend upward, while the outer 3 are actually sepals. The sepals are longer, bent backward, and have white patterning and a yellow stripe down the middle.

❖ *Sisyrinchium idahoense* var. *occidentale*
   (Idaho blue-eyed grass)   **FAMILY:** Iridaceae

DISTRIBUTION Occasional throughout, on both sides of the Sierra Crest
HABITAT Moist grassy areas, seeps
ELEVATION 2,000'–10,750'
SEASON Late June–early August
LOCATIONS Agnew Lake, Second Recess, Rock Creek Basin, East Lake (south of Bubbs Creek)

LEAVES AND STEMS: This relative of the iris usually reaches 20–30 cm in height. Like all members of the iris family, the stems are flattened. The leaves are long and narrow, like blades of grass, only stiffer. They can be as long as—or longer than—the flowering stems but are frequently hidden among the grass blades where this species lives.

FLOWERS: The flowers are a deep-periwinkle color. The sepals and petals are indistinguishable in this genus, instead appearing as 6 identical petals (or tepals, as they are technically known). The very center of the flower is yellow—as are the stamens.

Bibliography

Adler, Lynn S. 2000. "Alkaloid Uptake Increases Fitness in a Hemiparasitic Plant via Reduced Herbivory and Increased Pollination." *The American Naturalist* 156 (1): 92–99.

Adler, Lynn S. 2002. "Host Effects on Herbivory and Pollination in a Hemiparasitic Plant." *Ecology* 83 (10): 2700–2710.

Arnold, Sarah E. J., Vincent Savolainen, and Lars Chittka. 2009. "Flower Colours along an Alpine Altitude Gradient, Seen through the Eyes of Fly and Bee Pollinators." *Arthropod-Plant Interactions* 3 (1): 27–43.

Barbour, Michael G., Todd Keeler-Wolf, and Allan A. Schoenherr. 2007. *Terrestrial Vegetation of California*. University of California Press.

Becklin, Katie M., and Candace Galen. 2009. "Intra- and Interspecific Variation in Mycorrhizal Associations across a Heterogeneous Habitat Gradient in Alpine Plant Communities." *Arctic, Antarctic, and Alpine Research* 41 (2): 183–90.

Bhushan, Bharat. 2010. *Springer Handbook of Nanotechnology*. Springer.

Billings, W. D., P. J. Godfrey, B. F. Chabot, and D. P. Bourque. 1971. "Metabolic Acclimation to Temperature in Arctic and Alpine Ecotypes of *Oxyria Digyna*." *Arctic and Alpine Research* 3 (4): 277–89.

Botti, Stephen J. 2001. *An Illustrated Flora of Yosemite National Park*. 1 ed. El Portal, CA: Yosemite Association/Heyday Books.

Bradshaw, H. D., and Douglas W. Schemske. 2003. "Allele Substitution at a Flower Colour Locus Produces a Pollinator Shift in Monkeyflowers." *Nature* 426 (6963): 176–78.

Brandle, James R., William F. Campbell, William B. Sisson, and Martyn M. Caldwell. 1977. "Net Photosynthesis, Electron Transport Capacity, and Ultrastructure of *Pisum Sativum* L. Exposed to Ultraviolet-B Radiation." *Plant Physiology* 60 (1): 165–69.

Britton, George, Synnove Liaaen-Jensen, and Hanspeter Pfander. 2008. *Carotenoids, Vol. 4: Natural Functions*. Springer.

Brundrett, Mark C. 2009. "Mycorrhizal Associations and Other Means of Nutrition of Vascular Plants: Understanding the Global Diversity of Host Plants by Resolving Conflicting Information and Developing Reliable Means of Diagnosis." *Plant and Soil* 320 (1–2): 37–77.

Bunn, AG, LA Waggoner, and LJ Graumlich. 2005. "Topographic Mediation of Growth in High Elevation Foxtail Pine (*Pinus Balfouriana* Grev. et Balf.) Forests in the Sierra Nevada, USA." *Global Ecology and Biogeography* 14 (2): 103–14.

Caldwell, Martyn M., Ronald Robberecht, and Stephan D. Flint. 1983. "Internal Filters: Prospects for UV-Acclimation in Higher Plants." *Physiologia Plantarum* 58 (3): 445–50.

Caprio, Anthony C., Thomas W. Swetnam, The Sequoia, and National Park. *Historic Fire Regimes along an Elevational Gradient on the West Slope of the Sierra Nevada, California.*

Castellanos, Maria Clara, Paul Wilson, and James D. Thomson. 2002. "Dynamic Nectar Replenishment in Flowers of *Penstemon* (Scrophulariaceae)." *American Journal of Botany* 89 (1): 111–18.

Chittka, Lars, and James D. Thomson. 2005. *Cognitive Ecology of Pollination: Animal Behaviour and Floral Evolution.* Cambridge University Press.

Crimmins, Shawn M., Solomon Z. Dobrowski, Jonathan A. Greenberg, John T. Abatzoglou, and Alison R. Mynsberge. 2011. "Changes in Climatic Water Balance Drive Downhill Shifts in Plant Species' Optimum Elevations." *Science* 331 (6015): 324–27.

Cripps, Cathy L., and Leslie H. Eddington. 2005. "Distribution of Mycorrhizal Types Among Alpine Vascular Plant Families on the Beartooth Plateau, Rocky Mountains, U.S.A., in Reference to Large-Scale Patterns in Arctic-Alpine Habitats." *Arctic, Antarctic, and Alpine Research* 37 (2): 177–88.

Day, T. A., T. C. Vogelmann, and E. H. DeLucia. 1992. "Are Some Plant Life Forms More Effective than Others in Screening out Ultraviolet-B Radiation?" *Oecologia* 92 (4): 513–19.

De Luca, Paul A, and Mario Vallejo-Marín. 2013. "What's the 'Buzz' About? The Ecology and Evolutionary Significance of Buzz-Pollination." *Current Opinion in Plant Biology* 16 (4): 429–35.

Endress, Peter K. 2010. "Flower Structure and Trends of Evolution in Eudicots and Their Major Subclades 1." *Annals of the Missouri Botanical Garden* 97 (4): 541–83.

Franklin, Rebecca S. 2013. "Growth Response of the Alpine Shrub, *Linanthus Pungens*, to Snowpack and Temperature at a Rock Glacier Site in the Eastern Sierra Nevada of California, USA." *Quaternary International.* Accessed April 2.

Galsterer, S., M. Musso, A. Asenbaum, and D. Furnkranz. 1999. "Reflectance Measurements of Glossy Petals of *Ranunculus Lingua* (Ranunculaceae) and of Non-Glossy Petals of *Heliopsis Helianthoides* (Asteraceae)." *Plant Biology* 1 (6): 670–78.

Gardes, M., and A. Dahlberg. 1996. "Mycorrhizal Diversity in Arctic and Alpine Tundra: An Open Question." *New Phytologist* 133 (1): 147–57.

Germino, Matthew J., and William K. Smith. 2000. "Differences in Microsite, Plant Form, and Low-Temperature Photoinhibition in Alpine Plants." *Arctic, Antarctic, and Alpine Research* 32 (4): 388–96.

Germino, Matthew J., and William K. Smith. 2000. "High Resistance to Low-Temperature Photoinhibition in Two Alpine, Snowbank Species." *Physiologia Plantarum* 110 (1): 89–95.

Gould, Kevin S. 2004. "Nature's Swiss Army Knife: The Diverse Protective Roles of Anthocyanins in Leaves." *Journal of Biomedicine and Biotechnology* 2004 (5): 314–20.

Grossenbacher, Dena L., and Maureen L. Stanton. 2014. "Pollinator-Mediated Competition Influences Selection for Flower-Color Displacement in Sympatric Monkeyflowers." *American Journal of Botany* 101.

Grossenbacher, Dena L., Samuel D. Veloz, and Jason P. Sexton. 2014. "Niche and Range Size Patterns Suggest That Speciation Begins in Small, Ecologically Diverged Populations in North American Monkeyflowers (*Mimulus* Spp.)." *Evolution* 68 (5): 1270–80.

Grossenbacher, Dena L., and Justen B. Whittall. 2011. "Increased Floral Divergence in Sympatric Monkeyflowers." *Evolution* 65 (9): 2712–18.

Grotewold, Erich. 2006. "The Genetics and Biochemistry of Floral Pigments." *Annual Review of Plant Biology* 57 (1): 761–80.

Harder, L. D., and R. M. R. Barclay. 1994. "The Functional Significance of Poricidal Anthers and Buzz Pollination: Controlled Pollen Removal from *Dodecatheon*." *Functional Ecology* 8 (4): 509–17.

Havaux, Michel, Francoise Eymery, Svetlana Porfirova, Pascal Rey, and Peter Dormann. 2005. "Vitamin E Protects against Photoinhibition and Photooxidative Stress in *Arabidopsis Thaliana*." *The Plant Cell* 17 (12): 3451–69.

Heber, Ulrich, Wolfgang Bilger, Richard Bligny, and Otto Ludwig Lange. 2000. "Phototolerance of Lichens, Mosses and Higher Plants in an Alpine Environment: Analysis of Photoreactions." *Planta* 211 (6): 770–80.

Heuschen, B., A. Gumbert, and K. Lunau. 2005. "A Generalised Mimicry System Involving Angiosperm Flower Colour, Pollen and Bumblebees' Innate Colour Preferences." *Plant Systematics and Evolution* 252 (3–4): 121–37.

Hodges, Scott A. 1997. "Floral Nectar Spurs and Diversification." *International Journal of Plant Sciences* 158 (6): S81–88.

Hodges, Scott A., and M. L. Arnold. 1994. "Columbines: A Geographically Widespread Species Flock." *Proceedings of the National Academy of Sciences* 91 (11): 5129–32.

Hodges, Scott A., Michelle Fulton, Ji Y. Yang, and Justen B. Whittall. 2004. "Verne Grant and Evolutionary Studies of *Aquilegia*." *New Phytologist* 161 (1): 113–20.

Hodges, Scott A., Justen B. Whittall, Michelle Fulton, and Ji Y. Yang. 2002. "Genetics of Floral Traits Influencing Reproductive Isolation between *Aquilegia Formosa* and *Aquilegia Pubescens*." *The American Naturalist* 159 (S3): S51–60.

Hurteau, Matthew, and Malcolm North. 2008. "Mixed-Conifer Understory Response to Climate Change, Nitrogen, and Fire." *Global Change Biology* 14 (7): 1543–52.

Jackson, Louise E., and L. C. Bliss. 1984. "Phenology and Water Relations of Three Plant Life Forms in a Dry Tree-Line Meadow." *Ecology* 65 (4): 1302–14.

Jepson Flora Project (eds.). 2014. "Jepson eFlora, ucjeps.berkeley.edu/IJM.html." October 23.

Jorgensen, Tove Hedegaard, and Stefan Andersson. 2005. "Evolution and Maintenance of Pollen-Colour Dimorphisms in *Nigella Degenii*: Habitat-Correlated Variation and Morph-by-Environment Interactions." *New Phytologist* 168 (2): 487–98.

Jorgensen, Tove H., David S. Richardson, and Stefan Andersson. 2006. "Comparative Analyses of Population Structure in Two Subspecies of *Nigella Degenii*: Evidence for Diversifying Selection on Pollen-Color Dimorphisms." *Evolution* 60 (3): 518–28.

Kimball, Sarah. 2008. "Links between Floral Morphology and Floral Visitors along an Elevational Gradient in a *Penstemon* Hybrid Zone." *Oikos* 117 (7): 1064–74.

Kimball, Sarah, and Diane Campbell. 2009. "Physiological Differences among Two *Penstemon* Species and Their Hybrids in Field and Common Garden Environments." *New Phytologist* 181 (2): 478–88.

Kimball, Sarah, Paul Wilson, and J. Crowther. 2004. "Local Ecology and Geographic Ranges of Plants in the Bishop Creek Watershed of the Eastern Sierra Nevada, California, USA." *Journal of Biogeography* 31 (10): 1637–57.

Knudsen, Jette T., and Jens Mogens Olesen. 1993. "Buzz-Pollination and Patterns in Sexual Traits in North European Pyrolaceae." *American Journal of Botany* 80 (8): 900–913.

Kootstra, Arend. 1994. "Protection from UV-B-Induced DNA Damage by Flavonoids." *Plant Molecular Biology* 26 (2): 771–74.

Kopp, Christopher W., and Elsa E. Cleland. 2013. "Shifts in Plant Species Elevational Range Limits and Abundances Observed over Nearly Five Decades in a Western North America Mountain Range." *Journal of Vegetation Science*.

Körner, Christian. 2003. *Alpine Plant Life: Functional Plant Ecology of High Mountain Ecosystems*. Springer.

Körner, Christian, and Jens Paulsen. 2004. "A World-Wide Study of High Altitude Treeline Temperatures." *Journal of Biogeography* 31 (5): 713–32.

Körner, Christian, and Susanna Riedl. 2012. *Alpine Treelines: Functional Ecology of the Global High Elevation Tree Limits*. New York: Springer.

Koski, Matthew H., and Tia-Lynn Ashman. 2013. "Quantitative Variation, Heritability, and Trait Correlations for Ultraviolet Floral Traits in *Argentina Anserina* (Rosaceae): Implications for Floral Evolution." *International Journal of Plant Sciences* 174 (8): 1109–20.

Levin, Donald A. 1969. "The Effect of Corolla Color and Outline on Interspecific Pollen Flow in *Phlox*." *Evolution* 23 (3): 444–55.

Lunau, Klaus. 1995. "Notes on the Colour of Pollen." *Plant Systematics and Evolution* 198 (3–4): 235–52.

Millar, Constance, and Robert Westfall. 2010. "Distribution and Climatic Relationships of the American Pika (*Ochotona Princeps*) in the Sierra Nevada and Western Great Basin, U.S.A.; Periglacial Landforms as Refugia in Warming Climates." *Arctic, Antarctic, and Alpine Research* 42 (1): 76–88.

Millar, Constance I., Robert D. Westfall, Angela Evenden, Jeffrey G. Holmquist, Jutta Schmidt-Gengenbach, Rebecca S. Franklin, Jan Nachlinger, and Diane L. Delany. 2014. "Potential Climatic Refugia in Semi-Arid, Temperate Mountains: Plant and Arthropod Assemblages Associated with Rock Glaciers, Talus Slopes, and Their Forefield Wetlands, Sierra Nevada, California, USA." *Quaternary International*.

Miller, Renee, Simon J. Owens, and Bjørn Rørslett. 2011. "Plants and Colour: Flowers and Pollination." *Optics & Laser Technology* 43 (2): 282–94.

Miller, Carol, and Dean L. Urban. 1999. "A Model of Surface Fire, Climate and Forest Pattern in the Sierra Nevada, California." *Ecological Modelling* 114 (2–3): 113–35.

Pemble, R.H. 1970. "Alpine Vegetation in the Sierra Nevada of California as Lithosequence and in Relation to Local Site Factors." Davis, CA: University of California, Davis.

Phoenix, G. K., and M. C. Press. 2005. "Linking Physiological Traits to Impacts on Community Structure and Function: The Role of Root Hemiparasitic Orobanchaceae (ex-Scrophulariaceae)." *Journal of Ecology* 93 (1): 67–78.

Rausher, Mark D. 2008. "Evolutionary Transitions in Floral Color." *International Journal of Plant Sciences* 169 (1): 7–21.

Ronse de Craene, Louis P. 2007. "Are Petals Sterile Stamens or Bracts? The Origin and Evolution of Petals in the Core Eudicots." *Annals of Botany* 100 (3): 621–30.

Ronse De Craene, Louis P., and Samuel F. Brockington. 2013. "Origin and Evolution of Petals in Angiosperms." *Plant Ecology and Evolution* 146 (1): 5–25.

Rozema, Jelte, Jos van de Staaij, Lars Olof Björn, and Martyn Caldwell. 1997. "UV-B as an Environmental Factor in Plant Life: Stress and Regulation." *Trends in Ecology & Evolution* 12 (1): 22–28.

Rundel, Philip W. 2011. "The Diversity and Biogeography of the Alpine Flora of the Sierra Nevada, California." *Madroño* 58 (3): 153–84.

Rundel, Philip W., Michael Neuman, and Peter Rabenold. 2009. "Plant Communities and Floristic Diversity of the Emerald Lake Basin, Sequoia National Park, California." *Madroño* 56 (3): 184–98.

Schemske, Douglas W., and H. D. Bradshaw. 1999. "Pollinator Preference and the Evolution of Floral Traits in Monkeyflowers (*Mimulus*)." *Proceedings of the National Academy of Sciences* 96 (21): 11910–15.

Schmidt, S. K., L. C. Sobieniak-Wiseman, S. A. Kageyama, S. R. P. Halloy, and C. W. Schadt. 2008. "Mycorrhizal and Dark-Septate Fungi in Plant Roots above 4270 Meters Elevation in the Andes and Rocky Mountains." *Arctic, Antarctic, and Alpine Research* 40 (3): 576–83.

Sharsmith, C.W. 1940. "A Contribution to the History of the Alpine Flora of the Sierra Nevada." Berkeley, CA: University of California, Berkeley.

Stephenson, Nathan. 1998. "Actual Evapotranspiration and Deficit: Biologically Meaningful Correlates of Vegetation Distribution across Spatial Scales." *Journal of Biogeography* 25 (5): 855–70.

Stephenson, Nathan L. 1990. "Climatic Control of Vegetation Distribution The Role of the Water Balance." *The American Naturalist* 135 (5): 649–70.

Stoughton, Tommy. 2014. "Sierra Nevada—Claytonia.org." Accessed May 20. claytonia.org/tag/sierra-nevada.

Streb, P., W. Shang, J. Feierabend, and R. Bligny. 1998. "Divergent Strategies of Photo-protection in High-Mountain Plants." *Planta* 207 (2): 313–24.

Sugihara, Neil G. 2006. *Fire in California's Ecosystems.* University of California Press.

Swenson, Nathan G., and Daniel J. Howard. 2005. "Clustering of Contact Zones, Hybrid Zones, and Phylogeographic Breaks in North America." *The American Naturalist* 166 (5): 581–91.

Tanaka, Yoshikazu, Nobuhiro Sasaki, and Akemi Ohmiya. 2008. "Biosynthesis of Plant Pigments: Anthocyanins, Betalains and Carotenoids." *The Plant Journal* 54 (4): 733–49.

Taylor, L. D., and Thomas D. Bruns. 1999. "Population, Habitat and Genetic Correlates of Mycorrhizal Specialization in the 'Cheating' Orchids *Corallorhiza Maculata* and *C. Mertensiana.*" *Molecular Ecology* 8 (10): 1719–32.

Tesitel, Jakub, Lenka Plavcova, and Duncan D Cameron. 2010. "Interactions between Hemiparasitic Plants and Their Hosts." *Plant Signaling & Behavior* 5 (9): 1072–76.

Thomson, James D., and Paul Wilson. 2008. "Explaining Evolutionary Shifts between Bee and Hummingbird Pollination: Convergence, Divergence, and Directionality." *International Journal of Plant Sciences* 169 (1): 23–38.

Urban, Dean L., Carol Miller, Patrick N. Halpin, and Nathan L. Stephenson. 2000. "Forest Gradient Response in Sierran Landscapes: The Physical Template." *Landscape Ecology* 15 (7): 603–20.

Vignolini, Silvia, Meredith M. Thomas, Mathias Kolle, Tobias Wenzel, Alice Rowland, Paula J. Rudall, Jeremy J. Baumberg, Beverley J. Glover, and Ullrich Steiner. 2012. "Directional Scattering from the Glossy Flower of *Ranunculus*: How the Buttercup Lights Up Your Chin." *Journal of The Royal Society Interface* 9 (71): 1295–1301.

Weiss, Martha R. 1995. "Floral Color Change: A Widespread Functional Convergence." *American Journal of Botany* 82 (2): 167–85.

Wenk, Elizabeth. 2005. "Physiology and Distribution of Plants in Relation to Substrate on Coyote Ridge in the Alpine Sierra Nevada of California." University of California Berkeley.

Whittall, Justen B., and Scott A. Hodges. 2007. "Pollinator Shifts Drive Increasingly Long Nectar Spurs in Columbine Flowers." *Nature* 447 (7145): 706–9.

Whittall, Justen B., Claudia Voelckel, Daniel J. Kliebenstein, and Scott A. Hodges. 2006. "Convergence, Constraint and the Role of Gene Expression during Adaptive Radiation: Floral Anthocyanins in *Aquilegia.*" *Molecular Ecology* 15 (14): 4645–57.

Williamson, Sheri. 2008. "Do We See What Bees See?" *Life, Birds, and Everything.* fieldguidetohummingbirds.wordpress.com/2008/11/11/do-we-see-what-bees-see.

Wilson, Paul, Andrea D. Wolfe, W. Scott Armbruster, and James D. Thomson. 2007. "Constrained Liability in Floral Evolution: Counting Convergent Origins of Hummingbird Pollination in *Penstemon* and *Keckiella*." *New Phytologist* 176 (4): 883–90.

Wright, I. J., P. B. Reich, M. Westoby, D. D. Ackerly, Z. Baruch, F. Bongers, J. Cavender-Bares, et al. 2004. "The Worldwide Leaf Economics Spectrum." *Nature* 428 (6985): 821–27.

Zimmer, Carl. 2009. "Where Did All the Flowers Come From?" *The New York Times,* September 8, sec. Science. nytimes.com/2009/09/08/science/08flower.html.

Zimmer, Katja, Nicole A. Hynson, Gerhard Gebauer, Edith B. Allen, Michael F. Allen, and David J. Read. 2007. "Wide Geographical and Ecological Distribution of Nitrogen and Carbon Gains from Fungi in Pyroloids and Monotropoids (Ericaceae) and in Orchids." *New Phytologist* 175 (1): 166–75.

Ziska, L. H., A. H. Teramura, and J. H. Sullivan. 1992. "Physiological Sensitivity of Plants along an Elevational Gradient to UV-B Radiation." *American Journal of Botany* 79 (8): 863–71.

Scientific Name Index

Common Name Index

Check out this great title from
Wilderness Press!

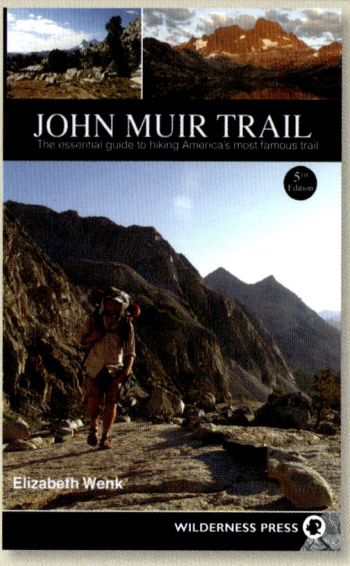

John Muir Trail

By Elizabeth Wenk
ISBN: 978-0-89997-736-2
$18.95, 5th Edition

5½ x 8½, paperback
296 pages
B&W photos and maps

Elizabeth Wenk's authoritative guide describes the 212-mile John Muir Trail, running from Yosemite Valley to the summit of Mt. Whitney. It provides all the necessary planning information, including up-to-date details on wilderness and permit regulations, food resupplies, trailhead amenities, and travel from nearby cities. Useful essentials are updated GPS coordinates and maps (along with an updated list of campsites along the trail), trail junctions, bear boxes, and other points of interest. The trail descriptions also include natural and human history to provide a workout for both body and mind—a must-have for any John Muir Trail enthusiast.

WILDERNESS PRESS
. . . on the trail since 1967

Ruler and Metric to English Conversion Table

inches	metric
¹⁄₁₆ in	1.6 mm
⅛ in	3.2 mm
¼ in	6.0 mm
⅜ in	1.0 cm
½ in	1.3 cm
⅝ in	1.6 cm
¾ in	1.9 cm
1 in	2.5 cm
1¼ in	3.2 cm
1½ in	3.8 cm
1¾ in	4.4 cm
2 in	5.1 cm
2¼ in	5.7 cm
2½ in	6.4 cm
3 in	7.6 cm
3½ in	8.9 cm
4 in	10.2 cm
4½ in	11.4 cm
5 in	12.7 cm
5½ in	14.0 cm
6 in	15.2 cm
7 in	17.8 cm
8 in	20.3 cm
9 in	22.9 cm
10 in	25.4 cm
12 in	30.5 cm
18 in	45.7 cm
24 in	61.0 cm
36 in	91.4 cm
40 in	1.0 m

metric conversions:
10 mm = 1 cm
100 cm = 1 m

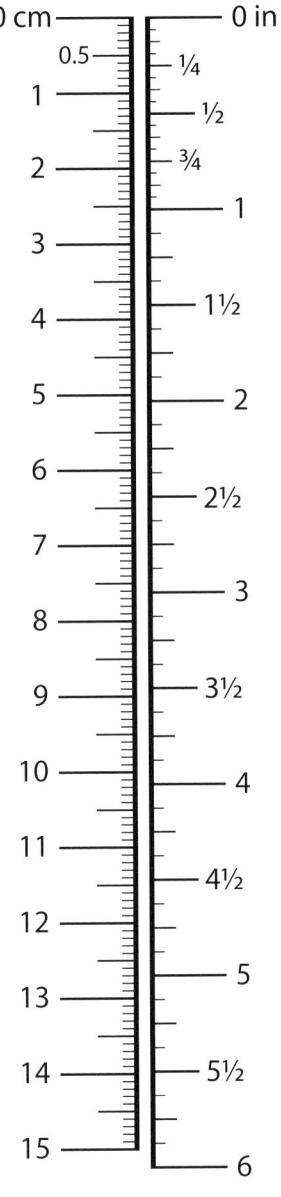

About the Author

From childhood, Elizabeth "Lizzy" Wenk has hiked and climbed in the Sierra Nevada with her family. Since she started college, she has found excuses to spend every summer in the Sierra, with its beguiling landscape, abundant flowers, and near-perfect weather. One interest lies in biological research, and she worked first as a research assistant for others and then completed her own PhD thesis research on the effects of rock type on alpine plant distribution and physiology. However, much of the time, she hikes simply for leisure.

photographed by Douglas Bock

Obsessively wanting to explore every bit of the Sierra, she has hiked thousands of on- and off-trail miles and climbed more than 600 peaks in the mountain range. Many of her wanderings are now directed to gather data for several Wilderness Press titles and to introduce her two young daughters to the wonders of the mountains. For them as well, the Sierra, and especially Yosemite, has become a favorite location.

Although she will forever consider Bishop, California, home, Wenk is currently living in Sydney, Australia, with her husband, Douglas, and daughters, Eleanor and Sophia. There she is working as a research fellow at Macquarie University and enjoying Australia's exquisite eucalyptus forests, vegetated slot canyons, and wonderful birdlife—except during the Northern Hemisphere summer, which she continues to spend exploring the Sierra.